Buddha Shakyamuni

The Padmakara Translation Group gratefully acknowledges the generous support of the Tsadra Foundation in sponsoring the translation and preparation of this book.

The Nectar *of* Manjushri's Speech

༄། །བྱང་ཆུབ་སེམས་དཔའི་སྤྱོད་པ་ལ་འཇུག་པའི་
ཚིག་འགྲེལ་འཇམ་དབྱངས་བླ་མའི་ཞལ་ལུང་
བདུད་རྩིའི་ཐིག་པ་བཞུགས་སོ།

པདྨ་ཀཱ་རའི་སྒྲ་བསྒྱུར་མཐུན་ཚོགས་ནས་
སྒྲ་བསྒྱུར་ཞུས།།

The NECTAR of MANJUSHRI'S SPEECH

A Detailed Commentary on Shantideva's *Way of the Bodhisattva*

Kunzang Pelden

Translated by the Padmakara Translation Group

SHAMBHALA · *Boulder* · 2010

Shambhala Publications, Inc.
4720 Walnut Street
Boulder, Colorado 80301
www.shambhala.com

9 8 7 6 5 4

Printed in the United States of America

⊗This edition is printed on acid-free paper that meets
the American National Standards Institute z39.48 Standard.
♻This book is printed on 30% postconsumer recycled paper.
For more information please visit www.shambhala.com.
Shambhala Publications is distributed worldwide by Penguin
Random House, Inc., and its subsidiaries.

Designed by Lora Zorian

The Library of Congress catalogues the hardcover edition of this book as follows:
Kun-bzan-dpal-ldan, Mkhan-po.
[Byan chub sems dpa'i spyod pa la 'jug pa'i tshig 'grel
'Jam-dbyans bla ma'i zal lun bdud rtsi'i thig pa. English]
The nectar of Manjushri's speech: a detailed commentary on
Shantideva's Way of the Bodhisattva / by Kunzang Pelden;
translated by the Padmakara Translation Group.
p   cm.
Includes bibliographical references and index.
ISBN 978-1-59030-439-6 (hardcover: alk. paper)
ISBN 978-1-59030-699-4 (paperback: alk. paper)
1. Santideva, 7th cent. Bodhicaryavatara. I. Comit de traduction
Padmakara. II. Title.
BQ3145.K7613 2007
294.3'85—dc22
2007015600

Contents

Foreword

In an age buffeted by the horrors of war and terrorism—to which the only response that most of us can imagine is retaliation with its endless consequences—what great good fortune it is, and how comforting to the mind, that there is still such a thing as bodhichitta! In times like these, even to hear of the idea of it is almost inconceivable. Yet here we have in our hands a manual that can actually teach us how to practice it and thereby lead us to buddhahood.

All the Buddhas and Bodhisattvas, including our teachers in the present age, have said that they started out upon their path by rigorously training in bodhichitta. I feel immense gratitude to all of them, first to Shantideva and then to our teachers: His Holiness the Dalai Lama, Kyabje Kangyur Rinpoche, Kyabje Dudjom Rinpoche, Kyabje Dilgo Khyentse Rinpoche, Kyabje Trulzhik Rinpoche, Dzongsar Khyentse Rinpoche, and my brother Pema Wangyal Rinpoche. All of them have taken these teachings beyond the stage of mere interest and inspiration; they have accepted them as their path and seriously pursued them. It is thanks to masters like these that this path is still available to us now.

What I most remember about my teachers is that they let their deep interest, their fascination with bodhichitta sink deep into the core of their being. And it was not interest alone that satisfied them; they let themselves be molded by these teachings, with results that became visible and tangible. They were not content to think what a beautiful path this is—while still continuing to resent and complain about others!

I am confident that this book describes the path that all our teachers have taken, and I am very encouraged that it is available for people like me, so that we can actually follow their example, train our minds, and cultivate compassion, humility, and the other Bodhisattva qualities.

I hope those who read this text will be inspired to receive direct instructions on the Bodhisattva path from authentic teachers. I pray that this text will not simply arouse admiration or interest in the ideas that it contains, but that its teachings will really sink into our minds and transform us—the sign of success being that we will apply them to ourselves without judging others.

I am grateful to everyone who has worked on this book. May it truly fulfill the aspirations that our teachers have made for all sentient beings.

JIGME KHYENTSE
Dordogne, 2006

Translators' Introduction

The *Bodhisattvacharyavatara* (conveniently abbreviated as *Bodhicharyavatara*) composed by the eighth-century Indian master Shantideva has occupied an important place in the Tibetan Buddhist tradition almost from its inception. Shantarakshita (725–783), the renowned abbot of the great university of Nalanda, invited by King Trisongdetsen to help in the establishment of the Buddhist teachings in Tibet, could scarcely have been ignorant of the life and achievements of his remarkable contemporary and confrere, and it is clear that when he inaugurated the great work of translation of sutras and shastras into Tibetan, the *Bodhicharyavatara* figured prominently among the many texts brought from India for that purpose.

Its first translator, Kawa Peltsek, was one of the first seven men (the so-called *sad mi mi bdun*) chosen to take part in an experiment to see whether Tibetans were capable of holding monastic vows. And since their ordination is said to have occurred in 767, we may conclude that he was born around 740.[1] We do not know exactly when Kawa Peltsek completed his translation. The first mention of it is in the Denkarma catalogue compiled probably in 824.[2] In any event, the fact that the *Bodhicharyavatara* should have been translated so soon after its composition (it is quite possible that Shantideva was still alive), on a par with other texts considered to be of the first importance for the propagation of Buddhism in Tibet, testifies to the speed with which the work had established itself already in India, or at least at Nalanda, as what we would nowadays call a "popular classic." Butön's statement, repeated by Kunzang Pelden, that a hundred and eight commentaries were composed on the *Bodhicharyavatara* in India alone is perhaps a pious exaggeration, but there can be no doubt of the esteem (following the universal astonishment that had greeted its first recitation) in which it was held, both in its native country and in Tibet. The Tengyur contains ten Sanskrit commentaries rendered into Tibetan, the most important of which, the *Panjika* of Prajnakaramati, has also survived in the original language. The translation of so many commentaries suggests that the *Bodhicharyavatara* was widely taught and studied. This is hardly surprising, for it is a detailed exposition of the gradual, systematic practice of the paramitas, and as such was tailor-made for the kind of Mahayana sutra tradition that Shantarakshita was at pains to transmit to the Tibetans, and which, a generation later, his disciple Kamalashila is said to have defended so successfully against the inroads of the Chinese Chan tradition.

Over a period of about three hundred years, the Tibetan version of the *Bodhicharyavatara* was revised twice: first by Rinchen Zangpo (958–1055) at the beginning of the New Translation period, and finally by Ngok Loden Sherab (1059–1109) about one hundred years later. That there should have been two widely spaced revisions to the translation is itself an interesting fact, pointing not only to the gradual discovery by the Tibetans of the existence of rival Sanskrit versions of Shantideva's work, but also to the sustained interest that its sublime message continued to excite. During the first three centuries of its existence in Tibetan, it was, in all probability, expounded and studied with the help of the Sanskrit commentaries just mentioned, aided by the oral tradition preserved from the expositions of the Indian masters present in Tibet during the early translation period, and again, following Langdarma's persecution of Buddhism, by Atisha (892–1054) and the panditas who assisted the later translators.

Atisha and the masters of the Kadampa tradition held Shantideva's shastra in particular veneration and numbered it among their "six indispensable treatises."[3] The evidence suggests nevertheless that, however popular it may have been, the *Bodhicharyavatara* did not stimulate scholarly commentary on the part of the Tibetans themselves. Historically speaking this is unsurprising, given that the scholastic and commentarial tradition, which was to become so much a part of Tibetan scholarship, really only began in the twelfth century with the founding of the monastery of Sangphu by the two masters from Ngok, Lekpa'i Sherab and his nephew, the translator Loden Sherab. According to the *Blue Annals*, the earliest Tibetan commentaries on the *Bodhicharyavatara* were composed by Loden Sherab himself, Chapa Chökyi Senge, and a contemporary scholar named Nyangdren Chökyi Yeshe. These three works have been lost, but commentaries by two of Chapa's disciples—Sonam Tsemo, the second hierarch of Sakya, and Tsang Nakpa[4]—still survive.

From these first beginnings until the present time, a series of important commentaries appeared, among which the most notable were composed by Butön Rinchen Drup (1290–1364), Sazang Mati Panchen Jamyang Lodrö (1294–1376), Ngulchu Thogme Zangpo (1295–1369), Sonam Gyaltsen Pal Zangpo (1312–74), Je Tsongkhapa (1357–1419), Gyaltsap Darma Rinchen (1362–1432), Pawo Tsuglag Trengwa (1504–66), Mipham Rinpoche (1846–1912), Khenpo Zhenga (1871–1927), Minyak Kunzang Sonam (Thubten Chökyi Drakpa) (nineteenth century), and Khenpo Kunzang Pelden (1862–1943).[5]

Although incomplete, this is nevertheless a representative and suggestive list.[6] The chronological grouping of the authors, moreover, indicates that interest in the *Bodhicharyavatara* was particularly strong in two periods—first in the thirteenth and fourteenth centuries and then much later in the nineteenth and early twentieth centuries—separated by a lapse of nearly three hundred years, from the death of Pawo Tsuglag Trengwa to the birth of Mipham Rinpoche. This apparent lull in scholarly activity coincided with a prolonged period of political unrest occurring in Tibet during the sixteenth and seventeenth centuries—a period of almost continuous crisis that must surely have been prejudicial to centers of learning. And the resulting intellectual stagnation could only have been aggravated by the increase in sectarian intolerance that followed the civil war in Tsang and the ensuing political settlement.[7] This unhappy state of affairs eventually provoked (in the nineteenth century) a reaction, in the form of the Rimé or nonsectarian movement, inaugurated by the combined efforts of a number of outstanding masters principally of the Nyingma, Sakya, and Kagyu schools. Their aim was to recover and preserve the many different streams of learning and spiritual practice of all traditions of Tibetan religion, the continued existence of which had been under threat owing to the social and political conflicts of the previous age, as well as to the oppressive spirit of religious prejudice that subsequently prevailed.

Another thing to notice in the earlier commentaries on the *Bodhicharyavatara* is the distribution of traditional allegiances that they reveal. In an earlier and more generous age, before relations had been soured by the antagonisms just mentioned, the different schools of Tibetan Buddhism, though distinct in their views and practices, enjoyed an easy coexistence. It was not unusual for keen students to receive teachings from a variety of traditions; and it was precisely this spirit of open, mutual respect and healthy eclecticism that the Rimé movement was intent on reviving. Once again, these facts are reflected in our list of commentaries. We find that in the early period, interest in the *Bodhicharyavatara* was broadly pervasive. Butön and Ngulchu Thogme Zangpo were Kadampas; Sazang was a Jonangpa; Je Tsongkhapa and his disciple Gyaltsap were Gelugpas; and Pawo Tsuglag Trengwa was a Kagyupa. By contrast, the four commentaries composed in the later period suggest a somewhat different picture. Although one was by the Gelugpa master Minyak Kunzang Sonam and the other three were composed by Nyingmapas, the inspiration for all of them derived from a common source, the teaching of Patrul Rinpoche. In other words, the existence of these commentaries—and they are the most important to appear in modern times—is evidence that, after a lull of nearly three centuries, and thanks to the Rimé movement, there occurred a resurgence of interest in the *Bodhicharyavatara*, which was in very large measure due to the activities and extraordinary personality of Patrul Rinpoche.

PATRUL RINPOCHE

Although the explanation lineage of the *Bodhicharyavatara* reaching back to Ngok Loden Sherab and beyond was never severed in Tibet, by the nineteenth century, the knowledge and study of Shantideva's text had almost fallen into abeyance, being confined to the scholarly environment of a small number of monastic colleges. It seems that even copies of the text had become a rare commodity.[8] This was a situation that Patrul Rinpoche was to change almost single-handedly. He devoted his life to the practice and propagation of the *Bodhicharyavatara*. Traveling all over the east of Tibet, he is said to have expounded it more than one hundred times, sometimes in detailed courses lasting many months. It was he, more than anyone else, who restored Shantideva's teaching to the important position that it now occupies in the sutra teachings of all schools of Tibetan Buddhism.

The strength of Patrul Rinpoche's influence, and the reverence in which he was held, derived not only from his great erudition and skills as a teacher, but also from the power of his personality and the purity of his own example.[9] Indeed, a profound knowledge of the *Bodhicharyavatara* and a lifelong dedication to the implementation of its teachings could not fail to produce an unusual personality. He seems in many ways to have been like another great monk and yogi, Shabkar Tsogdruk Rangdrol, an elder contemporary whom he much admired but never met.[10] Like Shabkar, Patrul Rinpoche combined the practice of the Great Perfection[11] with a tireless implementation of the Mahayana teachings on wisdom and compassion so powerfully advocated in Shantideva's verses and the mind-training instructions of Atisha and the Kadampas. Temperamentally too they were very similar. Untainted by worldly concerns of any kind, they were both free spirits unhindered by religious and social conventions. And both were renowned for their compassion toward human beings and animals alike.

Patrul Rinpoche was recognized at an early age as the third incarnation of a lama named Palge Samten Phuntsok, and his youth was spent at Palge Monastery (whence his name: Palge Trulku, or Patrul for short). In the Tibet of his day, monasteries were often large and wealthy establishments and the labrang, or residences of their abbots and lamas, were appropriately spacious and well-appointed—the perfect setting, one might imagine, for a relatively comfortable life of scholarship and contemplation. Such a prospect was of no interest to Patrul Rinpoche, and at the youthful age of twenty, he took advantage of the fortuitous circumstances occasioned by the death of the monastic administrator: He closed down the labrang and left. And for the next fifty years or so, he lived the life of a wandering hermit and yogi of no fixed abode, his belongings consisting of little more than the clothes he was wearing and a few books. He had no home, no property, no worldly responsibilities. It is said that whenever he wished to set off on a journey, all he needed to do was to stand up and he was ready to go.

He sought teachings at the feet of many masters and became a scholar of profound learning. A word-perfect knowledge of many texts, stored in his exceptionally powerful memory, allowed him to give lengthy and detailed teachings at any time and place as need arose. He traveled alone and without retinue. His appearance was unkempt and people often mistook him for a beggar and treated him accordingly. Many amusing stories were remembered about him, passed down lovingly by his disciples and their disciples to the present day. Often he would disappear for long periods, practicing in solitude, in caves or under rocky overhangs, or just at the foot of a tree.[12] His commitment to the path of renunciation, compassion, and bodhichitta were legendary—so much so that many people came to regard him as the incarnation of Shantideva himself. For it was difficult to imagine a more perfect embodiment of the teachings of the *Bodhicharyavatara*.

The reports that have come down to us of Patrul Rinpoche's life are largely anecdotal. They reflect the experience of those who knew him and describe the sides of his character that impressed them most. The degree to which these subjective accounts succeed in defining Patrul Rinpoche as he really was is difficult to assess, but the picture they convey is of a person who had completely abandoned the "eight worldly concerns." According to Buddhist teaching, these eight preoccupations or urges are the ways in which ego-clinging manifests in daily life. They consist of the desire for happiness, success, importance and good reputation, and the wish to avoid their opposites: discomfort, defeat, obscurity and disgrace. The fact that Patrul Rinpoche had abandoned or "leveled" these tendencies meant that whatever happened to him in the way of pleasure or pain, praise or blame, gain or loss, fame or neglect, was of equal consequence. He simply didn't care. He was without hope or fear—in life generally and especially in his relations with people. He never manipulated others to his own advantage and he was never afraid of telling them the truth. He had not the slightest use for recognition and reputation and was always direct and sincere, unmoved by considerations of spiritual or social rank. Behind the mask of famous lama, noble man, distinguished scholar, beggar, or brigand he saw only the living being, caught in the sufferings and delusions of samsara. He had an unnerving ability to see into the most secret recesses of those whom he encountered and he treated everyone according to their need with an equal frankness and familiarity. To those in difficulty, he was kindness and gentleness personified but with those who had the ability to profit from his guidance on the path, he was a formidable teacher, ferociously tearing away the facades and pretenses by which the ego defends and promotes itself. He had a reputation for being extremely fierce and it must have been devastating to be on the receiving end of one of his admonitions. Yet, as his disciples reported, his purposes were unfailingly compassionate and sincere; and for those who sought his guidance with a commensurate sincerity, he evoked a response of intense and lasting devotion. The reminiscences of Tenpa'i Nyima, the Third Dodrupchen Rinpoche, provide us with a fascinating vignette of what relations with Patrul Rinpoche were like.[13]

"Patrul," he writes, "uses fearful and overwhelmingly tough words, but there is no trace of hatred or attachment in them. If you know how to listen to them, they are, directly or indirectly, only teachings. Whatever he says is solid like gold—it is true . . . Whoever is involved in unvirtuous activities, unless the person is unchangeable, he digs out that persons' faults at once and exposes them."

No amount of familiarity with the master, Dodrupchen Rinpoche continues, could ever reveal the slightest inconsistency in his behavior. There was no guile, no deceit. What you saw was the man himself. "He seems hard to serve, yet however close you are to him, it is impossible to find a single instance of dishonesty ... he never deviates from the Bodhisattva activities." And then the telling remark: "It is hard to separate from him."

The *Bodhicharyavatara* was Patrul Rinpoche's constant companion. He taught it incessantly. Wandering all over Tibet, he expounded it in many monasteries of all traditions, following the Rimé practice of teaching according to the tradition to which the monastery belonged. When teaching Sakyapas, he would use the commentary of Sonam Tsemo; in Gelugpa monasteries, he would expound Gyaltsap's *Dartik;* and he would teach Kagyupas according to the commentary of Pawo Tsuglag Trengwa. His attentions, moreover, were not confined to monastic audiences. On many occasions he taught the *Bodhicharyavatara* to large gatherings of lay people, thereby providing a detailed explanation of the Mahayana path to the public at large, always emphasizing the importance of practice over mere learning.

Minyak Kunzang Sonam records in his biography of Patrul Rinpoche:

> Thanks to the kindness of Patrul Rinpoche, the entire region became filled with the explanation and study [of the great texts] and very many people, down to ten-year-old monks, were able to adorn their mouths with the recitation of the *Bodhicharyavatara* ... As a result, the whole land was gloriously transfigured through the enormous numbers of people who, from being complete beginners, aspired and turned their minds to the systematic implementation of the practice of the complete Mahayana path ... And the members of the black-clothed laity, both men and women, by attending for just a few moments the explanation of the *Bodhicharyavatara,* came to understand that the good heart and bodhichitta are the living roots of the Mahayana teachings.[14]

KHENPO KUNZANG PELDEN

The author, or rather the compiler, of the commentary translated in this volume, Khenpo Kunzang Pelden (or Khenpo Kunpel for short), was born in Dzachuka, Kham, in the east of Tibet, probably in 1862.[15] He spent a good part of his early life with Patrul Rinpoche, who, it is said, treated him like his own son and from whom he received many teachings. He completed his formal studies, however, under the guidance of Patrul Rinpoche's nephew Önpo Tendzin Norbu in Shri Simha College at Dzogchen Monastery, where he received full monastic ordination. He was also a close disciple of the great Mipham Rinpoche, whom he attended in his final years.[16] He was himself a great upholder of the Vinaya discipline and a distinguished scholar, and was invited to be the first professor at the scriptural college at Kathok.

Clearly, in commenting on the *Bodhicharyavatara*, Khenpo Kunpel could have produced a work filled with his own erudition and insights. Instead, as he explains in the colophon, his commentary is a compilation of the extensive notes that he himself took during a six-month course on the *Bodhicharyavatara* given by Patrul Rinpoche at Dzogchen Monastery. On this occasion, Patrul Rinpoche had used as his basic text the commentary on the *Bodhicharyavatara* composed by Ngulchu Thogme Zangpo, whose Kadampa tradition was especially dear to him. Khenpo Kunpel supplemented his notes with further explanations received from Patrul Rinpoche's other students, notably Önpo Tendzin Norbu and Mipham Rinpoche. Indeed, the presentation of the ninth chapter on wisdom follows closely, very often verbatim, Mipham's commentary, the famous *Norbu Ketaka*, which was itself closely modeled on Patrul Rinpoche's own teaching.[17]

In short, it is thanks to Khenpo Kunpel's devoted and self-effacing labors that a very full and faithful repository of Patrul Rinpoche's exposition of the *Bodhicharyavatara* has been preserved into our time. It could perhaps be said that *The Nectar of Manjushri's Speech* is the commentary that Patrul Rinpoche so often gave by word of mouth but never actually wrote. No doubt this is the reason why Khenpo Kunpel's text has attained such popularity among Tibetans and especially in Nyingma colleges. Avoiding long scholarly explanations that are unnecessary for the learned and confusing for the neophyte, he has instead tried to capture the direct, uncomplicated tone of Patrul Rinpoche's style, presenting Shantideva's teaching in a manner that may be most easily assimilated and implemented.

Although *The Nectar of Manjushri's Speech* is thus without extensive quotations of other works and supplementary disquisitions on subtle points, it is nevertheless a large work. Moreover, it presupposes a quite extensive basic knowledge of Buddhist teaching. This might prove problematic for readers who are new to the subject. However, instead of increasing the size of an already weighty tome through the addition of lengthy explanations in glossaries and endnotes, we have, where necessary, supplied page references to other works where the interested reader will be able to find the necessary details without difficulty. In particular, we would like to draw the reader's attention to the large body of information on all aspects of the *Bodhicharyavatara* generously provided by Andreas Kretschmar on his Internet website and especially to his translation of the extremely rich presentation of Khenpo Kunpel's commentary given by Khenpo Chöga of Shri Simha College, an exposition which is indeed a treasure trove of learning.

This translation has had a long gestation and is the result of the kindness of our teachers, to whom we wish to record our sincere gratitude. To begin with, most of Khenpo Kunpel's commentary was taught in detail in 1981, in the course of the first three-year retreat in Dordogne, by Lama Sonam Topgyal, a disciple of Nyoshul Khen Rinpoche, and the extensive notes made by the retreatants at that time eventually proved extremely helpful when the translation was finally made. Then in the spring of 1990, Alak Zenkar Rinpoche paid his first visit to the West; and it was in the course of his English lessons that we took advantage of his generosity in requesting the complete reading transmission of Khenpo Kunpel's commentary (a few pages at the end of every class). At that time, the translation of such a long text was no more than a sincere, but not very hopeful, aspiration. The idea took on more concrete form following the visit of His Holiness the Dalai Lama to Dordogne in 1991. On this occasion, on a hilltop overlooking the beautiful valley of the Vézère, His Holiness expounded the *Bodhicharyavatara*, explaining the first eight and then the tenth chapters, promising that he would return to France and give an extended teaching on the ninth chapter on wisdom. Thanks to the inspiration of that event, the decision was taken to make a new translation of Shantideva's *Bodhicharyavatara*. This project, which finally saw the light in 1997 in the form of *The Way of the Bodhisattva*, was initially postponed owing to the more pressing task of producing, at His Holiness' request, a translation of the explanations of the ninth chapter taken from the commentaries by Khenpo Kunpel and Minyak Kunzang Sonam in time for his next visit, which was to be at the monastery of Nalanda in the south of France in 1993 when he fulfilled his promise of two years before.[18]

Work on the *Bodhicharyavatara* and on the commentary on its ninth chapter made clear to us the desirability of a large-scale commentary to be made available in Western languages. From then on, the translation of at least Khenpo Kunpel's commentary in its entirety remained a Padmakara project, even though on several occasions, it was shouldered aside by other, more pressing projects. Now, finally, the task is complete—at the insistence, we may say, of Taklung Tsetrul Pema Wangyal Rinpoche. To him and to Alak Zenkar Rinpoche we owe a great debt of gratitude. We would like also to express our sincere thanks to Khenchen Pema Sherab, Jetsun Yangchen Chödzom, and Khenpo Shedrub for their precious assistance. This text was translated by Helena Blankleder and Wulstan Fletcher of the Padmakara Translation Group.

THE TEXTUAL OUTLINE

The textual outline, or sabche (*sa bcad*), is an important feature of Tibetan commentarial literature. It is the traditional means of showing the structure of an original or root text, marking out its divisions and subdivisions according to the perceptions and analytical skills of the commentator. Once created, it acts as a kind of interpretive lens through which one can identify, in light of the commentator's insights, the different parts of the composition, appreciating the way in which they relate to each other. Being itself a statement of textual analysis, and encapsulating as it does the commentator's overall approach to a given work, the sabche of a commentary can without exaggeration be regarded as the commentary itself in its most condensed form. It is for this reason that, as a means to assimilating the content of a text, students in the Tibetan scriptural colleges often commit its entire sabche to memory. Memorization still plays an important role in such a setting, where the texts studied are completely without footnotes, endnotes, tables of contents, indexes, and bibliographies—the comparatively modern inventions of Western scholarship. It is usual for a Tibetan khenpo to begin each teaching session with a recitation of the part of the sabche for the text already covered. This has the effect of reminding the students of the sections of the commentary already explained and of preparing them for the sequel.

Although the sabche is traditionally embedded in the text itself, it seems desirable, when making a translation into Western languages, to extract and present it separately in as clear and convenient a form as possible, thus giving the reader an immediate overview of how, in the commentator's opinion, the text is organized. The sabche can serve also as a useful revision tool, since it gives the structure and contents of the text in summary form. These can then be organized and fixed in the memory without too much difficulty.

To lay out a sabche in a user-friendly format that might fit comfortably on a standard book page is not an easy matter, the main obstacle being what may be called the "textual levels" of the commentary. To give an idea of what is meant by this term, let us consider how a textual outline actually appears within the fabric of a Tibetan text.

A Tibetan author might begin his commentary as follows: "This text is divided into three sections: the preamble, the text itself, and the conclusion. The first (i.e., the preamble) is divided into five." The author will then list the titles or subject matter of these five sections and then resume, "The first (that is, the first of the five subsections) is divided into two." These subsections will then be listed and the author will continue, "Now the first…" meaning the first of the two subsections. Let us imagine that this first subsection has no further divisions. The commentator will then begin an explanation of the point thus reached and when this is complete, will continue, "As to the second…" and move on to an explanation of the second of the two subsections.

So far, we have what may be regarded as three textual levels: (1) the tripartite division of the entire book into preamble, text, and conclusion; (2) the five sections of the preamble; and (3) the two subsections pertaining to the first of the preamble's five sections. When all the five sections of the preamble have been dealt with, together with however many subsections each of them may have, the commentary on the preamble is complete and the author will move onto the main part of the commentary. Here, the explanation may involve many more textual levels with any number of sections, subsections, further divisions, and subsidiary points. When the author has dealt with all these items systematically and in due order, advancing and retreating through all the different headings and subheadings, he will have completed the main body of the commentary and can then move onto the third main part of the book, the conclusion, which will then be expounded according to whatever divisions the commentator deems fit.

Given this method of analyzing the subject matter of a text, it is possible to create a diagram or wall-chart using symbols and indentations, in which the textual outline appears in the form of a tree-structure, thus allowing one to see at a glance how the text is divided and subdivided into its various parts. Naturally, a profound, intricate, or controversial text, requiring much learned commentary, will give rise to a textual outline of corresponding complexity. For example, the outline devised by Mipham Rinpoche for his commentary on the *Madhyamakalankara* (*The Adornment of the Middle Way*), has no fewer than twenty-one textual levels. Unfortunately, and for obvious reasons, the presentation of a sabche in extended chart format is impractical in the context of an ordinary book, where the physical considerations of page size preclude the use of indentation to any great degree. This is certainly true for a large and complicated work like the one just mentioned, but it is also true for the *Nectar of Manjushri's Speech*, which, despite its length, is of a comparatively simple structure. This is due to the fact that it is divided into separate chapters, each with a separate outline of its own, none of which has more than seven textual levels.

As a solution to the problem of indentation, we have resorted to the following scheme. The headings of the commentary are listed in the order that they appear in the book, and the figure at the beginning of each heading shows the textual level to which it belongs. All headings of the same level are indicated by the same figure, and each heading is subordinated to the heading of the earlier level that most closely precedes it. As an illustration of this procedure, let us consider the layout of chapter 1 of the present commentary. This chapter, "The Excellence and Benefits of Bodhichitta," is divided into two main sections, the headings of which are preceded by a figure 1, showing that they belong to the first textual level. The first of these, *1. The basis required for the generation of bodhichitta*, has only two subheadings, both preceded by the figure 2 to show that they are of the second level. By contrast, the second main section, *1. The benefits of bodhichitta* is more complex and has several more subdivisions. First come the three sections belonging to the second textual level: *2. The general benefits of generating bodhichitta*, *2. The specific benefits of bodhichitta in intention and the specific benefits of bodhichitta in action*, and *2. The greatness of a person who possesses bodhichitta*. Then come the three headings of the third level *3. Bodhichitta is superior to all other virtues*, *3. A change of name and of status*, and *3. The benefits of bodhichitta shown by means of examples*. According to the rule just enunciated, these three headings are all subordinated to the heading of the previous level most closely preceding them, namely, *2. The general benefits of generating bodhichitta*. On the other hand, the level three headings *3. Classification of bodhichitta in intention and action*, *3. The benefits of bodhichitta in intention and action*, and *3. Proving the benefits of bodhichitta by scripture and with reasoning* are all divisions of

2. The specific benefits of bodhichitta in intention and the specific benefits of bodhichitta in action. An examination of the textual outline will show that the same procedure is applied to the headings of the fourth and fifth textual level. For example, the six subheadings of level four dealing with the six examples of bodhichitta are all subsections of *3. The benefits of bodhichitta shown by means of examples,* whereas the level four headings *4. Plain or relative bodhichitta, engendered on the basis of prompting,* and *4. Subtle or ultimate bodhichitta, gained through [the recognition of] ultimate reality,* are subdivisions of *3. Classification of bodhichitta in intention and action.* Likewise, the two headings of level 5 at the end of the chapter are both subordinated to *4. Proving the benefits of bodhichitta with reasoning.*

Textual Outline

Chapter 8: *Meditative Concentration*   258

Prologue

NAMO GURU MANJUSHRI JNANA SAMAYA

Through marvelous prayers and bodhichitta born of your
    compassion,
More valiant than the other Buddhas of this Happy Age,
You have revealed enlightenment supreme and perfect in this
    time of ours.
Protect us, peerless Teacher, Lion of the Shakyas!

Ajita,[19] Manjughosha, and the others of the eight close sons,
The sixteen Arhats and the seven first fathers of the
    Doctrine,[20]
The world's adornments and the two supreme preceptors,[21]
    Shantideva and the rest—
These learned and accomplished masters of the noble land,
I honor them above my head with faith a hundredfold.

The eyes whereby the Snowy Land was filled with light,
The Abbot, Guru, Dharma King, translators and panditas:
Glorious emanations whom the Buddha had foretold,
Manjughosha's three embodiments[22]
And all the other holders of the New and Old traditions, free
    from sect and bias—
To these I bow in veneration.

Glory of the wisdom, love, and power of all the Buddhas,
Chökyi Wangpo,[23] from the lords of the three lineages never
    parted,

And all revered teachers, who are Buddhas come again,
Remain within the lotus of my heart until the essence of
  enlightenment is gained.

From all the words you spoke, essential nectar undefiled,
From all that I received, this fragment couched in written
  words,
Through blessings of the supreme lama and the Three most
  precious Jewels—
May there derive great profit for the Doctrine and all
  wanderers!

The glorious Dipamkara and all the Buddhas of the past; the supreme, unrivalled Lion of the Shakyas and all the Buddhas of the present; the regent, the great being, the venerable protector Maitreya and all the Buddhas of the future: In short, all the Buddhas of the three times have followed the Great Path. This path, the unique source of every joy and benefit without exception, both in the world of samsaric existence and in the peace of nirvana, is precious bodhichitta, the mind of enlightenment. This is the principal subject of the excellent treatise, the *Bodhisattvacharyavatara,* "The Entrance to the Activities of Bodhisattvas." This text, which is greater than the wish-fulfilling gem, the sovereign power, I shall now explain.

Introduction

1. The preliminary topics of the commentary

2. How a teacher sets forth the Dharma

3. How the Dharma is taught by a Buddha

When teachers who are Buddhas explain the Dharma, they use three kinds of miraculous display. First, by the miraculous power of their body, they project inconceivable rays of light from the strand of hair between their eyebrows. By this means, they gather to themselves an assembly of disciples to be trained—disciples who, as yet, have not been drawn to them. Then, by performing such feats as covering the three-thousandfold universe with the power of their tongues, they inspire the assembled disciples with confidence. By the miraculous power of their all-communicating minds, they are aware of the understanding, capacity, and dormant potential of the disciples they have gathered. Finally, by the miraculous power of their speech, which is perfectly attuned to their listeners, the Buddhas teach beings, gods, nagas, and so on, each in their own tongue and with the sixty qualities of melodious speech.[24] This is how they explain the Dharma in accordance with the needs of beings.

3. How the Dharma is taught by an Arhat

Teachers who are Arhats explain the Dharma by relying on the three purities. The first of these is the purity of the vessel or hearer. This refers to the fact that, thanks to their clairvoyance, such teachers know the minds of others. They are thus able to examine beings who need to be trained.

And if they find that the latter are appropriate vessels, they set forth the Dharma. The second purity is that of the teacher's speech. This means that, because these teachers are free from emotional obscurations like desire and the other defilements, they teach with words that are immaculate, in a manner that is perfectly correct and clear, and in a way that is melodious and pleasant. The third purity is that of the teaching. Thanks to their unforgetting memory, the Arhat teachers recall the Doctrine exactly as it was set forth by their own master, the perfect Buddha, and others. They then explain it without addition or subtraction, and without error. Their exposition is exact and unmistaken.

Why is it that the Shravaka Arhats do not explain the teachings by means of the three kinds of miraculous display? In fact, they are unable to do so owing to four cognitive limitations. To begin with, Arhats suffer from ignorance (in other words, an impediment in their knowledge) with regard to spatial location. This is exemplified by the story of Maudgalyayana, who was unable to see that his mother had taken birth in the buddhafield of Marichi. Arhats suffer also from a cognitive impediment with regard to time, as is shown by the fact that the noble Shariputra was unable to detect the root of liberation in the mind stream of the householder Shrija. They are limited, too, in being unable to perceive the endless sequence of causes and their results. As it is said in the verse:

> For a single iridescent eye upon a peacock's tail,
> The causes are both many and distinct.
> The one who knows them is indeed omniscient.
> Without all-knowing wisdom, they cannot be known.

Finally, Arhats are ignorant of very many of the qualities of buddhahood. They do not possess the ten strengths, the four fearlessnesses, the eighteen distinctive qualities, and so forth.[25]

3. How the Dharma is taught by a learned master

Panditas or learned scholars, for their part, expound the Dharma according to two traditions. In India, the noble land where the Dharma began, there were two very famous monastic foundations. It was the custom of the panditas of the glorious monastery of Nalanda to expound all the Buddha's words according to the five excellences and all the commentaries according to the five topics of presentation.[26] By contrast, the masters of the monastery of Vikramashila first prepared the student for the reception of the teachings and then explained the outline of the teaching by means of twofold confirmation.[27] Of these two traditions, we Nyingmapas follow the one propounded by the noble protector Nagarjuna and Padmasambhava.[28] We will therefore explain this great treatise, the *Bodhi-charyavatara*, according to the five topics of presentation: a discourse concerning the author, the scriptural sources of the treatise, its general tendency, an overall synopsis of the text, and its purpose.

4. The author of the treatise

The author of the *Bodhicharyavatara* was the learned master and noble Bodhisattva Shantideva,[29] who possessed in perfect measure the three qualifications necessary for the composing of shastras.[30] His life was marked by seven extraordinary events, in particular the fact that he was accepted and blessed by his supreme yidam deity, the venerable Manjughosha. The seven extraordinary events are listed as follows:

> He pleased his supreme yidam diety and at Nalanda[31] did
>   great deeds;
> He healed a conflict and accepted as disciples
> Those of strange beliefs
> As well as beggars, unbelievers, and a king.

The great being Shantideva was born in the southern country of Saurastra.[32] He was the son of the king Kalyanavarman and went by the name of Shantivarman. From his youth he was devoted to the Buddhas of earlier ages, and, having a natural affinity for the Mahayana, he held the teachers of religion and the monastic order in great respect. He was a benefactor to all, masters and servants alike, and he cared tenderly for the lowly, the sick, and the destitute. With his heart fixed solely upon the ways of enlightenment, he became expert in every art and science. In particular, he requested the *Tikshnamanjushri-sadhana*[33] from a certain ascetic mendicant. He practiced this and beheld the yidam deity.

When at length his father the king died, it was decided that the royal power should be conferred on Shantivarman, and a great throne made of precious substances was duly set in place. But in his dreams that night, the prince saw Manjughosha sitting on the very throne that he himself was to ascend the following day. Manjughosha spoke to him and said:

> My dear and only son, this is my throne,
> And I Manjushri am your spiritual guide.
> It is not right that you and I should take
> An equal place and sit upon one seat.

With that, Shantivarman woke from his dream and understood that it would be wrong for him to assume the kingship. Feeling no desire for the great wealth of the realm, he departed and entered the glorious monastery of Nalanda, where he received ordination from Jinadeva, the chief of its five hundred panditas, taking the name of Shantideva.

Regarding his inner spiritual life, he received the teachings of the entire Tripitaka, the three collections of the Buddha's teachings, from the noble Manjushri. He meditated on them and condensed their precious contents into two shastras: the *Digest of All Disciplines* (*Shikshasamucchaya*) and the *Digest of the Sutras* (*Sutrasamucchaya*). But though he gained boundless qualities of elimination and realization,[34] the other monks knew nothing of this, and, since to all outward appearances his behavior seemed to be restricted to the activities of eating (*bhuj*), sleeping (*sup*), and strolling around (*kutim gata*), they gave him the nickname "Bhusuku." Such was their estimate of his outward conduct. "This man," they complained, "performs none of the three duties[35] required of the monks of this monastery. He has no right to enjoy the food and alms offered in religion to the sangha. We must drive him away!"

Their plan was to take turns to expound the scriptures so that, when Shantideva's turn came round, he would be embarrassed and run away. They repeatedly urged him to preach, but on each occasion he refused, saying that he did not know anything. So they asked the abbot to order him to preach; and when the abbot did so, Shantideva immediately promised to give a teaching. At this, a few of the monks began to have misgivings, not knowing what to think. In order to put him to the test, they arranged a great quantity of offerings on the ground outside the monastery. They invited a large congregation of people and set up an enormously high lion throne in their midst. Then they sent for Shantideva, but most of the monks were thrown into confusion when they suddenly caught sight of him sitting high up on the throne, not knowing how he had managed to get there.

"Would you like me to recite some well-known teaching of the Buddha?" Shantideva asked. "Or would you prefer something you have never heard before?"

Everyone was thunderstruck. "Please tell us something completely new," they said.

Now the *Shikshasamucchaya* is too long, but, on the other hand, the *Sutrasamucchaya* is too short. So Shantideva expounded the *Bodhicharyavatara,* which, though vast in meaning, is quite brief. The noble Manjushri appeared, seated in the sky, and many of the people saw him and had great faith. Even more remarkable, when Shantideva came to the beginning of verse 34 of the ninth chapter, "When something and its nonexistence both are absent from before the mind," he and Manjushri began to rise higher and higher into the sky until at last they disappeared. Shantideva's voice, however, continued to resound so that the transmission was completed.

Those in the congregation who possessed extraordinary powers of memory wrote down the teaching as they had recalled it, but they produced texts of varying length: some of seven hundred stanzas, some of a thousand, and some of even more. The panditas of Kashmir produced a text of seven hundred stanzas in nine chapters, while those of Magadha (Central India) came up with a text of a thousand stanzas in ten chapters. Disagreement and uncertainty reigned. Moreover, they did not know the texts that Shantideva was referring to when he mentioned that they should read the *Shikshasamucchaya* repeatedly and occasionally consult the shorter *Sutrasamucchaya.*[36]

After a time, it was discovered that Shantideva was living in the south, at the stupa of Shridakshina. Two of the panditas who had supernormal powers of memory went to see him, intending to invite him back. But when they met him, it proved inconvenient for Shantideva to return. Nevertheless, in answer to their inquiries, he affirmed that the correct version corresponded to what the scholars of Magadha had produced. As for the *Shikshasamucchaya* and the *Sutrasamucchaya,* he said that they would find both texts written in a fine scholarly hand and hidden in the roof beam of his monastic cell at Nalanda. He then instructed the two panditas, giving them explanations and transmission.

Shantideva later traveled to the east where, through a demonstration of miraculous power, he resolved a serious conflict, creating agreement and happiness between the contending parties.

He also accepted as his disciples a group of five hundred people living not very far to the west of Magadha, who were holders of strange, non-Buddhist beliefs. There had been a great natural disaster, and the people were tormented by famine. They told Shantideva that if he could save their lives, they would respect his teachings. The master took his begging bowl filled with cooked rice received in alms and, blessing it with profound concentration, fed and satisfied them all. Turning them from their uncouth superstitions, he introduced them to the Buddha's Doctrine.

Some time afterward, in the course of another terrible famine, he restored to life and health at least a thousand beggars who were emaciated and dying of starvation.

Later, Shantideva became a bodyguard of the king of Arivishana who was threatened by Machala in the east (i.e., in Magadha).[37] Meditating upon himself as inseparable from Manjughosha, he took a wooden sword with its scabbard and imbued it with such tremendous power of Dharma that, so armed, he was able to subdue any and every onslaught. He brought about such harmony that he became the object of universal respect. Some people were, however, intensely jealous of him and protested to the king. "This man is an imposter!" they cried. "We demand an inquiry. How could he possibly have defended you? He has no weapon other than a wooden sword!"

The king was moved to anger and the weapons were examined one by one. When Shantideva was ordered to take out his sword, he replied that it would be wrong to do so since it would injure the king.

"Even if it harms me," said the king, "take it out!"

Going off with him to a solitary place, Shantideva requested the king to cover one of his eyes with his hand and to look with the other. With that, the sword was drawn, and its brightness was so intense that the king's eye shot from his brow and fell to the ground. He and his escort were overcome with terror and begged Shantideva for forgiveness, asking him for refuge. Shantideva placed the eye back into its socket, and, through his blessings, the king's sight was painlessly restored. The whole country was inspired with faith and embraced the Dharma.

Later on, Shantideva went to Shriparvata in the south. There he took to the life of the naked Ucchushma beggars, and sustained himself on the water thrown away after the washing of dishes and cooking pots. It happened that Kachalaha, a serving woman of King Khatavihara, once saw that if any of the washing water splashed on Shantideva as she was pouring it out, it was as if it had fallen on red hot iron. It would boil and hiss.

Now, at that time, a Hindu teacher called Shankaradeva appealed to the king and issued the following challenge. He said that he would draw the mandala of Maheshvara in the sky and that if the Buddhist teachers were unable to destroy it, then all Buddhist images and writings should be consigned to the flames and everyone obliged to accept the tenets of his religion.

The king summoned the Buddhist sangha and informed them of the challenge. But nobody could undertake to destroy the mandala. The king was deeply troubled, but when the serving woman told him what she had seen, he ordered that Shantideva be summoned. They searched high and low and eventually found him sitting under a tree. When they explained the situation, he announced that he was equal to the challenge but that he would need a jug filled with water, two pieces of cloth, and fire. Everything was prepared according to his instructions.

On the evening of the following day, the Hindu yogi drew some lines on the sky and departed. Everyone began to feel afraid. But early next morning, as the mandala was being drawn, no sooner was the eastern gate finished than Shantideva entered into a profound concentration. At once there arose a tremendous hurricane. The mandala was swept away into the void, and the crops, trees, and even the villages were on the brink of destruction. The people were scattered, the Hindu teacher was caught up in the wind like a little bird and swept away, and a great darkness fell over the land.

But a light shone out from between Shantideva's eyebrows showing the way for the king and queen. They had been stripped of their clothes and were covered with dust. And so with the fire he warmed them, with the water he washed them, and with the cloth he dressed and comforted them. When, through his power of concentration, the people had been gathered together, washed, anointed, clothed, and set at ease, Shantideva introduced many of them to the Buddha's teaching. He caused heathen places of worship to be demolished and centers of the Buddhist teaching to flourish, spread, and remain for a long time. As a result, the country came to be known as the place where the non-Buddhists were defeated.

Although for his own part Shantideva claimed to be no more than an ordinary man, Jetari tells us that he was considered to be an emanation of Manjughosha. In the estimation of Prajnakaramati, he was an Arya or noble being, and, referring to the excellence of his works, Vibhutichandra wrote:

Many beings have appeared,
Great lords of Buddha's teaching.
Yet in realization and experience,
None have I have found like Shantideva!

Master Krishnacharya spoke of Shantideva as one who had placed Manjughosha's feet upon the crown of his head. His excellence was indeed unbounded.

Shantideva left behind him three texts. Of these, two works, the *Shikshasamucchaya* and the *Sutrasamucchaya*, are respectively extensive and brief. The third work, namely the *Bodhicharyavatara*, is brief in form but extensive in meaning, and it is well known that in India no less than one hundred and eight commentaries were composed upon it.

4. THE SCRIPTURAL SOURCES OF THE TREATISE

The teachings contained in the *Bodhicharyavatara* are drawn from the Tripitaka, especially from the sutras.

4. THE GENERAL TENDENCY OF THE TREATISE

According to the general division of the Buddhadharma into the greater and lesser vehicles, the *Bodhicharyavatara* belongs to the great vehicle or Mahayana, and, of the sutra and tantra sections into which the Mahayana is divided, it belongs to the sutra teachings.

4. THE GENERAL SYNOPSIS OF THE *BODHICHARYAVATARA*

From the point of view of inner disposition, the *Bodhicharyavatara* explains the generation of bodhichitta, the supreme mind of enlightenment. From the point of view of spiritual training, it discourses extensively on how to train in the six paramitas or transcendent perfections.

4. THE PURPOSE OF THE TREATISE

This instruction on how to implement the complete and unmistaken path of the Bodhisattvas was expounded in the immediate term for the benefit of the five hundred scholars of the monastic university of Nalanda. Generally, however, it is addressed to all beings.

These then are the five preliminary topics of presentation, the purpose of which is to inspire disciples with confidence so that they become apt and suitable vessels for the teachings given in this text.

2. How disciples should attend to the teachings

3. Inner motivation

Beings of great scope[38] are utterly motivated by precious bodhichitta, the gateway to boundless merit. In this connection, we should reflect as follows. Of all the sentient beings who have existed in samsara from time without beginning, there is not one that has not been our father and our mother. And when they were our parents, they treated us with great kindness, just as our parents did in this present life. They gave us the first share of their food and clothed us with the best of clothes, and with deep love they nurtured us, showing us nothing but kindness. All these beings, once so good to us, have but one wish. They want to be happy. But having no idea of the causes of happiness, namely, the ten virtuous actions, they indulge instead in the ten nonvirtues, which are the causes of their suffering. The way they act is entirely at odds with their deepest wishes. They are confused and take the wrong path. Alas! They are like blind people left abandoned in the middle of an empty plain.

But now, at this present time, we have gained a human form with freedoms and advantages. We have met a fully qualified teacher, and the practice of the perfect Dharma is open to us. Now that we have such good fortune, we must not allow ourselves to sink into laziness and procrastination. We must study and implement the profound teachings of the sacred Dharma so that we will be able to free all living beings, our old mothers, from the karmic perceptions, the sufferings, and habitual tendencies of each of the six realms of samsara, and to place these beings finally in the state of perfect enlightenment. To generate bodhichitta by pondering in this way is a crucial point of the highest importance.

3. Outer conduct

4. Behavior to be abandoned

With regard to conduct that is to be avoided, one speaks of the three defects of a vessel, the six stains, and the five ways of misremembering.

The three defects of a vessel

Concerning the three defects of a vessel, it is said:

> Inattentive, you are like a vessel overturned.
> Forgetful, you are like a ruptured vessel.
> Stained by the afflictions, you are like a poisoned vessel.

When you are listening to the teachings, you should not let your ear-consciousness stray to some other object. For if you do not actually focus on the words of the explanation, but allow yourself to chatter or to look around, the situation is like someone trying to pour nectar into a pot that has been placed upside down. You may be physically present in the teaching assembly, but you are not listening to a single word. This is a defect.

Again, you may hear the Dharma, but if you leave it simply on the level of superficial hearing and understanding, and do not hold it in your memory, it is as though someone were pouring nectar into a pot with a hole in its base. Nothing remains. However many teachings you hear, you retain nothing and are still completely ignorant of how to put them into practice. This too is a defect.

If the reason for listening to the teaching is to improve your situation in life, to become famous or wealthy, or to attract the adulation of others, and if, while receiving the teachings, your mind is mingled with the five poisons (craving, anger, ignorance, and so on), it is like pouring a wholesome substance into a poisoned vessel. Far from bringing benefit to your mind, the Dharma itself will transform into its antithesis. This again is a defect.

Consequently, when receiving the teachings, it is essential to avoid such shortcomings. In the middle-length *Prajnaparamita-sutra*, Lord Buddha instructed us as follows: "Listen closely and well, and keep this in your minds, for I will speak to you." And the holy teachers have said, "If you do not practice the Dharma according to the Dharma, the Dharma itself will create the cause of your falling once more into the lower realms."

The six stains

It is said in the *Vyakhyayukti*:

> To be puffed up with pride, to have no faith,
> To have no yearning interest,

> Outwardly distracted, inwardly withdrawn,
> To listen with despondency: These are all impurities.

This refers respectively to the pride of thinking oneself superior to the teacher and to one's spiritual companions. It refers to a lack of confidence in the Dharma, the teacher, and one's fellow disciples. It refers also to an absence of keen interest and endeavor in the Dharma, and indicates distraction when the mind runs after the outer objects of the senses and is not concentrated, or when it sinks into a state of dullness and torpor. It refers too to the dismay one might feel at the length of the teaching session, or at the discomforts of hunger or thirst, or of heat or cold, on account of which one does not want to listen or else listens with displeasure. All these are, in the present life, hindrances to the teachings on concentration, wisdom, and liberation, all of which are perfect in word and meaning. As a result, one will fail to meet with the Dharma in one's future lives and will wander in endless samsara. Therefore one must control one's behavior, have an attitude of utmost respect, and listen to the teachings in the proper manner.

The five ways of misremembering

These are:

> To recall the words but not the sense,
> The sense but not the words,
> To remember without understanding,
> Or to turn the order upside down,
> To remember the reverse of what was meant:
> All these are faults you must avoid.

Consider these five points in order: (1) When you remember beautiful and elegant phrases without examining their profound meaning, your mind is not benefited. (2) When you dismiss the wording, thinking it of small importance, you may try to grasp the "profound meaning," but in failing to rely on the words, you will fail also to grasp the sense. (3) If you remember the various teachings without understanding whether they are of expedient or ultimate meaning, or whether they are indirect teachings to be interpreted,[39] you will certainly go contrary to the perfect Dharma. (4) If you remember in a confused, disordered manner, the sequence of the teachings will not be harmonious and contradictions will arise. (5) If, finally, you remember amiss, wrong ideas will proliferate and corrupt your understanding and you will bring the teaching into disrepute. Consequently, all such faults are to be rejected.

4. BEHAVIOR TO BE ADOPTED

This refers to the four attitudes, the six paramitas, and other rules of conduct.

The four attitudes

It is said in the *Gandavyuha-sutra,* "Son of my lineage, you should consider yourself as a sick man and the Dharma as your medicine. You should consider your assiduous practice as a medicinal cure, and your spiritual guide as a wise physician."

The six paramitas or transcendent perfections

The yoga of listening to the teachings with the three stages of preparation, the act of listening itself, and conclusion, is described in the *Tantra of the Effective Understanding of Instructions for All Dharma Practices:*

> Begin by cultivating bodhichitta
> And in the form of Tara visualize yourself.
> Consider your right ear a lotus flower,
> And meditate upon your teacher as Manjushri.
> Think that from your guru's mouth come rays of light
> That sink into the lotus blossom.
> Meditate upon all beings as Tara,
> And at the end, for just two instants meditate
> On emptiness devoid of thought.

Furthermore:

> Make offerings of seats and flowers,
> Clean the ground and let your conduct be restrained.
> Do no harm to any insect.

Supplicate the guru and receive his teachings
With an undistracted mind.
To clarify your doubts,
Ask questions on whatever is unclear.
Thus you have the six-branch discipline of Tara.

Accordingly, when the listeners offer a seat to the teacher who will explain the Dharma and when they make offerings of flowers and so forth, they are practicing generosity. When they clean the ground and restrain themselves from any disrespectful thought, word, or deed, they are practicing discipline. When they do no harm to the insects, bees, and so forth that are in the assembly, or when they put up with greater or lesser discomforts, like that of having fleas, they are practicing patience. When they supplicate the teacher and strive to listen to his explanations, they are practicing diligence. When, by being undistracted, they hear the teachings and retain them, they are practicing concentration. When they intelligently examine the meaning of the teachings, and come to a clear understanding by asking questions and discussing with the teacher when there are grounds for doubt, they are practicing wisdom. It is in such a way that they implement fully the six paramitas.

As for the teachers, when they explain the Doctrine, they are practicing generosity. They practice discipline when they teach in a manner free from afflictive emotion, and patience when they put up with fatigue and other irritants. They practice diligence through the joy they put into their teaching, and concentration by teaching without being distracted from the explanation of Dharma. Finally, by opening up the meaning of the words, they practice wisdom. Thus in the activity of the teacher also the paramitas are complete.

Other rules of conduct

It is said for instance:

Do not teach the Dharma to the disrespectful,
To those who, though not sick, wrap cloths around their
    heads,
To those who carry weapons, staffs, or parasols,
To those who are with covered heads.

2. THE METHOD OF EXPLANATION AND STUDY

The explanation (of the text) is given using five-point and three-point structures. With regard to the former, the *Vyakhyayukti* says:

> For those who wish to give essential teachings
> I shall give some brief advice,
> An instruction that shall be as follows:
> The purpose of the text, a digest of its contents,
> The meaning of the words, and proper sequence of the matter,
> Answers to objections—all these points should be set forth.

As for the three-point structure, the first is to make an outline of the text dividing it in sections, leaping like a tiger; the second is to comment on every word, proceeding slowly with the crawling gait of a tortoise; the third is to summarize the meaning from time to time in a single statement, surveying the text from above, in the manner of a lion. In the present context, we will not discuss these five-point and three-point structures further; but since they are occasionally referred to in the text, it is important to be aware of them.

My kind teacher Patrul Rinpoche, who understood the noncontradictory nature of the teachings, accepted all scriptural traditions as instructions for his personal practice. He was an impartial master of all doctrines, whether of the Old or New Translation schools. When he was asked how he taught the present text, I heard him say that with Sakyapas, he used the commentary of Jetsün Sonam Tsemo, with Gedenpas (Gelugpas) he used the *Dartik*,[40] and with Kagyupas he used the commentaries of Pawo Tsuglag Trengwa and others. Formerly, when teaching Nyingmapas in the Shri Simha college of Dzogchen Monastery, he used to teach according to our own Nyingma tradition. Later, he would base his explanation of the *Bodhicharyavatara* mainly on the commentary of Ngulchu Thogme, according to the special needs of time, place, and the people concerned. It was thus that he taught according to various interpretations. It was mainly on the basis of Ngulchu Thogme's commentary that he gave a six-month exposition of the *Bodhicharyavatara* to Chogyur Lingpa[41] (who was mentioned in the vajra prophecies), to the noble sons of his lineage, and to other masters and disciples such as myself. Regarding the explanations given in the present work, I was afraid of being excessively verbose, and in any case, a long disquisition laden with quotations would be superfluous for learned readers. I therefore decided on a simple word-for-word commentary that should be of interest for beginners, and which, being easy to understand, should be an aid to inner experience, while at the same time avoiding detailed discussions.

1. An explanation of the treatise itself

2. An explanation of the title of the treatise

3. The title itself

The title is given first in Sanskrit. In the noble land of India, there were four great canonical languages.[42] Of these, the title *Bodhisattvacharyavatara* is given in Sanskrit, the "well-constructed tongue," the language of the gods. This is translated into the best Tibetan,[43] which is easy to understand, as *byang chub sems dpa'i spyod pa la 'jug pa* (An Entrance to the Activities of Bodhisattvas). The word-for-word rendering is as follows: *bodhi / byang chub* / enlightenment; *sattva / sems dpa'* / heroic being;[44] *charya / spyod pa* / activities; *avatara / 'jug pa* / entrance.

Titles are applied according to four criteria: They are intended to express the meaning of a text; its range; its function; and such considerations as the place, time, or people referred to, and the metaphors employed. The title in the present case is of the first kind.

As to the meaning of the title, it is said in the *Net of Wisdom*:

Pure in being free from stain;
Accomplished through the waxing of good qualities.

[In the Tibetan word for enlightenment (*byang chub*), which is glossed here,] one speaks of purity (*byang*) because enlightenment involves the cleansing away of all that is to be discarded, namely, the two veils together with their habitual tendencies. Similarly, because enlightenment also involves the assimilation of all that is to be realized, namely, the qualities of primordial wisdom, one speaks of accomplishment (*chub*). In addition, those who strive for such a goal have great courage and do not shy away from actions that are difficult to perform, such as giving their heads and limbs to others—on account of which they are referred to as "heroic beings" (*sems dpa'*). As the *Sutralankara* says:

The stable ones (the Bodhisattvas) are unalarmed by
Pain or evil friends or hearing the deep teachings.

With regard to the word "activities" (*spyod pa*) used in the title, the all-
victorious Longchenpa said:

The Buddha's children must be trained in everything,
Especially the six transcendent perfections.

Every Bodhisattva activity is included within the six transcendent perfections. As for this treatise being an "entrance" to such activities, the text
is itself a perfect and unmistaken presentation (in a manner adapted to the
training of beginners) of the ways and means whereby the conduct of
Bodhisattvas is to be practiced.

There are two reasons for giving a title to a text and proclaiming it in the
beginning. Generally speaking, titles are necessary because, once one has
understood the relationship between title and contents, one can identify
the texts one wants to read and leave the others aside. It is said in the
Lankavatara-sutra:

If things were to be left unnamed,
Worldly folk would be confused.
Therefore our Protector, skilled in means,
Gave names to all his teachings.

More specifically, since in the present case, a title has been given that reflects the subject of the text, a person of superior capacity, merely on seeing it, will have a grasp of the entire message of the text. A person of
moderate capacity will understand its general gist, while a person of only
modest ability will be able to find the volume easily, just as one can identify a medicine by looking at the label on the bottle.

It might be objected that it is redundant to give the title in Sanskrit (as
well as in Tibetan). But this is not so. On the contrary, there are four reasons why titles are given in Sanskrit. First, because India was the pure wellspring of the Dharma, the Sanskrit title inspires the reader with confidence
in the perfect authenticity of the text. Second, all the Buddhas of the three
times set forth their Doctrine in Sanskrit, the divine and well-structured

tongue. Therefore if we ourselves pronounce and explain the title in that language, the enunciation itself will act as a vehicle of blessings for our minds. Third, in view of the fact that in the ages to come, the Dharma will again be taught in Sanskrit,[45] a predisposition for it is thus imparted to us. Finally, given that all the texts have, like this one, their names in Sanskrit, once we appreciate the difficulty even of pronouncing their titles, let alone the understanding and explaining of their contents, we will be inspired with gratitude toward the translators.

3. THE TRANSLATOR'S HOMAGE

This homage was inserted by the translator[46] and is called the "salutation imposed by royal command" or the "salutation indicating the section of the Tripitaka to which the text belongs." In the period of the ancestral Dharma kings,[47] the translators had the habit of paying homage to the yidam deity to whom they were personally devoted. There was no general practice established by law. But it happened that king Tri Ralpachen, having invited many panditas and translators to the temples Ushang Do and Pangthang Kamé, decreed that every revised translation, the text of which was established as final, was to contain a translator's homage that reflected the section of the Tripitaka to which it belonged, so that there would be no confusion as to its scriptural affiliation. This is why the homage is referred to in such a way.

Accordingly, in the case of the Vinaya-pitaka, since the subtle and precise teachings about the karmic law of cause and effect contained therein are the province of the Buddha alone, the homage is made to the "Omniscient One." Since the teachings of the Sutra-pitaka are present in the form of questions and answers between the Buddha and the Bodhisattvas, homage is made to "all Buddhas and Bodhisattvas." Finally, since the teachings contained in the Abhidharma-pitaka concerning such things as the aggregates (*skandha*), elements (*dhatu*), and sense fields (*ayatana*)[48] are to be realized by means of profound wisdom, the homage is made to the "noble and ever-youthful Manjushri (*Manjushrikumarabhuta*)."

In the present context, the homage is made in accordance with the Sutra-pitaka. The translator pays homage to the Buddhas (*sangs rgyas*): who have woken (*sangs*) from the deep sleep of ignorance and who have, like lotuses, blossomed (*rgyas*) with the understanding of all fields of knowledge. As it is said:

> Because they have awakened from the sleep of ignorance,
> Because their minds are amplified with all that can be known,
> The Buddhas are like lotus petals opened wide,
> Renowned as "the Awakened who have blossomed into
>   flower."

Homage is also made to those heroic, indefatigable beings, the Bodhisattvas, who generate the supreme thought of enlightenment and who strive in the practice of the six paramitas in order to attain enlightenment. To all these, and to the sacred Dharma residing in their mind streams, the translator pays homage before beginning his translation—lest there be any obstacle to the completion of the work.

2. An explanation of the treatise thus named

3. The preambles to the treatise

4. The expression of homage

[verse 1] Shantideva's objects of homage, when he says, "I bow down," are the Sugatas, "those who go in bliss." They are so called because they have journeyed to the state of perfect buddhahood, the blissful result of having relied upon the blissful path, namely, the vehicle of the Bodhisattvas. The object of homage is thus the Jewel of Buddha.

If the term Sugata is analyzed etymologically, we find that the element *su* means "well, beauteously, blissfully." And when this is conjoined with *gata*, which means "goes or gone," the resulting idea is, first, of one who goes or proceeds well or beautifully; second, one who goes without ever turning back; and third, one who goes perfectly or completely. The term therefore has three meanings, which are also interpreted in the teaching of the learned masters of Tibet and India as referring respectively to the qualities of elimination, of realization, and of elimination and realization taken together.[49] It is sufficient however to understand the word *sugata* in the following manner.

When one says that the Buddhas go well or beautifully, this means that, in being unstained by faults, namely, suffering and the origin of suffering (which belong to samsara with its defiled emotions), they are likened to beings who are endowed with beautiful and graceful forms. In this they are different from the denizens of samsara, for the worlds of existence are not beyond suffering and its causes.

When it is said that the Buddhas go without ever turning back, this means that, since they have extirpated the seed of the view of self, they never again return to samsara—just as there can be no more fire once the firewood has been consumed. They are like people who have been completely cured from smallpox [and cannot be reinfected again]. In this, their path is different from the paths of the non-Buddhists. For although non-Buddhist paths may lead to the very Peak of Existence, they are unable to go beyond the confines of samsara.

When it is said that the Buddhas have gone perfectly or completely, this means that there is not the slightest detail of the supreme qualities of complete elimination and realization that they have not realized. They are like vessels filled to the brim. In their manner of going, therefore, the Buddhas are different from the Shravakas and Pratyekabuddhas. For even though the latter do not fall back into samsara, their achievements are of a lesser kind precisely because their qualities of elimination and realization are not perfect and complete.

Now, since the Bhagavan Buddha mastered the dharmakaya, the body of the Dharma, in the twin aspects of transmission and realization, the root verse says that he possesses the "Dharma-body," namely, the Jewel of Dharma. It is said in the *Uttaratantra-shastra*:

> The dharmakaya should be understood as two:
> The dharmadhatu utterly unstained,
> And then the corresponding causes of the same,
> The teaching in its aspects both profound and vast.

In other words, there is the "Dharma-body" that is the realization of the ten strengths of a Buddha and so on, and there is the cause of this realization, the cause that is attuned to it, namely, the "Dharma-body" that is the profound and vast Dharma of transmission in all its categories. And all this, the Buddha is said to possess.

Finally, the "Buddha's heirs or offspring" refers to the supreme Jewel of

Sangha. It is generally said that the child of the Buddha's body was [his son] Rahula. The offspring of his speech are the Shravakas and Pratyekabuddhas, whereas the offspring of his mind are the Bodhisattvas. For just as the eldest son of a mighty king is the one who holds the lineage of his father, who takes responsibility for the latter's retinue and subjects, and who holds the key to the treasury, the supreme offspring of the Buddha's mind, the Bodhisattvas, are indeed the holders of the lineage of the Conquerors. They have in their possession the treasury of the sublime teaching. And they protect and care for the entourage of beings who are yet to be trained. Thus these same Bodhisattvas, the offspring of the Buddha's mind, are the Sangha of the Mahayana. To these Three Jewels—and not only to them but also to the Shravakas and Pratyekabuddhas, and indeed to anyone superior to him in even a single quality (such as slight seniority in training) or some benefactor—to all who are thus worthy of veneration, all without exception, the author bows down, paying homage with his body, speech, and mind.

The person who pays homage in this way is the master Shantideva; and he does so after the noble manner of his saintly forebears. As for the moment in which he does so, he pays homage just before composing his treatise. He does this, first, to dispel obstacles to the completion of his work; second, to inspire those who come after him with perfect confidence in the text, so that they will have faith and will gain a keen interest in its message; and third, to remove hindrances to the successful transmission and reception of his work. The noble Nagarjuna has said:

> The writer of a treatise who pays homage to the Buddha
> Cannot fail to have success.
> For he is stimulating faith and interest
> Both toward the Buddha and the text itself.

And the *Lalitavishtara-sutra* says:

> Full ripening of merit brings forth joy, dispelling every
> sorrow.
> People who have merit are the ones who gain their purpose.

The [Tibetan] continuative particle occurring at the end of the second line of the root stanza indicates that, having paid homage, Shantideva will now compose his treatise.

4. THE AUTHOR'S COMMITMENT TO COMPOSE

The activity or discipline of the Bodhisattvas, the offspring of the mind of the Sugata or Buddha, is threefold. It consists in the discipline of restraining from evil activity, the discipline of gathering virtue, and the discipline of bringing benefit to beings. The present demonstration (which is unmistaken and complete) of all the ways or means of embracing and implementing such a discipline is not in any way pretentious, neither is it the personal invention of the author. Shantideva announces that he will explain it in accordance with the teachings of the Conqueror, succinctly and in a manner easy to understand. And he will do so "according to the scriptures" so that we may have confidence in it. For it is said in the *Pramanavarttika:*

> The teachings of Buddha we may trust.
> For since he is exempt from fault,
> There is in him no cause for lies.
> Know therefore that the scriptures are exempt from error.

The immaculate teachings of the Conqueror (contained in the "unending knot"[50] of his heart), which arose from the vase of his throat, unfolded upon the lotus of his tongue, and issued from between his conch-white teeth, still exist undiminished. They are all the doctrines of the precious Tripitaka. This being so, it could be argued that the composition of the present text is a repetition of what already exists and is therefore superfluous. But there is no fault here. For the teachings of the Conqueror are vast and the scriptures are numerous, while the beings of this decadent age are short-lived and feeble both in understanding and application. They are overpowered by foolishness and indolence. It is difficult for them to assimilate all these teachings, and they are ignorant of how to combine and implement them. Thinking of such beings with great kindness, Shantideva pledges to compose a treatise that will describe the activities of the Bodhisattvas, completely and without error, in the form of a practical instruction, bringing together all the teachings, widespread as they are, in a manner that is easy to understand and practice.

Generally, there are four kinds of treatise: treatises that impose order on what appears disorganized, treatises that elucidate difficult points, treatises that bring together scattered elements, and treatises that are composed with a view to practice. The present text belongs to the third and fourth categories.

Supreme beings never give up their pledges. Thus the purpose of Shantideva's promise to compose the text is to ensure the completion of his work. As it is said in the *Prajnadanda* by Nagarjuna:

> Holy beings do not promise many things.
> But if they pledge themselves to some demanding task,
> It is as if they carve a picture on a stone:
> They do not turn from it though it may cost their lives.

4. The taking of a humble attitude

[verse 2] Shantideva says that he has no profound instructions to give that are not already to be found in the earlier teachings of the Buddha and of masters such as Nagarjuna and Asanga. Moreover, with regard to the art of composition, he is self-effacing. Yet Vibhutichandra has observed:

> Within the fold of Buddha's Doctrine,
> Many have appeared who were great masters, mighty beings.
> But someone to compare with Shantideva,
> In wisdom and experience, is nowhere to be found.[51]

This is very true. Nevertheless, Shantideva adopts an attitude of modesty. He says that, as far as the art of prosody is concerned, he has no literary skill that might distinguish him above others—the kind of stylistic elegance that one finds in such texts as the *Jatakamala* in thirty-four chapters by the master Aryashura, and the *Kalpalata* by King Kshemendra. For though these texts merely repeat what the sutras say about the Buddha's previous incarnations, they are so beautifully and poetically composed that they are a delight for the learned. For this reason, Shantideva says that in composing the *Bodhicharyavatara*, he does not claim to be of great help to others. He therefore rids himself of intellectual pride regarding the form and meaning of his words.

What, then, is the purpose of his writing? Shantideva says that he has composed his work in order to meditate upon and habituate himself to the conduct of the Bodhisattvas, which consists in the motivation of bodhichitta and the practice of the six paramitas. Moreover, of the three [schol-arly] activities, composition is more important than teaching and debate. For as the master Chandragomin has said:

> Therefore of the threefold craft of scholars,
> There may be some uncertainty in discourse and debate,
> But there's no room for this in commentary.

What is the reason for taking a humble attitude? It is said that "On the peak of pride, the water of good qualities does not stay." When the mind is puffed up with conceit, it cannot contain the water of the excellent quali-ties of the Dharma of transmission and realization. Rather it is liable to be deceived by Mara. While in this state, therefore, even if one composes trea-tises, they will be of no benefit to others. Accordingly, it is in order to elim-inate such faults that Shantideva adopts a humble attitude.

4. THE STIRRING UP OF A JOYFUL AND ENTHUSIASTIC ATTITUDE

[verse 3] Given that it is sufficient to understand the present subject for oneself, why, one might ask, is it necessary to compose a text? Shantideva says that, by such means, the strength of his vivid, yearning, and confident faith[52] in the activities of the Bodhisattvas will intensify for a little while, so that he can meditate upon and cultivate virtue, namely, the thought of bodhichitta and the six paramitas. For it is through continuous meditation and cultivation that bodhichitta is intensified. It is thus that Shantideva stirs up a joyful and enthusiastic attitude in his own regard.

Humbling himself once again, he says that other people, with a karmic fortune equal to his, who are sincere and take an interest in Bodhisattva activities—if ever they chance upon his *Bodhicharyavatara*—might also rejoice in the ways of the Bodhisattvas and so be happy to engage in them. He thus stirs up an enthusiastic attitude with regard to others, telling him-self that his work might be of some value to them. All this is necessary be-cause when the mind is depressed, it sinks into laziness and inactivity, becoming an unsuitable vessel for the acquisition of good qualities. There-fore Shantideva sets himself in a joyful frame of mind and stirs himself into a high spirit of enthusiasm. To be sure, the generation of any excellent quality is impeded when the mind falls to either extreme, whether of arrogance or of self-denigration. This can be seen in the *Pitaputrasamagamasutra*, in the part where the Lord set his father, King Shuddhodana, on the true path.

In conclusion, these four prerequisites (the homage, the promise to complete the work, humility, and enthusiasm) apply not just to the composition of treatises, but to any activity, whether of explaining or listening to the teachings, meditating on them, and so forth. They ensure that whatever one does will proceed without impediment and that one's task will be brought to a good conclusion. The two poles of intellectual arrogance and lazy depression will both be avoided. When these four features are present, everything one embarks upon will be brought to a worthwhile fulfillment. Such indeed is the practice of exemplary people.

These four prerequisites also exemplify the fourfold interrelated purpose.[53] The *subject to be set forth* is expressed in the root text as the practice of the Bodhisattva discipline. Its *immediate purpose* is expressed by saying that it will be meaningful to see the text because it is according to the scriptures. Its *ultimate finality* is the supreme result to be attained, namely, the condition of the Sugatas, who have gone in bliss, possess the body of Dharma, and are surrounded by their retinues of Bodhisattvas. And finally, with regard to the *connection* between these three features, it is clear that if the earlier ones are not present, the later ones cannot arise.

According to different masters, the fourfold interrelated purpose aims to inspire others with confidence, to remove doubts regarding the meaning, to obviate wrong thoughts, and to embellish the text.

3. The Main Body of the Treatise

The exposition of the treatise itself follows a structure taken from the Indian texts:

> May bodhichitta, precious and sublime,
> Arise where it has not yet come to be.
> And where it has arisen may it never fail,
> But grow and increase ever more and more.

Thus the ten chapters of the treatise are organized into four parts. Three chapters are devoted to the generation of bodhichitta where it has not previously existed; three chapters are devoted to the prevention of bodhichitta from weakening once it has been brought to birth; three chapters are devoted to the intensification of bodhichitta thus preserved; and finally, there is a concluding chapter in which the resultant merit is dedicated for the benefit of others. I propose to explain the *Bodhisattvacharyavatara*, the *Way of the Bodhisattva*, in the same way.

PART ONE

The Generation
of Bodhichitta Where It
Has Not Previously Existed

· 1 ·

THE EXCELLENCE AND
BENEFITS OF BODHICHITTA
Whereby the Heart Is Filled with Joy

1. THE BASIS REQUIRED FOR THE GENERATION
OF BODHICHITTA

2. THE HUMAN BODY AS A BASIS FOR THE GENERATION
OF BODHICHITTA

When describing the excellence of the human form in terms of the absence of unfavorable conditions, one speaks of "freedom, leisure, or ease." When describing it in terms of the presence of favorable factors, one speaks of "advantages, endowments, or wealth." Nagarjuna gives the following summary:

> To be in hell, to be a preta or a beast,
> To be a long-lived god or else a wild barbarian,
> To have false views, to live in ages when a Buddha has not
>   come,
> To have one's faculties impaired—all these are absences of
>   freedom.

To be exempt from the above shortcomings, on the other hand, is to possess the eight freedoms. Nagarjuna then goes on to describe the five personal advantages:

A human birth within a central land, with all one's faculties
   complete,
Faith in the Three Jewels, and freedom from unsuited karmic
   circumstances.

He defines the five circumstantial advantages as being when

A Buddha has appeared and taught,
The Doctrine still remains, and there are those who practice it
And who are lovingly disposed to others.

[verse 4] When we reflect in terms of causes, examples, or numerical
comparison, it becomes clear that this precious human life, endowed with
a full complement of eight freedoms and ten advantages, is extremely difficult to obtain. This is obvious when we consider its causes: the basic requirement of pure ethical conduct, the accessory requirement of
generosity and the other five paramitas, and the necessary connecting
principle afforded by pure aspirations.

   When we reflect with the help of examples, it is clear that the attainment
of a human existence is more difficult and rare than the chance occurrence
of a blind turtle that lives in the depths of the ocean rising to the surface
(which it does only once in a hundred years) to find its head inside a
wooden yoke floating at random on the sea. Alternatively, considered in
terms of numerical comparisons, the quantity of beings in the hell realms
are as the particles of dust upon the surface of the entire earth.
Proportionately, the pretas or hungry ghosts are like the grains of sand in
the river Ganges, whereas animals are like the grains in a vat of beer. The
asuras or demigods are like snowflakes in a blizzard, while the gods and
humans are like the motes of dust on one's fingernail. Again, another comparison may be made, this time according to the number of stars visible at
night, as compared with the stars that can be seen by day.[54] Reflecting thus,
we should be conscious of how difficult it is to acquire a human existence.

   Thanks to this achievement—to the compassion of our teachers and the
Three Jewels and to the power of our good karma—we are in a position to
achieve an objective corresponding to one of the three spiritual capacities
of beings: high rebirth in samsara or definitive benefit [namely, liberation
or enlightenment]. In this human state, however, death can strike at any
time, for its causes are uncertain and there is no saying that we shall not be

dead before this very evening. And if we fail to practice the sublime Dharma, which is so helpful to ourselves and others; and if we simply stay as we are, frittering away this human existence in distraction, rendering our freedoms and advantages meaningless, how can we possibly expect to find the excellence of this human form again? We shall certainly fail. Therefore Shantideva warns us not to render ineffectual these freedoms and advantages, not to let them go to waste.

To repeat, we have at the present time gained a human life endowed with freedoms and advantages; we have met with a qualified master and received profound teachings. Now that we have happened upon this situation, so hard to find, so easy to destroy, we must reflect again and again on the tremendous chance that lies within our reach. All the great exploits of worldly life we should just leave aside, and we should reject outright all trivial pursuits. And while we have the light of life, we should spend our time simply practicing the Dharma. We must be quick to seize the essence of our freedoms and advantages. As the glorious Atisha Dipamkara has said:

> This life so short, so many things to know!
> You have no notion of how long you have to live.
> So like the swan that milk from water strains,
> Pursue the goal that you yourself desire.

2. The Mind as a Basis for Bodhichitta

[verse 5] Here, Shantideva uses the image of the deep darkness of a sunless night unlit by any moon, when the sky is covered by thick clouds that hide the stars, and when everything is suddenly and for a split second illuminated by a flash of lightning. The present situation of beings is indeed like such a night, for the sun of omniscient primordial wisdom does not shine. It is a state of profound obscurity, for beings are ignorant of what they should do and what they should avoid. The sky moreover is covered with clouds, the obscurations brought about by the presence in their minds of the three or five poisons. It is in such circumstances as these that, by the coming together of two factors—the light of the Buddhas' bodhichitta and aspirations, and the merit of beings accumulated in the past—virtuous thoughts arise very occasionally in the minds of ordinary, worldly beings, overshadowed as they are by the gloom of ignorance. Such virtuous thoughts are simply the desire or willingness to do something good and

positive. They are fleeting impulses and they do not happen often (perhaps once in a hundred times, or twice in a thousand). They are extremely rare.

Therefore if the state of mind of actually wanting to accomplish something good occurs to you, you should be like a blind man who has managed to catch hold of a cow's tail. You should resolve never to lose it, but to develop it more and more. Don't ask your father. Don't discuss it with your mother. Don't let others decide for you. Just make up your own mind and be independent. Do not give yourself over to others, but be like a yak with its nose rope tied around its own head. Leave your enemies to their own devices; let your fields dry up. Practice earnestly, instead, the ten innermost riches of the Kadampa masters of old[55] and the famous three fierce mantras of the Dharma lord Tsangpa Gyaré. Tell yourself: "I will truly practice the sacred Dharma." And once the pledge is taken, it must be fulfilled!

The ten innermost riches are the three actions [of leaving, seeking, and obtaining], the four objectives, and the three vajras. The three actions are to leave the fellowship of humans, to seek the fellowship of dogs, and to obtain the fellowship of the enlightened. The four objectives are to turn your mind to the Dharma, to turn your Dharma to the condition of a beggar, to orient your beggarly condition toward your death, and to aim to die in a lonely cave. Regarding the three vajras, you start with the vajra of no procrastination, you conclude with the vajra of no need to be ashamed, and you take as your companion the vajra of primordial wisdom. The three fierce mantras are "Whatever has to happen, let it happen!", "Whatever the situation is, it's fine!", and "I really don't need anything!"

1. THE BENEFITS OF BODHICHITTA

2. THE GENERAL BENEFITS OF GENERATING BODHICHITTA

3. BODHICHITTA IS SUPERIOR TO ALL OTHER VIRTUES

[verse 6] As we have explained above, thoughts of wishing to accomplish something good are weak, like the flickering of lightning, whereas evil, nonvirtuous thoughts are like thick darkness and are our constant companions. They are so strong that they can throw us into the lower realms, and they are described as overwhelming because they are so difficult to reverse. Except for the precious mind of perfect bodhichitta, which shines brilliantly like the sun, what other ordinary virtue is able to overcome them? There is none. [verse 7] The reason for saying this is that for many

ages—three countless aeons and more—the powerful Sages,[56] the perfect Buddhas, deeply reflected upon one thing alone: the means to bring numberless beings to immediate benefit and ultimate bliss. And they have indeed found something that purifies evil committed in the past, that severs the continuum of evil to come, that overwhelms the defiled emotions of the mind, that nurtures and increases the tiny roots of virtue, and that brings the final achievement of great enlightenment. And seeing its benefit, they have taught it to disciples who might be trained. It is bodhichitta, the mind of enlightenment—the one factor that throughout the three times and for countless multitudes of beings secures easily and without travail an immediate benefit in the present moment and ultimately the supreme happiness of unsurpassed buddhahood.

[verse 8] Consequently, for those who wish and strive to halt the many ills of their own existence (the sufferings of birth, sickness, aging, and death), and for those who wish to clear away the sorrows of other beings in this and future lives—in short, for those who wish that, both now and ultimately, the myriad kinds of bliss be enjoyed by everyone, themselves and others—bodhichitta is the method to adopt. It must be seized by the mind and never relinquished.

3. A CHANGE OF NAME AND OF STATUS

[verse 9] It does not matter whether they are men or women, young or old, or whether their position in society is high or low. If the jewel of bodhichitta arises in the minds of suffering beings, who till then were languishing in the prison of samsara, bound by the chains of karma and defilement, they instantly undergo a change of identity. Henceforth, they are crowned with the name "Child of the Sugatas." They are called Bodhisattvas, heroes and heroines of enlightenment. Their status changes: they become objects of reverence and offering for the whole world, both gods and human beings. They are moreover said to be worthy of reverence even by the Buddhas themselves, for the latter have bodhichitta as their master.

3. THE BENEFITS OF BODHICHITTA SHOWN BY MEANS OF EXAMPLES

Here there are six sections: (1) the example of alchemy, showing that bodhichitta leads to the attainment of buddhahood; (2) the example of a jewel, showing bodhichitta's great worth; (3) the example of the miraculous fruit-bearing tree, showing that bodhichitta's root of virtue is inexhaustible and constantly increases; (4) the example of the heroic bodyguard, showing how bodhichitta overpowers the kind of evil that is definite [in being certain to ripen in an experienced effect]; (5) the example of the fires at the end of the kalpa, showing how bodhichitta eradicates the kind of evil that is indefinite [and may not itself ripen in a corresponding effect]. Finally, (6) there are further examples that are not found in the root verses but are mentioned in other texts.

4. THE EXAMPLE OF ALCHEMY

[verse 10] Here, bodhichitta is described using an example taken from alchemy, the point of comparison being the transformation of something bad into something good. By means of the supreme substance, the elixir of the alchemists (the gold-producing mercury), a single ounce of iron may be transmuted into a thousand ounces of pure gold. In the same way, if, with bodhichitta, one lays hold of this lowly human body composed of numerous impure substances, and if, instead of rejecting it as the Shravakas do, one adopts it throughout the course of many lifetimes in order to secure the welfare of others, this [human] body will itself become the body of the Buddha. It becomes something endowed with unimaginable qualities of excellence: a priceless wish-fulfilling jewel that protects from all the drawbacks of samsara and nirvana and grants the supreme perfection of the twofold aim.[57] Since it is able to effect such an extraordinary transformation, the extraordinary elixir of bodhichitta is something to be tightly grasped, never to be relinquished. We should therefore pledge ourselves to take hold of it as Shantideva says.

4. THE EXAMPLE OF THE JEWEL

[verse 11] The image adopted here is that of merchants journeying to an island somewhere in the ocean. They rely on a captain, in other words, a skillful leader, and hold in high esteem the jewels that he has appraised. In the same way, those who wish to make the voyage to the isle of liberation and omniscience first rely on the only guide, the peerless Buddha. With his boundless knowledge of omniscience, he has well examined, without error or confusion and for aeons of time, all the sublime teachings. And he has seen that, since bodhichitta is that by which buddhahood itself is obtained, it is supremely beneficial and more precious than any other teaching. For this reason, he has taught it to those who might be trained. Therefore, those who wish to dispel all the sufferings implicit in the condition of beings wandering in the six realms must take to heart this precious mind of enlightenment. And they must do this properly according to the three stages of preparation, actual commitment, and conclusion.[58] They must hold to it tightly and constantly with mindfulness, vigilant introspection, and carefulness, without ever letting it go.

4. THE EXAMPLE OF THE MIRACULOUS FRUIT-BEARING TREE

[verse 12] All other virtues of whatever kind that are not informed by bodhichitta are like the plantain tree, which bears fruit only once. When the fruit ripens, the tree gives nothing more and dies from its roots. Likewise, virtuous action tending to happiness gives its result in the form of high rebirth in samsara, but then it dwindles and is exhausted. Furthermore, the virtue of the Shravakas and Pratyekabuddhas ripens as the exhaustion of all the aggregates, which disappear without leaving any remainder. By contrast, virtue that is infused with bodhichitta[59] is like a perfect, miraculous fruit-bearing tree, the fruits of which never vanish but become ever more plentiful. Even after giving its fully ripened effect in the form of abundant but temporary happiness in the divine and human states, it is still not exhausted. Its (karmic) effects similar to the cause[60] continue to grow and increase without end, until a vast result is finally produced: the mass of merit that constitutes the body of a Buddha.

4. THE EXAMPLE OF THE HEROIC BODYGUARD

[verse 13] Unbearable and dreadful wickedness, such as the evil of rejecting the Dharma or harming the Three Jewels, or the sins of immediate effect,[61] are certain to produce the result of great suffering in the Hell of Unrelenting Pain.[62] Nevertheless, just like a murderer who, having recourse to the protection of a powerful escort, is instantaneously delivered from all fear of harm even if he meets the avenging son of his former victim, in the same way, whoever has precious bodhichitta is instantly freed from the sufferings of hell, which are the wages of great evil. Birth in hell does not occur; or if it does, one is instantly freed, having suffered no more than the time it takes for a ball of silk to bounce back up from the floor! This being so, how could those who are fearful of the effects of their evil actions not rely on bodhichitta? It is surely the rational thing to do!

4. THE EXAMPLE OF THE FIRES AT THE END OF TIME

[verse 14] The conflagration at the end of time consumes the world without leaving anything behind—not even the ashes of burnt grass. In the same way, and in addition to the evils described above, bodhichitta definitely and completely consumes or purifies in a single instant all other extreme negativities, such as slaughtering a hundred people. No remainder is left behind to be experienced. How, therefore, can anyone do without bodhichitta? It is surely a universal necessity.

4. THE BENEFITS OF BODHICHITTA EXPLAINED IN OTHER TEXTS

The other unbounded benefits of bodhichitta, which are beyond the mind's ability to calculate, were explained by the Buddha's great regent Maitreya, the loving protector, who in the fullness of his wisdom set them forth, with the help of two hundred and thirty examples, to the son of a wealthy merchant, the youthful Bodhisattva Sudhana. They are all to be found in the *Gandavyuha* chapter of the *Avatamsaka*. Since Shantideva has referred us to this text, here is the relevant passage. The *Gandavyuha* says:

> In the presence of the noble Manjushri, the Bodhisattva Sudhana generated the mind of enlightenment, whereupon Manjushri instructed him and sent him to the monk Meghashri. One by one, Sudhana attended one hundred and ten spiritual masters and each of them taught him a single aspect of the practice of the Bodhisattvas. Finally, he came again into the presence of the venerable Bodhisattva Maitreya, who was living in a southern land on the shore of the sea. Maitreya spoke to his attendants and said:
>
> Consider now the great perfection of his thought!
> Sudhana (the son of one so well-endowed with wealth)

Comes seeking now the Bodhisattva deeds.
He, the wise and learned, has now come to me.

Did you journey well, O you in whom
Compassion and a gentle love have sprung?
Did you journey well into Maitreya's mighty mandala?
Did you journey well, who are so peaceful to behold?
Accomplishing such hardships, are you not fatigued?
Approach, be welcome, you whose mind is pure!

Comforted and encouraged by these words, Sudhana gave an account of what he had experienced and requested Maitreya to speak about the deeds of Bodhisattvas. In reply, Maitreya told him to look into his palace, the name of which was "Essence Adorned by the Ornaments of Vairochana." Sudhana went to the palace and at each of its windows he saw one of the ways in which the venerable Maitreya had himself trained in the deeds of the Bodhisattvas, giving away his head and limbs. So it was that Sudhana learned all the Bodhisattva deeds and took them perfectly to heart.

The protector Maitreya taught to him the benefits of bodhichitta at great length: "O son of my lineage, bodhichitta is like a seed from which the qualities of the Buddhas grow. It is like a field, in which the goodness of all beings flourishes. It is like the earth, which is the foundation of the entire universe . . . Son of my lineage! These are the limitless qualities and benefits of bodhichitta, and even then there are more!"

There are, however, three main benefits of bodhichitta. It causes one to attain buddhahood; it increases virtue; and it purifies evil.

2. THE SPECIFIC BENEFITS OF BODHICHITTA IN INTENTION AND THE SPECIFIC BENEFITS OF BODHICHITTA IN ACTION

3. CLASSIFICATION OF BODHICHITTA IN INTENTION AND ACTION

Since all the qualities of the Mahayana path and its result arise from cultivating a state of mind turned to supreme enlightenment, one must generate bodhichitta at the very beginning. Bodhichitta is then classified, first, as "plain" [and easily cultivated] or relative bodhichitta, which is engendered on the basis of prompting; and, second, as "subtle" or ultimate bodhichitta, which is gained through [the recognition of] ultimate reality.

4. PLAIN OR RELATIVE BODHICHITTA, ENGENDERED ON THE BASIS OF PROMPTING

Maitreya said (in the *Sutralankara*):

> The power of a friend, the power of the cause, the power of
>   the root,
> The power of listening to the teachings and of virtuous
>   practice:
> From these it comes both stable and unstable;
> This, I say, is bodhichitta that is shown by others.

The "power of [meeting a spiritual] friend," as mentioned in the verse, can be illustrated by the story of an encounter in the past between three young men and a Buddha accompanied by his two main disciples. One of the boys made the aspiration to become like the Buddha, and the other two aspired to become like his disciples. Subsequently they became respectively our Teacher the Buddha Shakyamuni and his two great disciples, Shariputra and Maudgalyayana. The "power of the cause" refers to the awakening within oneself of the Mahayana lineage; the "power of the root" is the birth of compassion; the "power of listening" refers to the profound teachings; finally, "the virtuous practice" refers to the accumulation of merit. From all these is bodhichitta born. Whereas bodhichitta is considered unstable when it derives from the first strength, it is regarded as firm when it derives from the other four.

When a specific attitude of bodhichitta is generated, it is, according to Asanga and his brother Vasubandhu, a "mental factor." On the other hand, Vimuktasena and Haribhadra believe that it is the "main mind." The omniscient Longchenpa, for his part, says that, since it is taught that when the main mind is generated, mental factors are generated simultaneously, the former two opinions are not at variance. For their authors expressed themselves according to what they considered to be uppermost (the main mind or the mental factor). For when there is a main mind, mental factors also arise; when there are mental factors, a main mind must also occur.[63]

As for the defining characteristics of bodhichitta, it has two aims or features. Through compassion, it focuses on the welfare of others; through wisdom it focuses on perfect enlightenment. As it is said (in the *Sutralankara*), "It is a mental state endowed with two aims." And further, "The cultivation of bodhichitta is the wish to attain perfect buddhahood for the sake of others."

4. SUBTLE OR ULTIMATE BODHICHITTA, GAINED THROUGH [THE RECOGNITION OF] ULTIMATE REALITY

Subtle bodhichitta (in other words, bodhichitta that is difficult to realize) is born from the strength of meditation. Maitreya has said (in the *Sutralankara*):

> When the perfect Buddhas have been pleased,
> When the gatherings of wisdom and of merit have been made,
> Then nonconceptual wisdom with regard to all phenomena
> Is born, and it is known as ultimate.

Our sublime Teacher Shakyamuni delighted hundreds of perfect Buddhas, and, receiving their instructions, he amassed the supreme accumulations of merit and wisdom for one countless kalpa. It was thus that he attained supreme realization, namely, nonconceptual wisdom or knowledge with regard to all phenomena. And he beheld directly the truth of the first ground of realization.

[verse 15] Bodhichitta can be classified in other ways. For instance, it may be analyzed in terms of the first to the sixth (paramitas). In the *Prajna-paramita-sutras*, on the other hand, it is said that, according to the grounds of realization, there are twenty-two kinds of bodhichitta.[64] In the *Sagaramatiparipriccha-sutra*, bodhichitta is classified by way of eighty unceasing factors.[65]

There are many such divisions, but in brief, it should be understood that bodhichitta is essentially of two kinds: bodhichitta in intention (an aspiration for supreme enlightenment) and active bodhichitta (a practical engagement in the Bodhisattva activities). [verse 16] The difference between them is like the difference between the wish to go somewhere, and actually traveling to one's destination. It is thus that learned Bodhisattvas should understand the respective difference between bodhichitta in intention and bodhichitta in action.

Once again, there are several ways (using various examples) of explaining the difference between these two kinds of bodhichitta. Some, like the master Jnanapada, identify bodhichitta in intention with the bodhichitta of ordinary beings, and bodhichitta in action with that of beings on the noble grounds of realization. Others, like Abhaya(kara) and Jnanakirti, say that bodhichitta in intention is the bodhichitta associated with the path of accumulation, whereas bodhichitta in action is associated with the subsequent paths (from the path of joining onward). Shantipa, Ratnakara, and Sagaramegha say that a wish to attain enlightenment that is yet to be explicitly formulated in the ritual (of vow-taking) is bodhichitta in intention, while active bodhichitta comes into being when the wish is ritually expressed. For Prajnakaramati, bodhichitta in intention is a state of mind that does not eventuate in Bodhisattva activities, whereas bodhichitta in action is a state of mind that does so. According to Atisha, bodhichitta in intention focuses on the result, namely, buddhahood, while active bodhichitta focuses on the cause, namely, the path: They are defined as commitments related to the cause and to the result. Other authorities say that bodhichitta in intention is what beings may have until they reach the level from which there is no returning to samsara, whereas bodhichitta in action is what arises once this level is achieved—which is again to say that the two bodhichittas correspond to ordinary beings and to noble beings respectively. Given these variations in interpretation, most other authorities follow the teaching of Shantideva. The omniscient Longchenpa [agrees with Atisha] in saying that the commitment to achieve the result (buddhahood) is bodhichitta in intention while the commitment to the cause is active bodhichitta. [It is said furthermore that:]

> Divisions made by means of helpful images
> Are all contained in action and intention.

In brief, therefore, and in accordance with the distinction between intention and practical engagement, when one says "I will free all mother sentient beings, infinite in number as the sky is vast, from all the sufferings and shortcomings of both samsara and nirvana, and I will place them in the state of utterly perfect buddhahood," one is fervently wishing that one will also reach the resultant level of buddhahood. And one is making the pledge to do so. This is bodhichitta in intention endowed with two aims or orientations. When, after promising to undertake the path of the six paramitas (which are the cause), one engages and practices according to one's pledge, this is active bodhichitta. But just as when one sets off on a journey, the *wish* to go is not discarded; in the same way, where there is active bodhichitta, bodhichitta in intention is necessarily present.

One can, from the standpoint of their different aspects, distinguish two kinds of bodhichitta, three kinds of ethical discipline, as well as the bodhichitta vows or precepts. Nevertheless, they are all one according to their nature. For example, to practice virtue while wishing to attain perfect buddhahood for the sake of others is bodhichitta both in intention and in action. To bind one's mind with bodhichitta, to cultivate virtue, and to bring benefit to others are the three kinds of ethical discipline. And all of these restrain the negative actions and habitual tendencies of one's mind stream and are therefore referred to as the vows or precepts of a Bodhisattva. Although these are all essentially one, they are distinguished in a threefold manner according to aspect—just as a wishing jewel can be said to possess the three qualities of curing diseases, granting all one's needs and wishes, and shedding light in the darkness.

3. The benefits of bodhichitta in intention and in action

[verse 17] Simply to engender the bodhichitta of aspiring to supreme enlightenment produces, for those who wander in samsara, an immense result in terms of power and excellence: the states of Brahma and of Indra, kings of the gods, or of a chakravartin, a sovereign of the human race.[66] And yet a ceaseless stream of merit (in other words, the virtues of generosity, ethical discipline, and so on) does not flow from bodhichitta in intention, as it does from bodhichitta in action. [verse 18] When, however, one perfectly embraces the vow of active bodhichitta and keeps it unspoiled; when one intends never to turn away from the practice of the six paramitas but to liberate an infinity of beings from the sufferings of existence and peace and to bring them to enlightenment, [verse 19] from that moment on, the power of one's merit constantly increases and becomes inexhaustible—even when one is asleep, at play or in some other distracted state. It becomes as immeasurable as space itself. On the other hand, it is said that if one takes the vow of active bodhichitta but then neglects even a slight and sporadic practice of generosity and the other paramitas, not only is there no increase of merit, but the great downfall of failing to practice virtue occurs.

3. PROVING THE BENEFITS OF BODHICHITTA BY SCRIPTURE AND WITH REASONING

4. PROVING THE BENEFITS OF BODHICHITTA BY SCRIPTURE

[verse 20] Whether one thinks of the number of beings who are the object of one's concern or of the amount of their sufferings that are to be dispelled, and whether one thinks of the qualities of buddhahood to be gained or of the span of many ages required for such an accomplishment, the quantities one is dealing with are all are beyond measure. Accordingly, when the vow of active bodhichitta is taken and maintained unimpaired, the benefit that results from it is likewise immeasurable. On the basis of these four reasons, the Buddha has himself proclaimed this truth in the *Subahuparipriccha-sutra*. And this was not just an expedient teaching for those who only aspire to the lesser paths of the Shravakas and Pratyekabuddhas. The Buddha taught it precisely that they might understand and be certain about the qualities and benefits of bodhichitta.

As it is said in the above sutra, "If, for the benefit and happiness of infinite beings, I don the armor (of courage), the roots of virtue, which are forever directed at the benefit and happiness of all beings, will also be endless. They will increase and spread at all times, day and night, even when I am sleeping or being careless. It is thus that they will be perfected."

4. PROVING THE BENEFITS OF BODHICHITTA WITH REASONING

5. PROVING WITH REASONING THE BENEFITS OF BODHICHITTA IN INTENTION

The karmic principle of cause and effect is an extremely hidden object of knowledge. It is therefore the exclusive domain of the omniscient Buddha. Consequently, we can only distinguish between what is to be done and what is not to be done by trusting in the pure teaching of the Conqueror, for the karmic principle cannot be demonstrated by [the unaided power of] reasoning. Nevertheless, since the Buddha repeatedly praised the immense benefits of bodhichitta, these benefits may be logically deduced and are thus established. The text therefore makes as if to supply a reasoned demonstration.[67]

Once upon a time, when the son of Vallabha the householder—the son who was called "Daughter"—was setting off on a sea voyage in search of jewels, his mother wept and caught hold of the hem of his clothes. "Your tears," he cried, "will bring me bad luck on the journey." And with that, he kicked his mother in the head. In the course of his voyage, Daughter was shipwrecked, but holding fast to a spar, he was washed ashore on an island. He came to a town called Sukha and gradually moved on to other places, until finally he had to undergo the unbearable pain produced by an iron wheel spinning on his head. But then he thought to himself, "May the pain of other beings who are suffering for having kicked their mothers in the head ripen upon me. May they not experience it." At that very moment, his torture ceased and such was his bliss that he rose up in the air to the height of seven palm trees. And after his death, he was born among the gods.[68]

[verse 21] If one engenders the compassionate wish to soothe, with medicines for example, the aching heads of just a few people, this altruistic wish—even if it is ineffective—is productive of unbounded merit. [verse 22] What need is there to speak, then, of the boundless merit of the Bodhisattvas? They wish to remove the endless misery, in this and future lives, of all beings, who are as numerous as the sky is vast, bringing them immeasurable excellence both in the immediate term and on the ultimate level.

[verse 23] Nobody has good and altruistic attitudes equal to those of the Bodhisattvas, who want all beings to attain buddhahood. Even one's father and mother do not have it (and parents are well known in the world for the kindness they show to their children, wishing them long lives free from sickness, full of strength, wealth, and influence). One could argue that this is only because of their ignorance. But even the gods, who possess the five kinds of preternatural knowledge, and even the rishis or sages, who know the eighteen great sciences, are without this attitude. Again it might be thought that their lack of bodhichitta is due to a lack of kindness. But even Brahma himself, endowed as he is with love, compassion, sympathetic joy, and equanimity,[69] wishing happiness and freedom from suffering for all his subjects, is without bodhichitta, the wish that they should attain buddhahood. [verse 24] Our fathers, our mothers, Brahma, or anyone else have never even dreamt of having the wish to accomplish enlightenment—even for themselves. It is unreasonable to think that they could truly wish it for others.

[verse 25] This bodhichitta, turned as it is toward the good of all beings, which the gods and other beings do not conceive of even in their own regard let alone that of others, is the jewel of the mind. Of all thoughts it is the most precious, for it is the highest and most noble of all mental states. This truly wondrous attitude, never experienced before, now arises in the mind, thanks to hearing the teachings of the Mahayana and through the power of one's spiritual teacher. It is as astonishing as if the wish-fulfilling tree of the celestial realm had sprouted in the human world. [verse 26] For all beings, bodhichitta is the cause of every happiness, whether in the immediate or the ultimate term. It is the great panacea, the healing draft that thoroughly dispels the sufferings and ills of every being. How can the merit or benefits of this precious, jewel-like attitude of bodhichitta be gauged or measured? For the limits of the sky, the number of beings, the number of their sorrows, and the number of the Buddhas' qualities are all equally immeasurable. And so it is said in the *Viradattagrihapati-paripriccha-sutra*:

> If the merit of the enlightened mind
> Were to take material form,
> The whole of space would be replete with it
> And even then there would be more besides.

5. PROVING WITH REASONING THE BENEFITS OF BODHICHITTA IN ACTION

It is said in the *Samadhiraja-sutra*:

> The constant, daily worship of the supreme ones
> With countless gifts of all that may be found
> Within all buddhafields a hundred million strong—
> All this is nothing when contrasted with a loving mind!

[verse 27] If just the altruistic wish, the desire to bring happiness to others is far more noble than the offering of the seven precious attributes of royalty[70] and other gifts to the Buddhas, is there any need to mention the superiority of the actual practice of the six paramitas, generosity and so on, performed with the intention of bringing all beings, as infinite as space, to the true happiness of buddhahood?

[verse 28] Although beings want to free themselves from unwanted sorrows now and in the future (shortness of life, manifold illness, poverty, and so forth), their wishes and their actions are at cross-purposes. They kill, they steal, and they zealously indulge in the rest of the ten negative actions. By doing this, they hurry toward their miseries in this and future lives, like moths fluttering directly into a flame. Although they yearn for longevity and health and all other joys, they are ignorant of how to achieve them. For they have no understanding of what is to be avoided and what is to be accomplished. Not only do they fail to perform the ten positive deeds, but they commit various negativities, thereby destroying their happiness as though they regarded it as their very enemy.

[verse 29] Consequently, when those who are endowed with great love bring temporary and ultimate bliss to beings who are destitute of happiness and its causes, when with great compassion they cut away the pain and sorrow of all who are weighed down with misery and its causes, and when with wisdom they teach them what ought to be done and what ought not to be done, [verse 30] thereby remedying their ignorance of the karmic principle of cause and effect—what other virtue could be matched in strength with theirs? What other friends could bring beings so much good, placing them in a state of happiness, dispelling their sorrows, and teaching them what to do and what not to do? What merit is there comparable to bodhichitta?

In these verses Shantideva sets forth the benefits of bodhichitta. The reason why it is important for us to know about them is that if we actually have the thought that, come what may, we must give rise to bodhichitta both in ourselves and others, we will yearn for whatever will engender it wherever it has been previously absent. And we will intensify it where it has arisen, without ever letting it decline. When we have such an interest and longing, so great that none can prevent it—like hungry and thirsty people craving food and water—this is truly the result of understanding the benefits of bodhichitta. On the other hand, it has been said that simply to have an intellectual knowledge of all this and to explain it to others is of no help whatsoever. We must train our minds in bodhichitta over and over again.

2. THE GREATNESS OF A PERSON WHO POSSESSES BODHICHITTA

[verse 31] Those who acknowledge and repay the good that others have done to them in the past through the gift of such things as food or money are considered in this world to be worthy of praise. For as the saying goes:

> Honor and protection stay close by
> The man who recognizes and repays the favors done to him.

Those who show their gratitude are protected by the gods themselves, and they possess other great excellent attributes. This being so, what shall we say of the Bodhisattvas, who do good where no good has been done to them before and who strive only in the means to achieve the benefit of beings both now and in future lives, without ever being asked? What need is there to say that they are worthy of offerings and praise?

[verse 32] As the saying goes, "Know the meaning through examples." And indeed the meaning of anything is grasped more easily through such expedients. We may imagine therefore someone supplying food on a regular basis for, let us say, a year or month or just a day to a restricted group of people (a hundred or a thousand, who thus constitute a limited or inferior object of generosity). The period of time in which the act is performed is likewise inferior; it is the time it takes to complete the act of giving. The thing given is also inferior, for this is only a little food, and no great gift. We may imagine too that the act is performed in a disdainful manner, striking and hitting the beneficiaries, and is thus an inferior mode of giving. Finally, the benefit itself is inferior for the people in question are nourished for only half a day. Even so, many people in this world will consider such a donor to be worthy of praise and honor. "How virtuous," they will say, "to make such charitable donations!"

[verse 33] The gift bestowed by the Bodhisattvas, on the other hand, is not to just a few, but to all beings, the number of which is as infinite as the vastness of space. Their act of giving is not briefly done but lasts long, indeed until the very emptying of samsara. Their gift is no meager pittance, but the unsurpassable bliss of buddhahood, and their mode of giving is marked by serenity and devotion. Finally, the benefit involved is not small but thoroughly outstanding, seeing that it is the fulfillment of all wishes and is bestowed continuously and without interruption. What need then is there to say that the Bodhisattvas are generous benefactors worthy of respect and praise?

[verse 34] The Buddha has said that all those who have evil thoughts in their minds against the Bodhisattvas described above (sovereigns of generosity, who bestow on beings the state of buddhahood) and all those who do no more than wish that something unfortunate might happen to them (to say nothing of actual physical or verbal aggression), will remain in hell in great torment for aeons equal to the moments of their malice. And here, a moment is to be understood as the shortest possible unit, corresponding to one sixty-fourth of the time it takes for a strong man to snap his fingers. It is written in the *Prashantavinishchaya-pratiharya-sutra*, "Bodhisattva Manjushri, be forearmed! Those who show anger or contempt toward a Bodhisattva will have to stay in hell for as many kalpas as the number of their states of malice!"

[verse 35] By contrast, when one simply gazes upon the face of a Bodhisattva with an attitude of joy and sincere devotion, the effects are incalculable. One will have the joy of the gods of Tushita for more kalpas than there are instants of one's gazing. The outcome is even greater than the result of malevolence. As it is written in the *Niyataniyatagatimudra-vatara-sutra*, "Manjushri, if, for the sake of argument, all the beings of the entire universes of the ten directions were to lose their eyes and my noble sons and daughters, with their loving thoughts, were to cause them to grow again, even such merit, O Manjushri, would be unequal to that of my noble sons and daughters who watch with faith and devotion the Bodhisattva devoted to the Mahayana. For the merit engendered thereby is indeed beyond counting."

Even in times of famine; even when there is a dearth of clothing and possessions; even when there is loss of life of human beings and animals; even when there is disease, harm by negative forces, enemies and spirits, in all such terrible conditions, the Bodhisattvas, the offspring of the Buddha, are people for whom bad omens turn to good and for whom adversity becomes a friend. Such difficulties are no hindrance to their Dharma practice. Not only do they not give rise to evil deeds, but such troubles become a means for them to purify past evils and are an encouragement to virtuous actions. Positive attitudes, such as love, compassion, and the determination to abandon samsara, will naturally increase, as illustrated in the story of Prince Danarata and King Manichuda. On the other hand, Bodhisattvas who are without much courage and who are unskilled in means are unable to bear even the slightest difficulties. As the saying goes:

> When sun is warm and stomach full,
> You look like a practitioner.
> When setbacks and hard times befall,
> You're really very ordinary!

On the other hand, for those whose minds are stable and who are skilled in means, it is as Asanga has said:

> Even when the world is full of evil
> They turn hardship into the enlightened path.

Accordingly, when illness and sorrow, enemies and evil spirits and all such harms arise, if you do not fall beneath their power, they become an assistance on the path to enlightenment. They are like the wind, which can blow out a flame or cause a forest fire to blaze.

[verse 36] Shantideva pays respectful homage in thought, word, and deed to everyone, whether of high or low estate, in whose mind the precious mind of enlightenment has arisen, the state of mind that of all others is most sacred—the wish to dispel all the drawbacks of both existence and peace. And as the saying goes:

> When links are good, in one life buddhahood.
> When links are bad, samsara has an end.

Even when Bodhisattvas are attacked and reviled, it is through the strength of their compassion, bodhichitta, skillful means, and prayers of aspiration, that they forge links that connect their attackers with happiness both in the immediate and ultimate term. And they help them to attain it. This is illustrated by the story of the sage Kshantivadin and the king Maitribala.[71] Shantideva therefore takes refuge in the Bodhisattvas. For they are supreme beings, the source of happiness in this and future lives. Any kind of relationship with them is always beneficial. We should do as Shantideva does. We should make prostrations to the Bodhisattvas, the children of the Buddhas, and take refuge in them.

It may be thought that it is contradictory to say, on the one hand, that an evil intention against a Bodhisattva will lead to birth in hell, and to say, on the other, that even if one harms a Bodhisattva, one will be joined with happiness. But this is not so. The former statement is made from the point of view of the ineluctable karmic law of cause and effect, on account of which the evil attitude will give the immediate result of birth in an infernal existence. The latter statement takes into account the fact that the compassion of the Bodhisattvas, and their skillful means deployed through bodhichitta, together with the strength of their powerful prayers, afford protection and care even for beings who afflict harm on them.

The principal reason for acquainting oneself with the qualities of those who have bodhichitta in their minds is that one will then confess all the faults of thought, word, and deed that one has formerly committed against the Bodhisattvas. One will refrain from such faults in the future and take the Bodhisattvas as one's refuge. This in effect is what the result should be. On the other hand, simply to know about all this and to explain it to others is of no avail. It is vital to take all this to heart and to meditate on it.

It is generally said that Tibet is the field of the benevolent activity of the noble and compassionate Avalokiteshvara and that Tibetans belong to the lineage of the Mahayana. And on the whole, there is no one there nowadays who has not received an empowerment. They are consequently Bodhisattvas, worthy of the homage of both gods and humankind, and are thus an exceptional people endowed with many qualities.[72] Indeed they are the Buddhas of the future. Consequently, if one has entertained wrong ideas about them in the past, imputing faults and imperfections to them that they do not have, while denying the qualities that they possess, one should confess this and resolve never to repeat such an action. Henceforth, one should train in pure vision in their regard, pay them respect, and take refuge in them.[73]

It is said in the sutras moreover that, in the age of decadence, Bodhisattvas may make mistakes when they relate with other people. It is therefore important not to dwell on the faults of others, but to train in pure perception of them. It is said, furthermore, that we should revere the Bodhisattvas, imitating the brahmins of India who, taking the moon as their deity, venerate it while it is waxing, but not when it is full. Even if Bodhisattvas do have faults, they will nevertheless become Buddhas. Their faults, after all, are compounded phenomena and will consequently be worn away by dint of practicing the path. Nobody becomes enlightened by being faultless from the beginning. It is therefore said that to avoid dwelling on the defects and faults of others is a most important pith instruction.

This ends the first chapter from the *Bodhicharyavatara*, called "The Excellence and Benefits of Bodhichitta."

· 2 ·

CONFESSION OF NEGATIVITY

1. THE MAKING OF OFFERINGS

2. MATERIAL OFFERINGS

3. THE OFFERING OF ONE'S POSSESSIONS

Precious bodhichitta, which is endowed with such extraordinary qualities, does not arise in the absence of causes and conditions. All the causes for it must be complete. In this respect, the lord Nagarjuna says that bodhichitta occurs when the accumulation of merit is fulfilled. Asanga, for his part, says that it arises in a pure and limpid mind. Now the best of all ways of accumulating merit is to make offerings; moreover, the laying out of perfect offerings has the effect of rendering one's mind pure and limpid as well. Once, when the Tibetans asked the peerless lord Atisha for the vow of bodhichitta, he instructed them to prepare offerings. They did so, but Atisha found the offerings insufficient and refused to give the vow. Again the Tibetans prepared offerings and again Atisha refused. Finally, when they had laid out offerings on a far grander scale, Atisha said that they were just sufficient and gave the vow. It is clear that offerings are extremely important. Indeed, it is said that all one's possessions should be divided into three. One part should be set aside for one's subsistence and the other two should be used as offerings to the Three Jewels.

The offerings in question should be made in accordance with the "three purities." First, one's motivation should be pure. [verse 1] In other words, one makes the offerings in order to gain or generate precious bodhichitta in the mind. Second, the object or field of offering should be pure. The offerings are made to the Bhagavan Buddhas, those who have "thus gone," that is, those who have proceeded in accordance with ultimate reality. Likewise offerings are made to the stainless, supremely rare Jewel of the sacred Dharma, which is the truth of the path, delivering us from attachment, and also the truth of cessation, the state of freedom. As it is said [in the *Uttaratantra-shastra*]:

> Freedom from attachment and the freeing from the same,
> The Dharma has the nature of two truths.
> Deliverance from attachment in itself includes
> Cessation and the truth of path.

Finally, one makes offerings to the Bodhisattvas, the Buddha's offspring, who possess boundless, ocean-like qualities. On gaining the first ground of realization, for example, Bodhisattvas possess twelve groups of qualities, each group consisting of a hundred qualities. On the second ground, they possess twelve groups of a thousand qualities. And so on.

The third purity is that of the offering substances themselves. An excellent offering is one of good provenance and of immaculate quality, well-prepared or well-arranged. Good provenance means that the offerings have not been procured through wrong livelihood or evil actions. The offerings are of immaculate quality because they are clean, because they are offered without pride or ostentation, and because they are not spoiled by niggardliness and reluctance.[74] If we offer the best of what we have—of all that we hold most dear and rare—the offering itself acts as an antidote to avarice. If, on the other hand, we make offerings of things like moldy cheese, plants with withered leaves, and so on, our merit will diminish. This therefore is something to be avoided. Finally, the offerings should be well-arranged. The seven offering bowls should be clean and properly filled—set out evenly and in an orderly fashion. If they are insufficiently filled with water or grains, this will lead to poverty. If they overflow, our discipline will go astray. If the offered water is spilled, tumors will result, and so on. The preparation and arrangement of offerings should be free of all such faults.

3. The offering of things unowned

This refers to the offering of all the wonderful riches and commodities that we see or hear about in all the reaches of the universe spreading out in the ten directions. It is enough simply to offer them mentally, by recalling them or bringing their names and appearances to mind. Thus we can offer [verse 2] all the flowers—white lotuses, mandarava, and blue utpalas—that grow in the streams and meadows of the pure buddhafields or in the heavens of the gods, the lands of the nagas, and the human realms. To these are added all the fruits and grains that exist: the bilwa fruit, the mango, barley, rice, wheat, and so on. Bezoar, the best and most potent of medicines, is also offered, together with the six excellent substances[75] and other things such as medicinal substances, stones, herbs, and roots. We can make an offering of all the precious jewels to be found in world: the precious wish-fulfilling gem, which satisfies every need and desire, lapis lazuli, sapphire, and so forth.

And as it is said in the sutra:

Cool and tasty, light and soft,
Limpid water, free from all impurity—
When drunk, it does not harm the stomach
And to the throat it does no injury.

We can offer water endowed with these eight fine qualities, such as the waters of Lake Neverwarm, together with the great rivers that spill from it in the four directions—the Ganges to the east, the Sindhu to the south, the Vakshu to the west, and the Sita to the north, as well as the waters of the seven seas of enjoyment.[76] The peerless Atisha indeed spoke of the excellence of the water of Tibet, saying that the offering of it alone was enough to accumulate merit. [verse 3] We can offer Mount Meru, the king of mountains, composed of four precious substances, as well as the seven ranges of golden mountains and all the other peaks. We can offer all forest glades, pleasant solitudes encircled by groves of sandal trees, sweet and lonely places that are as clean as a mandala of turquoise and adorned with every kind of flower, places that are unfrequented by day and silent by night.

We can also offer trees garlanded with different-colored blossoms, beautiful like jeweled ornaments; and all kinds of fruit trees and vines with branches bending under the weight of their many delicious fruits and grapes perfect in color, fragrance, and taste. [verse 4] We can offer the scent of sandalwood and all the sweet-smelling trees to be found in the human world, as well as in the realms of the gods and the nagas. We can offer the natural incense of aloe, as well as perfumes contrived with human skill, and likewise every wish-granting tree, such as the celestial parijata, which satisfies every desire, together with the precious trees of Sukhavati, composed as they are of gold and other of the seven precious minerals. We can also offer the many harvests of crops like salu rice, which grow without the land being ploughed or the seed being sown, and everything else that is worthy to be offered but cannot be individually named. [verse 5]

Again, we can offer the four famous lakes[77] and immaculate turquoise meres adorned with lotuses of five different colors. We can offer the many lesser stretches of water embellished with lilies and resonant with the sweet and plaintive cries of waterbirds, swans and geese, with exquisite plumage of different colors—white as conch, yellow as gold, red as coral, and blue as turquoise. We can offer the brilliant light of the sun and moon rising in the east, the sweet fragrance of incense coming from the sandal groves in the south, the divine white butter offerings of the snowy mountains in the west, the blue cascading water, sparkling and pure in the north. And everything else, whatever there is.

These offerings, the flowers and all the rest, have four features in common. First, they are infinite in quantity, extending to the very limits of space. Second, they are untainted by negativity, for they are owned by no one, like the wealth and possessions of the people of Uttarakuru.[78] [verse 6] Third, they are offered in the imagination, keeping them before the mind. In other words, we act as if they were our own property and offer them without reserve. Fourth, they are offered to the Lord Buddha, the Powerful Sage, who, accompanied by his Bodhisattva children, is able to act spontaneously and unguardedly in body, speech, and mind,[79] and who is the most valiant of all the six classes of beings and the greatest of the human race. Moreover, the offering is well-made with the intention that precious bodhichitta take birth in the mind. And even if the offerings are modest, they give a great result, for the Buddhas are their perfect recipients. This is illustrated by the story of Mandhata, who became a chakravartin because he made an offering to a Buddha of only seven peas, or by the story of Ashoka, whose dignity as a Dharma king was due to the fact that he had [in a previous life] placed a handful of sand in the Buddha's begging bowl. This is why in the root text Shantideva prays to the Lords of Compassion, the sublime recipients of his offerings, who are without deceit and guile and are unchanging in their desire to help beings, that they might think lovingly of him and accept his gifts.

[verse 7] What is the purpose for the sort of offerings just described?

Shantideva explains that he is destitute of merit, which results from generosity and other virtues performed in the past. For this reason he is poor in his present life and is, as it were, the least among beggars. Apart from the items just described, he has nothing fit to offer. He therefore prays that his offerings be acceptable to the Buddhas our Protectors and their Bodhisattva heirs. From the first moment that they generated bodhichitta, they have—free from any kind of self-regard—thought only of how they might be of help to beings. They wish only that beings fulfill the two accumulations of wisdom and merit and purify defilements. Shantideva prays that, though they are free from clinging to the reality of things and have no needs of any kind, they might, through their miraculous powers and from their pure abodes, accept these offerings of all things wild and unowned, and that they might do so in order to allow him to purify defilement and accumulate merit. If, in our turn, we are able to make offerings in this way, it follows that, since the Buddhas and Bodhisattvas have wisdom and compassionate skill and are masters of inconceivable miraculous powers, they will also accept our oblation, thereby allowing us to fulfill our stock of merit and to cleanse our defilements.

3. The Offering of One's Body

[verse 8] To the Buddhas, the Victorious Lords, who have vanquished the four demons,[80] and to the host of their Bodhisattva offspring, Shantideva, henceforth and for all his lives to come, makes a constant and uninterrupted offering of his own body, which is so dear and necessary to him. He begs the supreme heroes, the Buddhas and Bodhisattvas, the lords of the three lineages[81] and so forth, to accept him completely and to adopt him as their own. Having thus become their respectful subject in body, speech, and mind, he pledges himself to fulfill their wishes. [verse 9] Now that they have fully accepted him as one of their servants and have made him their own, Shantideva promises that he will act according to their pleasure. For, although he is himself still in samsara, he will work for the benefit of others, undaunted by the sufferings of existence. He promises to accomplish the welfare and happiness of beings. But seeing that any negative action that he has committed is prejudicial to the good name and reputation of the Buddhas and Bodhisattvas, and since (on account of his sins) he is powerless to accomplish even his own good, let alone that of others, he

confesses all the evil of his past and resolves henceforth to abstain from it. In fact, it has been said that the offering of one's own body is the best way to protect oneself [from the results of former evil].

2. OFFERINGS MANIFESTED BY THE POWER OF THE MIND

3. THE OFFERING OF A CEREMONIAL BATH

This offering is made in accordance with the secular customs of ancient India and consists of the kind of ablutions performed before and after meals. It includes bathing the feet of one's guests, offering them perfume, and adorning their heads with garlands of flowers. As a means to purify himself and others, cleansing the impurities of thought, word, and deed, Shantideva offers a bathing ceremony to the Buddhas and Bodhisattvas, even though the latter are themselves quite unstained by any defilement. [verse 10] In the space before him, Shantideva imagines one or more bathing chambers, excellently perfumed with sandal, camphor, and the like. The floor is composed of five kinds of crystal, pure and transparent, beautifully wrought with inlaid patterns, sparkling and brilliant. Its surface is smooth and its draining conduits have been sealed with plugs. Four graceful pillars, colored according to the four cardinal directions, ablaze with the variegated shimmer of seven kinds of precious stone and crystal, are connected at their base by a low wall, reaching to the level of a man's waist, the purpose of which is to retain the water. Above this are four railings, and the whole is surmounted by a ceiling, its inner surface adorned with gleaming canopies of five sorts of pearl and other jewels, as well as banners, parasols, victory banners, pennants, silken frills, and pendant strings, whereby the whole is rendered extremely beautiful. The ceiling opens upward in the center, and above it, supported by small pillars, is a Chinese-style roof, adorned with a wishing-jewel as its crowning ornament.

Shantideva imagines that within these chambers thrones made of precious stones have been set in place. [verse 11] The Buddhas then arrive—the Tathagatas (those who have "proceeded in accordance with ultimate reality"). Although their minds never waver from the wisdom of the dharmakaya, they nevertheless appear according to the needs of beings in the rupakaya, or body of form, the illusory display of primordial wisdom. Accompanied by the infinite hosts of Bodhisattvas, they hang their garments on the railings just described.

Then, visualizing himself either in his own form or in the form of emanated offering goddesses, Shantideva clothes the Buddhas in the translu-
cent white bathing robes that he has offered. With tilted vessels—large,
exquisite vases of lapis lazuli and other precious substances, two-thirds
filled with water fragrant with cleansing unguents and perfume—he
bathes the Buddhas. All the while, offering goddesses of ravishing beauty
positioned on the radiant terraces outside the bathing chamber, sing melodious prayers and praises celebrating the high deeds of the Buddhas, accompanied by other goddesses on flute and drum. This then is the offering
of the bathing ceremony. When the plugs are drawn, it is imagined that the
bathing waters stream down from the sky and cleanse away all the evil
deeds and defilements of beings, oneself and others, who are beneath. In
particular, this water pacifies all the evil intentions and violent wickedness
of the local gods, owners of the ground—all spirits and bloodthirsty
demons, and all evil forces that are the source of epidemic diseases, thereby
bringing to an end the illnesses of both human beings and animals. And
one then imagines that precious bodhichitta takes birth in their minds.

[verse 12] Then with immaculate cloths of unexampled quality, heavenly
fabrics and Benares silk, with towels perfumed with sweet-smelling medicinal talc, Shantideva dries the bodies of the Buddhas and Bodhisattvas. All
these garments, bathing robes, and drying cloths now transform into a red
light of blessings and accomplishments and dissolve into the foreheads of
himself and others, specifically in the place between the eyebrows. With such
a thought it is understood that all the qualities of primordial wisdom have
been gained. Once their bodies have been dried, offerings are made to the
nirmanakaya Buddhas (who assume the demeanor of monks) of all the accoutrements of renunciants: the thirteen articles of ordained livelihood,[82]
such as the three Dharma robes, well-dyed with the three permitted colors
of red, blue, and saffron. Hundreds of thousands of such precious and
scented robes are offered. [verse 13] To the sambhogakayas, who appear in
the guise of chakravartins and who are given to the enjoyment of pleasures,
offerings are made of incomparable vestments of celestial and priceless ma-
terials, extremely fine, light, and soft to the touch, in various colors and de-
signs—all in all, the five silken garments: the short-sleeved garment that can
bestow upon the body the bliss of samadhi, the upper garment of white silk
wrought with golden traceries, the many-colored lower garment, the pendants of different silks, and a sash (there may also be a silken shawl instead
of the short-sleeved shirt). When making this offering of raiment, one should

wish that all beings, oneself and others, be clothed with a sense of moral conscience regarding their own conduct and the opinion and feelings of others.
As for ornaments and jewels, the eight precious adornments—the golden
diadem inlaid with lapis lazuli and so forth; earrings; the short, medium,
and long necklaces; bracelets; anklets; and belts—are offered many a hundredfold. With such as these, one adorns the noble Samantabhadra, Manjughosha, Avalokita Lord of the World, together with all the others:
Vajrapani, Kshitigarbha, Maitreya, Akashagarbha, and Sarvanivaranavishkambhin. So doing, one should wish that all beings be graced with the
major and minor marks of enlightenment.

3. OFFERINGS OF PLEASANT SUBSTANCES

In the *Abhidharmakosha* we find the following:

> The universe consisting of four continents, of sun and moon,
> Of Meru and the heavens of the gods,
> Of realms of both desire and of pure form,
> All this increased a thousand times defines the chiliocosm.
> This multiplied a thousand times is the dichiliocosm
> And as an intermediary universe has been described.
> And this once more a thousand times increased is the
>   trichiliocosm.

[verse 14] With vessels made of precious jewels, of conch or mother-of-
pearl, filled with the cool-scented water of white sandal and other exquisite
perfumes that penetrate even the boundless reaches of a thousand million
worlds, the offering goddesses anoint the bodies of the Buddhas and the
Bodhisattvas. The forms of the latter shine like pure gold sixteen times refined (its brilliance intensified by various agents and burnished with a
cloth of silk). Being lustrous in themselves, they radiate their light upon all
that surrounds them. It is thus that Shantideva says that he too will anoint
them, so that not the slightest blemish appears. Reflecting in the same way,
we should form the wish that all beings, ourselves and others, acquire the
golden skin that is a mark of buddhahood.

[verse 15] Before the Buddhas, Lords of Sages, who are the supreme recipients of offering, ravishing blossoms of perfect shape and hue are
placed: the celestial mandarava, the lotus and utpala of the divine and

human realms, together with all the brilliant, perfumed flowers that are to be found in the realms of gods, nagas, and human beings, as well as in the pure fields. Tossed into the sky, they take the form of palaces, canopies, banners and parasols, victory banners and mandalas—and all this is offered to the nirmanakaya Buddhas appearing in monastic guise. Flowers come showering down and go blowing in the wind as offerings to all the Buddhas of the ten directions. To the sambhogakaya Buddhas (appearing in the aspect of those who are given to enjoyment) garlands are offered made of five kinds of flowers, worked and expertly twisted together as though by skilled garland makers, together with other adornments. As we make such offerings, we too should wish that all beings, oneself and others, flourish with the blossoms of the seven elements that lead to enlightenment.[83]

[verse 16] Billowing clouds of the choicest incense are offered to the Buddhas and their Bodhisattva children—serpent-heart sandalwood, black akaru and the like, natural or manufactured, filling the whole of space in all directions, the merest scent of which ravishes the mind. These clouds of burning incense, whether in sticks or powder, which take the shape of seed-syllables or the seven attributes of royalty, are borne on the wind in the ten directions and all is respectfully offered as a pleasing oblation to the Buddhas and Bodhisattvas. Here the wish is made that this perfume might dispel the distress of beings and fill them with joy and that the minds of all beings, ourselves and others, be permeated with the fragrance of ethical discipline so pleasing to the enlightened ones. In addition, the best food is also offered: rice of a hundred savors and other dishes, drafts of nectar, the three white and the three sweet substances, and every delicacy contrived of perfect-tasting, aromatic ingredients. It is food worthy of a divine being (which in the present context means a king), prepared in water that is fresh and unsullied. In brief, an offering is made of all the food and drink that one could possibly desire. The Buddhas' begging bowls are filled with it and likewise all the jeweled dishes, plates, and other vessels. Thinking thus we make the wish that all beings, ourselves and others, acquire the supreme food of concentration.

[verse 17] A mental offering is made of the light of precious lamps of lapis lazuli, set within a host of beautiful, well-positioned lotuses all contrived of the purest gold, illuminating the whole world by day and by night. Each will be offered one by one, every lamp visualized as being as large as the three-thousandfold universe, its wick as high as Mount Meru, its molten butter as vast as the sea, its five-hued light filling the whole of space. And one makes the wish that, thanks to this offering, the darkness of all beings (their ignorance of the nature of phenomena) be dissipated and that the supreme light of omniscient wisdom be gained. Upon the even jeweled pavement, which has a checkered design and is soft and yielding to the step, and which is impregnated with sweet perfume to the thickness of an ox's hide, a carpet of ravishingly beautiful flowers is scattered, lying flat and even (without their stalks protruding) on the ground. Making such an offering, we should formulate the wish that all beings, ourselves and others, generate bodhichitta with an intent as immovable as the earth itself.

[verse 18] Palaces are offered that are incalculable in size, spaciousness, and design. They are made of jewels and constructed on five hundred different levels. Moreover, inside and on their outside terraces, offering goddesses sing melodious praises and play upon the lute and other instruments. These residences are adorned with loops and pendant strings of rosy pearls and other precious gems, which hang from the mouths of ornamental lions and sea creatures set upon the pillars both inside and outside the building. All these pendant ornaments are ravishingly beautiful; they sparkle with a myriad lights and are adorned with tassels, tiny bells and mirrors, with which the extremities of the strings of pearls are likewise decorated. The mirrors reflect, and the tinkling bells describe, the lives and exploits of the Bodhisattvas.

From the sandalwood spouts located at the corners of the roof, there flows a stream of scented water that collects in pools where various waterbirds play and sweetly sing. In certain of the palace halls, garments are laid out, in others, refreshments of food and drink. There are thrones and seats to sit on during the day, divans to sleep upon at night. They are piled high with many-colored cushions and pillows of heavenly fabrics together with every kind of precious accoutrement. Both by day and by night, jeweled lamps shed their radiance, shining in all directions, their light extending to the infinite reaches of space. They are thus the very ornaments of the sky. All this is offered to the compassionate Buddhas and the Bodhisattvas. Thinking thus we too should make the wish that, together with all other beings, we might reach the city of liberation.

[verse 19] Offerings are made of lovely parasols contrived of celestial silks and precious gems, golden shafts and exquisite jeweled fringes, unending knots, loops, and pendants. These are beautifully formed and delightful to behold. They are held aloft and carried around by offering goddesses, wise horses, and elephants. All these are constantly offered to all the Buddhas and their Bodhisattva children, just as in the past when Brahma, standing to the right of our compassionate Teacher, offered him five hundred parasols of lapis lazuli, while Indra, on the left, offered him five hundred parasols of the best refined gold. When the offering is complete, we too should make the wish that all beings, ourselves and others, be protected from the heat and vexation of samsara and the lower realms and that we all come beneath the cooling shade of the Three Jewels and the protection they bestow. We should consider that this twelvefold offering visualized by the mind pervades the three-thousandfold universe, even though such thoughts exceed the minds' imagination.

Shantideva himself was a yogi whose spiritual practice and manner of life were of an extreme simplicity. He did not teach extensively about actual material offerings. Offerings imagined by the mind, on the other hand, are the best way to complete the great accumulation of merit without difficulty. Such is the offering of a Bodhisattva skilled in means. We should therefore refrain from thinking that such offerings are unimportant and instead meditate upon them repeatedly. It is not necessary, however, to concentrate upon them uninterruptedly as we do with a yidam deity. If we hold the offerings to the Buddhas and Bodhisattvas before our minds for brief moments, it is not necessary to labor hard and exhaust ourselves in order to gather a great stock of merit. Thus the accumulations will be complete, defilements will be purified, and bodhichitta will arise in our minds. We will understand the teachings and remember them, and every other excellent quality will arise. It is important therefore to visualize all such offerings repeatedly, for this is of the greatest benefit and is easy to do. It is said that if we make such offerings, they are more vast and pure than any other offering deriving from wrong livelihood and negative actions, or from offerings made with pride and ostentation.

2. OFFERINGS MADE THROUGH THE POWER OF ASPIRATION

[verse 20] In addition, we should imagine that innumerable other magnificent offerings arise in the presence of the Buddhas and Bodhisattvas and remain uninterruptedly: the music of all sorts of wind and percussion instruments, such as cymbals endowed with eight qualities and so on, or the sweet music of the lute like that of Druma-kinnara (which sent even Mahakashyapa[84] helplessly a-dancing). And there are other entrancing sounds like the strumming of the tamboura of Prabha (king of gandharvas) and clouds of music, of dance, and of tuneful songs of praise—music the mere hearing of which can soothe the troubles of beings and inspire them with happiness. "Cloud" here has the connotation of something vast. We therefore make the wish that unbounded clouds of sweet melody, spreading to the ten directions, be constantly present before the Buddhas and their Bodhisattva children.

[verse 21] We then imagine that a shower of jewels and flowers and every precious thing falls unceasingly upon the Jewel of the sacred Dharma of transmission and realization, including all the volumes of the scriptures. It is said in fact that when the Buddhas and Bodhisattvas teach the Dharma, there falls a rain of flowers—a phenomenon called the "miracle occurring when the Dharma appears." Therefore let a rain of flowers fall whenever the teachings of transmission are given and received! Moreover, just as it is said that when the Buddha, the Blessed One, achieved perfect enlightenment, the gods of the Heaven of the Pure[85] caused a rain of flowers to fall, so too, whenever the Dharma of realization arises in the mind, may there fall a rain of flowers. Let it also fall upon all the supports of offering, such as stupas, the representations of the dharmakaya.

There are eight kinds of stupa, corresponding to the eight great deeds of the Tathagata. First, when our Teacher was born, Shuddhodana the king caused the Stupa of Heaped Lotuses to be built in Kapila. Second, at the time of the Buddha's enlightenment, the Stupa of Subjugation of Demons, otherwise known as the Stupa of Enlightenment, was constructed by Bimbisara and others. Third, when the Buddha turned the wheel of Dharma, his first five disciples built the Stupa of Many Auspicious Doors at Varanasi. Fourth, when the Buddha subdued the six non-Buddhist teachers, the Licchavis built the Stupa of Miracles in Jeta Grove. Fifth, when, after instructing his mother in the Heaven of the Thirty-three, the Buddha returned to the human realm at a place called Shankhashya, the local people erected the Stupa of the Descent from the Heavens. Sixth, when the Buddha repaired a schism in the sangha, the Stupa of Reconciliation was constructed in Venu Grove. Seventh, when the Buddha blessed the composite of his bodily form (in order to extend his lifespan), the Stupa of Victory was built by the Malla people in Vaishali. Eighth, the Parinirvana Stupa was erected, also by the Malla people, in Kushinagar.

As mentioned in the *Bhadrakalpita-sutra,* the relics of the Tathagata spread. Stupas were accordingly made for the Buddha's four canine teeth— one by Brahma, one by a naga living beneath the city of Rarok, another by the king of Kalinka, and yet another by the gandharvas of the city of Fair Gandhara. Eight stupas and other shrines were erected to house the eight large Magadha bushels that remained of the Tathagata's relics, as well as for his clothes, those that were burned and those that remained unburned. The Dharma king Ashoka accomplished the ordinary siddhi of bringing the yakshas or harmful spirits under his power, and, in a million locations in this world, caused a million stupas to be built containing the Buddha's relics. The bhikshu Akarmatishila, an emanation of the Dharma king Songtsen Gampo, brought relics of the Buddha from the Stupa of Heaped Lotuses in India. These relics are at present preserved between the eyebrows of the image [of Avalokiteshvara] called "Jowo Rangjung Ngaden." From this same stupa, Guru Rinpoche, the second Buddha from Oddiyana, transported by means of his miraculous power a full measure of relics that are now reposing in the white stupa of Samye. These relics are multiplying, and they can be found by fortunate beings even now.

May the rain of flowers fall upon all painted images and statues, be they cast in metal or carved in relief, such as the first picture ever made of the Tathagata, namely, the image "Created by Rays of Light," which gave teachings and brought the Singhalese maiden Vine of Pears to the realization of the truth [of the path of seeing]. May flowers fall upon the Buddha images made of precious gems by Vishvakarman, king of sculptors—for instance the one that depicts the Buddha at the age of twenty-five, now in the celestial realm of Tushita, the statue of the Jowo Rinpoche Shakyamuni showing him at the age of twelve, and the image called Jowo Mikyö Dorje preserved in the Ramoche, which depicts him at the age of eight (the latter two statues are now in Lhasa and the Jowo made of sandalwood by Vishvakarman is currently in China). According to the Vajrayana of the Secret Mantra, it is said that three things manifest when the Great Perfection teachings arise. The representation of the enlightened body is the self-arisen image of Vajradhara contrived of one hundred and one precious stones. The representation of the enlightened speech is the tantra entitled *The One and Only Son of the Doctrine.*[86] The representation of the enlightened mind is the five-pronged vajra, a cubit in size, made either of one hundred and one precious jewels or of gold. These objects appear in the sky above the twelve places[87] and other abodes where the teachings of the Great Perfection are propagated.

We should then make the wish that a rain of gems, flowers, perfumes, various garments, ornaments, grains, and medicines fall in an unceasing stream of offering upon all these representations. If our ethical discipline is pure, we will certainly accomplish all our aspirations. And even if this does not happen, we will be benefited.

2. THE UNSURPASSABLE OFFERING

The Bodhisattva Samantabhadra emanated from his heart hundreds of thousands of millions of many-colored lights, equal in number to the grains of dust in unnumbered buddhafields. At the end of each ray, he again visualized a form of himself and from the heart of each emanation, the same number of light rays were projected with another emanation of himself appearing at the end of each until they became unimaginably countless, with each emanation making an inconceivable array of offerings to the Buddhas and Bodhisattvas of the ten directions. Such is Samantabhadra's "cloud of offerings." [verse 22] And just as Manjughosha, Samantabhadra, and the other Bodhisattvas residing on the tenth ground of realization made offerings in infinite clouds of emanated gifts to the Buddhas of the ten directions, in the same way, we should aspire to make offerings to the Tathagatas our Protectors and to their Bodhisattva children. As it is said in the *Ratnolka-sutra*:

> Flowers everywhere and canopies of flowers,
> Flowers radiating myriads of beams
> Of every kind and color I spread out
> And offer to the Buddhas and their Bodhisattva children.

Moreover, since cultivation of bodhichitta, meditation on compassion, remembering the words, and understanding the meaning, of the Dharma are themselves unsurpassable offerings, we should persevere in them.

2. THE OFFERING OF MELODIOUS PRAISE

[verse 23] To those who are endowed with excellent qualities as abundant as the ocean, namely the Buddhas, whose bodies are adorned with the major and minor marks of enlightenment, whose speech is as melodious as the voice of Brahma, and whose minds are omniscient wisdom—to them and to their Bodhisattva offspring, Shantideva says that he will offer tuneful praises in the six methods of vocalization: rising, pausing, changing, slurring, high, and low—and any number of other ways. And he prays that clouds of tuneful eulogy rise up constantly and without fail before the Victorious ones and their Bodhisattva children.

1. AN ACT OF VENERATION

[verse 24] To the Bhagavan Buddhas of the past, present, and future, dwelling in infinite buddhafields in the ten directions, to the sublime Dharma of transmission and realization, and to the supreme Sangha, the assembly of those aspiring to virtue, who never forsake it once it has been gained, Shantideva prostrates, imagining that he has as many bodies as there are motes of dust in the universes of the ten directions. He reverently places his joined palms to the three places and stretches his body on the ground or touches it with his five limbs (hands, knees, and forehead). With devotion he recites the words of homage and respectfully recalls to mind the majestic qualities of the Three Jewels.

[verse 25] In the same way, we too bow down to what is referred to as the support of bodhichitta, that is, images of the Buddhas, collections of the Mahayana scriptures, the places where the Teacher was born and so on, the places where bodhichitta is cultivated, and all the places where the Dharma is proclaimed and heard. We bow to stupas and whatever representations of the enlightened body, speech, and mind exist. Likewise, we bow down to all teachers: preceptors who teach and transmit the pratimoksha vows (of individual liberation), those who give reading transmissions, and those who instruct the bhikshus and shramaneras,[88] and even those who teach people how to read and so forth. We bow down to the supreme Dharma practitioners who have put their old ways behind them and embraced a new way of life: to the sangha of the yogis, white-robed and long-haired, as well as to the sangha of the saffron-robed renunciants, and even to those who merely assume the outward demeanor of Buddha's disciples. With perfect devotion and respect in thought, word, and deed we bow down to them all. Of the different kinds of homage (physical, verbal, and mental), it is the mental homage that is the most important. Consequently, one prostration performed with an undistracted mind is much more effective and of much greater benefit than many prostrations performed while one is chatting and looking around.

When the bodily posture is straight, the subtle channels are also straight, as are also the wind-energies and the mind. Therefore, with these four items straight, we should visualize our father on our right, our mother on our left, our enemies and obstacle-makers in front, and on all sides beings as numerous as the particles of dust upon the face of the earth. All of them are holding a jewel between their reverently joined hands. It is said in the *Mahamoksha-sutra:*

> Like an opening lotus bud,
> Join your hands above your head.

Then, as we place our hands successively to the crown of our heads, to our throats, and to our hearts, we call to mind the qualities of the body, speech, and mind of the Tathagatas, and as we prostrate to them, we make the wish that beings purify their physical, verbal, and mental defilements and gain the invisible ushnisha upon their heads, the Dharma-conch of enlightened speech, and the unending knot of the enlightened mind. In other words, we wish that ourselves and others gain all the qualities of the "wheel of inexhaustible ornaments" of the enlightened body, speech, and mind. Then our entire body falls to the ground, or else our five limbs make contact with it. As our right knee touches the ground, we should wish and say, in conformity with the sutra, "May all beings proceed upon the right-hand path of integrity." As our left knee touches it, we should wish and say, "May all who are on the left-hand path of falsehood enter the true and noble path." When our right hand touches the ground, we should wish and say, "Just as when the Buddha, seated under the bodhi tree, pressed the ground with his right hand (which was itself the product of a hundred merits), subduing all negative forces and gaining enlightenment, may all beings overcome evil and adversity, and sitting under the bodhi tree, may they also press the earth with their hands and attain the primordial wisdom of buddhahood." When our left hand touches the ground, we should wish and say, "May I, by means of the four ways of attracting disciples, gather to myself all beings who are lost in the ordinary state of spiritual immaturity, who cling to negativity, and who are hard to benefit." When our face and forehead touch the ground, we should wish and say, "May beings, divested of their pride, serve their teachers, gain the invisible ushnisha, and be ennobled by every virtuous quality."

While performing the prostration in five points, we should wish and say,

"May the five defilements that afflict beings be dispelled! May they bring the five powers to perfection![89] May beings come to recognize the five sense objects for what they are! May they gain the five kinds of preternatural knowledge completely unimpaired! May they possess the five kinds of eye in all their purity![90] May they be supreme among all those born in the five classes of beings! May their ethics be supreme! May their concentration be supreme! May their wisdom be supreme! May their deliverance be supreme! May their knowledge of primordial wisdom of deliverance likewise be supreme!"

Regarding the benefits of performing prostrations it has been said that "through prostration you will be born a chakravartin as many times as there are atoms [beneath your outstretched body] from the surface of the earth down to the foundation of the universe;[91] and then finally you will attain to supreme peace."

1. TAKING REFUGE

Taking refuge opens the door to all the Buddhist teachings. It is the basis of all the vows and the source of all excellent qualities. It marks the difference between those who are inside the Dharma and those who are outside it; and through it one joins the ranks of those who are within.

Refuge is therefore of the greatest importance, for it is the entrance to the entire Dharma. In whichever kind of teaching one engages, one must first take refuge. It is the foundation of all the vows as the *Trisharana-saptati* says:

> All may have the vows
> Excepting those who have not taken refuge.

In fact, our Teacher the Buddha did not allow the vows to be given to anyone who had not taken refuge—from the eight-precept upavasa vow[92] up to the pledges of Secret Mantra. It was only to those who had the refuge commitments that he allowed the other vows to be given.

Again, refuge is the source of all good qualities. For if someone without refuge were to undertake any of the paths, whether the path of individual liberation, the Bodhisattva path or the path of the Secret Mantra, no benefit would come of it. As Drikung Kyobpa Rinpoche has said, "If you neglect refuge, the Dharma's foundation, there can be no benefit."

And indeed, when there is no foundation, there can be neither wall nor wall painting. On the other hand, someone who has the vows of refuge and who practices on any of these three paths will gain all the qualities of the path and its result, which are like walls and paintings built on strong and sure foundations.

As we have said, refuge marks the difference between those inside and those outside the Dharma. It is through refuge that one becomes a Buddhist. It may be observed that the line of demarcation between Buddhist and non-Buddhist lies in the affirmation or denial of the personal self. But if this were so, it would follow that the Vatsiputriya (which is a Buddhist school) would be accounted non-Buddhist. For by saying that there exists a responsible agent that cannot be said to be either permanent or impermanent, they affirm the existence of an inexpressible self.[93]

The term *tirthika* (holder of metaphysically extremist views) does not imply a complete absence of understanding. Kshitigarbha, an Indian disciple of the Lord Atisha, said that he had studied all the Buddhist and non-Buddhist texts, and yet he was still at a loss to say what differentiated them. And the glorious Atisha declared that since his teacher Shantipa had passed away and since he himself had come to Tibet, there was no one left in India capable of distinguishing the Buddhist from the non-Buddhist tenets. And he said this even though there were still the six great gatekeeper panditas (of Vikramashila) in the noble land.

As for himself, when in upper Tibet, in the region of Ngari, Atisha taught nothing but refuge—as a result of which, he was nicknamed the "refuge pandita." Moreover, when the scholars of Tibet pointed this out and asked him to teach something else, Atisha was delighted and said, "That means that even my name is working for the Buddha's Doctrine." As Drikung Kyobpa said, "In brief, all the sublime teachings can be condensed in refuge alone. Of all things, refuge is the most profound." The topic of refuge will be explained in two parts: a general outline followed by an exposition of the teaching on refuge in the present text.

2. THE GENERAL PRINCIPLES OF REFUGE

3. THE CAUSE OF REFUGE

Of the four kinds of faith: vivid faith, yearning faith, confident faith, and irreversible faith, the cause of refuge is irreversible faith.

3. THE ESSENCE OF REFUGE

The essence of refuge is to acknowledge [the Three Jewels], committing oneself to them in order to be free of something that one holds in dread. Refuge should not be mistaken for some kind of request or prayer. To make a request is like eliciting the assistance of someone, asking for protection when something untoward occurs—as when a malefactor suborns an official in the hope of not being punished. By contrast, taking refuge, as described in the *Sutralankara,* consists of an acknowledgement and a commitment. It is a commitment to the Three Jewels and a resolution to accept them as one's refuge. It is a clear decision that, henceforth, whatever happens good or bad, in joy or sorrow, whether one is raised up or brought low, one's hope and trust are placed exclusively in the Three Jewels. It is crucial to understand that the essence of refuge is an acknowledgment and a commitment.

3. THE DIFFERENT KINDS OF REFUGE

Although there is a way of classifying refuge according to the objects of refuge, the principal classification here has to do with the motivation with which one takes it. From this point of view, there are two kinds of refuge: worldly and world-transcending. World-transcending refuge comprises the refuge of the Hinayana and the refuge of the Mahayana. Mahayana refuge is further divided into causal refuge, which is provisional, and resultant refuge, which is ultimate.

It is said in the *Dhvajagra-sutra:*

> People when alarmed by fears
> Turn mostly to the hills or woods
> And have recourse to trees or sacred groves,
> In holy places taking sanctuary.
> All these are not the best of refuges
> And all who thus rely on them
> Will not be freed from suffering.

As it is said, when alarmed by minor and imminent adversities, such as illness or evil forces, people take refuge in the gods of the mountains or the forest, in Ishvara, Brahma, and Vishnu, as well as in the eight classes of spirits.

But how can such entities protect them from all their sufferings? It is not even certain that they can keep them from temporary dangers. They are not the supreme refuge. On the other hand, even refuge in the Three Jewels, if taken with an ordinary, worldly motive, is no more than a worldly refuge.

Concerning world-transcending refuge, the refuge of the Hinayana is the Three Jewels defined as follows. "The Buddha, the greatest of humankind" is the Victorious Shakyamuni, the supreme nirmanakaya—the Buddha, whose mind is the dharmakaya and whose body is the rupakaya. "The sublime Dharma, the highest peace and absence of all desire and attachment" is the elimination of all afflictive emotions and their seeds. The Dharma is thus nirvana or cessation. "The Sangha, the supreme gathering" refers to the realization that is "gathered" in the mind of a person (from which it had been previously absent). Now no one, whether human or divine is able to separate the truth of the path from the person who realizes it. It is for this reason that the supreme gathering is the Sangha (for "sangha" means gathering). Other gatherings are not supreme, for it is said, among other things, that "all that is born will die at last; whatever comes together will finally disperse." The Hinayana Sangha moreover consists of four groups of beings: the stream-enterers, the once-returners and the nonreturners, all of whom are on the path of learning; and the Arhats, who are on the path of no-more-learning.

When, in the context of the Hinayana, one takes refuge in the Three Jewels as just described, one is motivated by fear of the perils of samsara. The skandhas seem as terrible as an executioner armed with a knife, and the dhatus are like poisonous serpents. Wishing to be liberated from them, one takes refuge for as long as one lives, on the relative level, and until the result of the path is gained, on the ultimate level.

When, in the Mahayana, one goes for refuge, one cultivates an unbearably powerful compassion for beings, who have been one's mothers in the past and whose number is as boundless as the sky is vast. But it is not enough to feel compassion for them; one must be determined and decide to liberate them from their suffering. As long as one is not free oneself, however, one is powerless to bring others to freedom. Consequently, in order to free oneself and others from the perils of both samsaric existence and the peace of nirvana, one takes refuge in the Three Jewels, according to the Mahayana, until one gains enlightenment. This refuge consists of causal refuge, which is provisional, and also of resultant refuge, which is ultimate.

4. AN EXPLANATION OF PROVISIONAL CAUSAL REFUGE

In order to liberate oneself and others from the perils of existence and peace, one takes refuge in the Three Jewels [considered to be] outside oneself. How is this done? According to the general explanation, one takes refuge in the Three Jewels defined in the following manner. The Jewel of Buddha is the enlightened being who possesses the three or four kayas and is something distinct from one's own mind, such as the Teacher Shakyamuni. He first cultivated bodhichitta and accumulated merit for three countless kalpas. Eventually, he took birth as the son of King Shuddhodana, and at length attained enlightenment beneath the bodhi tree. The Jewel of Dharma is the sublime Doctrine of transmission and realization, which dwells in the minds of the Buddhas and Bodhisattvas. Finally, the Jewel of Sangha is an assembly that is different and separate from oneself, namely, the Bodhisattvas who have attained the ground of realization from which there is no regression, such as the venerable Manjushri, Maitreya, and so on.

4. AN EXPLANATION OF ULTIMATE RESULTANT REFUGE

As the Protector Maitreya said (in the *Sutralankara*), "It should be understood that resultant refuge is the resolution whereby one pledges oneself, out of love and compassion, to buddhahood." It is the *pledge* to accomplish within one's own mind the ultimate Three Jewels as a means to avoiding for oneself and others the shortcomings of both existence and peace. When one finally accomplishes the Three Jewels within one's own mind, one is delivered from all the fears and dangers of samsara and nirvana. Therefore resultant refuge is also ultimate refuge. As it is said in the Mahayana scripture, the *Uttaratantra-shastra:*

> Ultimately, only buddhahood is the refuge
> Of all wandering beings.
> For Buddha has the Dharma-body;
> And ultimately he too is the Sangha.

It should be understood that generally speaking, the subject of the entire *Uttaratantra-shastra* is none other than refuge. For it is said that the four chapters dealing with the Buddha-nature, buddhahood, the qualities of buddhahood, and the activities of buddhahood constitute an exposition of the resultant refuge.[94] Causal refuge is not ultimate precisely because it is unable to protect one from all the fears and dangers of existence and peace.

All this implies that resultant refuge and bodhichitta in intention are one and the same. One might therefore wonder whether there is any difference between them. The master Vasubandhu had four disciples by whom he was himself excelled. In his great commentary on the *Sutralankara*, Sthiramati, who was superior to Vasubandhu in his knowledge of Abhidharma, affirmed that resultant refuge and bodhichitta in intention come to the same thing. For he said, "The cultivation of bodhichitta is also called taking refuge." On the other hand, Atisha asserted a difference between them according to the presence or absence of the two hooks, or aims, of the commitment.[95] Finally, the omniscient Longchenpa said that the distinction between refuge and bodhichitta corresponds to the difference between aiming for the benefit of oneself and aiming for the benefit of others. It has been taught that if this view is examined, it may be reduced to the assertion that they are identical in their nature but different in their conceptual aspect. Insofar as there is the resolution to act "for the sake of all beings," it is bodhichitta; but insofar as one is resolved "to attain perfect enlightenment," it is (resultant) refuge. It is in this way that the two may be distinguished.

4. REFUGE ACCORDING TO THE *BODHICHARYAVATARA*

Although there are numerous ways of considering the taking of refuge, whether at the Hinayana or Mahayana levels, in the present text it is discussed in three stages. There is an explanation of the Hinayana and Mahayana refuge, followed by a general explanation of how refuge is taken.

5. AN EXPLANATION OF HINAYANA REFUGE

It is said in the texts of the Vinaya that one takes refuge for as long as one lives in order to free oneself from the sorrows of samsaric existence and to attain the peace of nirvana. With regard to the object of refuge, it is said in the *Abhidharmakosha*:

> Those who go for refuge in the Three,
> Take refuge in the Dharma of no-further-learning

And also in the Dharma of both learning and no-further-
learning—
And this respectively brings forth the Buddha and the Sangha.
They take refuge in nirvana.

As it is said (at the Hinayana level), the physical body of the Buddha was
the residue of the truth of suffering. In being the son of King
Shuddhodana, the Buddha was an ordinary man called Prince Siddhartha.
He traversed the five paths "on a single seat" [beneath the bodhi tree] and
attained perfect buddhahood. Because his body was that of an ordinary
person, propelled by the former karma of Prince Siddhartha, it was not, for
that very reason, an object of refuge. This is the belief of the Vaibhashikas.
Consequently, the Buddha as an object of refuge is none other than
the truth of the path of no-more-learning as realized by his fully enlightened mind. The Sangha as object of refuge consists of the realization of
the paths of learning and no-more-learning present in the minds of the
Sangha. For the bodies of the members of the Sangha are likewise the
residues of the truth of suffering. The Dharma as object of refuge is the absence of defilement (which is now overcome) from the mind of the
Buddha and from the minds of the Sangha—in other words, the state of
nirvana, beyond suffering, the absence of desire and attachment which
constitutes the truth of cessation. The Three Jewels are defined in this way
as the objects of refuge at the Hinayana level.

5. AN EXPLANATION OF MAHAYANA REFUGE

[verse 26] Shantideva says that we take refuge in the Buddhas who possess
the four kayas and the five wisdoms. We take refuge with the wish that all
beings, innumerable as the sky is vast, attain perfect buddhahood, and we
do so until we have gained ultimate enlightenment ourselves. In the same
way, we take refuge in the sublime Dharma of transmission and realization,
as well as in the noble Sangha of the Bodhisattvas. Regarding the length of
time during which we take refuge, we do so until, beneath a bodhi tree (on
the level of outer appearances), we too attain perfect enlightenment for the
sake of beings, and until, inwardly, our awareness, the sugatagarbha, becomes manifest in its natural state. It is said that all the Victorious Ones of
the past, present, and future attain enlightenment beneath a bodhi tree
(the bodhi tree at Vajrasana in India, in the case of the Buddhas of this

Fortunate Kalpa, or the tree called the Precious Illuminating Lotus, in the case of Amitabha and so forth). As it is said in the *Bhadracharya-pranidhana*:

> Promptly do they go beneath the bodhi tree
> And sit there for the benefit of beings.
> Attaining buddhahood, they excellently turn the wheel of
> Dharma.

The sugatagarbha in its true condition is perceived by the Buddhas alone. Not even the great Bodhisattvas can see it as the Buddhas do. The Lord Maitreya has said (in the *Uttaratantra-shastra*):

> Even noble beings see it like the sun is seen
> By newborn infants in their mother's bower.

The object of refuge comprises the Three extraordinary Jewels of the Great Vehicle. Buddha is, as the *Uttaratantra-shastra* says:

> Uncompounded and spontaneous,
> Realized not through an external cause,
> Possessed of wisdom, love, capacity:
> Such is Buddha who has gained this twofold goal.

Buddhahood is not compounded through causes and conditions, and its qualities are spontaneously accomplished. Neither is it realized through extrinsic circumstances; it is directly realized through self-cognizing awareness. Such are the three perfect qualities that apply to a Buddha's own benefit. Moreover, since Buddhas perceive phenomena both in their nature and in their multiplicity, they have a knowledge of everything that is knowable. With a great compassion that loves unconditionally and beyond reference, they teach the path and have the power to dispel all suffering and afflictive emotion. These are their three perfect qualities that have a bearing on the welfare of others. The perfected benefits of oneself and others are counted as two distinct bases for the classification of these two sets of threefold qualities. The Buddha is therefore endowed with eight qualities[96] and the three or four kayas.

With respect to the Dharma, the *Uttaratantra-shastra* says:

It is inconceivable, free from two, and free from thought,
Pure and lucent, with the nature of an antidote,
Free from all attachment and from all attachment freeing:
Thus the Dharma is defined as twofold truth.

As the text says, the Dharma is beyond all conception. It is the pacification of karma and defilements as well as of discursive thought. These three ultimate qualities refer to the truth of cessation, defined as freedom from craving and desire. The Dharma is pure of stain; it is endowed with the light of wisdom and is a counteractive force against all defilements. These three ultimate qualities refer to the truth of the path, which delivers us from craving and desire. This is the Dharma of realization, which is defined in terms of two [of the four noble] truths and endowed with eight qualities.

If this point is examined with care, it will be found that because the truth of cessation consists in elimination or absence (of impurity), it does not constitute a realization (in a positive sense). Why then do we call it the Dharma of realization? Cessation is the result of the truth of the path; the former occurs when the latter is realized. In other words, it is through the truth of the path that the ultimate expanse free from craving is reached. And this ultimate expanse or emptiness, indivisible as it is from primordial wisdom, is called cessation. It is therefore included in the Dharma of realization—and this is a very important point. Finally, the Dharma of transmission of the Mahayana scriptures is the favorable condition for the Dharma of realization, and this is defined in terms of two [of the four] truths.

The Sangha consists of the noble Bodhisattvas residing on the Mahayana grounds of realization whence there is no regression. Maitreya has said (again in the *Uttaratantra-shastra*):

Their knowledge of the nature and the multiplicity of things,
And their inward primal wisdom is unstained.
And so the Sangha of the wise who never will regress
Has qualities that cannot be surpassed.

As the text says, these Bodhisattvas possess the three qualities of primordial wisdom. Because they have a direct realization of ultimate reality, the sugatagarbha, they have the primordial wisdom that knows the nature of all things. And because they see that the sugatagarbha is present in all beings, they have the primordial wisdom that knows all that there is. These two wisdoms, which are inseparable, constitute awareness-wisdom. These three kinds of primordial wisdom constitute the qualities of the knowledge of the Bodhisattvas.

This primordial wisdom is free from the emotional and the cognitive veils, and also from the veil of meditative absorption. Being free from afflictive emotion, it is free from the obscurations arising from craving. Being free from the cognitive veils, it is free from the obscurations that are an impediment to knowledge. And being free from selfish aims, it is free from the obscurations of an inferior attitude. Thus the Bodhisattvas possess three qualities of freedom. All together, this comes to six qualities [three kinds of primordial wisdom and three freedoms], which, with the addition of the twin bases for the categories of knowledge and freedom, means that the Mahayana Sangha possesses eight qualities.

5. THE GENERAL WAY OF TAKING REFUGE

In accordance with the formula "The Buddha is the teacher unsurpassed; the sacred Dharma is the guardian unsurpassed, the Sangha is the leader unsurpassed," the actual protector or refuge *for beginners* is in fact the Dharma. The Buddha said, "I have taught you the methods that lead to liberation. Practice with diligence; your liberation depends on you." He also said:

> The Sage does not wash sins away with water,
> Nor wipe away the pain of beings with his hands.
> His realization he does not transfer to others,
> He frees by showing them the peace of ultimate reality.

This means that deliverance from the sufferings of samsara and the lower realms comes from accomplishing the sublime Dharma. Those who observe the eight-precept upavasa vow even for a single day protect their minds throughout that day from all faults and downfalls; and in a future life they will be born in a celestial realm. Therefore, the true refuge for beginners is the sacred Dharma. The other two Jewels are in themselves unable to give them such protection, and this is why the sacred Dharma is described as the unsurpassable refuge or protection.

In the Nyingma tradition of the Secret Mantra, on the other hand, it is said that the object of refuge is bliss, clarity, and absence of thought, or the channels, wind-energies, and essence-drops, or again the ultimate nature, its natural expression, and "compassion" [that is, its creative power] and so forth. [Refuge is thus] the wish and commitment to purify the channels, wind-energies, and essence-drops of the body. Through such a practice, the result is accomplished as set forth in the texts (for example, the nirmanakaya, that is, the purified channels).

Moreover, through being unaware of the difference between taking refuge and making prayers, one might pray the channels, wind-energies, and essence-drops, abiding in one's body, to afford some kind of protection for oneself and so on. But these are not things in which to place one's hopes. In brief, the difference between making a prayer and taking refuge lies precisely in the fact that the true object of refuge for beginners is the Dharma itself—the practice of the Dharma within one's mind. It is crucial to grasp this essential point. To fail to understand that the essence of refuge is a mental pledge, and that, of the supreme Three Jewels, it is the sublime Dharma that is the true refuge for beginners; to fail to understand that refuge means a commitment to implement the teachings leads to a repudiation of the Mantrayana refuge of the Nyingma tradition as mentioned above. This is the result of not knowing the difference between taking refuge and making prayers. Certain people in the Nyingma school, unable to deal with criticisms regarding this question, lose their tempers and start to have doubts regarding their own teachings, and end up by rejecting them. This sort of thing happens simply through a failure to understand the important points mentioned above.

Given that the true refuge is the Dharma, what is the point, one might ask, of describing the Buddha and Sangha also as objects of refuge? But the fact is that, if there had been no Buddha, we would still be in ignorance and would have no inkling of what we call the Dharma. Because he perfectly revealed to beings the faultless path that he himself had traversed, the Buddha is also an object of refuge. As for the Sangha, the truth is that we, the inhabitants of a decadent age, have not been fortunate enough to meet the Buddha in person. Nevertheless, the Sangha guides us on the authentic path of liberation. Therefore the Sangha too is our object of refuge. Consequently, we must take refuge in the Three Jewels, our Teacher, our Path, and our Companions. Since our teacher is the Buddha, we promise that we will only act and practice according to his instructions. We will pay no heed to the expositions of non-Buddhist teachers—or for that matter to the words even of those close to us, parents and relatives, should they be opposed to the Dharma. Since our path is the sublime Dharma, we pledge ourselves to the practice of it, according to the instructions of the Victorious One; and we will refrain from implicating ourselves in negative worldly pursuits, such as commerce, farming, the defeat of our enemies, and the biased protection of our friends.

Taking refuge in the Sangha (that is, the assembly of noble Bodhisattvas) and regarding them as our companions may be described in the following terms. If we go to Lhasa, our companions will be those who follow the lead of the caravan-chief. They will not be those who stay behind and do not make the journey, or who do not go the whole distance (though they may be traveling in the same direction). In the same way, we do not associate, whether in thought, word, or deed, with those (be they lay people or ordained clergy) who are swept away by evil, mundane activities associated with the eight worldly concerns. Similarly, we do not keep company with the Shravakas or Pratyekabuddhas. It is essential to train ourselves and follow in the footsteps of the noble Bodhisattvas, the children of the Buddha. For it is *they* who are our true companions. We should come to a firm decision and resolve to keep aloof from those who will lead us away from the path of Dharma. We can see therefore that to take refuge in the Three Jewels as our Teacher, Path, and Companions is a point of vital importance.

6. REFUGE PRECEPTS

It is not enough simply to know about refuge; we must actually take the refuge commitments properly in the presence of a teacher. And once taken, the commitments must be kept. The refuge precepts are of two kinds: common and particular, the latter having to do with actions to be avoided, actions to be implemented, and additional precepts.

The precepts concerning actions to be avoided are as follows. Once we have taken refuge in the Buddha, we should no longer take permanent refuge in the worldly gods (who are themselves caught in the circle of existence), nor should we pay homage to them. Once we have taken refuge in the Dharma, we should do no harm to any living being (even in our dreams) but protect them as much as we can. Once we have taken refuge in the Sangha, we should no longer associate with those who hold extreme views, nor with those who criticize our teacher and the teachings, and have no faith in them.

With regard to the precepts to be implemented, it is written in the *Pundarika-sutra:*

> Appearing in a host of different forms,
> The Buddha urges virtue on all wandering beings.

Accordingly, we should consider all likenesses of the Buddha, even a fragment of a clay image or *tsa-tsa,* as representations of the enlightened mind, as the Jewel of Buddha; and we should rid ourselves of any kind of disrespect. Instead, we should devotedly make offerings before them, lift them to our heads, and keep them in a clean place.

Once we have taken refuge in the Dharma, we should consider even a single syllable of the teaching as the Jewel of Dharma and avoid any kind of disrespect; we should never put texts on the ground and never walk over them. When turning the pages of the books, we should never lick our fingers and make stains on the text. Instead, books should be treated with reverence. As it is said in the *Ear-tip Jewel Scripture:*

> In the final cycle of five hundred years,
> I shall remain in form of written letters.
> Consider them as me and reverence them.

And in the *Ganti-sutra,* it is said that the Great Mother will take the form of the wooden ganti.[97]

Regarding the Sangha, we should consider any symbol of the monastic order—be it no more than the yellow belt of a renunciant, or only a patch or yellow or red cloth—as the Jewel of Sangha and we should treat such objects with respect. It is said in the *Ganti-sutra:*

> In future ages, at the sunset of the Sage's teaching,
> Any scraps of red or yellow cloth—
> The gods themselves will take and keep them as supports of
>   faith,
> And on the summit of Mount Meru they will worship them.

The additional or supplementary precepts are as follows. We should think of all our teachers and spiritual friends, all who reveal what is to be done and what is to be avoided, as the very Jewel of Buddha. And we should strive to please and honor them. Their instructions should be regarded as the Jewel of Dharma, earnestly accepted in their entirety without the slightest trace of disobedience. We should consider all our teacher's attendants and students as the very Jewel of Sangha, and we should keep them company, respecting them in thought, word, and deed, without irritating them even for an instant. It is written in the *Mahabheri-sutra*:

> Ananda do not sorrow!
> Ananda do not weep!
> In future I will come again, appearing as your spiritual friend
> To act for your and others' sake.

The common precepts of refuge are described by Ngari Pandita Pema Wangyal:

> For bribes, or even to preserve your life, do not give up the
>   rare and precious Jewels,
> And in the greatest need do not rely on any other means.
> Do not omit your offerings at the proper times.
> Take refuge and lead others to the same.
> Wherever you may go, pay homage to the Buddhas
> Who preside in that direction.
> These five are common precepts taught by Lord Atisha.

As explained, all this is what we should correctly implement or avoid. Taking refuge in the Three Jewels has the following benefits. It plants the seed of liberation; it places one within the Buddhist community; it protects from fear and from danger and brings about the attainment of buddhahood. Indeed, the benefits of refuge are unbounded. It is said in the *Suryagarbha-sutra*:

> Even myriad demons cannot slay
> The ones who go for refuge in the Buddha.
> Their discipline may fail, their minds may be disturbed,
> But it is sure that birth they will transcend.

Finally, the *Vimaladattaparipriccha-sutra* says:

> If all the merit that accrues from refuge
> Were to take material form,
> The whole of space would be replete with it
> And even then there would be more besides.

1. THE CONFESSION OF NEGATIVE ACTIONS

2. THE VISUALIZATION OF THE WITNESSES OF ONE'S CONFESSION

[verse 27] In the sky in front of himself, Shantideva visualizes the object of confession: all the perfect Buddhas, victorious, virtuous and transcendent, together with all the great Bodhisattvas, who reside in the infinite buddhafields in the ten directions and who are the sovereigns of great compassion. He prays to them with his palms pressed together.

2. THE CONFESSION ITSELF

Confession has four aspects or rather four strengths: the strength of regretting that one has done wrong, the strength of the support, the strength of the remedial practice, and the strength of amendment.

3. THE STRENGTH OF REGRETTING THAT ONE HAS DONE WRONG

[verse 28] What is it that Shantideva says? In this and all his other (that is, former) lives, while wandering in beginningless samsara, ignorant of what actions were to be adopted and what were to be rejected, disturbed by afflictive emotion, Shantideva admits that he perpetrated three kinds of evil deed: he performed actions that were evil by their nature; he transgressed the rules of discipline; and he incited others to do the same.

[verse 29] Deceived and overwhelmed by ignorance of the karmic law of cause and effect, and of the choice to be made between things to be done and things not to be done, Shantideva admits that he rejoiced in the evil committed by others. But now, seeing and acknowledging that these three kinds of erroneous conduct, whether serious or trivial, were indeed wrong, he openly confesses them—not just verbally, but sincerely from his heart—in the presence of the great protectors, the Buddhas and their Bodhisattva offspring, promising to refrain from them in the future.

[verse 30] In particular, Shantideva confesses the most serious faults he has committed with reference to the "field of excellence" (the Three Jewels of Buddha, Dharma, and Sangha) and to the "field of benefit" (his father, mother, and all who are rich in good qualities and are worthy of praise, such as learned spiritual masters and indeed all teachers). He confesses all the faults he has committed out of attachment, aversion, and ignorance: physically, by killing, destroying, and beating; verbally, by criticism, slander, and evil speech; and mentally, through wrong views, malevolence, and so on.

Of all such evil actions, attacks upon the Three Jewels or the spoliation of religious property (the stealing, robbing, or appropriating of it to oneself) are the most serious—religious property being all that has been associated with the Buddha, Dharma, and the teachers of the Dharma. The unvanquished Maitreya has said in the *Uttaratantra-shastra*, "How can freedom come to one who hates the Dharma?" There is also the story of the great adept Kyergangpa, who was tormented by the powerful sensation of his body being pierced by the white letter "A"—the fully ripened result, he said, of keeping the money a benefactor had given him to recite the *Ashtasahasrika* (the *Prajnaparamita-sutra* in eight thousand stanzas). It is said that stealing the property of the sangha, wherever it may be, and especially the provisions directly donated to it constitutes a very grave fault. In short, it is said in the sutras that to steal or traffic the property, great or small, of the sangha, or to appropriate it by dishonest means, cannot be purified even by confession and will surely lead to rebirth in the hell realms:

> The sangha's property is like diamonds;
> The sangha's property is like poison.
> But though for poison there's an antidote,
> To stealing of the sangha's goods there is no remedy.

There is a story about certain people who, after using the earthen vessels of the sangha, were reborn in the ephemeral hell of a cooking pot. Moreover, the Buddha, who knew all things, said that it is improper to give to the lower temple what is intended for the higher, or vice versa, or to keep the summer food of the sangha for the winter, or the reverse, or again to keep for tomorrow what is offered for today.

We can give some slight illustration of this by citing stories from the past. It is said in the Vinaya that if one fouls the wall and pillars of the monastic assembly hall with spittle or nasal discharge, one will be reborn in the ephemeral hell of a wall or pillar. If one uses for oneself a broom or a mortar belonging to the sangha, one will be reborn in the ephemeral hell of a broom or mortar. Again, if the monks hoard the summer food till winter, or the winter food till summer without distributing it, they will suffer greatly by being reborn as insects that have waists so tiny as to be like threads that are almost severed. In the *Damamako-sutra*, there is a story about a large tree that was entirely covered by worms that were devouring it. It was covered so that not even a pinpoint of its surface was exposed. The tree lamented for it was suffering intensely. It is said that this was the fully ripened effect of the actions of a monastic servant called Lita who embezzled the belongings of the monks and gave it as provisions to the laity. Lita was reborn in the tree and the lay people took the form of the worms. And after this, rebirth in hell awaited him.

Then there is the story about a filthy pond in the town of Rajagriha where for many years a four-legged, lizard-like insect lived in great suffering. When the Buddha came there with his disciples, he explained to them its karma. Formerly, he said, during the dispensation of the Buddha Vipashyin, in order to accumulate merit, five hundred merchants had offered some precious gems to the fourteen thousand monks abiding in the nearby monastery. The monks had accepted the offering, which they entrusted to the monastery bursar. Later, when the alms offerings had failed, the monks asked the bursar if he had sold the jewels. The bursar flew into a rage. He told them to eat their own excrement and said that the jewels had been given to him alone and not to the monastic community. Owing to this state of affairs, the monastic community had no option but to disband, each one going off by himself.

As a result of such a deed, the monastic bursar fell directly into the great hell, and for ninety-one kalpas was engulfed in vomit. Freed at length from that state, he was reborn in the evil-smelling cesspool from which he still could not escape, though he had been living there for many a long year. Already in the past, the Buddha commented, the Buddha Ratnashikhin had visited that place with his disciples and had explained to them the karma of this selfsame individual; and he was followed later by the Buddha Vishvabhukra, who did the same. And later, when the lizard-like insect eventually expired, it was reborn again in hell for an interminable lapse of time, after which, it appeared once again in the same unclean pond. Afterward there came the Buddhas Krakucchanda, Kanakamuni, and Kashyapa, all of whom explained the karma of the same creature. And likewise in the future, the Buddha said, all the thousand Buddhas [of the Fortunate Kalpa] will pass by here with their disciples and will explain this being's karmic destiny. In response to this explanation, the monks were so frightened that the hair on their bodies stood on end, and they strove diligently to tame their thoughts, words, and deeds. This story is also recounted in the *Damamako-sutra*.

Again, to the north of Nalanda, there lay the village of Katvam in the vicinity of which there was a subterranean cave. Once when a crowd of very young monks were playing there, a preta appeared in the form of a strange whirlwind all sparkling with firelight. The children threw stones at it and ran away, but one of the children who had thrown stones was possessed. His feet turned backward and his skin began to peel away, flames issued from his mouth and he began to yell at everyone in Sanskrit.

Now there lived a yogi nearby whose practice was to meditate on loving-kindness. He heard of what was going on, and, astonished to hear that the child was speaking Sanskrit, he went to listen. He questioned the preta and asked why the boy was burning. He was burning, the answer came, because he had welcomed the preta with hatred. By contrast, the yogi was not burning precisely because he had greeted the preta with love. The yogi then asked what action had caused the preta to be born in such a form. The latter replied that, since the yogi was a noble practitioner of loving-kindness, he would tell him, provided the monks were dismissed and sent away.

When the monks had gone, the preta described how he had once been Jinakara, abbot of Nalanda and, acting as though the place belonged to him, had once eaten unlawfully half a measure of old rice that belonged to the monks. On account of such an action, he had been reborn as a preta with a burning belly. The fire that incessantly consumed his entire vitals issued from his mouth in tongues of flame. In addition, because he had failed to remove his shoes on entering the temple that contained the Tripitaka, his feet were now bent backward. And since he had anointed his own body with the butter offered for light offerings to the Buddha image in the temple and had never repaid his debt, he was now obliged to suffer, his skin constantly peeling away. Religious property, the preta observed, is a perilous thing; and of all the Three Jewels, it is the property of the sangha that is most dangerous.

The yogi went on to inquire when the preta would be released from such an existence. The latter replied that this could only occur in approximately fifteen thousand years time, after which he would be obliged to go to the Hell of Unrelenting Pain. When asked whether there was a method for confessing his misdemeanor, the preta replied that since he had despised the karmic principle of cause and effect, there was no remedy. On the other hand, the preta said, a great benefit comes from refraining from using the property of the sangha. Indeed, his own attendant Gunashri had loved the monastic order more than his own life and had held its property in dread as though it were poison. When he came to die, he was welcomed by enlightened beings and dharma-protectors, with rainbow lights and music, and now he is liberated from samsara. Asked why it had been necessary to send the young monks away, the preta replied that they had all been his students in the past and that if they had heard the story, they would have been saddened and he would have been ashamed.

At that, the possessed child fainted. After a moment, when he was able to speak again, the yogi asked him what had happened and where the preta had been. The latter replied that he had been off to create difficulties for the virtuous practice of another yogi living further up the valley. When asked why he was behaving so badly—he who had been an abbot learned in the Tripitaka—the preta replied that though this had been so, he was unable to control his mind. He again possessed the child in such a way that its entire body became hot. Tongues of flame issued from the mouth and nose of the child, who began yelling at everyone. The yogi from higher up the valley was called and he visualized himself in a wrathful form. But the preta said that he himself had gained stability in the generation stage of wrathful deities and had no fear of anyone with worldly powers.

When the yogi who had been meditating on love asked the preta why it was that he went to the other yogi, the preta replied that though, when eating (be it never so much as the tiniest grain of barley), he felt that it was adding fuel to the fire in his belly, it was nevertheless because of his former habits that he went to the yogi up the valley in order to still his hunger, and that the trouble caused to the yogi was a means of removing his bad karma. When he was questioned further, the preta replied that at the time when he had been an abbot, the yogi from higher up the valley had come to Nalanda to study grammar. But he had neglected the rules of discipline while all the time taking advantage of his monastic state. He had availed himself of the monastic provisions of water and wood, and this was the reason for his now having to suffer such adversities.

When asked whether the yogi's bad karma would be exhausted through such trials, the preta answered that he had only begun to experience the results of this action and that in his next life, he would have to be born as a preta. When asked whether there was a means of purifying his negativity, the preta said that if the yogi were to pay homage to the sangha and make an open confession in their presence, his negative karma would be purified.

For a brief moment, the yogi cultivated loving-kindness toward the preta, who, pressing his palms together, said, "Are you not my mother come back to me?" And weeping, he vanished, never to return. Now, as the preta was recounting his story, most of the bystanders, who had formerly been his students began to weep. It is in light of such tales that one should understand the meaning of the Buddha's advice that the property of the sangha should be thought of as an ulcerated sore.[98]

Yet again it is recounted in a sutra how once upon a time, five hundred people polluted the water set aside for use in a monastic kitchen, with the result that it could not be used for cooking the monks' rice. Thus the Dharma teaching of the sangha was interrupted for that day. The karmic result of this act was that the five hundred people had to suffer by being reborn as five hundred loathsome pretas.

Again, it has been said that, once when the Lord Atisha was residing at Nalanda, there was a devout bursar. It was his duty, one day, to provide the monks with drinking water. He thought to himself, however, that if he were to distribute water on that occasion, there would be plenty to drink on that day, but not enough for the morrow. Believing that such a thing would be untoward, he decided to keep the water till the next day. Now during the night, he himself felt very thirsty and went to drink from a large copper tank, only to find that it was dry with not a drop of water remaining. Now the tank had just been filled, so the monk thought that he must be having visions since the water could not have evaporated so soon. He therefore decided to investigate the matter and put a stone in the tank. He then went to drink from a large pool at the gate of the monastery. He found however that this too was dry. Once again he thought that this must surely be an illusion since it was impossible for the water in the pool to have dried up as well. Therefore, in order to investigate further, he placed a large stone in the center of where the pool used to be. He then went to drink from the river, but found that the river also had run dry. Wishing to investigate further what must surely be a hallucination, the bursar wrapped his robes around the trunk of a tree on the far bank of the river. Then, still thirsty, he retired to bed. The following morning when he went to look, he found that the stone was still in the copper tank, which was now filled with water. There too was the stone marker in the pool in a place that was now inaccessible because of the depth of water. And then he saw his robes tied around the tree, now on the far bank of the river. It was said that the immediate ripening of his action implied that the fault was small.

Therefore, all those who are closely related with lamas and monks, and particularly those who hold positions of responsibility, high or low, such as ecclesiastical and monastic treasurers, bursars, and managers—all who are exposed to such temptations—should be scrupulous in their handling of the property of the Three Jewels and especially that of the sangha. For if they are careless, they will certainly have to suffer the unbearable pain of being burned and boiled in hell for many kalpas. It is therefore my request that they take kindly to these words (which are proffered in the hope that they might be of some benefit), and act with care and circumspection.

[verse 31] In the presence of his teachers, the Buddhas and Bodhisattvas, Shantideva goes on to confess openly and one by one all the evil deeds that he, the old sinner that he is, has committed in thought, word, and deed, and which cling to his mind as rust sticks to iron—unbearably grievous faults, the karmic fruit of which is to be reborn in hell. Why is it necessary to confess our faults swiftly? It is because we have no idea of when we shall die. The circumstances of death are uncertain and there is no surety that we will not die today. And the suffering experienced at the moment of death when life is severed, the suffering that occurs after death in the bardo, and the sufferings of the lower realms in the existence to follow, are all the results of negative action. [verse 32] This being so, Shantideva says, it may be that he will die before completing his confession, without feeling remorse for evils committed in the past, without making a resolution to abstain from such actions in the future, and without striving in positive actions, the antidote to evil. If this were to occur, he would be obliged to experience the pains of the lower realms, and what means would there be for his mind ever to be freed from them? Therefore, Shantideva prays that the Buddhas and Bodhisattvas swiftly grant him their protection.

We might well think that, although we have to die some day, it does not matter if there is no time today for the confession of our sins—we won't die without confession. [verse 33] But Yama, the demonic Lord of Death, is not to be trusted. He will not wait for us to finish what we have started (our confession, for instance), and he will not wait for us to do what we have planned but have not yet begun. And whereas it may be said that hundreds of healthy people may die within the lifetime of someone already suffering from a terminal illness, the fact is that whether we are healthy or ill, there is no certainty that we will not suddenly drop dead, like the sun breaking through the clouds or a lamp suddenly extinguished in the wind. Life is uncertain and the confident trust that we shall not die today is quite misplaced. Since there is no saying when, where, and how death may occur, it is impossible to be certain that we will not die today. As Nagarjuna has said (in the *Suhrillekha*):

> Life flickers in the flurries of a thousand ills,
> More fragile than the bubbles on a stream.
> In sleep, each breath departs and is again drawn in;
> How wondrous that we wake up living still!

[verse 34] When death arrives, we must leave everything behind: our home, our country, relatives and companions, our community, enemies and friends, family and possessions, clothes and sustenance, even our own bodies. We go forth into the next life completely alone. Shantideva confesses, however, that, forgetful of this; and in order to protect his family and those who are close to him (acquaintances, friends, and the people he likes), and in order to get the better of his enemies, he has committed many evils through attachment and aversion, killing, stealing, and so on. And it has all been so pointless. [verse 35] For even if he has failed to overcome them, his enemies will die in any case and cease to exist. Even if he is successful in guarding and caring for his friends and loved ones, nothing is achieved; they too will vanish in death. And he himself will die and cease to be. The entire universe, with its continents and mountains, with all the beings that it contains, friendly, hostile, or indifferent—be they as high-ranking as the heavens, as strong as thunder, as rich as the nagas, as beautiful as the gods, as fascinating as rainbows—all is destined to destruction. Whatever strongholds have been built, whatever wealth has been accumulated, whatever families have come together—everything will go. How absurd to do evil for their sake!

[verse 36] Shantideva gives the example of the objects of the five sense consciousnesses that he enjoyed the previous night in his dreams, together with whatever was done in their regard: enemies he defeated, friends he protected, the wealth, honors, and all the rest that he gained. He wakes in the morning to find he has nothing to show for it; everything is no more than a memory. In just the same way, he says, everything done the day before, all distinctions and discriminations made concerning the five objects of sense—accepting some, rejecting others, subduing rivals, supporting friends; everything done in the name of business, lands, wealth, honor, renown, food, and clothes; everything that was wanted and experienced— all is now no more than a memory: "This I did and this was done to me." Everything that has passed and no longer exists will never be seen again; it can bring no active benefit or harm. It is pointless to engage in action because of it.

[verse 37] Leaving aside the friends and enemies of our past lives, even in the course of the present existence, so many people whom we have liked or disliked have passed away. In so doing, they also are now no more than memories, unable to help or harm us in the slightest way. This being so, it might be tempting to think that the same applies to the evil actions perpetrated for their sake: They too are gone and can do no harm. This, however, is a mistake. The fully ripened, unbearable effects of all the evil deeds that we have perpetrated through attachment or hatred, on account of friend or foe, have still to be experienced. Our karma is like our shadow; it never goes away but lies before us as though in wait. It is written in the *Rajavavadaka-sutra:*

> When the dangerous moment comes, O king, and you
>   must go,
> You'll not be followed by your court, your wealth, your
>   friends.
> And yet wherever beings take their birth,
> Their karma dogs them like their shadow.

All that lies before us are the effects of positive and negative action. It is as when the Buddha took Nanda to the Heaven of the Thirty-three where he saw his future birthplace in the beautiful celestial pavilions, and then to the hell realms where he saw the copper cauldron that was prepared for him. Similarly, when the householder Shuka measured out the park that he was to offer to the Buddha, Shariputra declared that the results of such an act would be experienced in that very same life.

It is just as when important lamas or dignitaries travel, their monks and attendants go on before them to prepare the place and the kitchen so that they can welcome them. It is said that in exactly the same way, due to their specific karmic perceptions, evildoers will behold the henchmen of Yama welcoming them and leading them to hell, while those who have practiced virtue will be greeted by celestial beings and by their gurus, and will be led to the pure realms.

[verse 38] Summing up the situation, Shantideva says that the thought never came to his mind that he himself was only a brief and transient phenomenon—like a traveler passing through or an insect that lives for only a season. He does not know where he has come from; he has no idea where he will go. And the time will soon arrive when he will cease to be. Without knowledge or understanding, he says, he has clung to the notion that things are permanent; he was confused about what was to be done and what was not to be done. Through attachment to the things he wanted and to the people he perceived as close to him, and through aversion for what he disliked and whatever he perceived as alien, he killed, robbed, and all the rest. All these many negativities, he says, must now be confessed at once and without delay.

[verse 39] For the fact is that his span of life is not increasing; it diminishes constantly like a pond without an inlet. Never halting night and day, the moments that compose his life are slipping by. Not a single instant can remain. His span of life is constantly decreasing. As the saying goes, when the karma that propels the present life is spent, there is no way to prolong it even if the king of physicians were to appear in person. No external force, he says, can increase his span of life. For himself and everyone else, what is there to look forward to but death? All this points to the importance of confessing one's misdeeds. It is said in the *Anityartha-parikatha:*

> A pool whose inlet has been stopped
> Can only dwindle and can never swell.
> Just so for all who enter on the path that leads to death,
> How can they now rely upon this fleeting life?

[verse 40] So—Shantideva pictures to himself—when his span of life has come to term and death arrives, there he will be prostrate upon his last bed surrounded by those close to him, parents and siblings, doctors, friends and those he loves, all of whom will suffer as though they themselves were dying instead of him. They will do all they can to protect him, but all will be in vain. For, Shantideva says, no one can take from him the unbearable anguish that comes from the severance of life's thread. He alone will be the one to feel it. [verse 41] When the gradual process of dissolution sets in, the hallucinations produced by his evil karma will take the form of the terrifying messengers of the Lord of Death. They will seize and catch him by the neck with a black noose, and, in lonely torment, he will be bludgeoned with hammers. What help to him will be his close relations, his parents and family; what help will be his loving friends? No one, he says, will be able to protect him. For at that time, only the merit that derives from positive action—if it has been performed and accumulated—will be of any help. This is the best, indeed the only, protection; and yet it is precisely this, Shantideva laments, that in the past he neglected and shrugged away.

What can he do? [verse 42] Crying out in misery, he calls upon his protectors, the Buddhas and Bodhisattvas endowed with great compassion. For he failed to understand what was to be done and what was to be avoided. He had no faith in the karmic principle of cause and effect. He was careless of his actions in thought, word, and deed, and has done evil things. Not realizing the dreadful horrors in store—death, the bardo, and the lower realms in the next life—he killed and did many other evil things in order to get the better of his enemies, protect his friends, and accumulate wealth and sustenance. And it was all for the sake of this present life, so insubstantial, so transient! In the hour of his death, he will have to suffer terribly and his lot will be wretched indeed.

[verse 43] As an example, Shantideva considers the predicament of a man convicted of a serious crime and handed over to the king for punishment. He is dragged away to the scaffold by his fellowmen, who will do no more than amputate his limbs. Even so, he is terrified. His gaping mouth is dry, his eyes are glazed and protruding, his face is livid and his head downcast. He is completely transfigured by terror.

[verse 44] This being so, Shantideva reflects, how will it be for him when he is caught by the evil messengers of the Lord of Death? Hallucinations conjured up by his bad karma, these phantoms are naked and seven times the size of a human being. Their hair bristles and they have glassy, staring, triangular eyes. Their fangs are visible, biting down on their lower lips and their hissing breath is as strong as a hurricane. Ferocious and seething with rage, they are armed with iron hooks, nooses, hatchets, and hammers, and, as frightful as ogres with their dreadful grimaces contorted with rage, they will bind him with ropes and drag him off to his next existence. There the terror of infernal darkness and the burning ground of hell will come to meet him as he is propelled forward by the irresistible hurricane of his karma. With cries of "Strike him! Kill him! Cut him in pieces!" the servants of the Lord of Death will catch him with their hooks, bludgeon him with their hammers, cutting off his arms and legs. No need to speak of misery and fear, he will be subjected to the most horrible tortures.

[verse 45] It is at such times that people cry out "Rinpoche! Doctor!," calling to anyone who might have compassion. "Who," they cry, "can save me from the terror of life's end, from the horror of the servants of the Lord of Death?" They are terrified and gripped by panic. Because the skin of their faces is stretched toward the back of their skulls, their eyes are not closed but wide open and staring, looking desperately on all sides for help and refuge. But not even the Buddha can protect them from experiencing the bad karma that they have accumulated. When Devadatta fell into hell he cried, "Gautama, I am burning, I am burning!" [But the Buddha could not save him.] [verse 46] Then, when they realize that there is no protection, no escape, they will feel utterly abandoned. They will remember that they had been born in the southern land of Jambudvipa, a feat that was so difficult to achieve; that they had gained a human body endowed with freedoms and advantages, all so hard to gain; that they had met a holy teacher, so difficult to meet; that they had encountered the sublime Dharma, so difficult to find, and had even gained some slight understanding of what conduct should be adopted and what should be eschewed. Alas, the opportunity has been squandered in wrong action: Their conduct has been destitute of virtue, and much evil has been committed. There they are, defenseless and without a refuge. Death is now upon them, and there is nowhere to go but to the lower realms. Remembering all the evil they have committed, people tear at their breasts with their nails, their faces livid, their eyes brimming with tears. Their breath comes rattling in their throats, their heads and limbs shudder and twitch. And they die in great suffering. As it is said in the *Rajavavadaka-sutra:*

> Every wanderer must die.
> On your deathbed you will lie.

Just a little life remaining,
Fearful at Death's servants and despairing.
Now your panting breath will cease;
Your nostrils flare,
And in your gaping mouth your teeth are bare.
All around, your father, mother,
Son and daughter, sister, brother
Each to each they will declare,
"All his wealth we now shall share!"

"Father, mother, son, alas!" you cry,
But only in the Dharma does there lie
Protection; there's no helping grace,
No other refuge and no friendly place.
When this moment comes, great King,
The Dharma is the only thing
To shield and to protect you.
It's your teacher and your home!

So it is that at the time of death, there is no security apart from the sublime Dharma and one's good action. Shantideva wonders what a wicked person like himself will be able to do. For there is no escape; there is only misery and pain.

3. THE STRENGTH OF SUPPORT

The strength of support may be used either as the object to which confession is addressed or else as the support for purification. In the present case, we are concerned with the latter. [verse 47] When the time of death occurs, the hallucinations called up by negative karma—the messengers of the Lord of Death—appear. In terror people look everywhere for protection. But there is none is to be found. Consequently, it is essential to resolve that, from this day forth, we will take refuge in the victorious and perfect Buddha. He is the guardian of all beings without exception, who, in order to protect from sorrow beings as infinite as the sky is vast, first engendered the aspiration to supreme enlightenment. He then labored for the good of all that lives, and became the great and powerful Protector, the Buddha endowed with the ten strengths.

For it is said that the Buddha possesses many powers: his physical strength that he received from his parents, the strength of his miraculous power, the strength of his primordial wisdom, and so forth. The sutras explain that the strength inherited from his father and mother was such that every tendon in his arms and legs was a hundred and even five-hundred times stronger that those of Narayana. The *Shilakshipta-sutra* tells that when the Buddha went to Kushinagar, he encountered five hundred strong men, each one accompanied by a further five hundred. They were engaged in clearing a road but there was a great rock that they were unable to lift and move aside. The Buddha raised it with the big toe of his right foot, and with his hand he tossed it in the air. Such was the physical strength he inherited from his parents. Through his miraculous power, he reduced the bolder to dust and scattered it in all directions. Then, on discovering that this was not what the strong men wanted, the Buddha gathered all the dust together again and formed it into the rock just as it was before, setting it in a position out of their way. He did this, it is said, through the power of his meditation or primordial wisdom.

Most especially, a Buddha possesses ten kinds of strength with which he protects beings. As it is said:

> To know what is correct, and what is incorrect, and all the
>   ripening results of action;
> To know the different types of beings and their aptitudes and
>   interests;
> To know all different paths, absorptions, and the recollection
>   of past lives,
> Divine sight and the knowledge of exhaustion of defilement:
>   Such is Buddha's tenfold strength.

Possessing these ten strengths of knowledge, the Buddha perfectly instructed beings in the sacred Dharma. If we act according to his words, the fears and sufferings of samsara and especially the lower realms will be allayed. People who are confused about what is to be done and what is not to be done, and who fail to discern what is important, spend their entire lives in negative deeds. When death comes, they are filled with alarm and have no idea what to do. They look for protection, but there is no way to help them. It is just too late. This is not how we should act. If we hear about the Dharma in the morning, we must take refuge that very morning. If we hear of it at noon, we must take refuge at noon. If we hear about it in the evening, it is in the evening that we must take refuge, there and then, in the Buddha as our Teacher—and from that moment on until we attain the essence of enlightenment. This is the way to think. We should receive the teachings, reflect on them, and meditate on them by turns. And when teaching the Dharma, we should not content ourselves with fine words only; we should genuinely reflect about what we are saying. If we do so, it is said that our explanation will itself be a form of meditation.

[verse 48] While on the path of learning, the Buddha gathered the two accumulations of merit and wisdom for many immeasurable kalpas. At length, beneath the mighty tree of enlightenment, he attained omniscient wisdom and declared:

> Deep and peaceful, thought-free, luminous, unmade:
> The nectar-truth, this now I have discovered.

Accordingly, the Dharma that resides within the Buddha's heart, in other words, the Dharma that he realized, includes all the teachings profound and vast. If practiced, it scatters and pacifies all the terrors of samsara. Therefore from now on, we must take refuge in the Dharma of transmission and realization and take it as our path. Henceforth too, we must take refuge—perfectly, straightforwardly, and without hesitation—in the Sangha of the noble Bodhisattvas residing on the grounds of realization from which there is no regression. For they are our companions on the path.

[verse 49] Gripped by dread, Shantideva says, and beside himself with panic—at the thought of death, of the bardo that will follow, of samsara and the lower realms that are awaiting him in his next existence—he calls in distress to the noble Samantabhadra, the first of all the Buddha's sons, and offers him his body and all he has. We too must have this attitude. It is said furthermore that if, when making such an invocation, we are not genuinely afraid, we are in effect speaking falsely to the Buddhas and the Bodhisattvas, who are consequently saddened. In the same way, Shantideva offers his own body freely and without constraint to Manjughosha, the only sire of all the Buddhas.

[verse 50] Moreover, from the moment of first generating bodhichitta in the presence of the Buddha Ratnagarbha, the noble and compassionate Avalokita has labored lovingly for the benefit of numberless beings without the slightest trace of selfish desire or clinging. His inner qualities of compassion are thus harmoniously mirrored in his outer demeanor. At all times he watches over beings. His eyes never close, which is why he is called Avalokiteshvara, "the lord who sees." With confident and irreversible faith, Shantideva cries out to him from the depths of his being and with genuine, unfeigned sorrow—fearful of samsara and the lower realms, in terror at the approach of death and the bardo. In an agony of sorrow and in deep distress, he cries out to the noble and compassionate Lord Avalokita saying, "I pray, protect me now, the sinner that I am!" He confesses the karma accumulated through his evil deeds of body, speech, and especially mind—for it is from thought that words and deeds derive.

As [Dharmakirti] has observed:

> Discursive thought is ignorance, the mighty demon,
> That sends us falling down into samsaric seas.

Evil karmas arise from thoughts, and thoughts manifest because of ego-clinging—clinging to "I" and "mine," to self and other. And ego-clinging is nothing but ignorance. It is because of this that at all times, whether we are expounding the Dharma or listening to it, whether we are reciting prayers or meditating, our minds do not stay focused even for an instant but run after negative thoughts of attachment and aversion. This is why we fall into perpetual, interminable delusion. We accumulate negativity, which causes us to wander in the three lower realms in endless samsara. Shantideva acknowledges his wrongdoing and cries to Avalokiteshvara for protection from his evil karma.

[verse 51] Likewise, since we [monks] have all taken the full complement of vows but fail to keep them, we should rely on Akashagarbha, paying him homage, making offerings, and so on. This is important, for the Lord Buddha himself said that for beginners on the Bodhisattva path who commit downfalls, the noble Akashagarbha is like their walking staff.[99] Likewise we should invoke Kshitigarbha, the loving and caring protector of those who are destitute and in decline, such as beginners in the monastic life, whose conduct is infected with defilement and is as yet but a mere semblance of monastic discipline. And we should call upon Maitreya and Sarvanivaranavishkambhin and all the other powerful Bodhisattvas on the tenth ground of realization, who reside in the buddhafields of the ten directions and whose prayers and compassion are extremely vast. To all such beings, we should fly for refuge, calling upon them by name and imploring their protection from the depths of our hearts.

[verse 52] To Vajrapani also, the glorious Lord of Secrets, at the sight of whom the messengers and henchmen of the Lord of Death (as well as the dogs, birds of prey, and all harmful beings, who hate us as though our hands were red with the blood of their own fathers) flee in panic in the four directions—to him, Vajrapani, whose mere appearance drives away all terror, we should go for refuge with faith and devotion. According to the general explanation, it is said that all the Buddhas of the three times—from the moment they first generate bodhichitta until they achieve perfect enlightenment, turn the wheel of the Dharma, and pass into their parinirvana—are watched over and guarded by the glorious Vajrapani, who wields a blazing vajra in his hand and crushes the heads of all who try to attack them, whether in thought, word, or deed. He keeps them company like the guardian deities that stay with worldly people from their birth. Furthermore, he is called Guhyaka, "the Secret One," a name used to refer to yakshas. For he is indeed the lord of yakshas and is known also as Yaksha-Vajrapani. According to the particular explanation of the Secret Mantra, he is the spontaneous embodiment of the vajra-mind of all the Buddhas and has been empowered as the sovereign of the inconceivable secret of the enlightened body, speech, and mind. This is what "vajra in his hand" or "Vajrapani" signifies.

For us who practice the Mantrayana, it is essential to rely upon a yidam deity—one of the Bodhisattva lords of the three lineages, or any other yidam deity to whom we feel personally drawn. One deity is sufficient and is indispensable. We must request the empowerment of our yidam deity and practice the appropriate visualization and mantra recitation, without ever forgetting it. We must be able to recall it whenever frightening situations arise, even at night and in our dreams. It is said that if we do so, we will have the vision of the yidam deity coming to welcome us at the moment of our deaths.

[verse 53] Shantideva confesses that he, a sinner, has transgressed the words of the Buddhas and the Bodhisattvas, that he has failed to act virtuously and did not turn away from evil. Now that he can see the terrors of death, the bardo, and the lower realms that are in store for him, he takes refuge in the great and compassionate protectors just as a man who has fallen down presses on the ground in order to pick himself up. And he prays that they might save him swiftly from his fear and suffering, the wages of his sins.

3. THE STRENGTH OF THE REMEDIAL PRACTICE

In this chapter, as in the chapters on carefulness, vigilant introspection, and patience, the main point is the development of the appropriate qualities. In the present case, this means the creation in the mind of an antidote that will purify its negativity. To that end, we must meditate repeatedly on the karmic principle of cause and effect as well as on our life's impermanence. If we have not yet acquired this counteractive state of mind by which negativity is purified, we should now cultivate it. If we possess it to some extent but fail to apply it out of laziness and distraction, we should meditate upon karma and impermanence. This will encourage us to apply the antidote as soon as possible. When this understanding has been fully developed and implemented, any virtuous action, provided that it is performed in conjunction with the three supreme methods, will act as a purification for negativity.

The three supreme methods are as follows. The first is the wish and intention to perform virtuous action in order to make a break with negative behavior. The second is to maintain, in the course of the action, an attitude of confession of one's misdeeds. The third is to dedicate the accumulated merit to the purification of nonvirtue.

When accompanied by these three methods of preparation, the action itself, and conclusion, every virtuous action serves as a confession and thus constitutes an antidote. If we do not practice in this way, we may well spend our entire lives in solitary meditation, but unless we confess and purify even our smallest faults, using the practice as an antidote, we will have to experience their karmic results. As an illustration of this, let us imagine that a great many barley grains were planted in the ground together with a single pea. The barley will grow and the pea as well, for the growth of the barley will in no way hinder the growth of the pea. In the same way, it is said that however great may be our positive deeds, if we fail to focus on them with the intention that they act as a remedial force to our negativities, the latter will not be overcome thereby. Even good people can, in the next life, be reborn in the lower realms, for they may have in their minds the karma for such a destiny. In particular, their next existence will narrowly depend upon the mental attitude occurring at the moment of their death, for this will act as a bridge to their next rebirth. Those who do not know how to die properly should put every effort into the antidote to negative action, namely, confession. This is of the highest importance. Mindful of our negative emotions, the cause of lower rebirth, we should strive in their antidote, which is confession.

[verse 54] The reason why confession is necessary is illustrated by the example of a disease. If we are frightened by an ordinary illness, caused through the interaction of the three humors of wind, bile, and phlegm, we must rely on the medicine prescribed by a doctor and we must put up with whatever operations the latter performs on us: bleeding, burning, and all the rest. This being so, it goes without saying that, constantly afflicted from beginningless time by the diseases of craving, hatred, ignorance, and pride, we must follow the instructions of the Buddha, the supreme physician. We must reject what is to be avoided and implement what is to be accomplished.

[verse 55] Even one negative emotion, such as craving, or, otherwise interpreted, even one person whose mind is infected with defilement can bring low all those dwelling in the world, projecting them into the pains of the lower realms. But even if we were to search in all directions, other than the sacred Dharma, there is no remedy to be found that might heal the disease of the defilements. [verse 56] The best of physicians, he who has power to heal such ills, is the Buddha, the omniscient Lord. By means of his instructions, he uproots all the torments of body and mind. If therefore we neglect to follow the holy teaching set forth by him, and if we have false ideas about it, we are ignorant idiots on our own account and foolish in the eyes of the Buddhas and Bodhisattvas—as well as the protecting deities who will turn from us in contempt. The great master Nagarjuna has commented:

> More foolish than a man who takes foul vomit
> With a jeweled and golden scoop
> Are those who, gaining human birth,
> Defile themselves with evil deeds.

This is similar to the Buddha's saying that Devadatta was a foolish man, a drinker of filth. Jivakakumara was thrice honored by kings as the chief of all physicians. And he, in his arrogance, declared that whereas, in this world, the Buddha was a physician for the ailments of the mind, he, Jivakakumara, could attend to the illness of the body. The Buddha, however, thought to himself that if the pride of Jivakakumara were humbled and if the Dharma were taught to him, he would see the truth. He therefore transported him by miraculous power to the snowy peak of Himavat and told him to collect some medicinal herbs. Now Jivakakumara did not know what most of the plants were, but the Buddha, knowing them, explained them to him and thus humbled him. It was not enough, the Buddha told him, to have a modest expertise in medicine, which is but one of the minor sciences. Only the omniscient Buddha is the true physician, and apart from the sublime Dharma, there is no other medicine.

[verse 57] Thinking of the abyss of the lower realms, the result of evil action, Shantideva gives us a reason for the necessity of confession and purification. If, at the top of a flight of steps or on a small and ordinary cliff, we need to pick our way with special care (for if we fell, we might injure our heads or other limbs), it goes without saying that for fear of falling into the lower realms twenty thousand leagues below the earth—to the Reviving Hell and similar destinations (there to remain in dreadful pain for a long age, an intermediate kalpa or more)—we must act with the greatest care.

[verse 58] We are therefore advised to make immediate effort in virtuous living. This is the remedy. It is quite inappropriate to remain in a state of carefree nonchalance, telling ourselves that today at least we shall not die. For there is no doubt that death, the moment when we shall cease to be, is inescapable! We cannot be certain that death is not waiting for us this very night! As it is said in the *Suhrillekha*:

> Life flickers in the flurries of a thousand ills,
> More fragile than the bubbles on a stream.
> In sleep, each breath departs and is again drawn in;
> How wondrous that we wake up living still!

[verse 59] What guarantee can anyone give that we will not die today and that death is nothing to be afraid of? There is no one who can give us such assurance, not even a Buddha. What escape is there for us from the horrors of death? It is said in the *Bhadrakaratri-sutra*:

> What man is sure he will not die tomorrow?
> This very day you should prepare yourself.
> The great hordes of the Lord of Death—
> Are they not your faithful friends?

Death, our own death, is coming. How can we relax in careless ease? It is highly inappropriate to rest at our leisure, eating, drinking, and amusing ourselves. As Ashvaghosha once said in his *Shokavinodana:*

> Of all those born upon this earth
> Or in the upper realms,
> Did you see, or hear, or even doubt,
> That some were born that have not died?

It is essential to overcome our bad habits, our wonted clinging to the objects of the senses. We are like pieces of paper that, once rolled up, always tend to curl up again. Therefore we should reflect as follows: [verse 60] In the past, there was not a single object of the senses that we have not experienced. But nothing now remains of the ephemeral pleasure arising from the contact of consciousness with its object. The initial moment of pleasure was unable to remain for a second instant, and it is no longer here. The experience of happiness has no enduring core. Likewise, however much we now enjoy the objects of our senses, everything will go; nothing will stay. What pleasure is left over from it in the second moment? What is there that, different from what has gone before, does not disintegrate? There is nothing. Yet here we are, clinging to, and craving for, the objects of the five senses—on account of which we do not keep ourselves from evil and the sufferings that follow, ignoring every difficulty and fatigue, transgressing the words of our root gurus and of the Teacher of the triple world, the Lord Buddha, and his Bodhisattva children. It is thus that we are shipwrecked in this life and the next. We must not allow this to happen! In particular, because of our craving for meat, alcohol, and sexual pleasure, and the senseless practice of taking tobacco and snuff, we have indulged ourselves repeatedly. And since all such joys cease in the moment of their enjoyment, we yearn more and more for what is nothing but the bringer of ruin in this and future lives. This is why the teachings speak of the importance of cutting through all cravings for the objects of the senses, laying aside all important samsaric projects and simply forgetting about the smaller ones.

Realizing now that every pleasure is devoid of any abiding core, we must sever our attachment and craving. We are like children engrossed in play. There is no end to their games. Once we taste the objects of our desire, we are unable to drop them. Instead, let us cut through our clinging. Craving and grasping are the father and mother of existence. The extent of negative behavior is in proportion to the strength of our craving. On the other hand, if we sever the continuum of both craving and grasping, then even though an action is performed, its effects need not be experienced. It has been said that these last four verses constitute an essential instruction.

[verse 61] When we die, we will not be like modern lamas or men of state, who travel around with a large crowd of attendants. No, we will have to go alone. And this does not just mean that we will be without servants. When we leave our lives behind, we leave our parents, our children, our kith and kin, our pleasures and possessions. All that we have will be abandoned and left behind. A great king and a beggar are the same as two sticks: both must go alone, naked and friendless, their empty hands crossed on their chests, greeted by the approaching dark, thick and terrifying, pushed from behind by the red cyclonic winds of karma, with the dreadful heralds of Yama yelling, "Kill! Kill! Slash! Slash!" Through the force of karma we will be forced away to strange destinations we know not where, from the Peak of Existence down to the Hell of Unrelenting Pain. At such a time, we have no freedom of choice and we are beyond the help of friends or the attacks of enemies. Why then make so much of all our friends and foes?

[verse 62] What *will* harm us at that moment, however, is our own evil: the ten nonvirtues that we have committed through attachment and hatred toward friends and enemies, and on account of which we will have to suffer helplessly in the hells and other places of torment. So we should ask ourselves, how can we make sure to rid ourselves of evil, which alone is the cause of sorrow? This should be our only concern, as the text says—our sole and constant thought. This should be our daytime obsession and something that keeps us awake at night! It is thus that we should strive to confess our evil actions.

When cloth is being dyed, the preliminary washing is actually more crucial than the dying process itself. In the same way, it is because of [the dirt of] our nonvirtue that the qualities of study, reflection, and meditation on the teachings fail to appear in us. It is therefore said that it is vital to make an effort to cleanse our sins away. Once we have by various means awakened in ourselves the wish to confess sincerely and put an end to our evil behavior, we should bestir ourselves and get on with it.

Although there are all sorts of faults to be confessed and purified, everything may be summarized in two categories: actions that are evil by their nature and actions that are transgressions against established precepts. An action that is naturally evil is one that is negative regardless of who commits it. On the other hand, a transgression against the precepts or rules of ethical conduct is a violation by someone who is bound by such a rule. These two categories of misdeed are subject to four permutations. For example, if shramaneras or bhikshus, who have taken vows, kill someone, they do something that is both a transgression of their vow and also a naturally evil act. If on the other hand, they cut fresh grass, or eat in the afternoon, they transgress the rules but are not guilty of an action that is naturally wrong. If someone who has not even taken the vow of refuge kills a living being, that person has performed a naturally evil deed but not a transgression of the precepts. Similarly, if such a person cuts fresh grass, he or she performs a deed that is neither a transgression nor something naturally evil. Ordained people who fail in their observance of the monastic rule (even the prohibition to cut grass), are unable to keep to pure training. For the monastic rules are skillful means whereby the trainings are observed. They are like a fence with which the Buddha has enclosed the field of their discipline. The Buddha said:

> Those who break lightheartedly
> The instructions of their loving Teacher
> Will fall beneath the power of pain.
> They will be born as beasts, like him who, shaved and robed,
> Cut down the mango tree and later was reborn as naga
>   Elapattra.

[verse 63] Since therefore he has certainly acted in this way, Shantideva says that he is ready to confess all the evil, all the ten negative actions, that he has committed not knowing what was to be done and what was not to be done: evil actions that are said to be unspeakable and actions that are wrong because they are transgressions of the precepts, such as eating after noon. [verse 64] Whatever evil he has done, he will declare it in the presence of the protectors, the compassionate Buddhas and Bodhisattvas, with hands joined and with tearful eyes, the hairs on his flesh standing up. With a sorrowful voice he will pronounce the words of the confession in fear of the sufferings of death, the bardo, and the lower realms to come in future existences, with a mind filled with regret and remorse at the evil committed. Respectfully he will bow down repeatedly, confessing all his faults and downfalls, without concealing anything. The phrase *yang dang yang* (translated in the text as "ceaselessly") is an expression indicating the depth of the remorse that one must feel.

Even though we are unable to behold the Buddhas and Bodhisattvas, they can see us nevertheless. They are like well-sighted people standing in front of the blind. Consequently, if we declare and confess the innumerable faults that we have perpetrated, they will see us with the eyes of primordial wisdom no matter how many cosmic systems may lie between us. They will attend to us with their miraculous hearing, and will think of us in their omniscient minds. Indeed, it is said that they behold us directly and clearly.

[verse 65] Shantideva concludes therefore by praying to the guides and guardians of the world, imploring them to accept him as he is, a sinful man. It has been said that we should acknowledge and declare our faults as though the Buddhas and Bodhisattvas were questioning us about them.

3. THE STRENGTH OF AMENDMENT

To engage in evil action is like passing from light into darkness. It produces effects that are difficult to bear. For holy beings, such unwholesome conduct is an object of derision. Therefore, from now on, we must promise never to repeat such actions even at the cost of our lives. And when pronouncing such a resolution, we should consider that rays of many-colored light stream from the bodies of the Buddhas and Bodhisattvas and cleanse and purify our every fault and downfall—every negativity and obscuration of ourselves and other beings—like the sun rising in the midst of darkness.

There are two kinds of people: those who hoist aloft the victory banner of the Dharma and those by whom the banner of the demons is brought low. The former never commit any faults, whereas the latter commit them but then purify themselves with confession. The fact that negativities can be purified by confession is their (one) positive aspect. As it is said in the *Suhrillekha*:

> Those who once behaved with negligence,
> But later on assume a careful mien,
> Are handsome like the clear unclouded moon,
> Like Nanda and Angulimala, Ajatashatru and Udayana.

This ends the second chapter of the *Bodhicharyavatara*, called "Confession of Negativity," which is the main topic of the four discussed therein.

· 3 ·

TAKING HOLD OF
BODHICHITTA

1. Preparatory practice

2. The accumulation of merit

The explanation of the accumulation of merit has eight sections or "branches." Four of these have already been dealt with in chapter 2.[100] In the present chapter, we will consider the remaining four, which are rejoicing in virtue, the request that the Teachers should turn the wheel of the Dharma, the prayer that the Teachers might not pass into nirvana, and the dedication of one's roots of virtue for the sake of others.

3. Rejoicing in virtue

Positive actions may be distinguished according to the threefold classification of beings: those of lesser, medium, and great capacity. "Virtue tending to happiness," which belongs to beings of lesser scope, may be considered in terms of its causal and resultant aspects, both of which are a matter for rejoicing. [verse 1] From the causal point of view, Shantideva joyfully celebrates the practice of virtue—the ten positive actions and so on—that is not associated with the determination to leave samsara, nor with bodhichitta, nor with the practice of egolessness. It is this kind of virtue that releases samsaric beings from the suffering and torments of hell and the other evil destinies, and places them, for a time at least, in the bliss of the higher states. Shantideva rejoices also in the result of such virtue. For the situation of gods and human beings is happy by comparison with the three lower realms. And yet it too is marred by the three kinds of suffering: the suffering of pain itself, the suffering of change, and all-pervading suffering in the making. And so, with joy in his heart, Shantideva takes pleasure, untainted by jealous rivalry, at the happiness enjoyed by beings while they are in the divine and human realms, where—even though suffering is a constant liability for them—they reap the fruits of their positive actions accomplished in the past and have the enjoyment of physical beauty, youth, power, renown, wealth, and every perfect pleasure.

[verse 2] In addition, Shantideva rejoices in the cause and result of "virtue tending to liberation" (liberation in the Hinayana sense) of beings of medium scope. With regard to the cause, it is said:

> The knowledge that defilements are arrested, that there will be
>   no further birth:
> This wisdom is indeed enlightenment.

Shantideva therefore celebrates the virtue performed in conjunction with a determination to leave samsara and with the practice of egolessness, in other words, the cause of the enlightenment of the Shravakas and Pratyekabuddhas. With regard to the results of such virtue, beings are definitively freed from birth, sickness, old age, and death, and all the other sufferings of the three worlds of existence. They achieve the state of the various levels of the Shravakas on the paths of learning (stream-enterer, once-returner, and nonreturner) and the condition of Arhats on the path of no-more-learning. For them the ocean of blood and tears has dried up, the mountains of bones have been leveled. Remembering the qualities of realization and elimination attained by such beings, for whom gold is as valuable as a lump of earth, Shantideva has faith in them and rejoices. For it is due to their kindness that we can receive Vinaya teachings, which are sublime and worthy of praise, and which the Buddha in his compassion left for us as both teachings and teacher.

[verse 3] Shantideva also rejoices in the virtue tending to liberation that is possessed by beings of the great scope of the Mahayana, again in both its causal and resultant aspects. He delights in its final result, namely, perfect enlightenment endowed with the infinite qualities of elimination and real-

ization achieved by the Buddhas, the protectors and guides of beings. And he rejoices in recognizing its provisional, short-term result, namely, the qualities of elimination and realization achieved by the Bodhisattvas residing on the grounds of realization, from Perfect Joy, which is the first, to Cloud of Dharma, which is the tenth. [verse 4] Going on to consider the cause of such attainments, he delights sincerely and without envy in the oceanic virtues of bodhichitta, the mental attitude that, with buddhahood as its goal, is motivated by the aim to establish all beings, as infinite in number as the sky is vast, in the supreme bliss of buddhahood. Shantideva rejoices also in the training that consists of the six paramitas, which brings untold help to all beings. The benefits of such wholesome actions are as immense and long lasting as space itself, as the first chapter of the *Bodhicharyavatara* has already described.

The merit generated by rejoicing in this way even exceeds the merit gained by the perpetrator of the action in the first place. This is illustrated by the story of King Prasenajit, who invited the Buddha and his disciples to his palace and did them service with profound reverence. On seeing this, a poor beggar woman rejoiced in the king's actions, as a result of which the Buddha dedicated the king's merit to her. Concerning the benefits of rejoicing, it is said in the *Prajnaparamitasanchaya-sutra*:

> Meru and the universe three-thousandfold
> May all be weighed upon a weighing scale,
> But not the virtue that rejoicing gives!

To rejoice in the good deeds of others is an essential pith instruction for it allows us to accumulate a great deal of merit easily and swiftly without falling into arrogance and pretension. It is therefore said that when we see or hear of the virtuous actions of others, we should always rejoice in them.

3. Requesting the Buddhas to turn the wheel of the Dharma

When in the past our Teacher attained perfect enlightenment beneath the bodhi tree, he declared:

> Deep and peaceful, thought-free, luminous, unmade:
> The nectar-truth, this now I have discovered.

Were I to teach it, none would understand;
And so I will remain, not speaking, in the forest.

Because of the greatness of his Dharma and for very many other reasons, he remained silent and for several weeks seemed not to teach. At length, Indra, the king of the gods, offered him a white conch spiraling to the right, and Brahma offered a golden wheel of a thousand spokes. Beseeching him repeatedly to turn the wheel of the Dharma, they said, "That you might receive but four lines of teaching, you suffered untold difficulties, your body pierced with a thousand nails and a thousand flames of fire burning on your flesh. How is it that, having gained the treasure of the supreme Doctrine, you now draw back from turning the wheel of the Dharma?" The Buddha said:

For all those dwelling now in Magadha,
With wisdom, faith, and ears unstopped,
With hearts receptive to the Dharma, and who think no harm,
For them the doors of deathlessness, O Brahma, I throw open
wide.

And with that, the Buddha began to teach.

[verse 5] In the same way, to all the Buddhas of the past, present, and future—the enlightened lords dwelling in the ten directions, who look on Shantideva in their perfect wisdom (for indeed he is not hidden from them), and think of him with compassion and love—Shantideva considers that he respectfully offers a golden wheel and invokes them with joined hands. For all who are tormented by many sorrows, who have no knowledge of what is correct and incorrect,[101] who are unable to distinguish between the true path and the false and have no idea what is to be done and what is not to be done—for all who are thus enveloped in the gloom of ignorance, Shantideva prays that the Buddhas kindle the lamp of the sublime Dharma, thereby overcoming and removing the ignorance of beings in ways appropriate to their varying capacities. May the Buddhas reveal, he prays, the authentic light of primordial wisdom.

When we make such prayers, we should consider that the Buddhas promise to turn the wheel of the Doctrine. If we make such a request, the result will be that in all our lives, we will not entertain false views and wrong opinions, and we will never be separated from the light of the sublime teaching. This indeed, so it has been said, is the reason for making such a request.

3. PRAYING THAT THE BUDDHAS REMAIN AND DO NOT PASS INTO NIRVANA

[verse 6] When formerly the Buddha was requested by the upasaka Chunda not to pass into nirvana, he extended his life for three months. Likewise, although from the point of view of the ultimate truth, the Buddhas residing in the pure fields of the ten directions do not "enter nirvana," it may be that some Buddhas—once they have completed their work for beings—wish for various reasons to display their passing. Therefore, Shantideva joins his hands and prays them not to leave in blindness the infinite mass of beings, whose eyes of moral discrimination are darkened by the cataracts of ignorance. In order that they might further explain what behavior is to be adopted and what is to be eschewed, Shantideva requests the Buddhas not to pass into nirvana, but to remain for many countless kalpas. And as we also make such prayers, we should consider that the Buddhas accept them and agree to remain among us.

3. DEDICATION OF ROOTS OF VIRTUE FOR THE WELFARE OF OTHERS

In the Mahayana, dedication is generally made with a view to achieving great enlightenment. But in the present instance, in order to be inspired with bodhichitta, it is necessary to train oneself in the four immeasurable attitudes or simply in compassion. For this is said to be the root of bodhichitta. One is therefore inclined to think that dedication is perhaps taught here as an aspect of compassion.

[verse 7] Shantideva makes the wish that all the virtue amassed by him in the past, present, and future (which he exemplifies by the virtue accumulated by the seven branches previously explained) should clear away all the sorrows of samsara and especially of the three lower realms as experienced by beings who are as numerous as the sky is vast. [verse 8] In particular, because of the evil behavior of beings, the gods are losing the fight against the asuras.[102] And the latter, who are now in the ascendant, exhale a red cloud of pestilence, the source of eighteen kinds of plague. Beings, the object of Shantideva's compassion, are afflicted by these ailments, and

therefore until such time as they are cured of their sickness, he prays that he himself might become a perfect medicine to heal them. How he might do so is illustrated in the stories of the Buddha's earlier incarnations when on various occasions he saved the lives of others. For example, when he was King Padma, he willingly took birth as a rohita fish and cured the epidemic from which his subjects were suffering.[103] Indeed, generally speaking, all the medicines that exist have manifested thanks to the compassionate blessing of the Buddhas and Bodhisattvas. And so Shantideva prays that he might become a physician like Khye'u Chubep,[104] able to instruct beings and provide them with medicinal remedies. Moreover, our Teacher himself tended a sick monk, changed his bedding, and used a bamboo strigil to remove the excrement with which he had fouled himself. And since the Buddha made it a rule that we too should serve and care for the sick, Shantideva prays that he might himself become a nurse for those who are ill. We too should look after those who are ill and never neglect them.

[verse 9] Shantideva wishes that he may become a rain of sustenance with a hundred tastes, a nectar showering down unceasingly on all those in the world who are tormented by want of food and drink. He prays to be able to dispel their every ill of dearth and drought so that they will be satisfied and content. Likewise, in the intermediate kalpa of famine (an age marked by scarcity and want), the time of "secret eaters," "spoon eaters," and "eaters of bleached bones,"[105] he prays that he might himself become food and drink, tasty and nourishing, so that he might completely satisfy the hunger and thirst of beings. In the same way, Shantideva prays to become medicine in the ages of illness, and he prays to be able to transform the hail of weapons in the ages marked by war into a rain of flowers. It is said in the teachings that in order to avoid being born in a universe that is passing through the intermediate kalpa of disease, war, and famine, we should make offerings, here and now, to the precious Three Jewels of all the various kinds of medicine and weapons, and we should offer food and drink to the sangha, praying that we and other beings be spared from being reborn in such situations.

[verse 10] Again, for all those living in the world who are poor and destitute, without food, drink, clothes, wealth, and possessions, Shantideva prays that he might himself become an inexhaustible treasury of whatever they may wish for: food for the hungry and drink for the thirsty. "May I lie before them," he says, "closely in their reach, a varied source of all that they might need."

2. THE MIND-TRAINING

3. THE ACTUAL MIND-TRAINING

Bodhichitta is brought into being by mind-training. For if we do not cut through the shackles of desire, it is impossible for the altruistic attitude to occur. At the outset, therefore, mind-training is of crucial importance. As it is said:

> The sphere of living beings is unbounded,
> Likewise the desire to help them all.
> And even if you lack the strength for altruistic action,
> This is something you should constantly intend.
> In those who harbor wishes such as these,
> Bodhichitta will indeed be born.

The mind is trained by relinquishing, for the sake of others, the three foundations of ego-clinging (the body, possessions, and the roots of virtue). Beginners, however, should not actually surrender them in reality. For it is also said that if we try to do so without being truly able, the outcome will be nothing but a parody. If therefore we train and habituate our minds to the generous attitude of offering these three foundations to others, there is no contradiction in saying that we will perfect the paramita of generosity, even if in reality we do not actually give any of them even slightly. On the other hand, when people make charitable donations without having a generous attitude, their action is a mere imitation of generosity. It is therefore crucial to school and habituate ourselves in an openhanded and generous frame of *mind*. Of the three foundations of self-clinging, the body is most important. For we cling to our bodies as our selves or as our property, and we egocentrically seize upon possessions, enjoyments, and virtue as means to secure our physical well-being in this and future lives. In view of this, it is of vital importance to sever attachment to the body.

[verse 11] We must therefore reflect repeatedly and, following Shantideva's lead, declare that we will give away all that we hold dear: our bodies and our belongings (riches, clothing, and sustenance), as well as all our roots of virtue accumulated in the past, present, and future. We must relinquish everything for the benefit and happiness of all without exception—and we must do so sincerely and unparsimoniously, without counting the cost or expecting some recompense or karmic advantage in return. This is an essential pith instruction that drives out the fiend of ego-clinging, the root of samsara. Whenever thoughts of cherishing and attachment toward our bodies arise, we should face up to them squarely and at once, never losing sight of the view of No-Self, emptiness, and nonreferential compassion. This will ensure that we are on the supreme path and that beings, who are like illusory visions, will never be abandoned.

If, when fear falls upon us, as it might in dangerous places or in the solitude of the mountains, we remember that—having given away the three foundations of ego-clinging (body, possessions, and roots of virtue) to others—we have nothing left to cherish, a great load will be lifted from our minds. We will be at ease with carefree hearts. And if, while resting in this state, ego-clinging arises again, we should, as before, declare our abandonment of our bodies and possessions, imagining that physical beings like wild animals and disembodied phantoms like ghosts and demons feast upon our flesh and blood and steal away all that we have. And whether or not we actually shout "P'et," this constitutes both the mind-training and the practice of giving—and there is no higher chö practice than this.[106] For it is as the teachings say:

> To wander in a place of peril or in mountain solitudes
> Is outer chö.
> To give one's body up as food
> Is inner chö.
> To cut through ego-clinging
> Is the final chö.

Nothing is more important than this. It is said in the *Shikshasamuchaya*:

> Let this most crucial point be grasped
> Whereby no downfall will occur:
> My body and my worldly wealth
> And all my virtues gained and being gained and to be gained
> I give them all to everyone,
> Protecting, cleansing, and increasing them.[107]

As it is said, first one gives these three things to others, then one protects one's gift from whatever might damage it, then one purifies it from the stains of one's karmic burden, and finally, one skillfully increases it. The *Shikshasamucchaya* teaches that when these four factors are applied to the three foundations of ego-clinging, twelve elements result, and, within them, the practice of the six paramitas is included and rendered truly extraordinary.[108] As we find in the *Shikshasamucchaya*, "Once you have given your body and possessions to others, you should continue to use the food and clothes that were formerly yours only as servants might use the food and sustenance of their employers: solely to keep your body alive for the benefit of others. To do anything else is stealing." Indeed, if you use for yourself what has been donated to others, you are robbing beings of what has been given to them.

3. A REASONED DEMONSTRATION OF THE NEED FOR MIND-TRAINING

Two arguments are given to show the necessity of practicing the kind of generosity described above. [verse 12] In the first place, it is by giving up the three foundations of ego-clinging that nirvana, the state beyond suffering, is achieved. And since, as Buddha's disciple intending to leave samsara, Shantideva wishes and strives for nirvana, it follows that he must himself give them up.

But how is it possible to give up our virtue, since it is precisely through virtue that nirvana is gained? The accumulation of virtue or merit brings rebirth in the higher realms, and this is the foundation of the path. It is the necessary prerequisite for the occurrence in the mind of the truth of the path—the realization of the personal and phenomenal No-Self. [Now with regard to the personal No-Self,] it is said that when the emotional obscurations are discarded, the resulting "nirvana without remainder"[109] of the Shravakas and Pratyekabuddhas is like a fire or a butter lamp going out for want of fuel. By contrast, nirvana as understood in the Mahayana is the result of the removal of the two kinds of obscuration together with their habitual tendencies.[110] Therefore [as the *Sutralankara* says] liberation is no more than the exhaustion of error. Apart from the mere separation from the two obscurations, there is nothing extra to be attained. And as for the truth of the path, this is likened to a raft, which is to be left behind as soon as the far shore has been reached. Consequently, it is generally said that worldly virtue, bounded and confined by ego-clinging, is not actually effective in the attainment of liberation. In particular, since compounded virtue must be entirely relinquished if one is to attain the final result of perfect buddhahood, it definitely follows that we must give it all away.

In the second place, we might wonder why it is necessary to abandon the three foundations of ego-clinging even when we are not actually intending to achieve nirvana.[111] The answer to this is that, even if we do not give them away now, the fact is that when we die, we will have to leave behind both body and possessions. And as for our virtues, either these will have been exhausted by moments of anger experienced in the past or else (if this is not the case) they will be consumed by the single experience of their fully ripened result. It is certain therefore that everything is destined to be entirely and pointlessly lost. Therefore, in the present moment when we have freedom to act, it is best to give everything to other beings for their happiness and benefit. For in this way, the merit of such an action will not be exhausted but will become the cause of attaining the supreme goal.

3. The specific gift of one's body

[verse 13] Shantideva declares that he has given his body away to all beings (as infinite in number as the sky is vast) so that they may use it as they please. Let them forever kill it, slander it, beat it with sticks and stones, or do whatever else they wish. [verse 14] Let them treat it as their plaything or as the subject of all sorts of verbal asides, pleasant or unpleasant—made just to see what response they will get. Let them laugh at it, making it the butt of every mockery, ridiculing it in all sorts of ways. Now that he has given it away, why should he be so concerned about it, securing its advantage and fending off difficulties? For he has put an end to the thought that it is his to control.

[verse 15] Saying that he invites beings to do anything to him, good or bad, provided they do no harm or injury to themselves either then or later, Shantideva invites them to do whatever is fitting. He makes the general wish that whatever beings do in his regard should never be in vain, in the sense of being unprofitable to them, and that the thoughts that they have of him will not fail to benefit them. [verse 16] More specifically, whatever thoughts that beings entertain in his regard—anger and the wish to harm him, or kindness and the wish to do him good—he prays that they may always be the cause and means of the fulfillment of the desires and aims of beings, whether spiritual or temporal. Let none of these intentions be in vain. [verse 17] Here again Shantideva prays that the actions of beings should not fail to achieve their better interest. For he wishes that all who slight him to his face or who commit some other outrage toward his person and property—as well as all who blame and slander him when his back is turned—should also attain the fortune of enlightenment.

In short, as it is said in the *Pitaputrasamagama-sutra*, "May those who give me sustenance attain to perfect peace." We should pray that, whenever beings see us, hear our voices, touch or think of us, regardless of the connection good or bad that they may have with us, they may be brought to the accomplishment of their wishes and to temporary and ultimate happiness.

3. Dedication of the Results of Mind-Training to the Welfare of Others

[verse 18] Shantideva concludes by praying to become the best of guardians for those who are wretched because they are powerless, unprotected, and unimportant. He prays that he might be a sovereign guide for travelers on the road, merchants, and the like. For those who wish to cross the water, he prays that he might become a fine raft on rivers of medium size, a large ferry on great waterways, and a bridge across little streams. [verse 19] He prays that for those who, on long voyages, are weary of the sea and long for land, he might become an island, a place of dry earth where there are flowers and fruit-bearing trees. He prays that he might be a lamp for those who yearn for light, wishing to read at night and so forth, and for those who are in the darkness of not knowing what is to be done and what is not to be done. He prays that, for those who need a resting place and a bed, he might himself become these things, and for those who are old and infirm, that he might become a servant attending to their every need.

[verse 20] Shantideva aspires to be a sovereign wish-fulfilling jewel, which can bring rain wherever it is desired in the four cosmic continents, and a vase of plenty that pours forth a great treasure of all that could be wanted. When someone who has accomplished the vidya-mantras scatters substances blessed thereby, the beings that they touch become vidyadharas as fortunate as the gods of the desire realm, endowed with marvelous qualities. They have a life span longer than that of the sun and moon, they become more radiant than lotuses, and they grow stronger than elephants. Therefore, Shantideva prays that he might accomplish the vidya-mantra—which by simply being read gives rise to accomplishments—and thus be of benefit for others. May he also be the great panacea that soothes every disease and evil force; may he be the tree of miracles that gives every conceivable thing and satisfies every desire; may he be the abundant wish-granting cow, red-dappled, who with her milk satisfies the wishes of everyone.

[verse 21] Moreover, earth and the rest of the four elements are called *jungwa* (*'byung ba*) in Tibetan because they give rise (*'byung*) to all that manifests—not only in the sense of the material universe, but also in the sense of the beings that inhabit it. These elements are called "great" because everything depends on them and they are vastly pervasive. Earth is what provides support; water is the principle of cohesion; fire brings to ripeness; and wind staves off decay. In addition, space is an all-pervasive openness [in which phenomena are accommodated]. The elements therefore are what make life possible. In the same spirit, Shantideva prays that he might always be the ground or cause of the sustenance of countless beings, supplying them with a support, cohesion, warmth, movement, and space; providing them with food, clothes, wealth, and every amenity. Such is the immensity of Shantideva's aspiration.

[verse 22] For the infinite and inexhaustible number of living beings extending to the limits of space itself, and for the time it takes for all of them without exception to attain buddhahood, he prays that he might always be able to provide whatever they need and wish. Such is the time frame of Shantideva's immense aspiration. He prays that it will endure for a very long time.

This training of the mind acts as a preparation for the generation of bodhichitta, and, in addition, constitutes a practice to be implemented after bodhichitta has been generated. Thus we must strive to widen our perspective and make prayers of aspiration on a grand scale. For it is the greater or lesser breadth of our mind in the present moment and our prayers of aspiration that dictate the extent to which our Buddha and Bodhisattva activities will unfold. Mind-training is consequently of the highest importance.

1. THE ACTUAL VOW OF BODHICHITTA

This section concerns the ritual whereby the vow of bodhichitta is taken. There are three ways of generating bodhichitta: in the manner of a king, in the manner of a boatman, and in the manner of a shepherd. Whichever of these ways is adopted, the vow is pronounced either according to the tradition of Nagarjuna or according to the tradition of Asanga. In the tradition of Asanga, the vows of bodhichitta in intention and bodhichitta in action are taken separately, whereas in the tradition of Nagarjuna, they are taken together. To take the vow from a fully qualified teacher is the best way to engender within oneself a moral conscience and a sense of propriety with regard to the observance of the vow. It is said, however, that if one is unable to take the vow from an authentic master, if nevertheless one pronounces it in the presence of the three representations [of the Buddha's body, speech, and mind], or of a visualized field of refuge of the Mahayana, one does indeed receive the vow. One does in any case start simply by saying the phrase "Please think of me" three times.[112] One then lays the foundation of the vow by taking refuge three times. And if one takes the vows of bodhichitta in intention and in action separately, it is by reciting the first two lines of verse 23 ("Just as all the Buddhas of the past . . .") and the first two lines of verse 24 ("Likewise, for the benefit of beings . . ."), that one takes the vow of bodhichitta in intention. Then by reciting the last two lines of both verse 23 ("And in the precepts of the Bodhisattvas . . .") and verse 24 ("And in those precepts . . ."), one takes the vow of bodhichitta in action. [verse 23] If one takes these two vows together (as when the vows of individual liberation, of the Bodhisattva, and of the Secret Mantra are received on the same occasion),[113] one is also following the ancient precedent.

Just as the former Sugatas (for example, Buddha Shakyamuni who, as Abhakara the potter's son, engendered bodhichitta in the presence of Buddha Mahashakyamuni, or else the monk Akshobhya, who engendered bodhichitta in the presence of Buddha Mahachana, or indeed the Lord Amitabha, or the Medicine Buddha, and so on) embraced the awakened attitude of mind directed at unsurpassable enlightenment and just as they trained and abode, step-by-step, in the vast precepts of the Bodhisattvas (from being beginners until they attained buddhahood itself), Shantideva proclaims that, [verse 24] likewise, for the benefit of beings as infinite as the sky is vast, he too will adopt this attitude of bodhichitta in intention, wishing to assist beings to attain unsurpassable enlightenment. From that day forward, he says, he will train in the six paramitas and the other Bodhisattva precepts, step-by-step and according to his capacity. This is how bodhichitta in action is engendered.

The actual moment when the vow is received is at the third repetition of the formula. And at that time, one should have the conviction that the vows of bodhichitta in intention and action are obtained within one's mind. According to the teaching of the master Sagaramegha, one receives the vow of bodhichitta in intention with the first repetition and the vow of bodhichitta in action with the second repetition. The third repetition serves to confirm the reception of both vows. It is at that moment that one should be sure that one has received the vow.

One must be diligent in the bodhichitta training. The vow of bodhichitta should be taken at all times and in all circumstances. It is extremely important to persevere in this. The expression "step-by-step" in the root text is explained by the Sakyapas as referring to the discipline of avoiding negative actions as practiced by the Bodhisattvas of the highest, medium, and basic capacity. Those of the highest acumen are to eschew the eighteen root downfalls as explained in the *Akashagarbha-sutra*.[114] The Bodhisattvas of medium scope must keep themselves from the four root downfalls, such as the refusal to donate wealth or the gift of Dharma through a failure in generosity, as explained in the *Grihapati-ugrap aripriccha-sutra*. For Bodhisattvas of basic capacity, it is enough to preserve and not give up their bodhichitta in intention, as explained in the *Mahaguhyaupa yakaushalya-sutra*. Thus the progressive nature of the practice is understood in terms of a very detailed, moderately detailed, and summary gradation with regard to the avoiding of downfalls. The same tradition explains it also as referring to the training in the three kinds of discipline. The principal training of the Bodhisattvas is, on the path of accumulation, the discipline of avoiding negativity. On the path of joining, it consists mainly in the accomplishment of positive deeds. On the noble paths of seeing and meditation, it is mainly a question of benefiting others. The Sakyapas say also that one must train according to one's capacity, starting with the giving of food, such as vegetables, and progressing until one is able to give away one's very body.

In the Nyingma exegesis, the expression "step-by-step" is understood in light of the *Subahupariccha-sutra*, that is to say, as meaning "from time to time" or "little by little." Since it is impossible to train in the vast, ocean-like conduct of the Bodhisattvas from the very beginning, it is clearly stated that one should train in it "step-by-step." We find in the *Shikshasamuc chaya* that one should train in the precepts according to one's strength. Consequently, if one trains step-by-step and according to one's capacity, in the precepts of the Bodhisattvas, one's ability to observe the precepts will be gradually enhanced.

1. CONCLUSION

2. THE JOY THE AUTHOR FEELS IN HIMSELF

[verse 25] When wise people with clear minds have, with bright and lucid joy, engendered bodhichitta through the preparatory practice and the ritual of the vow as described above, they should, in order to intensify and increase their bodhichitta without letting it decline, lift up their spirits in acts of rejoicing. [verse 26] Therefore Shantideva exclaims that on the very day that he has generated bodhichitta, his life has given fruit. It has become meaningful. For it is as the saying goes, "If our ways are good, this body is a boat that carries us to freedom. If our ways are bad, it is a stone that pulls us down into samsara's pit." Here, then, Shantideva says, his human birth has now been well-assumed, meaning that it has not gone ill or badly. Today he has taken birth in the perfect lineage of the Bhagavan Buddhas and has become the dear son and heir of all of them. [verse 27] In whatever situation he finds himself, he will perform only what is beneficial for others and is in harmony with the lineage of the Mahayana. Moreover, from the Lord Buddha himself and the Bodhisattvas like Manjughosha down to himself, none of the teachers of the lineage has been stained by the root downfall of selfishness and the like. Therefore this lineage is noble and unstained; on account of which, Shantideva proclaims, he will persevere in the precepts of the Bodhisattva, like a son imitating his father. He will act in such a way that he will never pollute or compromise with faults and downfalls his high and faultless pedigree. These are matters on which we too must reflect again and again.

[verse 28] The fact that bodhichitta is difficult to find is illustrated by the example of a blind man, who is normally not supposed to be able to find anything, but who chances upon a wish-fulfilling jewel in a place where a heap of refuse has been swept and piled. It would be thought of as something highly extraordinary and a matter of great rejoicing. As the saying goes, "Writing formed by gnawing insects occurs by accident; it is not intentional." In the same way, Shantideva says, as if by some mere chance configuration of karmic merit, amid the refuse of the defilements that characterize an ordinary being like himself, the precious bodhichitta—the very thing that dissipates the drawbacks of both samsaric existence and peace—has arisen in his mind. This is something completely amazing, and he is exhilarated with joy.

[verse 29] The Bodhisattvas set forth the Dharma according to the aspirations of beings. In doing so, they crush the demon Yama, who is the bringer of death for every being without exception. Their bodhichitta is thus the draft of immortality that places beings in the undying peace of enlightenment. As it is said in the *Uttaratantra-shastra*:

> For those who gain immortal peace,
> The demon, death, no longer stirs.

Even in the immediate term, bodhichitta is indeed an elixir of immortality that drives away untimely death. The word "indeed" (*kyang*) in the root verse indicates that bodhichitta is even greater than the elixir of longevity brewed by the accomplished vidyadharas among the gods, nagas, and humans, and can preserve beings from death for many centuries.

Furthermore, on the eighth ground of realization, Bodhisattvas have power over material things.[115] They are able to dispel the poverty of beings. Bodhichitta therefore is the "sky-treasure" itself, a great mine of inexhaustible riches.

[verse 30] In response to the malaise of afflictive emotions like craving, aversion, and ignorance (which are the cause) and the malaise of suffering that is due to wind-energy, bile, and phlegm (which are the effects), the Bodhisattvas expound their teachings on the revolting aspects [of the body], on loving-kindness, and on dependent arising and the absence of self.[116] It is thus that they remove all the illnesses of beings without exception, in both their aspects of cause and result. Therefore of all the excellent medicines that exist, bodhichitta is supreme.

As it is said in the *Prajnaparamita-sutra* (that is, the *Abhisamayalankara*), "Those who seek the peace of Shravakas are guided to perfect peace by omniscience itself."[117] Accordingly, the Bodhisattvas, who know the paths of the three vehicles, set forth the ways of Shravakas and Pratyekabuddhas for those who, being of medium scope, belong to such lineages, and who, tormented and wearied by sorrows, wander long upon the pathways of existence. It is thus that the Bodhisattvas put an end to the suffering of existence. Bodhichitta is therefore like an excellent tree that, with the coolness of its shade, gives rest to those who are exhausted by suffering. Indeed, even the resultant achievement [the nirvana or cessation] of the Shravakas and Pratyekabuddhas arises thanks to the power of bodhichitta.

[verse 31] And for beings of lesser scope, the Bodhisattvas teach the path of virtue tending to happiness (in samsara)—the avoidance of negative actions and the practice of positive ones. Thus they liberate them from the states of loss and place them in the higher realms, in the conditions of celestial and human joy. Bodhichitta is consequently like a kind of palanquin, the universal bridge or causeway for everyone, in that it liberates beings from the lower realms. It is therefore described as a foundation for all paths because, in order to reach the ultimate goodness of liberation as envisaged in any of the three vehicles, it is necessary to be established first in the higher realms.

Having brought beings to the higher realms, to liberation according to the Hinayana, the Bodhisattvas have as their final intention the establishment of beings of the Mahayana lineage (but also, ultimately, those of the lesser and middle scopes) in the great vehicle itself. Therefore, they set forth the Dharma of the Mahayana. They teach bodhichitta, the supreme attitude of enlightenment, which cools the heat of desire and soothes the torments of other emotional defilements that are the principal obstacles to the liberation of unnumbered beings. It is thus like the naturally cool light of the rising moon. Speaking of the emotional obscurations, the Protector Maitreya has said:

> All thoughts of avarice and the like
> Are said to be emotional veils.

Thus, all the major adverse factors running against the six paramitas are emotional obscurations.

[verse 32] Within the mind streams of beings, the principal obstacle to omniscience, the awareness of all things, is the gloom of ignorance concerning the nature of phenomena. This is what is meant by the cognitive obscurations. Bodhichitta utterly removes them. It is like a great sun that dispels completely and at once the darkness of the three-thousandfold universe. As Maitreya has said:

> The thoughts referring to the three conceptual spheres
> Are described as veils upon the knowable.

If one cognizes something while believing in the real existence of the three spheres of subject, object, and action, one is obscured and limited thereby. It is this that prevents one from seeing all other objects of knowledge together and at once. This is what cognitive obscuration means.

Bodhichitta is the quintessential sap of the three turnings of the wheel of the Dharma. It is, in other words, the purest essence of the Buddha's words. It is like the creamy butter, rich and full, that comes from churning the abundant milk of the Dharma, of which it is the refined essence.

[verse 33] The numberless beings that live in the six realms are like wayfarers traveling upon the paths of existence, from the Peak of Existence down to the Hell of Unrelenting Pain. To help those who wish to enjoy the pleasure of a temporary and ultimate respite from the sorrows that they suffer, the Bodhisattvas are reborn in samsara through the power of their bodhichitta, and they remain with beings, staying close to them, in order to bring them to the undying state of supreme bliss referred to previously. They are like the people who pitch refreshment tents for the pilgrims traveling through Tsari. Bodhisattvas bring to beings whatever happiness they desire. Thus they satisfy these ceaseless wanderers who are constantly moving toward their deaths without a moment's respite, never finding a place of permanent repose. All this is thanks to bodhichitta. With these words, Shantideva brings into focus the teaching of the previous stanzas.

2. Exhorting Others to Rejoice

[verse 34] And so, in accordance with what has been said previously, within the sight of all the protectors, the Buddhas and Bodhisattvas whom he takes as his witnesses, Shantideva issues a summons on this very day to all beings as infinite in number as the sky is vast. He invites them to the highest bliss of ultimate buddhahood, and in the meantime—until such enlightenment is achieved—to a perfect feast of temporary happiness in the higher realms of gods and human beings. Let all the gods on the side of goodness, such as the seventy-five protectors of the Heaven of the Pure, as well as all the asuras and others rejoice! For by being thus called upon to rejoice at Shantideva's Bodhisattva vow, they too will be happy. They will gain their share of benefit and bestow their protection as well. The reason for taking the Buddhas and Bodhisattvas as witnesses of the vow of bodhichitta is that one will have a sense of propriety with regard to them and a feeling of moral conscience with regard to oneself.

Here ends the third chapter of the *Bodhicharyavatara,* called "Taking Hold of Bodhichitta."

PART TWO

How to Prevent Bodhichitta from Weakening Once It Has Been Generated

⋄ 4 ⋄

CAREFULNESS

The Attentive and Responsible Implementation of the Principle of Adopting and Rejecting

1. A BRIEF PRESENTATION

The whole of the Mahayana path may be summarized under two headings: motivation (the generation of the attitude of supreme bodhichitta) and application (the practice of the six paramitas or transcendent perfections). The development of bodhichitta and the practice of the perfection of generosity have already been explained in the foregoing chapters. Shantideva was himself a yogi of extremely simple practice. He therefore did not speak extensively about the practice of giving but did so only from the point of view of a monk staying in retreat. His teaching on the perfection of ethical discipline is to be found in the two chapters that deal with carefulness and vigilant introspection, whereas the four remaining paramitas are explained in the chapters that follow.

The present explanation of discipline is not concerned with the reception of the various vows, nor with their different precepts and the methods of repairing transgressions. Instead, Shantideva discourses upon carefulness, mindfulness, and vigilant introspection, which are the very factors that make the practice of discipline possible. It is essential that they be developed through repeated meditation and training in the way that Shantideva describes. For if carefulness is lacking and you simply imprison your body and speech—the vows will be a burden. You may put on an act of observing them for a while. But phenomenal appearances are deceptive and the mind is feckless and weak, and it is very quickly led astray by things and situations. In the end, you will fail. It is vitally important therefore to rely on carefulness and to strive zealously in the practice of discipline, the ground and basis of all the spiritual qualities that derive from study, reflection, and meditation upon the teachings. Nagarjuna has said:

> As earth is basis for the still world and its moving occupants,
> So discipline is said to be the ground of all good qualities.

Likewise, Vasubandhu says:

> Abide in discipline; study and reflect,
> And give yourself to meditation.

Discipline is thus the root or foundation of all positive qualities, but, as it is said, the astonishing thing is that people boast of their observance even when they have no idea what it is they should observe. Therefore, if you want to have good discipline, you must begin with a clear grasp of the precepts concerning what is to be done and what is to be avoided (the eighteen root downfalls and so on). Having understood that it is precisely the attentive and responsible implementation of the principle of adopting and rejecting that constitutes the essence of carefulness, you must cultivate it within yourself, striving to act or not to act as appropriate. It is said in the *Samadhiraja-sutra*:

> Study, discipline, patience, giving,
> Whatever can be qualified as virtue,
> The root of all of them is carefulness itself,
> For they are gained thereby, the Sugata has said.

[verse 1] It is therefore thanks to carefulness that virtues are acquired. And having clearly understood this, the Bodhisattvas, the children of the Conqueror, who "thus" (that is, through the threefold complement of preparation, the vow itself, and conclusion, as previously explained)[118] have firmly taken bodhichitta into their hearts—never to forsake it even at the cost of their lives—must never at any time diverge from it through laziness and procrastination. They should think that they will strive by every

means not to transgress or weaken the precepts regarding what is to be undertaken and what is to be spurned, such as the twenty root downfalls of the Bodhisattvas.[119]

Regarding the expression "children of the Conqueror," or Bodhisattvas, it is the actual occurrence of the supreme attitude that is most important, not the mere cultivation of it. Those who have no more than loving-kindness in their minds do not become Bodhisattvas merely by the fact of being called so by others. Only those who have the vast attitude (which focuses on perfect enlightenment and is endowed with the twofold aspect or aim),[120] who take the Bodhisattva vow according to an authentic ritual and observe it are entitled to the name "Bodhisattva." No one else.

The expression "firmly grasped" in the root text means that the Children of the Conqueror have assimilated the attitude of bodhichitta perfectly and irreversibly. Similarly, from the moment that we have generated the mind of enlightenment, we too must uphold it firmly, with the zealous wish that, come what may, we will never abandon it. If we have such a concentrated intention, telling ourselves that bodhichitta must be omnipresent even in our dreams, this will come about. It is therefore taught that the focusing of our earnest intention is of great importance.

When the root text says that Bodhisattvas "strive never to transgress" the disciplines of bodhichitta, this implies that it is pointless just to pretend to be learned and to make eloquent disquisitions tricked out with all sorts of examples concerning the Bodhisattva precepts, ocean-vast as they are. The important thing is to have a general knowledge of what the Bodhisattva precepts are and, in particular, to have a grasp of the crucial essence of these precepts. Regarding these same precepts, one speaks, once again, in terms of things to be avoided and things to be undertaken.

In the first place, the things to be avoided comprise the eighteen root or fundamental downfalls, together with the two downfalls of giving up bodhichitta in intention and bodhichitta in action. The eighteen downfalls mentioned in the *Akashagarbha-sutra* are summarized in verse in Shantideva's *Shikshasamucchaya*:

(1) To steal the Triple Jewel's possessions
Is said to be a downfall of complete defeat.
(2) The second downfall is to spurn the sublime Dharma,
   So the Sage has said.
(3) The third is to assault the monks or take their saffron robes—

Even from the ones who spoil their discipline,
To sentence them to jail, to kill
Or cause them to abandon the monastic state.
(4) The fourth is to commit five sins of instant retribution.
(5) The fifth is to espouse wrong views.[121]
(6) The sixth is to destroy a homestead and the rest:[122]
All these are fundamental downfalls, so the Sage has said.
(7) Then to set forth emptiness
To those whose minds are yet untrained;
(8) To turn those entering the path to buddhahood
Away from their complete enlightenment;
(9) To cause the ones who tread the path of pratimoksha
To leave it for the Mahayana;
(10) To hold, and to lead others to believe,
That on the path of (Hinayana) learning,
Craving and the like cannot be overcome;
(11) To praise oneself for sake of fame and wealth,
And likewise openly to criticize another;
(12) To claim untruthfully that one has gained
The realization of the view profound;
(13) To victimize the monks, imposing fines,
Thus causing them to take from the Three Jewels
Or else to take and use the offerings made thereto;
(14) To cause practitioners to give up calm abiding,
Or to give their sustenance to those who merely study or recite.

These then are the fundamental downfalls.
For beings they are causes of great hell.
I will confess them in my dreams
Before sublime Akashagarbha.[123]

It is thus that the eighteen downfalls (the five downfalls liable to be committed by a king, the five liable to be committed by a minister, and the eight associated with ordinary people) are expounded, together with a method for confessing them.[124]

Let us now consider the two remaining downfalls. In the *Mahaguhyau-payakaushalya-sutra*, we find: "O son of my lineage! If a Bodhisattva aspires to the attainment of the Shravakas or the Pratyekabuddhas, that is the gravest of all downfalls for a Bodhisattva!" To abandon beings in one's inner intentions by embracing the Hinayana attitude, is the root downfall associated with bodhichitta in intention. The second downfall is described in the *Ratnakuta* and consists in allowing one's training in active bodhichitta to diminish. If one lapses from one's pledge to practice the six paramitas of generosity and so on—deciding consciously that "I will not do even what I am able to do"—this is to abandon bodhichitta in action. On the other hand, the simple failure to apply oneself to virtue out of laziness and so on, does not imply a complete abandonment.

All the above-mentioned things to be avoided are summarized in the abandoning of negative action. In the second place, the things to be implemented consist of the trainings in the six paramitas and the activities aimed at benefiting others.

Finally and in particular, it is important to grasp the crucial essence of the precepts. As it is said in the *Rajavavadaka-sutra*:

> Great King, your tasks are many; you have much to do. In all circumstances and in all your doings, you are unable to implement the training in the six paramitas, from the perfection of generosity till the perfection of wisdom. Therefore, great King, never lose your yearning faith, your interest, and your aspiration, which are all directed to perfect enlightenment. Be mindful of them at all times, whether you are walking, standing, sitting, or sleeping. When you wake, when you eat and drink, think about it; meditate on it. Rejoice greatly in all the good actions of the Buddhas, of the Bodhisattvas, of the Shravakas and Pratyekabuddhas, and of ordinary beings. Rejoice too in the aggregate of your own good deeds past, present, and future. And having rejoiced, offer the merit [of rejoicing] to the Buddhas, Bodhisattvas, Shravakas, and Pratyekabuddhas, and share it with all beings. In order that the latter attain omniscience and bring the qualities of buddhahood to perfection in themselves, dedicate this merit three times a day to perfect and unsurpassable enlightenment. Great King, it is thus that you should reign. Your realm will know no decline and your accumulations leading to enlightenment will come to perfect completion.

We are thus exhorted in this sutra to aspire to enlightenment, to rejoice in virtue, to offer it to the Buddhas and their Bodhisattva offspring, and to dedicate it to the attainment of great enlightenment. In addition, it is said in the *Subahupariccha-sutra* that when the aspiration to attain enlightenment for the sake of all beings is never forgotten, it contains within it the six immaculate paramitas of the level of buddhahood.[125] It has therefore been said that this aspiration is itself a training in the six transcendent perfections. These two quotations from the sutras demonstrate the characteristics of bodhichitta very well. They are the best of instructions and are of great benefit for the people living in this decadent age.

1. THE DETAILED EXPLANATION

2. REFLECTING ON THE PRECEPTS TO BE IMPLEMENTED AS A MEANS TO INCULCATE CAREFULNESS IN ONE'S BEHAVIOR

3. PREVENTING THE ATTITUDE OF BODHICHITTA FROM WEAKENING

[verse 2] [In normal circumstances,] in the case of any action to which one has committed oneself, or has begun, recklessly and without due heed—as with everything that has only been summarily considered without a careful estimate of its profitability—it is right, even though a pledge has been given, to take stock in light of what should and should not be done and to decide whether to press on or to draw back.

[verse 3] But here the case is different. For the Buddhas and their heirs the Bodhisattvas, great beings like Manjushri and Maitreya, who are untouched by even the slightest delusion, have well pondered in their great wisdom and have taught that the precious thought of enlightenment is of great benefit. And in the chapter on the benefits of bodhichitta, Shantideva himself has weighed and examined it repeatedly. Moreover, it is said that in matters of great moment, the same word should be uttered twice; therefore he has "probed and scrutinized it." He has seen that the excellent qualities of bodhichitta are measureless. And having taken bodhichitta into his mind stream, how could he now procrastinate, telling himself that such a thing is beyond him? On the contrary, he says, he must diligently train in its precepts without delay.

[verse 4] Shantideva has now committed himself, as shown earlier, to deliver all beings from the sufferings of samsaric existence and the drawbacks of the peace of nirvana, and to place them in the state of buddha-

hood. If now he is not diligent in honoring his pledge, he will fail his invited guests, the entire multitude of beings—for he will not bring them to buddhahood as he promised. What destiny must lie in store for him, their betrayer? Nothing but hell and the other states of loss. Thus it is crucial to make a decision that one's promises will be fulfilled. [verse 5] For in the *Dharmasangiti-sutra* it is said that those who in their thoughts intend to give something away, even something as trivial as a handful of food, but then draw back will be reborn among the pretas. And the *Saddharmasmrityupasthana-sutra* also declares that those who fail to give the little that they intended will be born as pretas. But those who do not give what they have promised will go to hell.

[verse 6] This being so, Shantideva says, if he invites all beings, by whom the whole of space is filled, summoning them to the highest bliss of unsurpassed buddhahood, sincerely from his heart and not just with words, but then fails in his deeds and practice to bring them to such a state, he will have deceived and failed them all: the Buddhas and Bodhisattvas, the gods and asuras, and all other sentient beings. How then could he, their betrayer, expect to attain a happy destiny? Only failure must lie in store for him.

This point of view seems to be contradicted by the story of Shariputra as recounted in the *Pundarika-sutra*. He generated the enlightened attitude, venerated ten thousand Buddhas, and worked for the benefit of beings. But in the course of his life as King Vinasiva, he was approached by a malevolent demon who, appearing in the form of a brahmin, asked for his right hand. The king cut off his right hand and presented it with his left. "I will not accept," the demon cried, "an offering presented with such disrespect!" Shariputra was downcast and forsook his bodhichitta. He attained liberation nevertheless and, having become an Arhat, worked for the welfare of beings. Likewise in the *Kanakavarnavadana,* it is said that a man forsook his bodhichitta after practicing it for forty kalpas but became a Pratyekabuddha nevertheless. There is however no contradiction here. [verse 7] When those who, on losing their bodhichitta, do not fall into the lower realms, but on the contrary attain liberation and even lead others to deliverance, this is due to the karma they have previously accumulated.

The workings of karma, in all its different forms, are indeed beyond the conception of ordinary minds. As it is said:

> For a single iridescent eye upon a peacock's tail,
> The causes are both many and distinct.

One who knows them is indeed all-knowing.
Without all-knowing wisdom, they cannot be known.

Only the Omniscient can know the causes and effects of actions in all their subtle details; they are beyond the grasp of anyone else. Even the attempt to understand it is said to accomplish nothing but the mind's exhaustion. What therefore is the point in trying? For as the teachings say, the karma of beings, the activity of the Buddhas, the power of mantra, amrita, and concentration are all inconceivable. As it is said in the *Panjika* and the *Vritti*,[126] "We are ignorant with regard to these matters."

The pandita Kalyanadeva supplies the explanation that although Shariputra relinquished bodhichitta with regard to skillful means, since he had perfectly retaken the vow, he continued to work for the liberation of all beings. Furthermore, Vibhutichandra commented that although Shariputra had given up relative bodhichitta, he did not give up ultimate bodhichitta. And in the great commentary,[127] it is said that although Shariputra stopped cultivating bodhichitta, he did not relinquish his intention to achieve liberation. He was consequently not at fault; he attained liberation and did not fail to liberate others. With regard to the first of these three opinions, perhaps it could be said that this is a reference to the notion stated in the *Sutralankara* that "the Shravakas attain great enlightenment." It has been said in any case, that although Shariputra gave up bodhichitta under the pressure of the moment, he took the vow again. As to the second opinion, although it is accepted by some, how can it be admissible to say that relative bodhichitta can be relinquished by one who has realized the truth of the path of seeing, namely, the nonexistence of the two selves? There is much room for discussion concerning this matter, but the important thing is to grasp Shantideva's real intention.

Bodhichitta in intention may be lost in three ways. In the first place, if the occasion to help someone—even a mortal enemy—arises and one decides not to do so, or if, when there is a chance to save beings from harm, one has no thought of doing so, one is in effect turning away from them. Bodhichitta is also lost if [after entering the Mahayana] one engenders the Hinayana attitude. Finally, bodhichitta is abandoned when any of the root downfalls occur.

[verse 8] To abandon bodhichitta is the gravest and most negative of all the downfalls of a Bodhisattva. As it is said in the *Prajnaparamitasanchayasutra*:

If, after practicing the tenfold path of virtue for a million
    kalpas,
One wishes to become an Arhat or Pratyekabuddha,
Then discipline is faulty and has been perverted.
Such an attitude is graver than a root defeat.[128]

    The reason for this is that if such a downfall comes to pass, it casts down
[a Bodhisattva's] capacity to accomplish the good of all beings. For if the
downfall of abandoning beings occurs, then even if one attains liberation
as described in the Hinayana and one works for beings until achieving nirvana without remainder,[129] it will be impossible to benefit beings who are
present wherever space exists. The welfare of beings is consequently
thrown down. If, on the other hand, buddhahood is achieved, the benefit
of beings who fill the whole of space is accomplished on a vast scale.

    [verse 9] Furthermore, those who, even for a single moment, let alone a
protracted period, hinder the virtue and merit of a Bodhisattva, will be reborn endlessly in the lower realms because, by such actions, they bring low
the welfare of all beings. It is said in the *Prashantavinishchaya-pratiharya-
sutra* that when someone hinders the virtue of a Bodhisattva, even to the
slightest extent (like interfering in the act of giving a handful of food to an
animal), such a negative deed is far worse than killing or robbing the entire population of the earth. Such a person generates an unbounded sin, for
he or she impedes a positive action that will give rise to a Buddha. The
words "halts the merit" in the root text refer to creating an obstacle to bodhichitta. Anyone who does this commits the root downfall of hindering the
Bodhisattva's attainment of perfect enlightenment and of causing the
Hinayana motivation to arise instead. Given that the Bodhisattva who is
the object of such an action forsakes bodhichitta in intention, this is a further explanation of the words in the previous stanza to the effect that "the
welfare of all beings is reduced."

    [verse 10] The reason for saying this is that the sutras declare that if one
destroys the happiness of the higher realms for even one living being (let
alone many), one will certainly accomplish the ruin of oneself in the lower
realms. What need is there to add that if, by creating an obstacle to the
virtue of a Bodhisattva, one destroys the cause of the great happiness of all
beings who are numberless as the infinitude of space, one will sink from
the states of bliss and will be born countless times in the lower realms? For
if the generation of bodhichitta is not hindered, buddhahood will be

achieved. And once this is done, rays of light will emanate from the Buddha's body and, entering the lower realms, will instantly establish all beings in a state of well-being and gradually bring them to great enlightenment, the bliss of buddhahood.

[verse 11] It could be argued that even if a bodhisattva downfall occurs, this cannot be compared with the destruction of the vows of individual liberation. For if one confesses such a downfall, applies the antidotes, and generates bodhichitta again, all is restored. But as we have explained above, those who at one moment commit a heavy downfall of abandoning bodhichitta and at another moment vigorously embrace it, alternating back and forth, will long be prevented from attaining the Bodhisattva grounds, let alone great and ultimate enlightenment. For even if the downfall is purified through the force of confession so that they are saved from birth in the lower realms, a blockage is created nonetheless for the further appearance of good qualities in the mind stream, and this will delay the attainment of the grounds of realization and the other qualities. Take for example the story of Tilopa who is said to have been capable of achieving supreme accomplishment in seven days. But because he secretly took a handful of sesame seeds, he had to wait seven months. [verse 12] Therefore Shantideva declares that he will implement the precepts with devotion and care according to the promise he made when he conceived the attitude of bodhichitta.

3. OBSERVING THE PRECEPTS TO BE IMPLEMENTED WITHOUT RELAXING ONE'S DILIGENCE

Henceforth, Shantideva continues, if he is not diligent in the practice of the precepts concerning what is to be done and not to be done, he will, as a result of his downfalls, sink progressively from the human condition to that of an animal, and lower and lower from one state of misery to another. Suffering will be his lot. We may well tell ourselves that even if we don't make any effort at all, the Buddhas, the Bodhisattvas, and our teachers will surely not send us to the lower realms. Surely they will lead us on to more elevated states and to liberation. [verse 13] But the fact of the matter is that countless Bhagavan Buddhas appeared in the past. They were devoid of every self-centered aim and had the sole intention of securing the benefit and happiness of beings. And this they did before passing away. But, says Shantideva, because of his sins, he was like an incurable invalid beyond the doctor's power to save, and he failed to come within the sphere of those many enlightened beings and their healing works. They were unable to help or guide him. [It is worth remembering that] Devadatta, close as he was to the Buddha our master, the Teacher of the three worlds possessed of every excellence and free from every fault, could not be guided by him and, in his very presence, sank down into hell. [verse 14] So if, Shantideva reflects, he continues as before, acting in such an abject manner, immersed in evil and accomplishing nothing good, it will be his destiny, not just once, but time and time again, to sink lower and lower and take birth in the realms of sorrow. And even when he gains some respite in the higher states, his residual karma will cause him the suffering of many illnesses, imprisonment in chains, and the pain of being cut by swords and dismembered by axes.

2. Reflection on the freedoms and advantages of the precious human body as a means to inculcate carefulness in action

3. Carefulness in action resulting from thinking of the difficulty involved in gaining the freedoms and advantages of the precious human condition

[verse 15] The root text mentions three things: the coming of a Tathagata to the world (an event as rare as the appearance of an udumbara flower), the possession of faith in his teachings, and the gaining of a precious human body with freedoms and advantages. These factors refer respectively to the circumstantial advantages, the individual advantages, and the freedom to practice the Dharma (consisting in the absence of eight conditions in which there is no leisure to implement the teachings). It is indeed extremely rare to find oneself in a situation in which all favorable circumstances are gathered and from which all adverse conditions are absent—a situation, in other words, in which it is possible to practice virtue. Since these conditions will not be found again, it is essential to make the most of what we have, rendering our opportunity meaningful and fruitful.

[verse 16] On such a day as this, Shantideva reflects, he is free from illness and other adversity. He is blessed with favorable circumstances, in the sense of having food, clothing and so forth, and he is untroubled by the harms afflicted by hostile influences and other sources of danger. Yet this

life cannot be taken for granted even for an instant. It is fraught with uncertainty. Moment by moment it is draining away. This body does not last
for very long. It is like something borrowed, something on loan that cannot be kept forever. And there is no saying when the Lord of Death, will
take it back, as though he were its owner.

[verse 17] Previously and until the present time, Shantideva says that he
has been careless of what he should and should not do. He has indulged in
negative deeds. If he continues to behave in this way, not only can there be
no hope of liberation in the future, but he will not even obtain a human existence! [The fact that this can happen is illustrated by] the story of when the
naga king Sagara invited the Buddha to visit him in the ocean and said,
"When I was born here, there were only a few nagas, but now there are so
many that the sea itself cannot contain them. Why is this?" The Buddha
replied that it was due to the violation of precepts and other negative actions.

Moreover, if one fails to obtain a precious human existence and is born
in the lower realms, one can only ever accomplish evil; there is no opportunity to practice virtue. For instance, the majority of animals cannot live
unless they consume the flesh and blood of the species on which they prey.
And in the slaying of their quarry, they are far more skilled even than
human beings. [verse 18] The argument in the following stanzas continues
in the same vein. When one obtains a precious human existence endowed
with freedoms and advantages, one is fortunate in having the capacity to
do good with one's body, speech, and mind. But if, Shantideva says, he fails
to practice virtue even to the slightest degree, he will, as the result of his
evil actions, be tormented in subsequent lives in the hells and other of the
lower realms. And being ignorant of what to do and what to avoid, how
will he ever be able to accomplish virtue? It is impossible.

[verse 19] It will also be impossible to escape from the lower realms. For
if, Shantideva says, he does not perform even the slightest positive action,
but instead accumulates nothing but intensely negative acts for a long
time, it follows that he will continually wander in evil states for hundreds
of millions of kalpas. How could he possibly take birth in the realms of
happiness? He will not even hear of their existence.

[verse 20] For this reason, the Lord Buddha gave the hypothetical example, found in a sutra setting forth perfect instruction, in which the entire
earth is imagined to be covered by an immense ocean on the surface of
which there floats a yoke blown here and there by the wind. Coming to the

surface once in a hundred years, a blind turtle living in the ocean's depth could in theory find its head inside the yoke, adrift as it is upon the shoreless sea. But since the ocean is vast, the yoke mindless, and the turtle blind, the odds against such a thing happening would be immense. And yet to find a human birth is far more difficult than this!

3. CAREFULNESS IN ACTION RESULTING FROM REFLECTING ON THE DIFFICULTY OF ESCAPING FROM THE LOWER REALMS

[verse 21] Whether you consider it in terms of the shortest possible unit of time or as the period required for the completion of an action, a single instant of evil (such as a hostile impulse toward a Bodhisattva or one of the sins of immediate effect) is said to lead to the suffering of the Hell of Unrelenting Pain, where beings must stay for a very long time—an intermediate, or even an entire, kalpa. This being so, Shantideva reflects that the evils he has committed in samsara from time without beginning will cause him inescapable suffering for an immense duration. It is certainly not necessary to say that they will keep him from experiencing the states of bliss!

Generally speaking, a tiny cause can be productive of immense consequences. Even though their actions take only a brief instant, those who, for example, put someone to death will have to experience infernal suffering for a kalpa (which is a very long time). It is not the case that all our evil actions accumulated from beginningless time have already been exhausted through the experience of their consequences or through their being purified by confession. How many of them are still lodged within our mind streams! And, owing to the evil thoughts that constantly arise in the course of a single life, how many actions are perpetrated that will themselves lead to rebirth in hell? The negative deeds performed between the beginning and ending of this present life alone will render it difficult for there to be any moment of freedom from infernal existence.

As for the way in which the results of karma are experienced, it is stated in the *Abhidharmakosha*:

> Within the sphere of actions, those that are most grave
> Are first to ripen, followed by the deeds performed when
>   death is near,

Then by those arising through the force of habit.
The remaining actions ripen in the order they were done.

Accordingly, it is said in the teachings that there is an order in which the fruits of sin and virtue ripen. The actions performed nearest the moment of death ripen before all others.[130] In the absence of such actions, the results of actions that are most powerfully ingrained by habit will occur. Otherwise, actions fructify in the order of their commission. It might therefore happen that when death occurs, an evildoer may attain a favorable rebirth by dint of some early good action, and, conversely, there is no certainty that, on account of a negative action committed in an earlier life, a Dharma practitioner might not be born in the hell realms. For it is impossible to be certain that all past negative karmas have been purified by confession or exhausted through experience.

[verse 22] It might be thought that the results of earlier actions have been exhausted through their being experienced in the lower realms and that freedom will now follow. But the simple fact of suffering in hell and the other states of loss does not mean that the beings who have accumulated such evil karma are liberated from existence in the lower realms. The reason for this is that even while they are suffering the pains of the evil destinies, the fruits of their former misdeeds, karmic effects "similar to the cause," constitute a powerful stimulus for the occurrence of other negativities: aggressive attitudes, anger, acts of killing, and so on. Such a pattern is illustrated by the examples of the hawk and the wolf, as well as by the stories of Purnavasu and Ashvaka.

Generally speaking, manifest phenomena may be assessed by means of valid perception; hidden phenomena are known through valid inference; and extremely hidden phenomena, such as the karmic principle of cause and effect, are known on the authority of the Buddha's teaching. It is said that it is possible for the karmic principle to be logically established. And of the four principles of reasoning (the principle of causal efficiency, the principle of dependency, the principle of nature, and the principle of logical coherence), it is the fourth that is invoked here.[131] Be that as it may, if beings who are in hell (the place in which their karma has fructified) also accumulate karma while they are there—which will then be experienced in due sequence—it follows that there can be no chance of liberation from such a state. Personally, I do not see how this can be so and therefore respectfully request the learned to consider well what might be Shantideva's intended meaning here.

3. NOW THAT THE FREEDOMS AND ADVANTAGES OF THIS HUMAN FORM HAVE BEEN OBTAINED, IT IS IMPORTANT TO STRIVE IN VIRTUE

[verse 23] With regard to the practice of the sublime Dharma, it is difficult to find oneself in a situation in which one has an aptitude for its accomplishment. And having found such a thing—the freedoms of this precious human existence and the facts of discovering the Dharma and meeting a perfect teacher—one may, in the best of cases, achieve the ultimate goal in this very lifetime. In the next best case, one will be able to secure the human condition in one's next life and to awaken therein to the lineage of the Bodhisattvas. In the least of cases, one will have no regrets at the moment of death.

But if, Shantideva says, he fails to school himself in virtue and accomplishes nothing good, and if, under the influence of the eight worldly concerns, he consumes his entire life in distractions, he is deceiving himself. There is indeed no greater delusion than this. It is also stupid, and there is no greater ineptitude than the failure to distinguish between what is to be done and what is not to be done. We should not follow after the objects of sense since they are crafty in misleading us. And since our awareness is feeble, we should not let it be enslaved by confusion. Instead, we must cultivate carefulness and practice Dharma purely.

[verse 24] Here Shantideva remarks that if, having found the freedoms and advantages (of a precious human existence), he fails to accomplish virtue, he is being extremely foolish and is greatly deluding himself. For, at the same time as being fully aware of his situation, he is like an animal led astray by a mirage of water; he thirsts for the objects of the senses and tries to secure wealth, respect, and a good reputation. Tricked and beguiled by silliness, he tells himself that the likes of him are unable to practice Dharma, whether now or in the future, and he allows himself to sink into depression and idleness. This is how people put an end to their fortunate opportunity in spiritual matters. They put themselves down, thinking that they are stupid and unable to study, telling themselves that they have too much anger, that they are without compassion, that they are distracted and incapable of diligence, and so on. But if, Shantideva tells himself, he fritters away his life, he will bring ruin on himself, and at the time of death, he will feel great regret. After all, he has succeeded in the difficult task of being born in this world, he has gained the freedoms and advantages of a human existence, which are so difficult to gain, and he has found the teachings and a teacher, all so difficult to find. If therefore he fails to practice the sacred Dharma whereby attainment is to be had, he will feel great remorse at the moment of death; he will tear his breast with his nails, his mind in an agony of distress. And after death, he will fall into hell.

[verse 25] It is said that the fires of hell are seven times more fierce than the fires at the end of time, which are themselves seven times hotter than the ordinary fire of burning sandalwood. The experience of hellfire is therefore said to be unbearable and protracted. And when, Shantideva says, his body (which will then be much more sensitive to pain than it is now) experiences the agony of being burned, there is no doubt that his mind too will also be tormented, scorched in the flames of unbearable regret. For, either the thought will come to him that it is because of his failure to practice the Dharma that he must now undergo such experiences, or else the guards of hell will tell him that his pains are the result of this or that deed.

[verse 26] Whether in terms of causes, examples, or numerical comparisons, a human life endowed with freedoms and advantages is extremely difficult to achieve. It is the foundation for all positive works, it is what makes the practice of Dharma possible, and it is something, Shantideva reflects, that he has not attained in a very long time. It is by some accident of merit that he has gained it now and it is vital that he should not again fall victim to the same senseless conduct. Instead, he should have a clear discernment of what is beneficial and what is harmful. For what if he again commits negative actions, he asks, and is once again led back to the very hells where he has been before?

How do we know that we have come from the hells into this life? As he was about to enter his parinirvana, the Buddha, like a father who, before embarking on a sea voyage leaves his will and testament for his young son in the safe keeping of his relatives, said to the supremely noble Avalokita and Manjughosha and others, "When beings now in hell who have some slight connection with me are freed from their sufferings and gain a human form, give them this treasury of knowledge that I have accumulated for three countless kalpas."

Therefore Shantideva reflects that if, in view of all this, he falls yet again into the situation of allowing himself to be destroyed, [verse 27] it is as though he has been dazed by witchcraft, or else he is like a mindless person unable to tell the difference between help and harm. The omniscient Longchenpa has said:

We do not grasp things when explained;
We do not understand when things are shown to us.
Great balls of iron are our hearts, great lumps of flint.
We're mindless—there's the honest truth!

Are we truly as mindless as the verse says? Obviously, our hearts are neither iron balls nor pieces of stone, yet how is it, Shantideva asks, that we do not recognize our stupidity and confusion? Though we think that we will practice the Dharma, that we will keep the discipline, that we will study and reflect upon the teachings, the fact is that we don't. We are helplessly out of control. What is it that is making us so stupid? For sure, there must be something that we have failed to recognize. We should ask ourselves again and again: What is it?

2. REFLECTING ON THE AFFLICTIVE EMOTIONS TO BE DISCARDED AS A MEANS TO INCULCATE CAREFULNESS IN ONE'S BEHAVIOR

3. THE DEFECTS OF THE AFFLICTIVE EMOTIONS

[verse 28] What is it, we may ask, that renders us so stupid? Aversion and craving are indeed the parents of samsaric existence. Together with ignorance and the other afflictions, they are our own inner enemies. But these enemies are not like soldiers with physical bodies, heads, and limbs, armed with chain mail and every kind of weapon, and equipped with helmets decked with ensigns. They are not by any means courageous heroes. On the contrary, they are lazy. Moreover, they are not clever or skilled in deceiving. In fact, they are quite stupid. How is it then, asks Shantideva, that these afflictions have reduced him and everyone else—teachers, lords, high or low, strong or weak—to this abject condition of slavery and suffering, deprived of every freedom? How is it that, in the pursuit of honor and fame, wealth and enjoyment, we neither rest by day nor sleep by night? We are slaves to our desire; we are slaves to our aversion—to the point where we do not even shrink from actions that will cost us our lives. Powerless, we are at the beck and call of our emotions, which torment us with all the sufferings of slavery. [verse 29] And these emotions have no dwelling place other than the temple of our own minds. It is *here* that we actually entertain our emotions of attachment and hatred as though they were our guests. We are their slaves and lackeys. Whatever they want, we enthusiastically accomplish, even though, by way of recompense, they harm us unrestrainedly at their pleasure in this and future lives. Yet we bear it all. We put up with these afflictions, our enemies, without the slightest resentment. This is the sort of patience we have, completely abject and wrongheaded. It is an object of contempt for the Buddhas and their Bodhisattva children.

[verse 30] Shantideva reflects about the terrible damage that his enemies, the emotional afflictions, can wreak. Even if the kings of the gods and lords of the asuras were to come against him with all their retinues, renowned as the most powerful forces in the world, each of them able to defeat multitudes of many thousands, and even if their aggression were directed at him alone, they could certainly do no more than harm his body and belongings. They would be unable to throw him into the blazing fiery Hell of Unrelenting Pain. [verse 31] By contrast, the emotional afflictions, such as attachment and hatred, which are indeed his most powerful enemies, are able in a single instant (such as a moment of malice toward a Bodhisattva) to cast him down into the fires of Unrelenting Pain, in which the firm majesty of Mount Meru, the king of mountains, eighty thousand leagues in height, would be instantly reduced to ash—to say nothing of anything else. It is therefore essential to overcome such enemies.

[verse 32] Turning now to the long duration of the damage inflicted, Shantideva reflects that these enemies of his, namely, his negative emotions, have long harmed him—indeed from beginningless samsara until the present. And if he does not manage to vanquish them now, they will continue to harm him for a long time in this and future lives, indeed, for as long as samsara continues. No other enemies—such as the thieves of his possessions—are able to cause him injury over such an extended period. It is therefore essential for him to apply the necessary countermeasures.

[verse 33] There then follows a reflection on the difficulties that ensue from relying on such foes. For Shantideva says that if he were to appease ordinary enemies by giving them the material goods that they want, they will always act favorably to him and give him their assistance. But however much he serves his enemies the afflictions—his craving, hatred, ignorance, and the rest—and yields to their demands, not only will they not show him any favor or give him any help, but they will drag him down to grief both in this life and the next. He must therefore repudiate them instead of aiding and abetting them.

[verse 34] For a very long time, indeed for endless and beginningless time, our afflictions are, without the slightest interruption, our unprovoked and natural enemies—just as fire is naturally hot. And it is from them alone that the various sorrows of this and future lives evolve. Moreover, they make their abode in the very temples of our hearts. If we serve them perfectly, it is sure that they will harm us perfectly. If we serve them moderately, they will harm us moderately. If we serve them little, they will do us little damage. And if we serve them not at all, they will leave us completely alone. The basic reason for all these ills, which dwell in our hearts, is the fact that we do not fear samsara though it is like a ditch of fire or a den of venomous snakes and is suffering by its very nature. On the contrary, we take pleasure in it. There lies the blame. How can we enjoy and be attached to samsaric things? It is completely senseless.

Although they have no desire for the sufferings of samsara, Bodhisattvas take birth there and strive for the welfare of beings. This is because they are moved by compassion. It is not that they take pleasure in samsara, for if they did, they would want beings to stay there and not be liberated. But this is not the case. It is said that the Bodhisattvas themselves cannot stand the unbearable sorrows of beings in samsara. They therefore make little of their own suffering and remain in samsara for the sake of others.

[verse 35] Our negative emotions are like jailers that imprison us in the three worlds of samsara. It is they that allow us no escape. It is they that appear to us in the form of the killers who slay us in the hell of Reviving and the other infernal states. And they lurk within our minds—in the web of our very cravings—without our even wanting to repudiate them. If we get caught in them, like birds tangled in a fowler's net, what chance do we have of joy in this and future lives? These are the enemies that we must strive to overcome!

3. Putting up with the hardships involved in abandoning the afflictions

[verse 36] Merely to recognize afflictive emotions and to acknowledge their defects is not enough. They must be rejected. This is why Shantideva says that until he has definitely destroyed his enemies, his defilements, and not merely suppressed them, he will cultivate within his mind their antidotes and steep himself in them. To that end, he will strive and never allow his diligence to weaken even at the cost of his life. That is the meaning of his promise. Shantideva then gives the example of someone slightly injured by an ordinary enemy, perhaps through the theft of his horse or some other property. The fury of the injured person's pride will be intensely aroused. And until he has got the better of his adversary, he will not even sleep, so great will be the energy that he puts into his plans for vengeance. There is no need to mention that great efforts must also be made in overcoming negative emotions, which are so hostile and cause so much mischief. The kind of comparison being used here is technically referred to in poetics as a "simile of correspondence."

[verse 37] But even if one does not put a great deal of effort into defeating one's ordinary enemies, the fact is that they are going to die anyway. It is in the nature of things that they will have perished before long. Such ordinary foes are themselves the victims of suffering, which is why they are unflatteringly referred to as "wretched or miserable." They are themselves weak and are the objects of compassion.

When one battles against enemies in the hope of victory, one ignores all the horrible sufferings that one knows are in store, the wounds of arrows, of swords and spears, and so on. And until one accomplishes one's aims (the destruction of one's opponent), one must stand one's ground refusing to give way. [verse 38] This being so, Shantideva tells himself that he too must fight and vanquish his afflictive emotions, those enemies for whom it is as natural to hurt him in this and future lives—unprovoked and with terrible pain—as it is for fire to be hot. These are the natural enemies of us all, high or low. Whenever they appear, they labor for our destruction, and it is essential to make the greatest effort to destroy them.

Therefore, Shantideva declares that from then on, and for the sake of striving in the antidote, whatever adversities present themselves (poverty, lack of provisions), all of which are a source of a hundred vexations, he will not allow himself to be depressed or to lose heart. He will not allow himself to think that he has never before succeeded in eliminating emotional defilement despite the use of antidotes and that he will be unsuccessful once again. He will not allow himself to adopt such a defeatist attitude. Instead, he will take joy in applying the antidotes. Needless to say, he will remain unflinching until his enemies, his defiled emotions, are all brought low. He will not listen to the voices of depression and idleness.

[verse 39] Soldiers flaunt as trophies the scars and wounds on their heads and limbs made by swords and other weapons—wounds that their enemies have inflicted in wars fought to no great purpose. They show them off as badges of heroism. If this is the case, why should he, Shantideva, regard as harmful and injurious the trials and hardships that arise while he is persevering in the remedial practices, while he is striving in the Bodhisattva trainings for the sake of the great goal of enlightenment both for himself and other beings? Not only are they not harmful, they are extremely beneficial. For it is by them that his defilements are purified!

[verse 40] Fishermen, butchers, and workers on the land, in order just to scratch a living, go without rest the whole day long, and at night they do not sleep. The stones are stained by their bleeding feet, the trees by the blood of their hands. They must patiently ignore all the discomforts of cold and heat, the wind and the rain. This being so, says Shantideva, why should he shrink from the hardships encountered on the path, in his wish to bring beings to happiness in the immediate term and then to the ultimate great bliss of buddhahood? Of course, he must shoulder all such hardships.

[verse 41] When previously he generated bodhichitta, Shantideva says he made a promise involving all beings in the ten directions to the very limits of space. He undertook to take to the other shore those who have not yet crossed over, to free those as yet unfreed, to rouse those who are still not roused, and to establish in the state beyond suffering those who have yet to reach it.[132] In other words, he made a promise to liberate them from all their obscurations: karma and the afflictions. When he made this pledge, he himself was not free from negative emotions, not even to the slightest extent. [verse 42] He did not have the measure of his own capacity and to make such an ill-considered promise was, to be sure, an act of madness. For it was as if he had promised to save someone while he was himself bound and drowning in the water. But pledges are to be honored nevertheless! Therefore Shantideva tells himself that he must never draw back from his task but must apply antidotes in order to overcome his enemies, his defilements. Now that he has promised, he must strive with utmost diligence.

3. HOW EMOTIONAL DEFILEMENT IS TO BE ABANDONED

[verse 43] He therefore decides that he will vanquish his enemies, the defilements, by means of remedies to which he has grown accustomed. This will become his all-consuming passion! The defilements have harmed him from time without beginning. He is therefore filled with rancor against them, and he will conduct a war in which antidotes will fight against defilements. For defilements must be abandoned.

It could be argued that passion and rancor are themselves types of attachment and aversion, and that they must consequently be rejected. But defilements such as these, namely passion for the antidotes and rancor against defilements, are, in the early stages, means by which the negative emotions are to be destroyed. This is why, for the time being, they are not to be regarded as things to be rejected. They should not be spurned. All the same, they do constitute cognitive obscurations and at some point, they too will have to be abandoned.

[verse 44] From the very first, we should emulate the attitude of Shantideva. It would be better to perish in the fire, he says; it would be better for his head to be cut off and fall to the ground, or for some other dreadful thing to happen to him, than that he should ever surrender to his mortal enemies, his defiled emotions, and that he should serve and grovel before them. This is the kind of pledge that we should make again and again.

[verse 45] When enemy forces, in the ordinary sense of the word, are forcefully driven from the state, they retreat and base themselves in other countries, where they regroup their forces, mustering many bands of robbers and thieves—the better to return and wreak havoc in retaliation. But negative emotions are not like ordinary enemies. Once they have been driven out through [realizations gained on the] noble path, they can never return.

[verse 46] How then are they to be discarded? If examined, defilements such as craving are easily removed. For when they are scrutinized by the eyes of wisdom that understands their lack of inherent existence, these same defilements, contemptuously referred to as "miserable" in reference to their baseness, are scattered like darkness at the rising of the sun. Where will they run to, Shantideva asks himself, now that they are driven from his mind? They have nowhere to go. From where will they return, their strength restored, to launch further attacks against him? The fact of the matter is that previously, when his understanding was weak, he had made no effort to eradicate them. If only he had had wisdom and perseverance, emotional defilement would have been much easier to dispose of than other enemies.

[verse 47] This is how we should scrutinize the nature of the afflictions with the eyes of wisdom. When attachment or hatred arises in our minds, we should not allow ourselves to be overpowered by it, but should examine it in the following way. The defilements of craving and aversion are not to be found in objects external to us, whether in our enemies or our friends. We know this because the defilements still arise even when external objects are absent. Moreover, if they were actually based in such objects, it would follow that when other people encounter our enemies and friends, they would experience aversion and attraction in the same way that we do, but this is not the case. Therefore defilements do not dwell in the outer objects.

But neither do they subsist within the conjunction of the sense organs and consciousness. For even when sense power and consciousness meet, defilements do not automatically arise. If the defilements were intrinsic to such conjunctions, it would mean that whenever we see or hear anything, attachment or aversion would be felt, whereas this does not happen. Nor can the defilements somehow exist in the interstice between object and consciousness, for space is empty. Therefore such defilements have no dwelling place whatsoever. And since they cannot abide elsewhere, whether in beings or in the outer universe that contains them, we may well wonder where they actually are—these same defilements that have been our enemies from time without beginning! How is it that they do so much damage to ourselves and other beings in this and future lives?

Analysis reveals that the defilements appear and yet lack inherent reality. They are like insubstantial visions, mirages of things that do not exist. Such illusions display three properties. First, they appear when certain conditions arise, second, they are perceived by the mind, and third, they are without intrinsic being. Defilements arise thanks to the circumstantial causes provided by enemies and friends; they appear to our mind, and yet they lack inherent existence. We should take comfort from this fact and not allow ourselves to be alarmed at the thought that we can't get rid of them. We should not follow after sense objects like dogs running after stones. Instead we should be like lions. Whatever defiled thoughts of craving or aversion arise in the mind, we should recognize them for what they are, in their nakedness. First we should search for where they have come from, then we should search for where they dwell in the present moment, and finally we should search for where they go. If we do this, if we strive to see, by means of this technique, that the defilements are without inherent existence, it will be easy to discard them, for they are without intrinsic being. This being so, Shantideva asks himself why he should stand by and do nothing, allowing them to torment him—all so needlessly—with the pains of hell and other lower destinies? It is said in the *Ratnakuta*:

In future times, O Kashyapa, there will be conceited monks who will be like dogs running after stones. Excited by [the throwing of] a stone, a dog will chase after it; it will not chase the person who threw it. In the same way, O Kashyapa, certain monks and practitioners will persistently discriminate between forms, sounds, smells, taste, and textures. They will understand that these are impermanent, deceptive, and liable to destruction, yet they will not know whence they arise. Therefore, when they go to villages, towns and cities, provinces and royal palaces, they will be wounded by forms, sounds, smells, tastes, and textures. Even if they stay and die in solitude, since they abide by precepts limited to the world,[133] they will be reborn in the higher destinies and will continue to be harmed by the objects of the five senses. And when their minds leave that condition at death, they will not find freedom from the evil destinies. And what are these evil destinies? They are the hell realms, the states of animals, the world of the Lord of Death,[134] and that of the asuras. It is thus that these monks are like dogs chasing after stones.

In times to come, however, O Kashyapa, there will be other monk-yogis who will not be like dogs chasing after stones. If you throw a stone at a lion, it will know where the stone has come from. It will chase not the stone but the one who threw it, with the result that no more stones will be thrown! In the same way, when monks who practice yoga behold the outer objects of the senses, they know that the latter take their origin in the mind. And having examined the mind, they know that it is not truly existent, and thus they are free.

[verse 48] In the spirit of what has been discussed above, Shantideva resolves to reflect well on the instructions on carefulness as set forth in the scriptures and the commentaries. He determines to strive to apply them in the practice of the three higher trainings of the superior path: ethical discipline, concentration, and wisdom.

It is said metaphorically that the Buddha should be regarded as a physician and the sacred Dharma, in its aspects of study, reflection, and meditation, should be looked upon as a medicine. The principal training in discipline is like following a special diet and behaving appropriately in the event of illness. The negative emotions of attachment and aversion are like diseases, whereas we ourselves are like invalids. If we fail to observe the discipline, if we fail to implement what is to be done and avoid what is to be avoided, the Dharma will do us no good whatsoever. We are like people who ignore the advice of a learned physician who tells us how we should eat and act: Do this, and avoid that. How can we expect to be cured from the diseases of heat and cold and so forth, even when we actually take the right medicine against such ailments? It is impossible. On the other hand, if we correctly observe the doctor's advice and, moreover, take a suitable medicine, our illness will be cured. In the same way if we practice the Dharma with effort, training in discipline, we will be freed from every suffering and attain to great bliss. This is why we must strive to train ourselves in carefulness. As it is said in the *Suhrillekha*:

> Carefulness brings life, the Sage has said,
> And carelessness is death.
> Therefore to increase your virtue,
> With devotion always practice carefulness.

Here ends the fourth chapter of the *Bodhicharyavatara*, the instruction on carefulness.

· 5 ·

VIGILANT INTROSPECTION

The Repeated Examination of the Mind and Body in Their Various Situations

1. GUARDING THE MIND IN ORDER TO IMPLEMENT THE TRAININGS

2. A BRIEF EXPOSITION

It is important to understand that mindfulness consists of not forgetting those actions that are to be implemented and those that are to be avoided. Vigilant introspection or inner watchfulness is the repeated examination in all circumstances—whether we are alone or in the company of others—of our physical, verbal, and mental behavior, and the conscious implementation of the principle of adopting what is to be done and rejecting what is not to be done. We must first study at the feet of an authentic teacher in order to understand, train ourselves, and become adept in "adopting and rejecting." Otherwise, how would we be able to apply it without forgetting? As it is said:

> Strange it is that many who declare themselves observant
> Do not even know what is to be observed.

Nowadays, there are many monastics, both bhikshus and shramaneras, as well as those who claim to be tantrikas, who enjoy a good reputation in the estimation of other people but do not even know what most of the defeats, residual faults, and root downfalls are.[135] This is a disgraceful state of affairs.

Therefore it is in full knowledge and with the constant mindfulness of the principle of adopting and rejecting that we should properly check the state of our minds and, standing guard over them, act or refrain from acting accordingly. It is said in the *Shikshasamucchaya*:

> Who will know the contents of my mind
> Better than myself, my own preceptor?

Since others are unaware of our negative states of mind, how can they set us on the path? For even if they have some slight knowledge of our physical and verbal misdeeds and tell us to refrain from them, they succeed only in irritating us and not in placing us on the path. By contrast, if we ourselves have brought our thoughts, words, and deeds onto the path, we will not be irritated when we make mistakes and we will be able to return to the path again. In other words, we should be teachers unto ourselves. For example, if the mind is compared to a horse, mindfulness will be its rope and introspection its keeper. If we fail to keep a guard over our minds with mindfulness and introspection, we will be unable to persevere in the training.

[verse 1] So people who wish to implement the three precious trainings of the excellent path correctly should not fall into the power of distraction but should strive one-pointedly to guard their minds from every fault, gaining mastery over them through mindfulness and vigilant introspection. Whatever we may think to the contrary, if we do not preserve our minds from defiled emotion through the practice of mindfulness and introspection, we will be unable to prevent our training from regressing. Indeed, if we neglect to keep a guard on our minds and manage for a time to control our body and speech merely out of fear of authority, the vows and precepts will become a burden and we will get nowhere. It is therefore essential to keep watch over our minds.

2. A DETAILED EXPLANATION

3. ALL HARM COMES FROM THE MIND

[verse 2] The mind, which Shantideva compares to an elephant, follows after the habits of the past and eagerly anticipates future thoughts. And caught up in the mental states and circumstances of the present moment, it is lost and

dissipated in whatever arises. Left running wild to its own devices, it accumulates bad karma, which in future lives will result in the intense pain of being boiled and roasted in Unrelenting Pain and the other hells.

In India, wild elephants were used for military purposes. They were maddened with alcohol and unleashed against the enemy, whose towns they were able to reduce to total ruin. Even so, they were powerless to inflict on human beings any harm comparable to the Hell of Unrelenting Pain. Therefore every effort should be made to control the mind.

[verse 3] If the elephant of the mind, which can be driven wild by desire, is tethered with the rope of mindfulness (so that it remains aware of the principle of adopting and rejecting with regard to the actions of body, speech, and mind); and if it is bound to the post of correct mental behavior, and prevented from following past experience, inviting future thoughts, and straying to the objects and conditions of the present, all fears and dangers of this and future lives will be brought to nothing. All altruistic virtues will be gained without difficulty. They will drop into our hands like gifts.

[verse 4] What are the fears and dangers of this and future existences? In our lives at present, they are whatever is hostile: tigers, lions, elephants, bears, snakes, and [dangerous humans like] thieves, robbers, and so on. The terrors of the life to come are the dreadful henchmen of the Lord of Death, the guards of hell, and so forth. The fears that threaten us both in our present and future existences are the evil forces and demons summoned and sent by the magical power of others, as well as all devilish influences that rob beings of vitality and shorten their lives.[136]

[verse 5] But if, Shantideva says, he manages to do no more than just tether his own mind, it is as if all such evil harm-doers have been secured. They will be powerless to injure him. As it will be explained in due course, if on a journey one surveys with mindfulness and vigilance the road in front and behind, one will not come face to face with tigers and other dangerous things. Moreover, people who are mindful and vigilant are accompanied by spirits that take pleasure in goodness, such as tutelary deities,[137] as a result of which they do not encounter such beasts. And even if they do, if they pray to Guru Rinpoche, the great master from Oddiyana, they will come to no harm. As Shantideva says, if just the mind is tamed with loving-kindness, compassion, and bodhichitta, all such dangers are subdued and rendered harmless. It is just as with Ngulchu Thogme Zangpo, in

whose presence sheep and wolves would be friends and play together, or with Simha, the Indian mahasiddha who used to ride a lion using poisonous snakes as ropes to tie his saddle.

[verse 6] Proofs for this contention can be found in the scriptures, which declare that all the myriad fears and sufferings of mind and body in this and future existences arise from minds overpowered by delusion and distraction and from the negative actions to which they give rise. This was said by the Buddha himself, who spoke the truth and was free of every falsehood. It is said in the *Ratnamegha-sutra* that power over one's mind confers power over all phenomena. And it is further said in the *Saddharmasmrityupasthana-sutra:*

> The mind's our enemy, our mighty foe;
> No enemy exists apart from this our mind.
> Like tinder burned by flames itself has kindled,
> The mind is scorched and burned by mind itself.

It stands to reason. [verse 7] All the infernal instruments used to torture beings—the saws and swords, the groves of razor-sharp blades, the pestles and mortars in which beings are pounded—who created them for the purpose of such torment? No one other than the mind itself. Who was it that forged the burning iron ground, and why? Whence, Shantideva asks, have all these women appeared (the very ones after whom he had lusted and with whom he had committed acts of sexual misconduct in the past), calling to him from the top, and then from the foot, of the shalmali trees? They come from his mind and nowhere else. [verse 8] All such terrifying apparitions are but the offspring of his sinful mind; they are what appears to a mind that is steeped in nonvirtue. This is what Lord Buddha himself has said in the scriptures. It is written in a sutra that distinguishes the different kinds of beings:

> The iron pavement blazing hot,
> All burning round with fiery flame,
> The iron saws so sharpened fine
> That cut one body hundredwise—
> From minds of those do they arise
> Who sin in body, speech, and mind.

Thus, throughout the three worlds—understood either as the desire, form, and formless realms or as three dimensions above, upon, or beneath the earth—no harm or fear arises except from the mind overpowered by delusion. Therefore, if one manages to guard the mind effectively, not allowing it to stray into the power of distraction and delusion, every danger and injury in this and future lives will come to nothing.

3. ALL VIRTUE COMES FROM THE MIND

[verse 9] Generosity too derives from the mind. For if the paramita of generosity were to consist in the actual distribution of great gifts leading to the complete elimination of poverty without a single beggar remaining, how can it have been achieved by the Buddhas of the past (for still to this day there are many beggars and starving people)? The fact is, however, that it has been achieved by them.

What then is the perfection of generosity? [verse 10] The teachings explain that generosity is perfected by training oneself in the attitude of openhandedness, in the genuine intention, wholly without miserliness and cupidity, to give to all beings—high and low, rich and poor—one's every possession: body and belongings, along with the merit of such a gift, without any expectation of recompense whether in this or future lives. It is said in the *Akshayamati-sutra*, "What is the paramita of generosity? It is the sincere wish to give to others whatever one has, together with the karmic result of such an act." The term *paramita* implies that the act of giving is performed in a manner free from the assumption of the real existence of the subject and object of the action, as well as of the action itself. The same is valid for the other five paramitas. Therefore generosity does not depend on the objective value of the gift. It depends on a generosity of attitude untrammeled by any kind of attachment that would prevent one from making a gift of one's external possessions or of one's inner qualities and merit. It follows that generosity is in the mind.

[verse 11] Ethical discipline likewise comes from the mind, as can be seen in relation to the act of killing. It is impossible to find a place to put living beings (such as fish and other animals) where they will be protected from being killed. But regardless of whether other beings put them to death, if we are determined to refrain from doing so, thinking that we will not kill even at the cost of our lives, this is said to be the perfection of ethical discipline. The sutras define this paramita as the *decision* to refrain from harming others. In the same way, the vow [of chastity] cannot be observed simply by doing away with objects of lust. Ethical discipline subsists in the attitude of restraint, in ridding oneself of desire. If this attitude is absent, mere abstention from untoward activities does not constitute discipline. Therefore, once again, discipline comes from the mind.

[verse 12] Patience also arises from the mind. Dangerous and unruly beings are everywhere like space itself, and wherever you go, you will never find anywhere that is outside space. In other words, there is nowhere that is free of beings liable to inflict harm on others. It is impossible to get rid of such harm-doers. It is impossible to do away with the objects of our anger. But even though there are always enemies who will injure us, if through the practice of patience we are able to subdue our own enraged minds, it will be as if we had succeeded in overcoming all such foes. [verse 13] Shantideva illustrates this with the idea of covering the entire earth with leather, with sheets of soft hide, in order to protect ourselves from thorns and the like. Where could such quantities of leather be found? Obviously nowhere. On the other hand if we were simply to cover our feet, by putting on shoes with leather soles, it would be as if the whole earth had been covered with it and our purpose would be achieved. [verse 14] In the same way, although it is impossible to avert or do away with every external source of harm, all we need to do is remove our inner attitude of anger. What need is there to get rid of outer irritants?

[verse 15] Diligence too is founded on the mind. If we generate a clear, unequivocal attitude of kindness or compassion, like the loving thoughts of a mother for her only child, this state will fructify as rebirth in the Brahma-world, which is a heaven of the form realm, and in all the exalted states of bliss associated with such a state. It is said in the *Mahaparinirvana-sutra*, for example, that the great compassion felt by a mother for her dying child and the vivid intention of love felt for each other by a mother and her daughter when they were both carried away by a river resulted after death in their being born in the Brahma-world. Thus no matter what good deeds of body and speech we may diligently perform, this will not automatically result in rebirth in the Brahma-world, because physical and verbal actions are weak in the results that they give. It is the *mind* that is the chief criterion. This text defines diligence as a state of mental joy, though there are numerous ways in which diligence might be discussed.

[verse 16] Generally speaking, concentration is also a practice of the mind. It is true that one may for a long time undergo every kind of physical austerity as a means to bring about the birth of concentration in the mind stream (such as recitation, or going without food or clothing). But if the mind is distracted by objects of desire, fluttering like a scrap of paper caught in a tree, no matter what recitations or austerities are performed, their hoped-for aim will not be achieved. This was said by the Buddha himself, who has a direct unmediated vision of the nature of all things. In the sutra *Distillation of Concentration,* the Buddha said, "O monks, if your mind is distracted by desire, none of your austerities and prayers will give any result." And as we find in the *Prajnaparamita-sutra:* "Through my mind's distraction, I fail to accomplish my own good, let alone the good of others. Therefore, I will not allow my mind to be distracted even slightly."

[verse 17] As for wisdom, the most important thing for everyone to understand is the nature of the mind, which is empty, devoid of self, and luminous. Although everyone possesses it, not everyone knows or realizes it—which is why it is described as a secret. All external phenomena arise in the mind like reflections in a mirror. They are mental fabrications. They are the mere display of the mind and do not extend beyond it. The principal task therefore is to understand the mind clearly, and to that end we must use reasoning. We must examine the mind. We must look for its shape, its color, and so on. We must search for the place where the mind arises, where it dwells, and where it ceases. If we fail to understand that the mind is beyond every concept of origin, dwelling, and cessation; if we fail to penetrate this secret of the mind (its emptiness and lack of self), then however much we long to achieve the joy of nirvana and to uproot the sorrows of samsara, we will wander uselessly in misery. Concerning this secret of the mind, the Shravakas and Pratyekabuddhas fully understand only the personal No-Self; they do not understand the No-Self of phenomena, which remains hidden from them, a secret.

To sum up therefore in the words of the *Gandavyuha:* "All Bodhisattva conduct is founded on the mind."

3. THE NEED TO KEEP WATCH OVER THE MIND

[verse 18] All the sorrow and fears of this and future lives, as well as all merits and virtues, arise from the mind. We should therefore, by applying mindfulness (in other words, not forgetting the principle of adopting and rejecting), take possession of our minds and guard them well with vigilant introspection, repeatedly examining our physical and mental behavior. All trainings are contained in such an endeavor. For all the discipline of the white-robed, long-haired yogis, as well as of the saffron-robed monastics, should be a means to guard the mind with a sense of moral conscience—both with respect to oneself and to others. For of what use otherwise is a multitude of different and arduous disciplines, of donning the white robes and tying up one's locks, or of wearing the saffron robe? They are all pointless.

[verse 19] When we find ourselves in wild and unruly crowds (of people who are without mindfulness and whose attention is scattered toward outer objects, people whose minds are not restrained by discipline), we would take the greatest care to shield whatever physical wounds we might have, for fear of further injuries. The same is true when we are in bad company, with people who are rough and cruel and who rouse us to anger, or when we are with people who are sexually attractive and who might stimulate our desire—we should at all times guard the "wound" of our mind with extreme care, protecting it from the great suffering that will come from damaging the vows, which after all we wish to observe. Just as adverse circumstances aggravate our physical injuries, when the mind falls into the power of things wished or unwished for, craving or anger arises. This is why we should avoid company liable to excite our desire or aversion. [verse 20] For if we take special care to protect our injured bodies, in fear of the comparatively minor sufferings of this present life (which might occur owing to the worsening of our physical condition), why shouldn't we also use mindfulness and introspection to protect our minds from becoming defiled with afflictions, for fear of the pain of being ground and bludgeoned later on in the Hell of Crushing? It stands to reason that we should.

[verse 21] If, by using mindfulness and vigilant introspection, we keep a ceaseless guard over our minds, the result will be that, whether we find ourselves with difficult people liable to stimulate aggression or with attractive people liable to excite desire, our firm commitment to the observance of the vows and precepts will not decline as a result of such circumstances. This shows how good and useful mindfulness and vigilance are.

[verse 22] In conclusion, Shantideva reflects that it is fine for him to lose his property and everything that has been offered to him. It is fine for him to lose whatever esteem he may enjoy in terms of honor or respect. It is fine for him to lose even his body, the support of his life; and it is of no importance if his livelihood in terms of food and clothes just disappears. In short, even if he dies and all other merits accruing from his body and speech perish—none of this signifies. But he will never give up the practice of carefully and vigilantly guarding his mind so that he can continue to observe the precepts.

1. USING MINDFULNESS AND INTROSPECTION IN ORDER TO GUARD ONE'S MIND

2. A BRIEF EXPLANATION

[verse 23] Consequently, Shantideva addresses all his followers who wish to guard their minds. He begs them to preserve diligently and by every means—even at the cost of their lives—an attitude of mindfulness, never forgetting what is to be done and what is not to be done. He begs them to maintain a state of vigilant introspection and to examine their conduct in thought, word, and deed constantly. And when Shantideva speaks with his hands joined in supplication, he is not making a gesture of respect toward his hearers but indicating the extreme importance of his message.

2. A DETAILED EXPLANATION

3. THE DRAWBACKS OF HAVING NO INTROSPECTION

[verse 24] Even though they may be very clever and in the bloom of youth, when people suffer imbalances of the humors of wind, bile, and phlegm and are afflicted by disease, they are able neither to walk, sit, or speak. In just the same way, people may be very intelligent and clearheaded, but if they lack mindfulness and have no self-scrutiny, their minds are scattered. And if they are ignorant with regard to what behavior is to be adopted or avoided, their minds are confused. The result is that, whatever virtuous actions they undertake (such as studying the Dharma or avoiding evil), they are unable to bring them to the desired term.

[verse 25] Wisdom is nothing where vigilant introspection is lacking. The wisdom that comes from receiving the teachings from a spiritual master, the wisdom that results from reflecting on them by dint of repeated examination and analysis, and indeed the wisdom that comes from meditating one-pointedly upon their meaning—all these will be short-lived in those whose minds are without vigilant introspection and are therefore distracted. When water is poured into a pierced vessel, it gradually leaks out and drains away. Similarly, the three kinds of wisdom will not remain long in people who have only mindfulness. They will be forgotten. For when there is no vigilant introspection, mindfulness alone is powerless to retain them.

[verse 26] Discipline likewise is brought to nothing. Many people who are perfectly knowledgeable with regard to their precepts and the principle of adopting and rejecting, who have confident faith in the karmic principle of cause and effect, and who are joyful and diligent in discerning what they should and should not do are occasionally stained by downfalls, and their discipline comes adrift, through a failure in vigilant introspection.

[verse 27] Whenever one is at fault through lack of vigilant introspection, the bandits of desire and hatred and the thieves of pride and jealousy come in pursuit; and they gain an entry whenever the guard of mindfulness (the remembrance of what is to be adopted and rejected) is allowed to lapse. And all the merit gathered in the past (all the riches of one's virtue) they steal, severing the life force of the happy destinies and sending beings down to the lower realms in the same way that thieves and robbers take the belongings of their victims and even murder them.

[verse 28] Craving and aversion and all the other defilements are like a band of thieves and brigands who first spy on people—travelers and so on—to check whether they are vulnerable or not. If they are, the thieves watch for a favorable moment to attack, whether by night or by day. Functioning in exactly the same way, the defilements of desire and hatred are always on the watch for an occation to harm us. They behave just like thieves and brigands. When they get their chance, they snatch away the wealth of virtue that we have accumulated in the past and they destroy its effects—the happy destinies—with the result that we fail to attain them.

3. How to practice mindfulness

[verse 29] For the reasons just given, mindfulness—the state of mind in which the principle of adopting and rejecting is not forgotten—must be placed at the door of the house of the mind, that is, the door through which the mind engages in improper objects. So positioned, as a protection against the thieves and brigands that are the defiled emotions, it must never be allowed to stray outside or wander elsewhere. In other words, we must use mindfulness to protect our minds from being distracted by the objects of the six consciousnesses. If this reliance on mindfulness is forgotten, and if the mind strays and scatters toward sense objects, we should immediately recall that it is through neglecting to maintain mindfulness that the mind falls into the power of defilement and will bring about the experience of injury and suffering in the lower realms. And once again we must establish firmly a state of close mindfulness.

[verse 30] For beginners, who are unable to maintain such a state, the way to cultivate mindfulness and cause it to arise is to rely on, or to keep the company of, a fully qualified teacher, who himself possesses both mindfulness and vigilant introspection. It is therefore said in every system of teaching in the Buddhist tradition that one must never separate from one's teacher. Lamas and abbots need to teach their disciples correctly about the principle of adopting and rejecting; and for their part, the disciples need to act according to the teachings they receive. Disciples who respect the precepts dread the reproaches of their teachers as well as the ensuing defects that arise when the precepts and trainings are transgressed. Such fortunate people will easily generate mindfulness; they will experience no difficulty in doing so.

[verse 31] Moreover, the Buddhas and Bodhisattvas are in constant possession of an unobstructed primordial wisdom. There is not the slightest thing that they do not see and know, and we should therefore consider that we are always in their presence. Indeed, they are like people who can see standing in the midst of the blind. They have a direct and unmediated knowledge of all our shortcomings of thought, word, and deed, great or small, and it would not be right to offend them by our conduct. [verse 32] If we think of this repeatedly and do not forget it, we will feel a certain conscientiousness, as well as a respect for the precepts, and we will, for our own part, shrink from bad behavior. Externally also, with regard to others, we will be apprehensive of giving offence and will thus gain a sense of moral propriety, which will also put a break on unwholesome activities. We should always keep ourselves in this state of mind. If we succeed in doing so, not only will mindfulness take birth in us, but of the six recollections associated with the Bodhisattva precepts (that is, the thought of Buddha, Dharma, Sangha, generosity, discipline, and the yidam deity), the recollection of the Buddha will also occur frequently to our minds.

[verse 33] When mindfulness (that does not forget the principle of adopting and rejecting) is placed as a sentinel upon the threshold of the mind to prevent the latter from slipping into objects of defilement, a vigilant introspection that scrutinizes all activities of thought, word, and deed will naturally arise. And even if it is sometimes forgotten or scattered, it will return.

1. SCHOOLING ONESELF IN THE MIND-TRAINING BY
MEANS OF MINDFULNESS AND VIGILANT INTROSPECTION

2. THE DISCIPLINE OF AVOIDING NEGATIVITY

3. PURIFYING THE ACTIONS OF BODY, SPEECH, AND MIND

[verse 34] We should rely on mindfulness and vigilant introspection at all times and in all situations. At the outset, we should inspect our minds to see the kind of thoughts that are arising. We should check whether our state of mind is positive or negative. If it is negative, we should recognize that this is a defect and that it is harmful both for our present and future existences. We should then refrain from all action, whether physical or verbal and should not allow ourselves to follow this unwholesome mental state. Instead we should be like the trunk of a mighty tree unmoving in the wind. Our minds should be unshakeable and we should not allow them to fall under the influence of negative thoughts, involved as such thoughts are with the objects of the senses. We should act in accordance with the proverb "Clean the lamp while it's still warm. Club the pig right on its snout." As soon as bad thoughts arise, we must beat them down without delay.

[verse 35] Shantideva goes on to say that he will never allow his gaze to wander vacantly around. In other words, he will never look at things that are futile or are not in harmony with the Dharma. He will not pretend to be other than he is; he will not create a facade for others to see. Being convinced of the principle of adopting and rejecting and of the ultimate nature of phenomena, he will look with lowered gaze and half-open eyes fixed upon a point past the tip of his nose or at the distance of a yoke's length. For as it is said, whatever thoughts of craving, aversion, and so on, arise in the mind, the eyes are drawn toward [the associated object] and the defilements themselves can be visibly discerned in the eyes' expression. It is consequently not good to look around with distracted gaze.

[verse 36] If he gets tired when walking or sitting with such a focused gaze, Shantideva considers that he will raise his eyes and look around—albeit with mindful vigilance and without distraction—in order to relax his eyes and mind. And if there is someone in his field of vision, he will not put on an expression of annoyance but, with eyes cast down and looking at a point a yoke's length away, he will, according to the local custom, greet him with a friendly word of welcome.

[verse 37] Nevertheless, when on dangerous paths, he will look to the east and in all the four directions one by one, slowly, repeatedly, and with undistracted mind in order to see whether there is any risk. Especially when he is relaxing, he will not behave in an agitated and careless manner, creating a poor impression in the eyes of others—playfully capering around and turning only his head to look behind while still walking. Instead, he will turn his entire body carefully and slowly to look back along the path, to make sure that there is no danger from hostile sources, whether robbers or wild beasts. [verse 38] He will therefore look around, in front or behind, to determine whether to press on or to return home. Likewise, in every situation (whether he is in town or sitting in the rows of the monks, whether eating or sleeping, walking or sitting), his task is to recognize the prime needs or aims of himself and others and to act accordingly and with vigilance.

[verse 39] Whether he is in a town or a monastic assembly or in his meditation session, he will begin every action by consciously deciding on the physical attitude he should adopt (for example the seven-point posture of Vairochana with legs crossed in the vajra position and hands in the mudra of equanimity). And from time to time he will vigilantly check it.

[verse 40] If a wild elephant breaks loose from its fetters, it can do enormous damage. It must therefore be tethered very securely. In the same way, says Shantideva, if this mind of his—a wild and rampant elephant indeed—dominated as it is by craving and aversion, is distracted toward objects of desire and anger, it will draw him into torment in the lower realms, the regions of hell and of the pretas. Therefore, not letting his mind stray distractedly to external things, he will tether it with mindfulness and vigilant introspection to the sturdy post of concentration, focusing on exposition, study, and meditation upon the Dharma—binding it just as one might tether an elephant to a post so that it does not get away. He will devote his every effort to restraining his body from all movement, to abstaining from speech, and to reflecting concentratedly upon the view, meditation, and action of the sublime Dharma—without allowing himself to be distracted even for a moment. He resolves to be vigilant in examining his mind, guarding it so that it might never slip its bonds and escape.

[verse 41] Those who strive to master profound concentration should have their minds focused solely on that objective and should not be distracted by anything else even for a single instant. If they wander slightly into distraction, they should immediately look to see what their minds are doing instead of concentrating. And coming back to the point, they should set themselves undistractedly in meditative equipoise.

[verse 42] In dangerous situations, however, when one's life is threatened for instance by tigers, leopards, or other wild animals, or else in times of celebration, when offerings are made to the Three Jewels, or again on the occasions when one is involved in activities the purpose of which is to bring great benefit to others—on all such occasions, when it is impossible to remain one-pointedly in meditation, one is allowed to act in the manner that seems best, provided one does so without distraction and in a spirit of mindfulness and vigilant self-scrutiny. For although it is taught that discipline is superior to generosity, it is nevertheless true that in times when offerings on a vast scale are being made, one may relax the lesser precepts of one's discipline—for example, the rule against making expansive gestures with one's hand or the offering of alcohol. It is written in the *Akshayamati-sutra* that in times when generosity is being practiced, [certain minor aspects of] discipline may be relaxed and suspended.

[verse 43] Whatever we may have planned or actually begun—for example, the study or practice of the *Bodhicharyavatara*—we should decide that, from having begun it until the task is complete, we will not allow ourselves to think of other projects, such as all the various things that are to be recited, all the different things that we might do or study, all the places that we might visit, and so on. When we start something—for example, the study of the present text—we should keep our minds fixed concentratedly upon it and should be determined from the beginning and for as long as necessary to strive until it is completed. On the other hand, when we manage to achieve something, we should not rest on our laurels. When one thing is properly done, we should start on something else.

[verse 44] If we act in this way, a whole succession of tasks will be brought to term. By contrast, if we fail to follow such a plan of action—if after beginning one thing, we stray to something else—neither task will be accomplished. As the proverb says, "Always leave one foot upon the ground; you'll fall if you lift both." If, however, we proceed in stages as described and properly complete the earlier task before launching into the next, this will prevent the fault of inattention, the lack of introspection (one of the twenty lesser defilements), from growing.[138]

3. PROTECTING THE PRECEPTS FROM DEGENERATION

[verse 45] In order to be of comfort to people, such as the sick or the aged, it may be necessary to amuse them by chatting and indulging in various kinds of light conversation or to attend lots of shows like the performances that beggars put on in order to gain their sustenance: amusing routines with trained monkeys, music, dancing, or conjuring tricks. One does this kind of thing just to make others happy. For one's own part, one should cast aside all interest and taste for them. For it is inappropriate to take pleasure in such chatter or to be fascinated by such spectacles. Nevertheless, when lamas and important persons attend the entertainments given by beggars and so on, they should remunerate and congratulate them.

[verse 46] Unless there is some important reason for their actions, Bodhisattvas, lamas, and tulkus must avoid doing anything that might cause others to waver in their faith. Therefore, when they feel the urge to grub in the soil with their fingers or with sticks, or when they want to pull up grass or trace patterns or draw pictures on the ground simply because they cannot keep their hands from fidgeting, they should remember that the Tathagata has laid down rules specifically to discourage such behavior. And alarmed by the fact that transgression of such precepts will lead to the lower realms, they should immediately restrain themselves.

[verse 47] When the desire arises for physical movement, whether to travel far or near, or when one even wishes to move one's arms or any other part of one's body, or when one wishes to speak and indulge in conversation with others, one must first examine one's mind and ask oneself whether one's motives for doing so are good or bad. For Bodhisattvas, those with stable minds, must act correctly and with due reason. In other words, they must reject negative action and engage in good works. If the twenty-seven sources of mistaken conduct—even the most subtle ones—are truly absent from the mind, the faults and downfalls related to the Individual Liberation, Bodhisattva, and Secret Mantra vows will not occur. It is therefore important to make an effort to find out what exactly these "sources" are and commit them to memory and then to make an effort in correct conduct.

[verse 48] Shantideva mentions these twenty-seven sources as follows. The first is (1) delight and attachment for what we like (our friends and possessions), and the second is (2) aversion and repugnance toward enemies and other unpleasant objects from which our minds draw back. When such urges and longings arise in the mind, we should do nothing with such a motivation: We should not walk, move around, speak, or allow the mind to pursue such objects. Instead, we should remain unmoving like logs of wood. We should not allow our body, speech, and mind, to run after what attracts or repels us.

[verse 49] We may also be afflicted with (3) frantic behavior of thought, word, and deed, where we do not realize what we are doing, especially when our minds are in the grip of attachment, giving rise to uncontrolled and compulsive behavior. We may have (4) the will to make fun of others or to play tricks on them. We may be (5) arrogant with the seven kinds of pride: the pride of ego-clinging, simple pride [of thinking that we are special], the pride of thinking that we are better or greater than others, the "pride of pride,"[139] the pride of thinking that we are only slightly inferior [to someone obviously exceptional], perverted pride [when we are proud of something reprehensible], and blatant arrogance [deluded self-confidence]. We may be (6) infatuated with ourselves, self-satisfied because of our families or our physical appearance, our youth, our learning or our wealth. We may also feel (7) the urge to expose the hidden faults of others whether directly or indirectly. We may feel (8) the repeated urge to irritate people, which is explained as wishing to revive old conflicts that have been reconciled in the past or never being content with the alms donated, always wanting and asking for more. Finally, we may have (9) the wish to deceive and cheat others.

[verse 50] When (10) we feel the desire to speak highly of our own good qualities or those of the group to which we belong; when (11) we want to criticize and put down those whom we do not like; when we find ourselves (12) using insults, wounding others with our words; and finally when we notice that we are (13) picking a quarrel between others and ourselves or creating divisions—it is at all such times that we must refrain from every act of body, speech and mind. We should remain just like logs of wood.

[verse 51] When (14) we find that we have a desire for things—food for instance, or clothes; when (15) we feel the wish to be looked up to (to be given a good seat and to be respected by others); when (16) we would like others to know how good we are, or when (17) we would like to be surrounded by efficient people who would serve and wait on us, fetching water, attending to the fire, and so on; and when (18) we wish to be served immediately: to have our beds prepared and to be tucked into the blankets—it is then that we must not allow our body, speech, or mind to follow after such things. Instead, we should remain like logs of wood.

[verse 52] When (19) we feel like neglecting even some small action that would be of benefit to others (which we are nevertheless perfectly able to do), such as helping someone who is sick, and when (20) we want to get the best for ourselves (even something trivial like a good place in the temple), we should conduct ourselves like Geshe Ben, subjecting all our self-interested efforts to mindfulness and vigilant introspection. And since the mouth—with all its talk full of attachment or anger, and all its futile and meaningless chatter—is a treasury of nonvirtue, the very gateway of faults and downfalls, when (21) we have the urge to speak, we should instead stay like logs of wood.

[verse 53] When (22) we are full of intolerance (the antithesis of patience) and when (23) we are sunk in laziness (the reverse of diligence) and when (24) we feel fainthearted and put-off when we hear about the teachings on emptiness and practices that are difficult to do; or again when (25) we are boastful, that is, arrogantly pretentious, or (26) given to various kinds of light and ill-considered chatter, without care and reflection; and finally, when (27) we have attachment to our own groups (institutions, traditions, etc.) thinking that they are the best in both a worldly and a religious sense—when all such attitudes arise, we should remain like logs of wood. To put on a show of devotion to the lamas of one's own tradition is mostly a species of attachment. It has consequently been said that there should be no confusion between genuine devotion and sectarian bias.

[verse 54] It is important therefore to examine whether the mind is caught up in attachment and anger and the other of the twenty-seven sources of negative behavior, to investigate whether or not one has strayed into meaningless actions such as digging in the soil, cutting grass, tracing patterns in the dust, and so on. On discovering that they have fallen into such a state, courageous Bodhisattvas should rely upon the appropriate antidote, for it is thus that their minds will remain undistracted and will keep from straying into things that are either meaningless or [productive of] emotional defilement. Bodhisattvas must get a grip on their minds and must not allow themselves, either in word or deed, to indulge in bad thoughts.

[verse 55] Whatever Dharma practice we do physically, verbally, and mentally—staying in retreat and so on—we should not act simply in imitation of others. Instead our practice should be marked by nine factors that are productive of virtue. These are as follows: (1) Whatever practice we perform, we should have great certainty about it. We must understand its preparatory, principal, and concluding stages and have no hesitation about them. (2) We should rely on the practice and have complete trust in it. (3) We should be firmly resolved to perform it and should not allow ourselves to be influenced by adverse circumstances, such as illness or lack of food. (4) We should approach the practice with joy and with feelings of respectful devotion. We should honor both physically and verbally all who are worthy of homage: abbots, masters, and teachers. (5) With regard to ourselves, we should have a sense of moral conscience, the ability to feel ashamed of ourselves. And with regard to others, namely, our teachers and the Buddhas and Bodhisattvas, we should feel a certain awe and apprehension.

(6) We should in general be quiet and peaceful. That is, we should place restraints on our five senses, in particular those of the eyes, ears, and mind. For if we fail to keep them under control, attachment and aversion will arise. Perhaps we are in the habit of belittling ourselves, thinking that, because our attachment, our anger, and our mental wandering are too great, we are incapable of keeping our senses under control. But it is a mistake to be so defeatist, becoming thus the cause of our own ruin. No one ever received the prophecy (that they would gain control of their senses and become superior beings) who was free from desire and anger from the very beginning. Take for example the lustful Nanda, the aggressive Subhuti, and the ignorant Chudapanthaka. Instead, we should be diligent and make an effort. Our behavior should be disciplined and calm. We should work quietly for the happiness of others. For Bodhisattvas are "perilous" objects and it is therefore important to protect others from losing faith in us.[140]

[verse 56] Ordinary people—who are like children—are at odds with each other in their tastes and desires. They disagree. Something that amuses one person will irritate another. This being so, it follows that, when we practice the way of the Bodhisattva, some people will be delighted and full of praise, while others will be displeased and critical. (7) We should not allow ourselves to be dismayed by such things; otherwise our bodhichitta will be impeded, as is recounted in the story of Shariputra and his attainment of arhatship.[141] Indeed, not only should we not be downcast, but we should be aware that such circumstances arise from desire, anger, and the other defilements, which are the result of the various yearnings of childish beings. Because they are overpowered by defilement, the resentment they feel toward a Bodhisattva's activity and the Dharma practice is beyond their control. For this reason, the Bodhisattvas should treat such difficult individuals with an even greater tenderness.

[verse 57] We should be beyond reproach in the things we do both for our own sake (such as feeding ourselves or listening to the Dharma teachings) and for the sake of others (teaching the Dharma or the giving of alms and so on). (8) When we do these things, we should think that all that we have done, all that we are doing, and all that we will do has the nature of a magical apparition. We should thus be without clinging to "I" and "mine," and maintain this attitude at all times.

[verse 58] As Shantideva observes, we have waited so long to attain a precious human existence, which is so hard to find. Now that we have obtained it, we must strive to make it meaningful. (9) By mulling over this time and time again, by thinking of the difficulty of obtaining all the freedoms and advantages of such a condition, our minds will become determined and as unshakeable as Meru, the king of mountains. It is essential to keep our minds firmly set, not allowing them to stray from the object of meditation owing to the influence of nefarious company and the like.

2. THE DISCIPLINE OF GATHERING VIRTUE

3. WHY IT IS NECESSARY TO ABANDON ATTACHMENT TO ONE'S BODY, WHICH IS THE CAUSE FOR NOT TRAINING IN THE PRECEPTS

[verse 59] The mind cherishes the body. When the latter is hungry, it provides it with food; when it is thirsty, it gives it something to drink. When people discuss its defects, even those of its eyes and nose, the mind springs to its defense. This attitude of protecting the body is a state of mind that is to be abandoned. It should be earnestly challenged by counteractive thoughts that cut through such attachment. Addressing his mind, Shantideva observes that, when the vultures and jackals, with their love of flesh, will be tugging at his body, pulling out its intestines and other organs here, there, and everywhere, and devouring it, his mind will not be unhappy on that account. Why then is it so besotted with the body now, lavishing such care on it, nurturing it with food and clothing, and protecting it from injury? It does not make sense.

[verse 60] Shantideva pursues the following reflection, questioning his own mind: "Why, O mind, do you think of this body as yourself or as your property and protect it with food, clothing, and the rest? This is illogical, for you are a completely different entity from the material body, the essence of which is the semen and ovum of its parents. Of what possible use, therefore, can this body be to you? You have no need of it.

[verse 61] "If you say that you need it as your dwelling place, then you are a fool and do not know what you should and should not do. If you need a support in which to dwell, why not take as your body a clean human form carved in wood? For that indeed would be reasonable. By contrast, [your present] body is a machine composed of bones joined together by tendons that can stretch and contract; it is essentially an accumulated mass of thirty-six impure substances like meat and blood. Nothing but filthy substances issue from its nine orifices. How can it be reasonable to protect such a thing, repugnant as it is, unclean and decaying?" The body is said to be decaying because, whereas the wholesome and essential derivative of the food that one consumes becomes flesh and fat, its putrid residue remains in the greater and smaller intestines, where, according to the *Nandagarbhavakranti-sutra,* the eighty thousand bacteria dwell and are responsible for the foul stench of excrement and urine.

[verse 62] "And if, O mind, you think that, although the body is an object of decay as just described, you will nevertheless protect it on account of its wholesome core, then you should, with your sharp, blade-like discernment, separate the covering of skin from the flesh and look! All that you will find is something frightful, filthy, and foul-smelling. There is nothing else. Again, with the blade of intelligence, strip the flesh from its bony frame and examine it.

[verse 63] "And when you have separated the bones, pulling them apart at the joints and so on, examine carefully right down to the bone marrow. Ask yourself, where is the pleasant and desirable essence of the body to be found? Is it inside the body or outside? This is something that you yourself should investigate with your own intelligence, examining each and every detail.

[verse 64] "If, persisting in the search, you find nothing that is pleasant or desirable, why, O mind, do you persist in clinging to this body? Why do you protect this impure, decaying, foul-smelling form? It does not make sense.

[verse 65] "You may think that you need the body and that therefore you should of course protect it. But what is it that you need? You cannot consume this impure body; you cannot drink its blood and pus. You cannot suck its stomach or intestines. What, O mind, are you going to do with this body? You have not the slightest need of it!

[verse 66] "From one point of view, there is no reason for you to protect this body. But from another point of view, it would be quite reasonable and appropriate for you to save and keep it as food for the vultures, foxes, and other animals that are without any concepts of clean and unclean!"

Of course, these are Shantideva's words of scornful irony. It is true that when this body is examined outside and in, it is found to have no essential core of any kind. And yet an essential benefit is to be extracted from it nevertheless. How so?

> The mind is like a king omnipotent.
> The body is his servant both in good or ill.

As it is said, if one is able to use one's body as a servant in the performance of good works, then of all the physical forms to be found among the six classes of beings, this human form is the best for the practice of the Dharma. Therefore in order to "extract its essence," the human body—and this applies to everyone: lamas, monks, high or low, strong or weak—should only be used as a servant in the performance of virtuous deeds. Apart from that, there is nothing else to be done with it.

[verse 67] Again addressing his own mind, Shantideva points out that it strives to protect his body—just like people who are strongly attached to their bodies and indulge them with whatever they want, whatever pleases them: food for their mouths, clothes for their backs, ornaments, and so on. "But what," he asks, "will you do when the Lord of Death, who knows neither love nor compassion, takes it from you, helpless as you are, and throws it as food to the vultures and dogs? What, O mind, will you do then? You will be powerless to do anything."

[verse 68] "Servants and slaves," he continues, "who are unable to work or who do their work poorly are not supplied with food or clothing by their masters. But, O mind, even though you lavish both food and clothing on this body, in the end the mind and body separate; they go their different ways. Since therefore the body is of no benefit to you, O mind, why do you pamper it with food and clothes, serving it with such great effort and labor? It makes no sense at all."

[verse 69] Therefore, instead of clinging to the body as in the past, we should not fall into the opposite extreme, but provide it with food, clothing, and so on, with which to fill its stomach and protect it from the wind—just so that we can use it to practice the sacred Dharma properly. We should do this in the same way that we would pay someone for work to be done—but then we should make sure that the body works for us, listening, reflecting, and meditating on the sublime teaching. And if it fails to practice the teachings that will help us in the life to come, we should not provide it with food and clothes or anything else that we might have. We should not just feed and clothe this body, taking care only of its stomach and its back!

[verse 70] Instead, let us regard this body as a simple support—a boat for making the journey to liberation and omniscience, and for coming to the rescue of beings. And just as we might look after a boat, without falling into extremes [of neglect or extravagant care], we should sustain our bodies with food and clothing, avoiding all excess. In order to accomplish well the benefit of all beings, let us, with the perfect attitude of bodhichitta, train ourselves properly in the six paramitas, making of this body a wish-fulfilling gem (the sovereign power that can bring benefit to anyone who sees, hears, remembers, or touches it). In other words, let us transform this human body into the body of a Victorious Buddha.

3. Becoming skilled in one's way of behaving

[verse 71] Body and speech should be placed in the power of the mind, and the mind should itself be placed in the power of the remedial attitude. Whenever we look at someone, we should have a smiling expression and should completely avoid any angry frowns and sullen looks. We should be true and honest friends to everyone, helping them and speaking to them with candor and without deceit.

[verse 72] When picking up furniture, chairs and beds, pots and pans, for instance, and putting them down, we should not do so carelessly and inconsiderately, throwing them around and making a commotion. Such a thing is displeasing in the eyes of others and will cause them to lose their respect. Neither should we violently throw open the door of the house and so on. Since this interrupts the concentration of abbots and lamas, it should not be done. We should constantly be mindful of our own shortcomings; we ought to behave in a subdued manner so that whatever we do will not be seen or heard by anyone. We should actually take pleasure in humility. Wherever we are living, be it monastery or mountain hermitage, we should take care to be neither seen nor heard.

[verse 73] Herons, cats, and burglars, whom the world does not normally regard as peaceful creatures, go about their business very softly, moving stealthily with soundless limbs. This is how they get what they want: their food and all the rest. They would not succeed if they acted in any other way. There is no need to say that when working for their own or others' sake, wise Bodhisattvas must act in the same way: quietly and with disciplined care.

[verse 74] When we receive an admonition, for instance when someone who is skilled in beneficial counseling in spiritual and worldly affairs says to us such things as, "Stop behaving so badly. You really ought to take an interest in the teachings and study them," we should not react with pride and arrogant disdain. Instead, we should at once accept the advice with humble respect, regardless of whether it can be implemented or not. We should follow any unsolicited advice that is in tune with the Dharma and leave aside whatever is not.

[verse 75] When people say things that are useful both in the immediate and long-term, we should heed them as though we were the speaker's disciples, and we should do what they say. We should praise everyone who says something that is true and is of spiritual value; and instead of answering back in an untoward manner, we should be nice to them, telling them that they have spoken well. Similarly, when we see people doing something virtuous, such as making offerings or giving alms, we should not be jealous and try to put them down. We should praise them openly instead, telling them that their actions are excellent and worthy; and we should encourage them in words of warm approval.

[verse 76] In order to avoid flattering people, Shantideva says that we should extol their qualities discreetly by mentioning them to others. And when people mention the qualities of those whom we do not like, we should not speak to the contrary, but should concur and give support to their words of approval. On the other hand, when we find that people are praising our own qualities, we should not be proud but should instead appreciate their pure perception, which enables them to discover such qualities in us.

[verse 77] Generally speaking, the aim of every undertaking, whether of ourselves or of others, is to achieve happiness. Yet [genuine] happiness is very rare; it is not something that can be bought even with great wealth. This being so, we should take heartfelt and unjealous pleasure in the good qualities of others, whether on the worldly plane or on the spiritual level of study, reflection, and meditation on the teachings. [verse 78] If we do, we will lose nothing in this life (our own happiness and joy will not at all be lessened), and the result of such a perfect attitude, unstained by envy, will be that in our lives to come, we will have the great happiness of the higher realms. By contrast, if on seeing the good qualities, wealth, and enjoyments of others, we have feelings of irritation and jealous rivalry, these will exhaust all the positive qualities of our present life and the weapon of such an evil state of mind will turn against us. We ourselves will suffer and be unhappy, and once this life is over, the great misery of the lower realms will be the wages of such an attitude.

[verse 79] When we speak, for example in answer to the questions of others, we should be vigilantly aware of our own inner motives, and we should reply agreeably, accommodating ourselves to the people addressed whether their inclinations are positive or negative. We should inspire confidence by making sure that our words are consistent with what we have said on previous and subsequent occasions. We should express ourselves clearly, so that our meaning is not in doubt, and we should speak pleasantly, so that our interlocutor is happy—avoiding all passionate expressions of attachment to our own position and repugnance toward that of others. We should speak softly, gently, and with moderation.

[verse 80] When we catch sight of others (regardless of whether they are great or unimportant, powerful or weak), we should recognize that it is through them that we are, in the first place, able to engender bodhichitta; it is through them that we are then able to practice the Bodhisattva activities related to the two accumulations as expressed in the six paramitas; and it is through them too that we will ultimately attain buddhahood. We should therefore acknowledge them as friends and helpers on the way of the Bodhisattva, and we should never look at them with angry eyes. We should gaze on them as a mother might look at her baby, with open, honest, and loving hearts.

[verse 81] In the case of virtuous action, great merit will be gained if the action has four distinctive features. From the point of view of time, the action should be constant and uninterrupted. From the point of view of motive, it should be informed by a resolute attitude—of faith, compassion, and so on. From the point of view of antidotes, it should act as a remedy [to its contrary, that is, negative action]. In the practice of generosity, for example, if we give away the thing that is most precious and dear to us, this will certainly counteract our avarice. In the case of discipline, the relinquishing of whatever we are most attached to is sure to counteract whatever is contrary to discipline, and likewise for the rest of the six paramitas. From the point of view of the field or object of action, if the action—giving, for instance—is performed in relation to the "field of excellence" (the Three Jewels), the "field of benefit" (our parents), or the "field of suffering" (travelers from afar, the sick, and so forth), it will be far more meritorious than if it were done in relation to other beings. The same principle applies (mutatis mutandis) in the case of nonvirtue.

Whatever positive deeds are performed, it is not sufficient just to imitate mechanically the conduct of others. Especially in the case of the Bodhisattva practices of generosity and the rest, if we are unaware that there are different kinds of generosity (both pure and impure); if we do not know the proper motivation, the way in which generosity is to be practiced, as well as the need to dedicate the merit, our practice of giving remains quite ordinary, no different, for instance, from the way that animals give things. Therefore we must know how to practice generosity; our actions must go to the vital point.

[verse 82] Whatever Dharma practice is performed, it is first important to have a perfect understanding of its purpose and to have faith or confidence in it. It is thus that, at all times, good deeds like the six paramitas of the Bodhisattvas are to be performed. It is just as in the account of how Atisha used to make tsa-tsas himself—in all actions of offering and giving, and so on, we should not depend on others: people exhorting us or people who would do them on our behalf. If we ourselves are able to do them, we should. But if we are not able, it is not at all appropriate to rely on others (to do them for us).

[verse 83] The paramitas of generosity, discipline, and so on, are arranged in a sequence of gradual elevation so that the higher ones are considered to have priority over the lower ones—to such an extent that the contrast between each of them is like the difference between the water contained in the ocean compared with the water contained in a cow's hoofprint. Greater benefit results from observing discipline for a single day than from practicing generosity for a hundred years. It is said in the *Sutralankara* that the paramita that follows depends on the one preceding it, for they are set forth in sequence, being successively more elevated, successively more subtle [that is, more difficult to practice]. As a general principle, the greater paramita should not be sacrificed for the sake of the lesser one. In particular cases, however, the Bodhisattva should consider as more important whatever is of greater benefit to beings. This should be the motive behind a Bodhisattva's thoughts and deeds. As it is said:

> The general and specific
> Are, in every treatise, of the highest moment.

2. The discipline of working for the benefit of others

3. Earnestly working for the welfare of beings

[verse 84] Understanding and undertaking the disciplines of avoiding negative action and of accumulating virtuous action, one should abide with constancy and diligence in the discipline of bringing benefit to others. One must strive to achieve the welfare of others in a manner that is completely free from self-interest. To great Bodhisattvas, who labor in such a way and are completely free from selfish motives, the Buddha, greatly compassionate, allowed the seven negative actions of body and speech (which are forbidden at all times to practitioners of the lower vehicle and to novice Bodhisattvas). He did this because he saw that the sacrificing of trivial and ephemeral joys, and the provoking of lesser suffering can lead to lasting happiness and to the removal of greater suffering. This may be illustrated by the story of Captain Goodheart who killed Black Spearman in order to protect him from falling into hell, or by the story of the young brahmin Tararamana who wedded a merchant's daughter in order to protect her from the horrors of death. It is said that, by their actions, both these Bodhisattvas gained a degree of merit that otherwise would have taken many kalpas to accumulate.[142]

3. Drawing beings to the Dharma by the gift of material things and of the teachings

[verse 85] When one is living in the solitude of the mountains, for instance, whatever alms one has should be shared with [three categories of beings]: those who have fallen into the lower realms, such as animals like birds and dogs; those who have no protection, like beggars; and those who are engaged in the outer and inner yogic disciplines, namely, solitary meditators. In addition, one should offer the first part of one's own share to the Three Jewels, and ignoring one's likes and dislikes, one should take just enough to sustain one's body, dedicating the leftovers and donating them to the spirits. For if one eats too much, one will be heavy and dull; if one eats too little, one will be weak and unequal to the practice of virtue. Apart from the three Dharma robes that monks must wear (the tunic, the upper robe, and the patched shawl), one should give everything away to beggars. The three Dharma robes, however, should not be given. Indeed, as it is stipulated in the *Bodhisattva-pratimoksha:* "Do not give away the Dharma robes. For if you have less than the required three, on what basis can you practice pure conduct?"

[verse 86] At the present moment, when one is a novice Bodhisattva, one should not damage one's body (cutting off one's hand for example) for some altruistic but trivial reason. For it is with the body that one is able to practice the sublime Dharma properly. One should instead take care of one's body so that it is able to work for the good of others—eating just enough to fill one's stomach and dressing sufficiently to keep out the cold, without falling into either extreme of excess. One should fulfill the activities of a Bodhisattva and, with prayers of aspiration, dedicate the merit to the gaining of omniscience for the sake of all beings. If one acts in this way, one's wishes for immediate and ultimate happiness of all beings will be swiftly fulfilled one after the other.

[verse 87] The compassionate attitude of a beginner is not pure. Therefore until one reaches Perfect Joy, the first of the Bodhisattva grounds, one should refrain from actually giving away one's body (one's head or one's limbs), which is the basis for the practice of the sublime Dharma. For it is not certain that such actions will be of benefit to others. It is also possible that one will have regrets, which will in turn create obstacles to the practice of virtue. As it is said in the *Shikshasamucchaya:* "It is taught that the body should be protected as though it were an important medicinal tree." But such sacrifices can be made when they are beneficial for the teaching and for beings in this and future lives, and when they are not an obstacle to virtue, as when the lama-king Changchub Ö surrendered his body.[143]

[verse 88] Teachings should not be given to people who show no respect, with their mental attitude or behavior, toward the teachings or the teacher. If the teachings are bestowed in such circumstances, the greatness of the Dharma will be diminished and the listeners will not be benefited. What is more, the lack of respect shown by such people toward the teachings will cause them to fall into the lower realms. Neither should the teachings be given to those who, even though they do have a respectful attitude, nevertheless keep their heads covered though they are not sick; keep their hats upon their heads; carry parasols or walking sticks, or swords, spears, and other weapons. One should not explain the teachings to those who cover their heads with their monastic shawls or who are seated on lofty seats. Of course, allowances are to be made in the case of the sick.

[verse 89] It is inappropriate to expound the profound teaching on emptiness and the vast teaching on the grounds and paths of the Mahayana to those who have the lesser attitude (of the Hinayana) and who aspire to the path of the Shravakas and Pratyekabuddhas. Furthermore, an ordained monk should not instruct a woman alone and unaccompanied by a man. And when one expounds the Dharma, one should not [in a partial, sectarian manner] be interested only in the doctrine of the Mahayana to the detriment of the teaching of the lesser doctrine of the Shravakas and Pratyekabuddhas, and vice versa. For such teachings are like different kinds of food, suitable either for adults or for children. They are not to be judged in terms of good or bad. On the path of liberation they are the same, like the taste of molasses and salt [one cannot say that one is right and the other wrong]. With this understanding, one should respectfully expound them. In the *Sarvadharma-vaidalyasamgraha-sutra* the Buddha said: "O Manjushri, if some people consider some of the Tathagata's teachings as good and others as bad, they have rejected the holy teachings."

[verse 90] People who are of the Mahayana type, who are endowed with sharp faculties and are suitable vessels for the vast and profound teachings, should not be directed toward the lesser teachings of the path of the Shravakas and Pratyekabuddhas. To do so is to commit a downfall, for it is not right that those with wisdom should be fettered and those who have faith should be confused. Aside from exceptional situations in which the profound view should be explained, it is essential to set forth the law of karma in relation to virtuous and nonvirtuous actions. In other words, the principles of moral conduct based thereon should not be neglected. One must not mislead those who are able to practice the way of the Bodhisattvas by telling them (according to a literal interpretation of the scriptures) that in order to gain liberation it is enough simply to read a few good sutras and to recite a few dharanis and mantras. One must distinguish between the teachings of ultimate meaning, the teachings of expedient meaning, and the teachings of indirect and implied meaning, and so on.[144] One must take care to teach disciples according to their capacity.

3. AVOIDANCE OF GIVING SCANDAL TO OTHERS

[verse 91] If Bodhisattvas do not avoid doing things that give scandal to others,[145] they will be an occasion for the latters' nonvirtue. Therefore when they dispose of toothpicks, spittle, nasal discharge and phlegm in the presence of lama, in a temple, or in some other dwelling place, they should do so unobtrusively. Neither should they soil commonly used sources of clean water or good fields with urine and excrement. This is wrong and is forbidden.

[verse 92] When they eat, Bodhisattvas should not gobble noisily, cramming their gaping mouths. Wherever they are, they should never sit with legs outstretched, and when they wash their hands, they should not rub their hands together but wash each hand individually.

[verse 93] Lay Bodhisattvas should not sit on the same horse, bed, or seat, nor in an empty house, alone with a woman of another household; and ordained monks should never be alone with women who are not of their family. In short, any behavior that the Bodhisattva understands to be offensive in a given social setting—whether on the basis of personal experience or as a result of advice solicited from knowledgeable sources—should be abandoned.

[verse 94] When someone asks them directions, Bodhisattvas should not indicate the way rudely with their left hand or just by pointing with one finger. Their way of speaking and their gestures should be respectful, and they should indicate the way with all the fingers of their right hands. They should do so cheerfully and in a manner that encourages their interlocutors with faith.

[verse 95] Bodhisattvas should avoid making expansive and affected gestures when picking up or putting down comparatively minor objects. Instead, they should move gently, making themselves understood verbally or by snapping their fingers. If they behave otherwise and in an unrestrained manner, people will no longer respect them on account of such faults.

[verse 96] When Bodhisattvas lie down to sleep in the middle period of the night, they should remember to do so in the posture assumed by the Lord Buddha, the protector of all beings, when he displayed his passing into nirvana—that is, in the position of a sleeping lion, lying on his right side, his head pointing to the north and his face to the west. It is thus that they will be mindful of the Buddha. Therefore, they should lie facing whichever direction they like and is without danger, the north, east, and so forth. They should lie with their right side to the ground, their legs laid one on top of the other, their right hands beneath their cheeks, and their left arms stretched out along their thighs. This is how they should sleep, with their bodies covered with the Dharma robe. Just before they fall asleep, they should focus carefully with mindfulness and inner watchfulness on luminosity, remembrance of death, and the thought that they will rise quickly the following morning. If they do this, even their sleep will be virtuous.

We should make a practice of harmonizing the periods of our life with the periods of a single day. We should consider that daybreak corresponds to our birth, midday to adulthood, and evening to old age. When we lie down, this corresponds to the afflictions of illness that lead to death, and sleep is death itself. Dreams correspond to the intermediary state or bardo, whereas waking up the next day corresponds to rebirth in the next existence. And we are advised never to forget the practices related to precious bodhichitta.

1. OTHER ELEMENTS OF A PERFECT PRACTICE

2. THE PERFECT PRACTICE ITSELF

[verse 97] As it has been said in the *Bodhisattva-pitaka*, the deeds of Bodhisattvas (such as the six paramitas and the four ways of gathering disciples) can be divided into innumerable categories. Of these, moreover, novice Bodhisattvas must meditate on and implement the practices aimed at cleansing and training the mind (such as those set forth in the *Bodhicharyavatara*), until such time as their minds are definitively purified.

[verse 98] If they commit a root downfall, they should confess it in accordance with their capacity, whether high, medium, or basic.[146] And they should once again take the Bodhisattva vow. If they have committed other faults, they should recite the confession of Bodhisattva downfalls called the *Triskandha-sutra*, which includes the three sections of confession, rejoicing, and dedication. They should do this three times by day and three times by night. Taking thus the support of the thirty-five confession Buddhas, the Bodhisattvas, and bodhichitta itself, they should purify all remaining faults, in addition to their root downfalls, with the strength of this remedial practice.

[verse 99] Therefore in whatever they do, whether for their own good or for the good of others, and in whatever circumstances, Bodhisattvas must diligently and confidently put into practice the Buddha's teachings, which were bestowed so that Bodhisattvas might train themselves in whatever situation they happen to be. Shantideva condenses all such teachings in his text. For example, when one walks, one applies the teaching contained in verse 37 (of the present chapter); when one sits, one applies verse 93; when one finds oneself in the solitude of the mountains, verse 85 is relevant, as also is verse 92 when one is eating; verse 79 when one is speaking; verse 80 when one is looking at others; or verse 96 when one composes oneself for sleep. Further instructions are found in the chapter on perfectly pure action [in the *Avatamsaka*].

[verse 100] There is no field of knowledge or science with which the offspring of the Conquerors should not familiarize themselves, be these the five great sciences (crafts, medicine, grammar, logic, and the inner science of Dharma) or the five lesser sciences. For those who train in all fields of knowledge, who abide in mindfulness and vigilance, and who are skilled in the ways of the Bodhisattvas, there is no action (even the lifting and placing of their feet or the stretching and contraction of their arms) that is without merit. Even "nonvirtues" take on a virtuous complexion, to say nothing of actions that are morally neutral.

[verse 101] All one does, whether directly or indirectly, must be for the sake of others: directly, through the gifts of Dharma or material things, or indirectly, as when one practices a sadhana in retreat, dedicating such activities for the benefit of others and making aspirations for their sake. One should not do anything simply for oneself. And it is solely for others' sake that one should dedicate all positive actions (the six paramitas and so on) performed by oneself and anyone else in the past, present, and future to the gaining of enlightenment. It is thus that merits should be dedicated and prayers of aspiration made.

[verse 102] At all times, from first generating bodhichitta to the attainment of great enlightenment, one should take the support of a spiritual guide respectfully with one's body, speech, and mind. For it is by frequenting such a sublime master that one will come to possess every kind of excellent quality. A vehicle (*yana* in Sanskrit) may be considered from the point of view of those who are transported in it, the destination to which it brings them, and the actual means of conveyance.[147] Of the three aspects, the great vehicle or Mahayana refers to the third one and is described by the *Sutralankara* in the following terms:

> Its scope is great indeed,
> And likewise is its twofold practice,
> Its wisdom, and its diligence.
> Superior also is its skill in means,
> As also is its great attainment,
> And the great enlightened deeds of buddhahood.
> Great therefore in seven ways,
> The Mahayana is indeed termed great.

Spiritual masters, who are learned in, and set forth, the profound and vast aspects of the Mahayana, endowed as it is with such sevenfold greatness, and whose practice of the Bodhisattva discipline excels through their observance of all the vows—spiritual masters such as these should not be forsaken even at the cost of one's life. Even if one's very life were at stake, one must never grieve them or go against their word. One must never stop relying on one's teacher.

[verse 103] As for the way in which such a master is to be followed, a description can be found in the *Gandavyuha* chapter of the *Avatamsaka* scriptures, where an account is given of how the Bodhisattva Sudhana followed a great number of teachers (one hundred and ten in fact). And in the passage about the life of Shrisambhava one finds a description and appreciation of how Sudhana met the young Shrisambhava and the young woman Shrimati and served them with respect, thus showing how a spiritual master should be served. "O noble son," it says, "look upon yourself as an invalid and upon the spiritual teacher as a physician, upon the teaching as a medicine and upon the earnest practice as a cure." The way in which a teacher should be served is described in this text with great detail. It should be taken to heart and one must follow one's teacher accordingly. One should read this chapter together with other sutras taught by the Buddha. And one must study (and understand) all the Bodhisattva trainings in respect of what is to be adopted and rejected in the service of a spiritual teacher.

[verse 104] Indeed, since it is by the study of the sutras that a knowledge of the Bodhisattva precepts is gained, these scriptures are to be read. In particular, given that the *Akashagarbha-sutra* teaches clearly the eighteen root downfalls of a Bodhisattva and the manner in which such faults can be repaired, it is said that this sutra should be studied first. [verse 105] Shantideva's own *Shikshasamucchaya* sets forth clearly and in detail the conduct that Bodhisattvas should embrace at all times—such as how to give, protect, purify, and increase one's body, possessions, and virtue. One should therefore read this text, not once, but again and again.[148] [verse 106] Alternatively one might also read the *Sutrasamucchaya*, which is a condensed description of the activities of the Bodhisattvas extracted by Shantideva from the sutras. And the two identically named works composed by Nagarjuna should also be diligently studied.[149]

[verse 107] All activities allowed and not forbidden in the sutras taught by the Buddha and in the two treatises *Shikshasamucchaya* and *Sutrasamucchaya* should be properly embraced and undertaken by Bodhisattvas. In short, in order to protect the minds of worldly beings from a loss of confidence in the Bodhisattvas, and in order to be a source of joy for them, one should learn the precepts of the Bodhisattvas and strive to implement them perfectly, for the sole purpose of benefiting beings.

2. A SUMMARY OF THE CHAPTER

[verse 108] The practice of vigilant introspection can be briefly defined as the examination (performed repeatedly and not only once) made to discover whether one's actions in thought, word, and deed are positive, negative, or neutral, combined with the alert and enthusiastic implementation of the principle of adopting and rejecting. [verse 109] All these trainings in body, speech, and mind should be earnestly put into practice as we have explained. For what is to be gained by simply parroting the words of the text? We must strive to implement their meaning. Indeed, what invalid was ever helped merely by reading or listening to an explanation of the four medical tantras, without submitting to the remedy? Help comes only from taking the medicine and following the proper cure.

Here ends the fifth chapter of the *Bodhicharyavatara*, the instruction on the practice of vigilant introspection.

⋅ 6 ⋅

PATIENCE

Eliminating Anger,
the Antithesis of Bodhichitta

1. THE REMOVAL OF ANGER

[verse 1] A kalpa is a lapse of time embracing the four periods in the life of a universal system: formation, duration, destruction, and the period of voidness.[150] Each of these four stages lasts twenty intermediate kalpas, and all eighty of these taken together are referred to as one great kalpa. The sutras declare that the merit of all good works accumulated in the course of a thousand such great kalpas—the practice of generosity toward beings, the taking of refuge in the Three Jewels (the Buddha or Sugata who "proceeds in bliss," the sacred Dharma, and the Sangha) and the making of offerings to them, the keeping of discipline, and so forth—all is shattered by a single instant of fierce anger. Now in the *Manjushrivikridita-sutra,* we find the text, "Manjushri, what we refer to as anger destroys virtue gathered in a hundred kalpas." In other words, we are told that anger destroys the virtue sometimes of a hundred and sometimes of a thousand kalpas.

The commentaries on the *Bodhicharyavatara* explain that when ordinary beings succumb to anger, they destroy merit accumulated in a hundred kalpas, but that when Bodhisattvas succumb to anger, they destroy the merit of a thousand kalpas. In addition, the *Prajnaparamitasanchaya-sutra* states that Bodhisattvas who have yet to receive the prophecy[151] destroy as many kalpas of merit as the moments of anger they feel toward a Bodhisattva who has obtained the prophecy. This interpretation is also found in the great and medium length compilations of the *Prajnaparamita-sutra*. Some commentaries, on the other hand, express doubts concerning this matter and object that if a single instant of anger destroys the merit of practicing generosity for a thousand kalpas, it follows that, since ordinary beings are never without anger, no one can ever attain liberation. This being so, the kind of instant referred to must be the so-called "instant as time required for completion of an action."[152]

Regarding this matter, some authorities reflect as follows. There are three kinds of virtue. There is virtue tending to happiness in samsara, which is marked by neither skillful means nor wisdom. There is virtue tending to liberation, which is informed by the wisdom of understanding the nonexistence of the self. Finally there is the virtue of the Mahayana, which is performed with both wisdom and skillful means. In the present case, it is the first kind of virtue (tending to samsaric happiness) that is destroyed. And the agent of destruction is violent aggression that, directed toward an exceptional object, is not offset by feelings of remorse or some other counteractive remedy. Regarding the manner of destruction, the seed of virtue is not completely destroyed, but its power to emerge into experience is temporarily overwhelmed and deferred until another lifetime. The reason for this is that [in the unfolding of the karmic process] the results of the heaviest actions make their appearance first. As it is said in the *Abhidharmakosha*:

> Within the sphere of actions, those that are most grave
> Are first to ripen, followed by the deeds performed when
>   death is near,
> Then by those arising through the force of habit.
> The remaining actions ripen in the order they were done.

This is the view of the authorities just mentioned.

Nevertheless, Gyalse Rinpoche[153] refutes this interpretation, for, in view of the fact that a delay in the moment of experiencing the karmic result may also affect the virtue tending to liberation, there is uncertainty about the kind of virtue that is susceptible to destruction by anger and about the way in which this destruction is brought about. In the *Arya-sarvastivada*, we find the text: "O Upali, since anger diminishes, removes, and completely annihilates even great roots of virtue, do not allow yourself to get angry even at a stump of charred wood, let alone a body endowed with consciousness."

Although Gyalse Rinpoche says that it is uncertain what kind of virtue is destroyed, he gives no reason at all for supposing that anger can destroy virtue tending to liberation. He says that the manner of destruction is uncertain, and he is not specific about the agent by which such destruction is effected. On the other hand, since it is said that one should refrain from anger even against a wooden stump, it follows that it is not certain that the anger in question must be felt toward an exceptional object. His refutation of the opinion of the earlier authorities therefore leaves the issue unresolved. On the other hand, I have not found any other answer to this question.

From the actual wording of the root text, it would seem that all good works—making offerings to the Three Jewels and so on—are affected. But when one reflects upon the meaning, it appears that whereas anger destroys the virtue of word and deed (as present for example in the practice of generosity), it is unable to destroy the virtue of the mind. [This implies that] the merit arising from the practice of generosity, whether in the form of offerings or of charitable donations, and all the merits arising from discipline (perfect observance in thought, word, and deed) are destroyed by a single flash of real anger toward a Bodhisattva and others. On the other hand, anger cannot destroy the merit that accrues from the practice of patience, diligence, concentration, and wisdom because the paramitas are distinguished hierarchically.[154] Moreover, patience is the direct antithesis of anger, and it has been said too that if the merit gathered through the practice of generosity and discipline is accomplished within the framework of the three supreme methods,[155] it too is protected from destruction by adverse conditions.

[verse 2] But since anger does destroy virtue and causes birth in the hell realms, no other negative action is to be compared with it. Conversely, no other virtue or "austerity" is to be compared with patience, which is the reverse of anger. As the sutra says:

> Patience is sublime ascesis, patience is supreme;
> It is supreme transcendence of all sorrow, so the Buddha said.

Therefore it is to be earnestly cultivated. We must strive to give birth to patience within ourselves by every means, as will be explained in due course.

[verse 3] Those who are tormented by the pain of anger (whose minds are irritated by their enemies and other people) will never know the bliss of concentration, a state of perfect mental happiness. It will be impossible for them to achieve concentration of mind and they will know neither mental joy nor physical well-being, even at night—for sleep will desert them. They will feel completely insecure and will lose all stability in body and mind. [verse 4] Kings and chieftains who are full of hate may well provide their servants and ministers, the minions who depend on them, with gracious gifts of wealth (gold and silver, and robes of silk and satin) and positions that bring them the deference of others. But even these ministers, let alone other people, will forget the favors done to them and will turn against their lords, attacking and even murdering them. [verse 5] A man of anger brings grief to his family and friends through his harsh language and violent behavior. They will dislike and turn away from him. And even if he surrounds himself with a circle of helpers by unstintingly lavishing money and property on them, they will not stay with him and will not serve him. In short, an angry person is like a vicious snake, completely destitute of happiness and well-being. It is thus important to rid oneself of anger.

[verse 6] All who hate will have their every virtue ruined by the enemy that is their own anger. They will be brought down to hell because of it, as has been explained above. Their anger will bring them sorrow in this and future lives. By contrast, those who take control of their minds and school themselves in patience will achieve the opposite. They will destroy the enemy that is their anger and attain great happiness both now and in their lives to come.

[verse 7] Everything that produces uncomfortable and unwanted situations (such as the loss of possessions) both for ourselves and our sphere of interest, and all that is a hindrance to getting what we want in terms of property and well-being—all these produce a state of mental annoyance, and this is fuel for anger and hatred. For just as it is food that makes the body grow, it is unhappiness of mind that gives rise to anger and resentment. And anger it is that lays in ruins every kind of mental goodness. Thus it is essential to overcome such states of unhappiness, for they are the food on which our anger feeds.

[verse 8] And just as it is possible to sap the strength of enemies by intercepting their food supply, in the same way we should completely destroy our unhappiness of mind, which is the food of anger, our enemy. For this enemy has absolutely no other aim than to injure us in all sorts of ways,

now and in our future existences, through the destruction of our roots of virtue. [verse 9] And so, come what may, whatever harm or adversity may befall us in the way of unwanted situations, or hindrances to desired situations, we must resolve again and again never to allow them to disturb our mind's cheerful disposition, which is itself the remedy for depression. It might be thought that if we simply put up with adversity, the result will be that everyone, good and bad, will look down on us. But the fact is that if our minds are disturbed, and if we allow ourselves to be depressed by the injuries we receive, not only will we fail to accomplish our aims, but the virtue of our minds will be weakened and destroyed.

[verse 10] To be sure, if there is a remedy—if something can be done to change the situation when injuries are done to us—what reason is there for depression and resentment? And similarly, if there is nothing that can be done to mend the situation, the broken cup for instance, what good does it do to be unhappy about it? Indeed, not only will this be of no help, but it will aggravate the situation further on account of the suffering produced by the conflict arising in ourselves and others.

1. Cultivating patience

2. Identifying the object of patience

[verse 11] It is said that there are twenty-four objects to which patience is to be applied: twelve things that we do not want and twelve things that hinder our desires. There are four things that we do not want either for ourselves or for those who are close to us (our parents, our teacher, our tradition, and so on). These are (1) suffering, (2) the disadvantages that come from such things as contemptuous discrimination, (3) direct verbal aggression such as being called a thief, and (4) the destruction of good reputation through the spreading of malicious rumors. Applied both to ourselves and to our loved ones, this comes all together to eight unwanted things. In addition, there are four things (the opposite of the four mentioned previously) that we do not wish our enemies to have. We don't like them to be happy or to be praised or to have any kind of material success or good reputation. Consequently, there are all together twelve things that we do not want.

The twelve things that prevent us from getting what we want consist of obstacles to our happiness and so forth (the reverse of the things previously named), occurring four by four in the experience of ourselves and those who are on our side (therefore eight), together with obstacles to suffering and so forth in the experience of those whom we dislike. Thus there are twelve of them and these, taken with the previous twelve, make twenty-four objects in relation to which patience is to be exercised. When considered from the point of view of past, present, and future situations, these twenty-four items constitute all together seventy-two causes of anger. It is said that we should cultivate patience in their regard; we should be able to accept what we do not want, and even consider the fact of wanting as itself a defect.

2. CULTIVATING PATIENCE

3. CULTIVATING PATIENCE WITH REGARD TO WHAT WE DO NOT WANT

4. CULTIVATING PATIENCE WITH REGARD TO WHAT BRINGS US SUFFERING

5. THE PATIENCE OF ACCEPTING SUFFERING

The cultivation of patience with regard to what brings us suffering will be explained in detail. This same explanation is to be adapted to the other objects of patience, upon which it is important to meditate. These points are indicated in a summary fashion in the textual outline [of the commentary itself].

[verse 12] In this world of samsara, the causes of happiness (wealth, honor, and so on) are few and appear only sporadically. On the other hand, there are many causes for our various unwanted sorrows and we are powerless to stop them from happening. This is the very definition of samsara; and as long as we wander therein, the causes of suffering—however much we may kick against it—are endless and we have no choice but to submit to it. For those who understand this, however, there is a positive aspect to pain. For without suffering, we will never have renunciation, the determination to free ourselves from the sorrows of samsara. By contrast, if we do have suffering, a longing for definitive freedom will arise in us. Therefore, addressing his own mind, Shantideva tells himself to stand firm and accept his sufferings patiently. For they are a spur urging him to get out of samsara—an exhortation to virtue and a broom to sweep his sins away. Suffering does have its positive side.

[verse 13] The devotees of Gauri, the goddess Uma, practice austerities by impaling themselves on the tridents that are her emblems or burning themselves in the fire of the homa offering. Likewise, certain of the non-Buddhist practitioners of Karna, in order to attain the realm of Brahma, have their heads cut off at the eclipses of the sun and moon. Also, fired by mutual envy, they quarrel and burn each others' houses down, and use their weapons to cut each others' limbs. If they are prepared to undergo such great pain, which is so hard to bear and so futile as a means to achieving what they want, why, Shantideva asks himself, is he so chicken-livered when it comes to working for the supreme Good: the state of liberation beyond all suffering?

[verse 14] There is nothing that familiarity and force of habit do not make easy to accomplish. It is thus that even adversity can be tolerated. Therefore Shantideva tells himself that it will be by accepting minor discomforts now that he will be able to bear great hardships in the future. [verse 15] After all, he asks, does he not already have to put up with the pointless irritations of life: the bites and stings of snakes and flies, the sensations of hunger and thirst, painful infections on his skin and other disorders? How can he not see that he has no choice but to endure such meaningless discomforts? Looked at from this point of view, it is easy to see that it is perfectly reasonable to endure hardships in the interests of the great goal.

[verse 16] The heat of summer and the winter's cold, the wind and the rain, various illnesses and such hardships as beatings and imprisonment—Shantideva declares that he will not allow himself to be so thin-skinned on their account. For, to the extent that he frets about them, his troubles will be aggravated, and his discomforts will only increase until they become unbearable. [verse 17] Moreover, it is from habit that one acquires the strength to bear with all adversity. For example, there are some whose courage increases when in the thick of battle they are wounded and they see their own blood flow. Others, by contrast, faint even when they see other people bleeding, let alone themselves. [verse 18] All this is the result of how the mind is set, oriented whether to stouthearted valor or to the timidity that is its opposite. Yet everything is made easy through habit. Therefore Shantideva tells himself that when striving for the great goal, he will make light of every injury great or small, never allowing himself to be overwhelmed or to wallow in resentment.

[verse 19] When sharp sufferings and injuries inflicted by others occur, wise Bodhisattvas should keep their minds serene, joyful, and untroubled by sorrow. The understanding of the Dharma should act as a remedy for the afflictions. Every effort should be made to combat anger and the other defilements through the use of antidotes—in this case, patience. It is just like fighting a war. When defilement and antidotes clash on the battlefield, that is, when the Dharma strikes at the vital point and evil karma from the past rises up to retaliate, it is only to be expected that there will be a great deal of discomfort and plenty of wounds.

[verse 20] Those who scorn every discomfort for the sake of accomplishing the supreme goal, those who vanquish their enemies, namely, their anger and other defilements—they are the ones who are the best and strongest, the truly victorious heroes. But those who vanquish only external enemies, massacring men and horses and so forth, do no more than wound and kill what is lifeless already. Heroism in such situations is no more than an empty boast.

[verse 21] In any case, suffering has its good and useful side. For when we suffer, we will have feelings of renunciation and world-weariness, and arrogance will be driven from our minds. Thanks to our own suffering, we may experience unbounded compassion, wishing to free others who are also suffering in samsara. Similarly, we will reject and shun the negativity by which suffering is caused, and we will be enthusiastic in the pursuit of goodness, the cause of happiness, thus becoming meticulous with regard to the karmic principle of cause and effect.

5. PATIENCE THAT CONSISTS IN CERTAINTY WITH REGARD TO THE ULTIMATE REALITY OF THINGS

[verse 22] We may think that, whereas we do indeed put up with our sufferings, we are nevertheless indignant at the people who make us suffer. But if we are not angry at our humors, the wind, bile, and phlegm and other important sources of disease and pain, why should we be angry at the animate beings who cause us injury? Illness arises from four causes: conditions related to time, evil influences, food, and personal behavior. Since a disease is not an independent force, what use is there in being angry with it?

But why, it will be argued, should we not resent those who throw stones at us, for they do it on purpose? The answer is that our attackers are not independent agents either. The enemies who do us harm are themselves driven by anger and the other afflictions—just as the occurrence of illness is dictated by time of life, evil influences, the things we have eaten, and the way we behave. In neither case is there an independent agent. Both are acting under the influence of something else that is controlling them. And because they are dependently arising, they are empty [of real existence]. We should understand that there is neither a real injury nor a real injurer to be resented. This is how we should deflect our anger.

[verse 23] For it is just as with different diseases, which arise through the power of causes and conditions, the humors of wind, bile, phlegm, and so on. They do not do so intentionally, for they are not autonomous agents. The same applies to the enemies that torment us. They too are without autonomy. They do not fall victim to the experience of hatred and the other defilements willingly, but through the power of unhappy mental states. Diseases and enemies are on the same level in that neither is an independent agent.

[verse 24] It will be argued that they are not the same, for diseases have no intention to harm us, whereas enemies do. To this Shantideva replies that when people get angry, they do so simply on the basis of ordinary circumstances. They do not premeditate their rage, saying, "Now I will get angry with this person." And although these same circumstances never decide and plan to cause anger in a person, it is nevertheless on the basis of them that anger arises. It is just as when a reflection appears in a mirror: The mirror has no intention of producing the reflection on its surface. Nevertheless, a reflection appears through the coming together of different factors. And although a form does not intend to produce a reflection in the mirror, the reflection just appears owing to certain conditions. It is the same both in the case of a disease and of an enemy.

[verse 25] Anger and all the other afflictions, and the whole panoply of negative actions motivated by them—killing, stealing, and so on—are also brought about by circumstances. When the latter are absent, the faults (anger and so forth) are powerless to act intentionally on their own. It follows from this that we should not react to our enemies with hatred and anger but should generate compassion instead.

[verse 26] When no physical object is present, the experience of seeing (on the part of the eye consciousness) does not occur. The same is true mutatis mutandis with hearing and all the other senses. And when there is no seeing or hearing and the like, there is no engaging in positive or negative deeds. Therefore, although anger arises on the basis of the coincidence of an object, the sense power, and the sense consciousness, the gathering of these three conditions does not itself intend to produce anger in a given person's mind. And the resulting anger is not an entity that regards itself as produced by such conditions. In all of this, there is no trace of an independent, autonomous agent.

[verse 27] The Samkhyas, Naiyayikas, and other non-Buddhists may consider that not all contributory factors are without independent existence. For they believe that purusha, prakriti, and so on, are autonomous entities and that they are the origin of such phenomena as the aggressive attitude of an enemy. This however is not true. What they consider to be prakriti, with its five features, and what they conceive of and label as purusha (also endowed with five features) do not arise out of some preexistent state in order to do harm, or anything else, to others. They do not arise with such a premeditated intention for the simple reason that they are themselves unborn, as unborn as a barren woman's son. For if purusha and prakriti (which are held to be permanent and independent entities) can "come into being," they are in fact impermanent and dependent upon extraneous causes and conditions.

[verse 28] If, on the other hand, they are unborn (if they do not come into being), purusha and prakriti have no existence. This being so, there is nothing that could come into existence or that could wish to come into existence as an aggressor or something else. It may be argued that the conscious self or purusha, asserted by the Samkhyas, enjoys the objects presented to it by prakriti. But if purusha knows and apprehends an object such as sound, it must perceive or "stray toward" the object (here, sound) permanently and exclusively. Purusha can never stop perceiving this one thing, because [according to the Samkhyas] it is permanent as a perceiver.

[verse 29] As for the refutation of the belief of the Naiyayikas that the self is permanent and unconscious, Shantideva argues that such a self cannot function as a malevolent mind. Indeed, since this permanent self is, on account of its permanence, like space, it is certainly devoid of causal efficiency or action. [The Naiyayikas argue that] although the self is permanent, when it meets with impermanent circumstantial conditions, such as manas (mind),[156] which are extraneous to it, it becomes causally effective. But this is untenable. Even if it encounters other factors, like the mind, the permanent self is by nature immutable and does not change. Therefore, Shantideva asks, what causal efficiency could these conditions produce that was not previously there? Indeed, none at all.

[verse 30] Therefore even if the mind and other circumstantial conditions were to assist it, if the self cannot change from what it was previously, what property could these conditions or mind elicit from it that was not already present? None at all. Indeed, if they *did* succeed in doing so, this would disprove the self's permanence. Thus even though the Naiyayikas claim that such conditions are auxiliaries to the self, what connection can there possibly be between these two in terms of assistant and assisted? For whatever is permanent cannot be assisted by circumstantial conditions.

[verse 31] Consequently, all agents of harm are without autonomy. They arise through the power of circumstantial conditions. And these same conditions arise successively owing to the influence of still earlier conditions and are thus themselves without autonomy. For example, the enemy declares himself through the power of his hatred. His hatred arises owing to certain conditions, and these conditions arise through the power of still earlier karmic circumstances. And so on ad infinitum. There is an endless regression of foregoing causes. A wholly autonomous entity is thus impossible. Everything arises in dependence on something else and is therefore empty. When we understand this, we will also understand that every agent of harm, being devoid of real existence, is like a mirage, a dream image, or a magical apparition. The object of anger and the agent of anger are both unreal—interdependence means emptiness—and therefore we should not allow ourselves to become angry.

[verse 32] Given that all things are like magical apparitions, without true existence, it could be argued that it does not make sense to oppose anger with patience. After all, what anger is there to be opposed by what antidote or person—for there is no doer and nothing done? On the ultimate level, this is quite true. But if we confine ourselves to the conventional level, the relative truth, it is on the basis of the cultivation of patience that the continuum of infernal suffering and so forth (which is the consequence of hatred) is severed. There is nothing inappropriate in this; on the contrary, it is indeed highly reasonable.

[verse 33] Since all things are "other-powered," that is, dependently arising, when we come across someone, enemy or friend, doing something untoward or harmful, we should call to mind that this has arisen from conditions; it is not a freestanding, autonomously existing event. And following the explanation given above, we should remain calm and not respond with anger, as is described in the tale of the Shravaka Purna when he went begging for alms.

5. THE PATIENCE OF MAKING LIGHT OF WHAT CAUSES HARM

[verse 34] If beings had the freedom to be as they wanted without depending on conditions, it would follow that no one would suffer even slightly. For no one wants to suffer or to be unhappy even to the smallest extent. Everyone wants happiness.

[verse 35] But this is not how things turn out. It is through inadvertence that beings helplessly injure themselves, tearing themselves on thorns and briars. Others, ardent in pursuit of wives, riches, and possessions, starve themselves of food and drink and inflict great suffering and discomfort upon themselves. [verse 36] People even destroy themselves, some by hanging themselves, others by leaping off cliffs, others by eating bad food or swallowing deadly poison. Still others, by their evil conduct—killing, stealing, sexual misconduct, lying, and so on—bring ruin upon themselves in this and future lives.

[verse 37] As has been explained, if while they are helplessly under the power of hatred, attachment, and the other afflictions, beings destroy themselves—their own selves whom they cherish so much—how can those who are in the power of the defilements be expected not to harm the bodies of others? It is certain that they will. [verse 38] Those in whom hatred or the other negative emotions have arisen are no more free than if they had been possessed by demons. They have no mastery over themselves and are even capable of suicide. So Shantideva reflects that when they try to injure others (including himself), since he is a Bodhisattva, it is appropriate that he should have compassion for them. And even if he feels no compassion, what justification does he have for reacting angrily? What point is there in being angry?

[verse 39] In the case of ordinary people who behave like foolish children, the question is: Are they *by their very nature* prone to injure others, or not? If they are, what point is there in being angry with them? It does not make sense. It is like being annoyed with fire when we touch it and get burned. [verse 40] On the other hand, if these faults of theirs (all their aggressive attitudes) are adventitious—whereas their real nature is to be gentle—it follows that resentment against them is equally senseless. For that would be like someone who is annoyed when the sky is filled with smoke but then blames not the smoke but the sky!

[verse 41] When aggressive people intentionally take hold of sticks, stones, or swords and strike us on the body, we say that we are angry at those who strike us. However, these attackers are themselves driven by their anger. They have lost control. It would make more sense to be angry first with what actually hurts us, namely, the stick or the stone, and second with the anger itself.

[verse 42] In the end, all the blame comes back to ourselves. For in our past lives, we were the ones who injured others in the same way that they are injuring us now. It is only proper that as retribution we should now suffer the harms inflicted by others in return for the violence that we did to them in the past. [verse 43] Their weapons, the cause of injury, and our bodies, the objects injured, are the same in being equally the sources of our suffering. Our enemies drew their weapons to cause us pain, while we held out our bodies to receive it. Since this is how suffering arises, whom should we be angry with? Since the fault belongs both to ourselves and to someone else, it is out of place to resent only the latter.

[verse 44] Our bodies, which are easy to destroy and difficult to sustain, which are composed of substances like blood and lymph, are like running sores in human form. They are unable to bear the slightest sensation of cold or heat. They crave for food, for clothes, and for the company of a mate. Yet left to themselves, they are unable to satisfy these needs. It is the mind that must make contact with objects [for satisfaction to occur]. By itself, the body is as though blind. Therefore, since the body is something that we ourselves have assumed, whom should we resent when pain occurs? We should not be angry with others so much as with ourselves.

[verse 45] We who are like silly children shrink from suffering both now and in the future, and yet we love the things that cause it (acts of killing or stealing, and the other nonvirtues). Thus it is that we injure ourselves by our own wrongdoing. Our pain is self-inflicted. Why should others be the objects of our anger? [verse 46] In the same way that the terrifying janitors of hell and all the groves of razor-trees are the results of our own actions, all the pain in this and future existences is all of our own making; it is produced by our own deeds. Who else is there to be angry with? Indeed, no one.

[verse 47] Those who injure us, who now come against us (to rob and to despoil), do so summoned by our own evil and aggressive behavior in the past. Drawn to us by the actions of stealing and robbery that we ourselves have formerly inflicted upon them, it is now their turn to do us injuries—which, in due course, will throw them (thieves and robbers that they are) into the hells. So are we not the ones who bring ruin upon our enemies? Yes, we are indeed the tormentors of our foes!

[verse 48] But if we are able to practice patience toward the enemy who harms us, our many evil actions of the past will be cleansed and a great accumulation of merit will be brought to completion. It is thus that our enemies bring us benefit. But they, because of the harm they do to us (the cause and condition of their negative actions), will have to languish, so it is said, for kalpas in the Hell of Unrelenting Pain, all for the sake of an aggression that it has taken only an instant to accomplish. They will have to suffer the long-drawn agonies of hell.

[verse 49] Therefore it is *we* who are *their* tormentors while it is *they*, our enemies, who do good to *us*. For we are able thereby to repay what we owe, to purify our karmic debts and blood feuds, to complete our accumulations of merit, and to dispel our obscurations. Our understanding of what is to be done and what is not to be done is completely inverted. How pernicious our minds are! What reason do we have for being angry with our enemies?

[verse 50] In view of all this, we might think that if we thus bring ruin on the enemies that do us harm—a harm on account of which they will be cast down into hell—we will have to go to hell as well. But it is taught that if we possess the quality of patience in our minds, we will not do so—the implication being that if we are without patience, we will. [Conversely,] it could also be argued that our enemies will not go to hell either, since they bring us benefit. But it is the cultivation of patience that saves us from going to hell. On the other hand, what is there that can save our foes from such a destiny? There is nothing.

[verse 51] We may well reflect that, as Bodhisattvas, we are in the wrong if we fail to protect our aggressors. But while, at the moment, we are indeed unable to provide them with adequate protection, the fact is that if we actually harm them in retaliation [for what they do to us], it is certain that we will be giving them no protection at all, for the anger and the other negativities in their minds will greatly increase. And we in turn will ruin our four virtuous disciplines (never to repay abuse with abuse, never to be angry in return for anger, never to strike back when struck, and never to expose the faults of others when they reveal our own). And thus even patience, the best of Bodhisattva austerities, is utterly destroyed. In this connection, it is said that there are four possible situations in which

Bodhisattvas may find themselves. They can protect both themselves and others, they can protect themselves but not others, they can protect others but not themselves, or they can fail to protect either themselves or others.

4. Cultivating patience toward those who treat us with contempt

[verse 52] Perhaps we think that we get angry when contemptuous treatment results in injury to our minds or our bodies. But we should remember that our minds—that is, our thoughts—are bodiless; they have no physical form. Therefore no one can in any way destroy them with weapons and other things. On the other hand, the mind cherishes and clings powerfully to its bodily support with the result that we are attached to our bodies and claim them as our own. That is why we suffer when our bodies are attacked and beaten. If there were no clinging to the body, no injury would be felt.

[verse 53] It could be argued that when injury is sustained, it is both the mind and the body that suffer. But angry looks and other affronts—insults, as when someone accuses us of being a thief, a liar, or an old swindler, or other calumnious talk behind our backs—do not harm the body in the slightest way, still less the mind. So what reason, Shantideva asks, does the mind have for being so resentful? Such an attitude is quite illogical.

[verse 54] It might be thought that, while scorn and contempt do not harm our bodies and minds directly, nevertheless we are averse to such things because they show that we are disliked by others. But the dislike of others can do no actual harm to us—after all, it cannot devour us whether now or in the future. Why then is it so hard to accept that others should take no pleasure in us and show us no respect? We ought to [be able to] bear with it.

[verse 55] Perhaps we think that when we are despised, we are disliked and mistrusted by others and that this will be to our material disadvantage. Such scorn is an obstacle to our well-being, and that is why we cannot accept it and become resentful. But we are to consider that however much wealth we accumulate in this life—gold, silver, horses, stocks of tea, and so on, we will have to leave it all behind at the moment of death. None of it can be taken with us to the next life. We must go forth naked, our empty hands tucked under our armpits. On the other hand, it is then that all the negative deeds of hostility and aggression perpetrated in the past for the sake of material gain will keep us steady company. They will not be removed (by death) and we must suffer the consequences.

[verse 56] Perhaps it will be argued that if we are without possessions, we will have no food or clothing and will soon die. It is because we do not want this that we get angry when others treat us with contempt. But as Shantideva says, it is better for us to die now, this very day, than to live a long life sustained by wrong livelihood. For it is taught that, if there is a choice between a long but evil life or death this very day, death today is the better option. The sutras define wrong livelihood in terms of all kinds of clinging to the objects of the six senses. The *Ratnavali* stipulates that wrong livelihood is to be summarized under five headings. It is an attempt to secure a living by flattery, hypocrisy (i.e., pretending to be a good practitioner), self-interested generosity, putting forward one's status or position [as being a person worthy of support], and indirect theft (e.g., pretending that one has nothing).[157]

Perhaps we will think that since we want to live, it is better not to die today. But however long our or anybody else's life may be, however many years may lie before us, the pain of death will finally come and there is no escaping it. So it is better to die now than live a long life sustained by evil means. Indeed, if an extremely wicked person has a long life, his or her suffering will be far greater when the time of death arrives. Death today would be far preferable.

[verse 57] We can look at the following example: One man may have a dream, and in his dream he may think that he lives a hundred years filled with the pleasures of the five senses. But then he wakes up. Another man may think in his dream that he has experienced these pleasures for only an instant, and then he too wakes up. When they wake, the happiness that both have felt in enjoying such pleasures—whether it seemed short or long—will not return for either of them. [verse 58] Similarly, when the hour of our death comes round, whether we have lived a long and pleasure-filled life or whether we have lived only a short while without much joy, the happiness, whether short or long, is over—just like someone waking from a dream. The happiness that we have previously felt will never return and no further experience of it will be possible. There is only the pain of death—which is the same irrespective of whether life has been short or long.

[verse 59] We may be rich in worldly goods—stocks of tea, horses, gold and silver, silken clothes; we may delight for many a long year in the pleasures of the senses made possible by our possessions. But when tomorrow we die, despoiled and stripped as though by thieves, we must go forth naked and empty-handed into our next life. However many horses, mules, riches, food, clothes, and friends we may have, whatever companions may be ours—retinues of monks, students, or subjects—we can take none of them with us when we die. We must go forth alone.

[verse 60] Once again, it could be argued that if we are rich, we are likely to live for a long time and not die. And by making offerings and charitable donations; by having sacred images painted; by creating representations of the Buddha's body, speech, and mind; by making prostrations and circumambulations, and so on, we will purify our negative karma and will accumulate much merit. It is for this reason, we tell ourselves, that we are irritated when we encounter hindrances to such a course. But if we are irritated with what prevents us from getting what we want (given that one instant of anger or hatred destroys merit accumulated in the course of a thousand kalpas), does not this mean that all our merit will be dissipated and a great evil increased?

[verse 61] In that case, what use will our lives have been when the only real reason for living—the purification of evil and the accumulation of merit—has been ruined, when merit has been exhausted and there has been a great increase in negativity? What is the point in living such a life; what point is there in *not* dying, when evil is the only consequence? Surely there is no point at all.

[verse 62] It could be objected that if we patiently put up with all kinds of unpleasant speech, other people will entertain wrong ideas about us and will criticize us. And since we are Bodhisattvas, they will destroy their own merit and throw themselves into the lower realms. It is for this reason, we tell ourselves, that we resent their unpleasant speech. But how is it that we do not resent the same kind of unpleasant talk, criticism, and wrong thoughts when they are directed at others, even sublime beings superior to us? We ought to resent it!

[verse 63] Perhaps we will claim that we are not upset when unpleasant words are addressed to others because those who say such things do so because they have lost faith owing to the apparent misbehavior of the people in question (who may even be sublime beings). It is because of the latter that the situation has arisen. But if this is the case, why is it that we are impatient when they insult *us*? For when such people say unpleasant things, it is dependent on the arising of negative emotions and they have no control over it. Therefore we ought to bear with it. In short, when others dislike us, when they create obstacles to our success, when they insult us to our face or slander us behind our backs, we should take pleasure in cultivating patience.

4. Cultivating Patience toward Those Who Ill-Treat Our Loved Ones

[verse 64] Even people who are outside the Buddhadharma and those who, out of attachment to their own tenets and aversion to those of others, vilify and destroy sacred images, stupas, and the scriptures of the sublime Dharma—thus performing the extremely negative actions of abandoning their own Dharma tradition and committing the sins of immediate effect and so on—should only ever be the objects of our compassion. We should not be angry with them. The Buddhas are themselves unaffected by such behavior, for their nature is uncompounded. As for Buddha images and representations of the Dharma, they, being material and inanimate, can feel no pain when damaged.

[verse 65] And even when our teachers, parents, family and so on, members of the monastic order, and Dharma friends become the object of incorrect attitudes—when they are criticized, robbed, or harmed in some way—it is their karma that has summoned such actions from their aggressors. Understanding that these sufferings arise from conditions, as was explained earlier in verse 31 ("All things, then, depend on other things etc."), we should check our anger.

[verse 66] Injuries are inflicted both by animate agents like human beings or by inanimate entities like fire, water, wind, falling rocks, and so on. Animate and inanimate are both alike in inflicting harm. They are also alike in the sense that both are conditioned. And they are the same too in being devoid of self. Why do we select only animate agents as the special objects of our anger? It is quite illogical. We should simply bear with injuries regardless of their provenance, animate or inanimate.

[verse 67] Some people, in their ignorance, perpetrate evil actions (stealing, entertaining wrong views, belittling others, abandoning the Dharma, and committing the sins of immediate effect). Other people who have no compassion toward them are, in their ignorance, moved to anger and retaliation. Which of the two parties is guiltless? To whom should error be ascribed? Both accumulate great evil, and both are equally at fault.

[verse 68] The question is: Why did those in the first category (our teachers, friends, and so on) do evil in the past, which is now the cause of their being harmed at another's hand? The effects of their past actions cannot be averted and are now ripening on them. We should not be resentful in such situations. Since everything derives from karma, what reason is there to resent the harm-doer?

[verse 69] Having now arrived at this understanding, Shantideva declares that, come what may, he will not be resentful when others do harm to his relatives and loved ones. He will not get angry but will persevere in virtuous ways, calming the resentment that exists between his friends and their enemies. And he will do this in order to foster in the hearts of everyone (his relatives and their enemies) an attitude of mutual love that banishes all hatred and anger.

[verse 70] How is one to pacify resentment, or how is one to act so that anger and hatred do not arise? Shantideva takes the example of buildings that are on fire, when the flames go leaping from house to house. The wise course is to take and fling away anything inflammable that might assist the speedy propagation of the fire—straw and other things that, though useful, are of lesser importance. [verse 71] Similarly, when our friends or close associates, to whom we are attached, are attacked, first the fires of hate spring up between these same friends and their assailants. Fearing that the conflagration of hatred might spread also to our minds and the merit of a thousand kalpas be consumed, it is said that we must at once cast away whatever we are attached to: friends, close associates, and so on. The meaning here, it is said, is that we must at once cast away our attachment.

[verse 72] It might be thought that if we do not help our friends when they are assailed, people will gossip maliciously about us and we will become contemptible in their eyes. In answer to this, Shantideva cites the example of an extremely guilty person who, when being led away to execution, is set free after having only his hand amputated. He is surely better-off. In the same way, it is surely better to endure merely human injuries like scorn, rather than suffer the pains of hell. [verse 73] If the present pains inflicted by our enemies on ourselves and our friends are beyond our power to tolerate, how much more intolerable will be the pains of hell? This being so, why do we not remove the anger in the minds of ourselves and of our friends that is the cause of future sorrows in the unbearable torments of hell? We should certainly get rid of it.

[verse 74] We may well think that the sufferings of the human state that are inflicted by enemies are unwanted and therefore intolerable. But right until the present time, for the sake of objects to which we have been attached and which we have desired, we have experienced the fierce, unbearable pain of being burned by fire and cut by swords in the realms of hell thousands and thousands of times over. And in all this time, nothing was achieved either for ourselves or for others. The suffering was completely pointless.

[verse 75] The hardship implied in cultivating the patience of accepting the difficulties inflicted by aggressors and of making light of them is as nothing compared with the agonies experienced in the hells. In addition, great benefits will come from the hardships of such patience, both for ourselves and for others. The harm inflicted on beings in the lower realms is dispelled thereby; and suffering, once accepted, is like a broom that sweeps away our negativities and is a stimulus to goodness. Thus we should not shy away from it but instead should embrace it joyfully.

4. CULTIVATING PATIENCE WHEN PEOPLE DO GOOD TO OUR ENEMIES

[verse 76] When others speak well of his enemies, of the rivals of whom he is jealous, and so on, praising them for their qualities, and, when, in praising them, they experience a certain mental gratification, why, Shantideva asks, does his mind not take pleasure in praising them as well (in accordance with the principle "When good is talked about, you should follow suit")—instead of speaking in a contrary sense? He ought to be happy; resentment is quite out of place.

[verse 77] It should be understood that those who praise their enemies and rivals have a state of mind that is happy and joyful. Indeed the mental pleasure that derives from praising one's enemies is not like the pleasure that comes from such things as indulging in meat, alcohol, and contact with a sexual partner. *This* pleasure is the source of suffering in this and future lives and is therefore a serious failing. For that reason, the Buddhas and Bodhisattvas, endowed with every excellence, have deprecated and forbidden it like poison. It creates conflict between beings and drives them apart. The pleasure that derives from praising one's enemies, on the other hand, has four beneficial qualities, which are the reverse of the previous defects. First, it is the source of all happiness in this and future lives. Second, it is not negative but virtuous, for it is a source of unbounded happiness and rejoicing. Third, the Buddhas and Bodhisattvas, who are endowed with perfect qualities, do not forbid it but urge it on us. Finally, it is the most perfect way of winning people over, because praise that is joyous and without jealousy is the best kind of pleasing speech, a fact that is illustrated by Dromtönpa when he praised the qualities of Lama Khuwa.

[verse 78] If, owing to jealousy, we do not want such a pleasure, thinking that if we praise others (including the people we do not like), they will be the ones to experience happiness and contentment, we should also give up remunerating our servants, since their wages make them happy. But we will certainly be the loser both now and in the hereafter. For in the present life the work will not be done, and in the next we will not be able to enjoy the fruits of generosity.

[verse 79] In other words, our perception of what is to be done and what is not to be done is completely inverted. When others (including those we dislike) see and hear that our qualities are being praised, we are keen that everyone should be happy by joining in the eulogy. But when the compliments are paid to our enemies, we are unwilling to enjoy the celebration by joining in their praise, for we are afraid that they will be made happy by it.

[verse 80] We have cultivated the attitude of mind that is oriented toward enlightenment, wishing to establish the infinite multitude of beings in the unsurpassable happiness of buddhahood. If now we find that, without needing our help, beings gain for themselves some slight contentment in the way of clothing and sustenance, why should we resent it? It is quite improper to be displeased and annoyed. [verse 81] We have cultivated bodhichitta, wishing that beings attain enlightenment and thus become objects of veneration for the three worlds of desire, form, and no form. Why should we find ourselves in a torment of resentment when petty marks of favor (to say nothing of veneration) come their way? How is it that we are unable to accept this? Such a situation is wholly out of place. [verse 82] Take the example of our dependents, our parents or relatives who rely on us and whom we have the constant duty to support, providing them with food and clothing. Should it happen that they find a means of livelihood for themselves, will we not be happy? Will we once again be resentful? Such a thing would not at all make sense.

[verse 83] To be sure, if we do not want even these paltry favors to come to others, how can we possibly want buddhahood for them? How can anyone have bodhichitta (the attitude of mind that is oriented toward enlightenment) and at the same time jealously resent the spiritual and temporal benefits that others enjoy? It is clear that such a person has no bodhichitta at all.

[verse 84] When lamas and tulkus are jealous of each other and find it intolerable that others of their rank should be honored and served, resenting thus both the benefactors and the beneficiaries, they should counteract their mental attitude by consistently reflecting as follows. Whether the horse or pack animal is gifted, or whether the benefactor keeps it for himself and it stays in his stable, in neither case will it come to the lama in question. Whether the benefactor gives or does not give his horse to his rival, how can it be a matter of concern to the lama? What sense does it make for him to wish enviously that the horse goes not to his rival but comes to him? It would make more sense to rest in a state of indifference.

[verse 85] We get angry out of jealousy when others acquire possessions, and we wish even more of them for ourselves. But the cause of others' wealth is their previously accumulated merit, their present devotion to the Dharma and the teachers, and their qualities of learning and discipline. These are the sort of qualities that benefactors appreciate, and this is why such people are sponsored. We too can accumulate merit by making offerings and giving alms and so on; and we too can inspire clear confidence in others through the strength of our faith in the Dharma and the teacher and through being quiet and disciplined thanks to the practice of mindfulness, vigilant self-scrutiny, and carefulness. We may also possess a pure observance of monastic discipline. Through our study of the teachings, we too can acquire the skill to discriminate properly between what is to be done and what is not to be done; and we too may soften our hearts with compassion and bodhichitta. And as a result of all such qualities, we too may discover an effortless source of provisions. Why in our jealousy do we find such causes of wealth so intolerable when they occur in others? Why, by our resentment, do we cast these same causes so far away from us? On the contrary, we should grasp them to ourselves. Indeed, if we wish to enrich ourselves by every means, why are we not angry with ourselves for not seizing upon such causes? For they are what benefactors regard as the most worthy reason for making offerings, and are thus the source of abundant wealth. We should blame our own jealousy. We should resent ourselves and no one else.

[verse 86] We may consider that we and the people that we envy are all the same and equal. Therefore when we don't have something, they shouldn't have it either! But the very cause of our poverty is the fact that, ignorant of what should be done and what should not be done, we have committed evil actions such as stealing. Not only are we without any repentance and remorse, but we even have the effrontery to vie with those who have knowledge of correct conduct, observance of the discipline, and accumulation of great merit, because of which their wealth has appeared. Our attitude is wrong! And if we cannot help competing with others, then let us observe the discipline, accumulate merit, and understand the proper rules of conduct.

When the objects of patience were identified above, mention was first made of oneself and of one's close associates, and this was followed by mention of enemies. Of the twelve undesirable factors that were thus revealed, the way to cultivate patience with regard to the causes of our suffering was explained in detail under three headings.[158] The cultivation of patience with regard to those who treat us with contempt and so forth,[159] patience with those who mistreat our loved ones, together with patience toward those who do good to our enemies—all this is set forth concisely and should be explained as it was before. And once it is explained, we ought to meditate and familiarize ourselves with it. In the condensed exposition given below of the twelve obstacles that prevent us from getting what we want, the question of enemies is addressed at the beginning. The *Bodhicharyavatara* does not say a great deal about these obstacles and so they should be expounded in the same way as the first [three] topics.

3. Cultivating patience toward obstacles that prevent us from getting what we want

4. Cultivating patience toward obstacles that prevent unpleasant things from happening to our enemies

[verse 87] We are irritated with what prevents those we dislike from suffering and being scorned by others. On the other hand, when our adversaries are unhappy or suffer, when they are affected by a bereavement or a loss of livestock, or when their enemies attack, we should ask ourselves why this should be a cause of rejoicing for us. We are in no way benefited by it.

And if, thinking that we might be, we express such a wish and say how much we would like such things to happen to our enemies, such verbalizations cannot cause them the slightest harm, either now or in their future lives. Such behavior is completely futile! [verse 88] And even if our hostile wishes were to occasion harm, once again, what reason is that for us to rejoice? We might tell ourselves that we would be happy if our wish were to be fulfilled before we die. But what manner of happiness could that be? Indeed, could there be anything more ruinous either in the present life or in the life to come? Not only will our malevolence do nothing to ruin our enemies, but the weapon of our evil wish will turn against us, attracting every kind of misfortune like a magnet drawing iron to itself.

Since such an attitude constitutes the downfall of abandoning beings, it follows that in our next life we will fall into the hells and will have to endure great suffering. [verse 89] Just as when a fish is caught on a hook by a fisherman who cooks it in his pan (the fisherman in this case being the defiled emotion who casts the hook, namely, the evil wish), we too are caught on the hook, unbearable and sharp, and flung into the burning copper cauldrons of the hells, sure to be boiled by the workmen of the Lord of Death and to suffer pain for long ages.

4. CULTIVATING PATIENCE WITH THOSE WHO OBSTRUCT WHAT WE AND OUR FRIENDS DESIRE

[verse 90] It is inappropriate to be irritated with those who throw obstacles in the way of our acquiring honors and renown in a worldly sense. For indeed, all the veneration of praise and celebrity paid to us by others will do nothing to increase the merit that will be of help to us in our future existences. Nor will it increase our span of life; for it brings neither health nor strength and nothing for the body's ease: no food to still our hunger, no drink to slake our thirst.

[verse 91] If we are intelligent enough to know where our advantage lies and how to secure it, we will ask ourselves what good there is to be had in such things (as praise and renown). The answer is that there is none at all. It could be argued that although they do not benefit the body, they are good for the mind in that they make us happy. That is why such things are desirable. But if it is only pleasure that we want, we [monks] might as well make ourselves beautiful and go in for gambling, women, and alcohol. It is thus that Shantideva places the desire for a good reputation and praise on the same level as all the things that should not be done in a monastic setting.

[verse 92] The actions of ignorant people are completely pointless. In order to secure a reputation for magnanimity and for being victorious in every dispute, they squander everything they have. In order to gain renown for courage, they go to war and risk their lives. But when one is dead, what use are such pleasant-sounding words as "He's won; he's a hero"? Who will there be to take pleasure in them? No one.

[verse 93] For example, children amuse themselves by building sand castles. But when the latter come crumbling down, these silly, ignorant children burst into tears and cry inconsolably. It is the same with us. When our fame and good reputation start to fail and are damaged, we are unhappy; we suffer. Our minds are as deluded as silly children.

[verse 94] We might wonder whether the joy we have in being well-spoken of derives from the pleasure taken in the words of praise or from the state of mind of the person who praises us. Of course, the short-lived words spoken by another person, being devoid of intellect, cannot intend to praise us. It therefore does not make sense to be pleased by them. Words are just abstractions, "nonthings." It is out of place to be happy at them.

We therefore say that we are made happy by the joy that others have when they praise us. It is this that causes our happiness. [verse 95] Perhaps this is so. But of what benefit to us is the pleasure others take in praising our friends and even ourselves? It cannot be of any good to us. For their pleasure is theirs and theirs alone. We cannot experience even a part of it. [verse 96] It could be argued that when a mother is happy, her child is happy also. In the same way, when those who praise us are happy, we are happy too. But for us who are practicing the way of the Bodhisattva, the happiness of any being ought to be a cause of our own joy. Why then is it that, when praise is directed toward those whom we dislike, for instance, and gives pleasure to them, our jealous minds are made miserable? There is something wrong here; the two attitudes are in contradiction.

[verse 97] When we investigate to see whether the satisfaction we feel on realizing that we are being praised and that others are speaking well of us is caused by the actual words or by the state of mind of those who praise us, our pleasure is shown to be completely pointless. It is unacceptable to common sense and is like the silly behavior of children who are happy with their sand castles and are attached to them.

[verse 98] Whether we are teachers or practitioners of the sacred Dharma, if praise comes our way, if we are venerated or become famous and wealthy, our minds will become excited and arrogant, and we will become more and more attached to possessions. And in order to secure both wealth and respect, we will not have time or interest either in teaching or practice. We will be involved in distracting activities and will be carried away by the eight worldly concerns. Such straying into the objects of desire will destroy the slightest thought of weariness with samsara and the determination to leave it.

It is said too that samadhi or concentration dwells in minds that are weary with samsara. But if our minds are not weary, then—no need to speak of concentration—we will not even accomplish the virtues of body and speech. If we do possess a few qualities worthy of appreciation, our envy of those who are praised for their excellence increases and we are irritated and distressed by the worthiness of others. This is how the excellence of this and future lives is utterly destroyed.

Of all defilements, jealousy is the worst. For when the lustful Nanda, the angry Subhuti, and the ignorant Chudapanthaka beheld the qualities of the Tathagata, it was possible for them to be tamed and to be transformed. By contrast, Devadatta, who in fact possessed a few supernatural powers and was able to subjugate King Ajatashatru, was not only incapable of perceiving the Buddha's qualities (because he was jealous of him), but through sheer malevolence he committed a sin of immediate effect and was born in the hell realms.

We too have this kind of defilement. [verse 99] Therefore, all those unpleasant people who stay close by in order to annul whatever praise is given to us—together with all veneration, good reputation, and prosperity—are surely there to guard us from falling into ruin in the hells or the other realms of sorrow. For praise is indeed something to which we get attached. Rather than being angry with such people, we should be grateful to them for their kindness and the good they do to us.

[verse 100] After all, we are striving to gain liberation from the prison of samsara where we are bound by afflictive emotion. We surely have no need of the praise, gain, and reverential treatment that increasingly imprison us in such a state, any more than a prisoner chained in prison has need of further shackles. How can we be resentful of those who labor to release us from the fetters of respect and wealth, the very bonds of samsara? It makes no sense.

[verse 101] Opening the door to wealth and honors and clinging to them is an omen foretelling a descent into the lower realms. Given that we are thus determined to plunge ourselves headlong into the sorrow of the states of loss, Shantideva reminds us that those who hinder us from acquiring fame and fortune bar the way to such a destiny. They are like the Buddha's very blessing. How can we possibly be angry with them, seeing the benefit that they bring to us? We ought to be grateful instead.

[verse 102] We should not be irritated, claiming that, if they take our possessions, they will be obstacles to our virtuous activities, such as having pictures painted of the Buddhas or creating representations of their body, speech, and mind, or that they will hinder us from making offerings and distributing alms or from practicing meditation in retreat. But as it has been explained already, since patience is the supreme and peerless austerity or virtue, how can we not devote ourselves to it? For if we wish for virtue and merit, we should dwell in patience.

[verse 103] If, through our own shortcomings of anger, jealousy, and so on, it happens that, while our enemies are at hand as the very causes of our patience—supreme merit and virtue that this is—we fail to practice forbearance toward those who harm us and obstruct our material gain and good reputation, we are indeed hindering ourselves. Some commentators interpret the word "cause" in the root stanza as meaning "patience."

[verse 104] If there are no aggressors or harm-doers, patience does not arise. It appears only in the presence of those who attack us. Given therefore that it is precisely an enemy that is the definite cause for the practice of patience, how can it possibly be said that the enemy is an obstacle to our merit and virtue? It does not make sense, for the former is the cause of the latter. It is the *absence* of the enemy that prevents patience from appearing.

[verse 105] If beggars arrive asking for alms just at the time when alms are being distributed, they actually facilitate the practice of generosity. Since they do not hinder it in the slightest way, how can they be regarded as obstacles? Similarly, for someone who wants to receive the monastic vows, it would be absurd to say that the abbots and monks are impediments to ordination. For they themselves constitute the right conditions for receiving the vows.

[verse 106] At the present time of degeneration when the kalpa is in its period of decline,[160] the poor—the helpers of our generosity—are legion. On the other hand, the abbots and monks who bestow ordination are few. And even rarer are the assailants that are the source of patience. The reason for this is that since Bodhisattvas do not injure beings in the slightest way, but only help them, the latter cease to be aggressive and become well-disposed. As soon as they meet Bodhisattvas, even malicious beings become loving and respectful. Their violent thoughts and behavior subside. For example, both deer and hounds listened to Dharma in the presence of the venerable Mila, and wolves and sheep played happily together in front of Ngulchu Thogme Zangpo.

[verse 107] The causes for practicing patience, supreme merit and virtue that it is, are rare. Therefore, just like a man who, being destitute, is overcome with joy on discovering easily and without travail an inexhaustible treasure of food and clothing in his own house, in the same way, when we come upon that extreme rarity, an enemy or obstacle-maker—a support for patience, the best of Bodhisattva practices—joy must be the only result. We ought to be like the great lama Serkhangpa, who said that his teacher was Nyathubten—a bandit who had robbed him of everything that he had. From that moment on, Serkhangpa abandoned his ecclesiastical rank and became a yogi free from all mundane activity.

[verse 108] If we have no one against us, patience cannot arise in our minds. Consequently, since we have brought forth patience thanks to the people who harm us and whom we dislike, it is fitting that we make offerings to them of its first fruits, for they indeed have been the cause of it. [verse 109] And if we think that such offerings are not due to our enemies because they never had the conscious intention to engender patience in our minds, why, by the same token, should we make offerings to the sacred Dharma as being the proper cause for the accomplishment of great virtue in our mind stream? We ought not to, because the sublime Dharma never consciously intends to induce us to virtue.

[verse 110] We may protest against such a conclusion, saying that the sublime Dharma is without malice, whereas our enemies conspired to do us harm and are therefore undeserving of any recompense. But if our enemies were like good doctors and, without malevolence, tried only to benefit us and make us happy, how could we possibly have developed patience? It would have been impossible, for there would have been no cause for it. [verse 111] If they were to strive to benefit us, we could not engender patience. Conversely, since it is in relation to their harm-doing motivated by intense anger that we do engender it, our enemies are indeed the cause whereby our patience is perfected. And though this is not their intention, they are nonetheless suitable objects of veneration, as much as the sacred Dharma itself. For it is they who are the causes of our doing something virtuous.

1. RESPECT FOR BEINGS

2. REVERENCING BEINGS, CONSIDERING THEM AS THE FIELD OF MERIT

[verse 112] Because it is in relation with hostile beings that we accomplish patience and the other virtues, it follows that the fertile ground in which the seed of buddhahood (the perfection of the twofold aim) is perfected consists of beings and Buddhas. Since the harvest of virtue will burgeon and grow on the basis of both of them, they are like fertile fields. This is something that the Sage, the Tathagata, has himself declared. For in the *Sutra of Perfectly Pure Aspiration*, he said:

> Formerly upon the field of beings
> And on the field of Buddhas did I base myself.
> 'Tis thus that I have harvested
> The endless qualities of buddhahood.

These two "fields" are specified because in the beginning, when sublime bodhichitta is first cultivated, one focuses on beings through compassion, and one focuses on perfect Buddha, or buddhahood, through wisdom. Subsequently, Bodhisattva practices such as the four immeasurable attitudes and [the paramitas of] generosity, discipline, patience, and the rest are based mainly on beings, whereas practices like the taking of refuge are based mainly on the Buddhas. Finally, within perfect, fully manifest buddhahood, there remains the imperative of placing every living being in that same level of enlightenment.

Since the meaning of the scriptures is to be substantiated by reasoning, an argument is supplied regarding this question. This consists of pointing out that by making beings happy through their practice of love and compassion and by rejoicing the hearts of the Buddhas, many holy beings have perfectly secured their own and others' benefit; in other words, they attained buddhahood.

[verse 113] Therefore, in order to achieve the qualities of perfect enlightenment (such as the ten strengths and the four fearlessnesses) within our mind streams, we must depend upon beings and Buddhas equally. What sort of practice is it then to serve and respect only the Buddhas and not beings?

[verse 114] Of course it could be objected that Buddhas and beings are not on an equal footing, since the former are without defect and are endowed with every excellence, whereas beings are a mass of faults. But no claim is being made that the Buddhas and sentient beings are on a par in terms of their qualities. They are equal in the sense that it is through depending on them both that we accomplish the qualities of buddhahood. The excellence of beings is like that of the Buddhas in that it is thanks to them too that we are able to bring forth the enlightened state. From that point of view, therefore, beings and Buddhas are indeed said to be similar or equal.

[verse 115] Let us consider those whose minds are absorbed in love, the essence of the fourth samadhi. If we make offering to such practitioners promptly, when they have arisen from their meditation but not yet from their seats, the result of such an action will ripen quickly and will be experienced in this present life. This reveals the eminence of living beings. Through having their loving minds focused on beings, such meditators become perilous objects.[161] Again, merit that derives from faith in the Buddhas, the offering of a single flower or a single drop of water, the holding up of just one hand in a gesture of homage and so on—all this will turn into inexhaustible virtue tending to liberation. And this reveals the eminence of the Buddhas.

[verse 116] In short, since it is through beings also that we can achieve the resultant qualities of enlightenment, we consider that the Buddhas and beings are equal. They are not, of course, equal in their qualities. For the Buddhas are oceans of unbounded excellence: the ten strengths, the four fearlessnesses, the eighteen distinctive qualities,[162] and so forth, none of which qualities are present in beings. [verse 117] The ten strengths and other supreme qualities of buddhahood are unique and without compare. If the tiniest part of such qualities were to appear in ordinary beings, then even if the three worlds replete with all riches and the seven kinds of precious substance were presented to them alone, the offering would be too small.

[verse 118] Thus, although from the standpoint of their qualities, beings and Buddhas are not the same, nevertheless, a part in eliciting the supreme state of buddhahood within our minds is also possessed by beings. And on account of just this similarity, beings, as much as the Buddhas, are the proper objects for our veneration. They constitute a field that is to be respected and gratified.

2. Reverencing beings with the wish to rejoice the Buddhas

[verse 119] Another reason why it is necessary to treat beings with respect and kindness is that the Buddha is the greatest friend, without pretence or insincerity, of every being (including his own enemies) who wanders in samsara—so much so that he had the same regard for Devadatta as he had for Rahula [his own son]. How else are we to repay the benefits—indeed the incommensurable happiness—that the Buddhas and Bodhisattvas secure for us in this and future existences, except by coming to the aid of beings and benefiting them? Since there is no other way to recompense the kindness that the Buddhas have shown to us, we must—in acknowledgment and repayment of it—make living beings happy.

[verse 120] When the need arises, the Buddhas and Bodhisattvas are even ready to give away their bodies (the product of a hundred merits) and plunge into the Hell of Unrelenting Pain in order to bring about the good and happiness of beings. If we revere and have faith in the Buddhas and Bodhisattvas, we will repay their kindness by bringing benefit to beings in our turn. For this reason, even if beings do great damage to our wealth and happiness, we should think only well of them and submit to it, just as good disciples interpret in the best light whatever their teacher does.

[verse 121] And if on occasion the Buddhas and Bodhisattvas, the Lords and teachers of ourselves and others, are careless even of their own bodies for beings' sake, how can we, inept and stupid as we are in discriminating between good and bad behavior, act with such conceit toward others? We ought not to do so. Instead we should become their respectful servants. Like faithful attendants, we should strive to bring happiness to beings.

[verse 122] The enlightened ones are made happy when beings, who are to them as their only children, are made happy. They sorrow when beings are harmed. By benefiting beings, therefore, and by bringing joy to them, we please the Buddhas also. And when we offend beings and cause their sufferings, we offend the Buddhas as well. [verse 123] In order to illustrate this point, Shantideva gives the example of a man whose entire body is being tormented with fire. Even if all the pleasures of the senses were presented to him for his enjoyment, not only would he remain unmoved by such a gift, but his distress would only be aggravated thereby. In the same way, even if we make offerings to the Three Jewels, there is no way to please

the greatly compassionate Buddhas and Bodhisattvas when we are ourselves the cause of others' pain.

People who perform the so-called "red rituals" (offerings of meat and
blood) place these substances in a mandala. And they claim to invoke the
presence of the Buddhas and Bodhisattvas and to make such oblations to
them. But this is like killing a woman's beloved child and then inviting her
to partake of its flesh and blood. The wisdom deities will be unable even to
approach. Instead, all the powers of darkness, which crave and delight in
meat and blood, will draw near and devour them. This is how both the cel-
ebrants and benefactors [of such rituals] bring ruin upon themselves both
in their present and future lives.

[verse 124] All the harm in thought, word, and deed that has been done in
the past and until the present moment to beings wandering in samsara is a
source of grief to the most compassionate Buddhas and their Bodhisattva
offspring. Therefore, in their presence and with bitter remorse, Shantideva
confesses every one of these great sins without dissimulating or concealing
any of them. And he takes the pledge never to repeat them in the future,
praying that the Buddhas and Bodhisattvas will forgive him for whatever he
has done to displease and sadden them.

[verse 125] And so from this day forward, in order to rejoice the hearts
of the Buddhas and their children, Shantideva declares that he will subjugate every kind of malevolence that he might feel toward beings, as well as
all his pride. He will be the servant of the entire world. Therefore, whether
people kick the highest part of him, namely his head, with their lowest
member, namely their feet; whether they cut or slay him, he says that he
will not retaliate even when he is in a position to do so. He is resolved to
accept everything with reverence. And so, he proclaims, "Let the great and
compassionate guardians of the three worlds rejoice!"

[verse 126] There is no doubt that the Lords of great compassion consider all wandering beings without exception as their very selves. It is just
as when the Buddha took to himself the swan that had been shot down by
Devadatta. It is taught that when the Buddha first engendered the attitude
of bodhichitta, he considered all beings in general as his fathers and mothers. More specifically, he looked upon all those older than himself as his
parents, all those who were his age as his brothers and sisters, and all those
who were younger than him as his sons and daughters. It was thus that he
took them all to himself. When he was traversing the paths of accumula-

tion and joining, he regarded them as himself through the process of equalizing and exchanging self and other (a practice that will be explained later). When he reached the path of seeing and realized ultimate reality in which self and other are the same, he claimed all beings for himself in a manner devoid of all duality. And when, having discarded the two veils together with their associated habitual tendencies, he achieved buddhahood—when, that is, the dharmadhatu (the object) and primordial wisdom (the subject) mingled, like water with water into a single taste free from all duality and there was not the slightest trace of dualistic phenomena—Buddha and buddhafield were apprehended as a single whole.

The enlightened body, speech, and mind of the Buddha embraces the whole of space, wherever it extends. As it is written in the sutras:

> However far the sphere of space extends,
> Thus far is the extent of living beings.

And:

> Wherever space pervades,
> The enlightened body likewise spreads.
> Wherever the enlightened body lies,
> Is present also the enlightened speech.
> Wherever the enlightened speech pervades
> Enlightened mind is present too.

As the text declares, beings dwell wherever space pervades, and they are all embraced by the enlightened body, speech, and mind. Therefore, from the very beginning, beings are never separated from the enlightened mind. Knowing this, those great beings who have attained enlightenment take beings as themselves.

For there is not the slightest difference between what is called "Buddha" and what is called "beings" in that all are endowed with the Buddha-nature. The Buddhas are totally free from apprehending a duality between self and other. For if they were to apprehend this duality, it would follow that they had not realized the absence of self, which is absurd. Therefore, as explained earlier, those who appear to deluded perception as beings possess the same nature as the Buddha, the protector. Since they are pervaded by the sugatagarbha, they are indeed the Buddhas of the future. For as the sutra says, "All beings are permeated by the sugatagarbha," and:

> Pure and limpid, luminous,
> Untroubled, uncompounded,
> The nature of the Buddhas, gone in bliss,
> Is present from the outset and is thus defined.

And supporting such passages with reasoned argument, the Lord Maitreya has also said in the *Uttaratantra-shastra*:

> Because the perfect Buddha's kaya all-pervades,
> And suchness is undifferentiated,
> Because they all possess the Buddha's lineage,
> All beings, always, have the Buddha-nature.

Since it is demonstrated both by scripture and by reasoning that beings are indeed Buddhas, how is it possible for us not to treat them with respect? As much as we reverence the Buddhas we must also reverence beings. For there is no such thing as buddhahood if beings are abandoned.

[verse 127] It is said that to accomplish the happiness of beings is the best way to rejoice the hearts of the Buddhas. And it is also taught that to benefit beings is itself the highest way of accomplishing one's own benefit and happiness. Moreover, when beings are happy, they are able to act correctly. This therefore is the supreme way of removing the sorrows of the world. Making beings happy must therefore be something that we should do diligently, all the time.

2. PRACTICING RESPECT FOR BEINGS, THINKING OF THE CONSEQUENCES OF THE GOOD AND EVIL DONE TO THEM

[verse 128] We may imagine a person, such as a royal minister, who does harm to a multitude of beings (by imposing exorbitant taxes, perhaps, or by inflicting punishment on them). People with foresight will refrain from retaliating even if they are able to do so. On the contrary, they will bend to the minister's will and make sure they please him. [verse 129] For they know that the minister is not acting on his own account and without support. Indeed, he is seconded by the power of the king and his other ministers. In the same way, we should not retaliate even against the most feeble of our tormentors, such as lice and their eggs, contemptuously destroying them. [verse 130] For it is as though they have as their allies the terrifying guardians of hell (who can boil and burn us in revenge), as well as the compassionate Buddhas and Bodhisattvas, who will be grieved at our mistakes, with the result that we will fail to meet them and cease to be an object of their compassion. Therefore Shantideva declares that he will respect and please all living beings, just as subjects might serve a ferocious and wrathful king (who imposes severe reprisals and exacts the death penalty for the slightest offence). Shantideva will strive to placate beings in all sorts of ways.

[verse 131] The reality moreover is far greater than this example might suggest. The degree of benefit or harm involved is not at all comparable. For however much we may displease and anger a king, he can do no more than kill us or confiscate our possessions. By contrast, if we offend beings, we will suffer in the hells in our next lives. Obviously, a mere king is unable to inflict such suffering. [verse 132] Conversely, however much we may please a king, he can only reward us with possessions, power, riches, and the enjoyments of this present existence. But he is powerless to bestow on us what is to be gained through pleasing beings and securing their happiness, namely, the ultimate condition of buddhahood.

[verse 133] Therefore, Shantideva tells himself that, by bearing with all things and by pleasing and bringing happiness to beings, he will achieve in the future the final fruit of such practices: the state of perfect enlightenment. And in addition to that, why should he not also see its temporary fruits in this present life too, namely, general appreciation and an increase in glory and wealth as the foundation of every excellence, as well as the increase of his fame. On this basis, in whatever situation and company he finds himself, he will only ever help beings and do good to them, and will therefore be serene in body and mind. [verse 134] Throughout his future lives, while he remains in samsara and until he achieves the fully ripened effect of enlightenment, he will, as a result of cultivating patience, enjoy a handsome and attractive body with its parts and senses all complete. And because he does no harm to others, he will not be afflicted by different illnesses. Because he pleases and benefits beings, he will have an excellent renown; his happiness will increase, and he will have a long and happy life.

He will enjoy the vast and perfect contentment of a chakravartin, a universal king rich with the seven precious attributes of royalty and able to establish his subjects in the practice of the ten virtues.

Here ends the sixth chapter of the *Bodhicharyavatara,* on patience. This is to be cultivated when the venom of anger appears, the result of feelings of dissatisfaction arising through the subtle experience of attachment and aversion, which, hard to recognize, derive from the eight worldly concerns.

PART THREE

How Bodhichitta Is to Be
Developed and Intensified

· 7 ·

DILIGENCE

The Support of the Practice

1. A BRIEF EXPLANATION OF THE NEED FOR DILIGENCE

[verse 1] As it has been said, "The paramita that follows depends on the one preceding it." Accordingly, the six paramitas are arranged in such a way that each paramita stands in a relation of cause and effect with the one following it. When people are generous, they are not attached to possessions, and this makes possible the practice of discipline. When discipline is acquired, so too is the ability to cultivate patience; and once patience has been achieved with regard to the great and difficult practices, it is possible to apply [enthusiastic] diligence. Why is this last paramita so necessary? Because it is through such diligence that one obtains the fruit of great enlightenment—as if it lay within one's fingers' reach. When there is no wind, nothing either inside or outside the body can move.[163] In the same way, without diligence, nothing positive relating to the two accumulations can occur. But, where diligence is present, great enlightenment is swiftly obtained through the wholesome power of the two accumulations.

1. A DETAILED EXPLANATION OF DILIGENCE

2. DILIGENCE IDENTIFIED

[verse 2] Diligence is defined as a state of mind that takes joy in virtue. Here, the mention of virtue indicates that diligence implicitly excludes all

states of nonvirtue and indifference, whereas the mention of joy excludes the virtues of body and speech, and indicates the nature of diligence [as a mental disposition]. For although positive physical and verbal actions are regarded as diligence, this is only because they are referred to with the name of what causes them.

2. REMOVING THE CONDITIONS INIMICAL TO DILIGENCE

3. IDENTIFYING LAZINESS AND ITS CAUSES

Here we will identify the contrary of diligence and then explain how it can be removed. The reverse of diligence is laziness, of which there are three kinds. First, there is the laziness of indolence; second, there is the laziness that consists in an inclination to unwholesome actions; and third, there is the laziness of self-depreciation and defeatism.

[verse 3] In itself, laziness, whereby the mind takes no joy in virtue, is caused by three things. These are first, the failure to strive in goodness, accompanied by an interest in idle entertainment; second, an indulgence in sleepiness and an increasing desire to lie in bed upon one's pillow; and third, the failure to be saddened by the sufferings of samsara. As we find in the detailed commentary, "Because they have no sorrow at the sufferings of samsara, people indulge in indolent pleasures and yearn for sleep." But although we enjoy the pleasures of distraction, and so on, and take delight in sleep, when all grosser cogitation is suspended, all such bliss transforms at length into suffering. So it is that, hankering after such sensations and feeling no sorrow at the ills of samsara, we engage in the activities of this life, getting the better of adversaries and protecting friends. However much we work at such activities, there is no end to them—and yet we do not grow weary of them but boast of all we do!

3. AN EXPLANATION OF HOW TO RID ONESELF OF THE THREE KINDS OF LAZINESS

4. CULTIVATING AN ANTIDOTE TO THE KIND OF LAZINESS THAT IS A YEARNING FOR IDLENESS

[verse 4] When we grow lazy, we should meditate on impermanence and drive away our laziness with the whip of diligence. We should meditate on impermanence by reflecting on the image of a fisherman and his net. Our

defiled emotions—attachment, anger, and the rest—are like trappers and fishermen who go in search of fish, ensnaring them and killing them in their nets. They enmesh and catch us in the toils of rebirth in the three worlds of samsara, which are pervaded by death, the inescapable destiny of us all.[164] This is how we fall into the mouth of Yama, the merciless Lord of Death. It is certain that we must die. How is it possible that we can still ignore this fact? We must face up to it and immediately strive in virtue.

[verse 5] We should also meditate on impermanence using the image of a buffalo and its butcher. Death comes for all humanity: our friends in the monastery and our companions in the Dharma, those who are older, those who are younger, and those who are of the same age. The Lord of Death spares none. He takes us all one by one. Can we still not see this? If we *do* see it but continue in our lazy attachment to sleep and to distraction, if we fail to make effort in virtue, we are indeed incredibly stupid—just like buffaloes that, without the slightest qualm, sleep next to their own butchers, who kill them one after the other.

[verse 6] We should meditate too on impermanence, using the example of an ambushed wayfarer. Like highway robbers who kill travelers, blocking all paths of escape and watching and lying in wait ahead along the road, the pitiless Lord of Death seals off all the ways that we might flee from him. He leaves open only the high road that leads to death itself. And there he waits for us. He has us already in his sights. How can we continue to delight in food and drink by day and in sleep at night? How can we be happy when our days and nights are racing by? Instead we must diligently persevere in virtuous action.

[verse 7] We should remember, too, that death will come soon. Generally speaking, in this age of decline, our lives are not long even if we manage to live out a full span of years. More to the point, the adverse circumstances of disease and negative influence are abundant in our time. We cannot even be certain that we will not die tonight. Death will be so quick to swoop down on us. Therefore let us put a joyful effort into virtuous action, gathering the two accumulations of merit and wisdom till that time comes. If we give up being lazy only when the moment of death has arrived, there will be no time to accumulate merit even if we feel inclined. What will be the point of abandoning laziness then?

[verse 8] It is not at all certain when we will die. Of all our life's activities, some we have only thought of doing and have not yet put into action. Some we have premeditated and are in the act of doing. Some we have left

unfinished and are only half complete. But the pitiless Lord of Death will arrive suddenly without our even having time to think that he is on his way. And it is only then—when death is certain—that we will suddenly realize that we have failed to strive in virtue and avoid evil when we could have done so. Instead, we have done the reverse, committing evils and doing nothing good. With deep regret, we will weep and cry, "Alas!" We will think, "The Lord of Death has done for me!" And with a mind as heavy as Mount Meru, we will leave this body and go forth into death.

[verse 9] When death arrives, our friends and dear ones and all that we possessed and could never part with—none of it can go with us. We have to leave everything behind and set out all alone on the path to the next life. We will have to watch our parents, our children, and our friends, who will have lost hope of our ever recovering. They will have red and swollen eyes (so strong will their sorrow be), and tears will glisten on their cheeks. And we will have to look, too, into the frightful and hideous faces of the messengers of the Lord of Death. Sometimes memories of our past life will occur to us, and brief glimpses of our parents and relatives; sometimes visions of the next life will appear, and also the servants of the Lord of Death.

[verse 10] We will be tormented by the recollection of our former sins. Our chests will bear the scratch marks of our nails. Screams of lamentation and the din of hell will break upon our ears. We will hear voices shouting "Kill! Kill! Cut! Cut!" and in sheer terror we will foul ourselves with excrement. We will be confused in all we do, say, and think; we will fail to recognize others and even ourselves. What will we do when that hour arrives? We shall be powerless to do anything. Therefore it is *now*, when we have the freedom to do so, that we should strive in virtue.

[verse 11] And if we are so unbearably terrified even while we are still alive, like living fish writhing on hot sand, what need is there to speak of the feeling of horror and intolerable pain of the next life, in the hells created by our evil deeds from time without beginning? As it is written in the *Suhrillekha:*

> If seeing pictures, carved or painted, of infernal realms;
> If thinking, hearing, reading of them frightens you,
> What need is there to speak of when you'll feel
> Their pain unbearable in fully ripened fruit.

[verse 12] How can we lie back, so lazily and in careless ease, when we have perpetrated the evil deeds that have created the Hell of Great Heat where our bodies, tender and sensitive as a baby's flesh, will be burned beyond all endurance in boiling molten bronze? It is certainly not reasonable to do so!

[verse 13] There is no need to speak here of the kind of diligence that leaves time neither for relaxation during the day nor even for sleep at night. We have no diligence at all, whether in study (even for the space of a year or a month) or in the approach and accomplishment phases of practice in retreat. How can we possibly hope for great results: for the qualities of erudition and accomplishment in this life or for rebirth in a pure field in the next? As the saying goes, "Less tolerant than new and tender flesh, more angry than an evil wraith." Because we are so sensitive and short tempered, unable to tolerate even the slightest discomfort, we will come to many harms both in this life and in our lives to come.

Whatever is born in the samsaric state must die; therefore it is certain that we are in the power of the Lord of Death. And yet, just like the gods transported by their pleasures, we do not give death a moment's thought. Delighting in distraction as if the hour of death will never come, we indulge in nonvirtue. Alas! How we will lament when we are beaten down by the dreadful agonies of death in this and future existences. How pathetic we are! The only sensible thing is to remember that we must die, and thus, strive diligently in positive action.

[verse 14] Now that we are in possession of this physical support, this human body endowed with freedoms and advantages, which is so difficult to find and is like an excellent ship, we must strive in virtue, thereby freeing ourselves from the great river of suffering in the three worlds of samsara. If we do not persevere in diligence now, it will be incredibly difficult to find such an excellent vessel again. What a fool he is, Shantideva tells himself. He is all confused about what should be done and what should not be done. The time at hand is not for sleep; it is for diligently cultivating positive action and avoiding negativities!

4. CULTIVATING AN ANTIDOTE TO THE KIND OF LAZINESS THAT CONSISTS IN AN INCLINATION TO UNWHOLESOME ACTIONS

[verse 15] It has been said that Shantideva's words in this verse are to be construed as meaning that the sacred Dharma is the cause of boundless joy. In brief, when the sacred Dharma is heard in the beginning, it is like a nectar for the ears, bringing inspiration and faith where there had been no faith before. Later, when one reflects on it, it dispels all the wandering thoughts of the distracted mind. Finally, when one meditates upon it, it causes the primordial wisdom of liberation to be born in the mind. Virtuous in the beginning, middle, and end, the Dharma is a supreme joy.

Therefore, how is it possible for us to turn away from listening to the explanation of the Tripitaka and from practicing the three trainings? How is it possible that we should take delight in what is contrary to the Dharma and is productive of unbearable suffering both in this and future lives? How is it possible for us to take pleasure in getting the better of enemies and in favoring friends; to take pleasure in trade and farming, in family and household, in being enslaved to religious wealth, horses, and possessions, and in providing for one's family? How can we indulge in all such distractions, which run counter to the study and practice of the Dharma and leave time neither for leisure during the day nor sleep at night? How can we take pleasure in the reckless agitation of body, speech, and mind: in games and sports, in floods of unvirtuous talk motivated by desire and aversion, in pointless chitchat that is neither positive nor negative, in jokes and loud, raucous hilarity, and in all kinds of mental distraction with our thoughts chasing pointlessly after the things of the past, present, and future?

[verse 16] But what is it that we *should* take pleasure in? As will be explained, with regard to virtuous conduct, we should not allow ourselves to fall into a defeatist attitude. Instead, we should don the armor of diligence, and we should summon all our strength, namely, the four counteractive forces. With mindfulness and vigilant introspection, we should earnestly adopt positive, and reject negative, behavior. And by implementing the antidotes, we should bring our body, speech, and mind under control. (These are two strengths that relate to each other like king and minister respectively.) And we should strive with joy and diligence in the trainings of bodhichitta. To begin with, we should meditate on the equality of self and other and then progress to the exchange of self and other.

4. CULTIVATING AN ANTIDOTE TO THE KIND OF LAZINESS THAT CONSISTS IN SELF-DEPRECIATION AND DEFEATISM

[verse 17] We must not put ourselves down by telling ourselves despondently that we are such great sinners and that we have so many emotions—

wondering how *we* could ever attain enlightenment, the state of unsurpassable buddhahood. For the Tathagata, the omniscient Buddha, who speaks only the truth and never lies, has proclaimed with undeceiving words that if they are able to bring forth the strength of perseverance, even weak and feeble beings like gnats and stinging insects that fly in the air, like bees that drink nectar from the flowers, and like every kind of dung-eating beetle—even they can gain unsurpassable enlightenment that is so hard to find. [verse 18] As we find in the *Subahuparipriccha-sutra,* "This, moreover, is how Bodhisattvas should perfectly train themselves. They should reflect that if even lions, tigers, dogs, jackals, vultures, cranes, crows, owls, worms, insects, flies, and stinging gnats will awaken into the state of unsurpassable buddhahood, why should they, human beings, allow their diligence to weaken—a diligence that will lead to buddhahood? They should never allow this to happen even at the cost of their lives." The idea that underlies this argument is that all beings are in primordial possession of the Buddha-nature. And when they encounter the Buddhas and Bodhisattvas, their Buddha-nature awakens, the seed of liberation is nourished, and, gradually, as they progress in the succession of their lives, they attain buddhahood.

[verse 19] If we and those like us, who have attained the best of all the six kinds of existence, who have the faculty and understanding of speech and are able to distinguish good from bad—if we cultivate bodhichitta without succumbing to despondency, if we do not relinquish the practice of the Bodhisattvas, why ever should we *not* be able to gain enlightenment? Surely we will achieve it! For it is said that even those who have been inconstant in their cultivation of bodhichitta will attain enlightenment.

[verse 20] We may accept that by striving in this way we will indeed attain great enlightenment. All the same, we are still alarmed and frightened at the prospect of having to give away our life and limbs. To speak like this shows that our fears are all misplaced. For we are failing to distinguish between the kind of intense suffering that we ought to dread and the slight discomforts that it is unnecessary to fear. We are confused about what to adopt and what to abandon, and we are frightened by things of which there is no reason to be afraid.

[verse 21] What we ought to fear is the failure to generate bodhichitta. We ought to fear the thought that it is *unnecessary* for us to suffer the pain of having our heads and limbs cut off [for the sake of others]. But this is not something that scares us. Nevertheless, from time without beginning, for myriads of innumerable and measureless periods of time, our heads and members have been repeatedly cut with swords, impaled upon spears, burned in infernal fires, and torn apart with incandescent saws. But the enduring of all these pains has been completely futile. No accumulation of merit has been gained from it, no enlightenment has been achieved!

[verse 22] Compared with all this, Shantideva remarks, the hardships suffered for the sake of accomplishing unsurpassable buddhahood are indeed limited. And therefore we should bear with them, knowing that the suffering in question is circumscribed and confined to the span of three countless kalpas. It is just as when the tip of an arrow pierces the body and causes great pain. In order to put an end to such intense and destructive suffering, it is necessary to make an incision, cutting away some skin, flesh, and bone. Come what may, we have to put up with the discomfort of the operation.

[verse 23] Furthermore, the doctors of this world and those who are skilled in the arts of healing use unpleasant methods in order to cure our ailments (painful treatments such as bleeding, cauterization, and amputation). And we must bear with the distress of being bled and burned. Thus, in order to overcome and banish all dreadful sorrow (the multitude of long-lasting ailments of the three worlds), we should accept and put up with what are indeed but minor discomforts.

[verse 24] By contrast, as a remedy for our ills, the Buddha, the greatest of healers—unlike the physicians just mentioned—does not make use of the kind of harsh and drastic treatment just described. The healing he prescribes is of the greatest excellence and mildness. It consists in sitting cross-legged on a comfortable seat and exercising strong and perfect mindfulness! It is thus that he soothes away the intense and unbounded diseases of the two kinds of defilement, such as the chronic diseases of the eighty-four thousand afflictive emotions, from which the beings in the world all suffer.

[verse 25] Of course, people will wonder how the giving away of one's flesh can be described as gentle treatment. The answer is that there is no need to do this in the beginning. When people are completely incapable of being generous, they must train themselves by passing something from their right hands to their left and back again, thus gradually getting used to the act of giving. They should think to themselves that they are [truly] giving, accompanying their gesture with a verbal expression. Subsequently, they should make little gifts of food to others: fragrant herbs and so on. For this is what the Buddha, who guides beings along a gradual path, instructs us to do at the outset. Gradually, as we acquire the habit, we will be able to give more and more until at length the time will come when we are able to make the great gift of our flesh and blood without holding anything back.

[verse 26] At such a point, when the habit has been acquired and we are free from all attachment, we will be able to consider our bodies as of no greater moment than a plant. We will then experience no difficulty in giving away our flesh and blood. For when we have realized the natural equality of all phenomena, gold and clods of earth will be of equal value for us, space and the palm of our hands will be the same. The pleasure of being anointed with water of sandalwood on our right side and the pain of being cut with a knife on our left will be all the same. All will be equal, both good and bad. We will fully understand the dream-like quality of all phenomena, and we will be free from every fear. As it is said in the *Sutralankara*:

> For those who know that all is like a mirage—
> That birth is like the entrance to a garden paradise—
> In times of plenty and in times of dearth,
> No fear of pain is there, no dread of the afflictions.

[verse 27] Of course it could be argued that even if we are able to give away our heads and members, we are still dismayed and afraid since, for the sake of beings, we will have to remain, through birth and death, for a very long time in samsara, which is like a pit of fire or a cage of venomous snakes. But the answer to this is that, although Bodhisattvas remain intentionally in samsara, they are not stained by its defects, just as a lotus is not defiled by the ooze in which it grows. Bodhisattvas abandon every negativity, and therefore they no longer have the experience of physical pain. They have understood that the nature of all knowable phenomena is the absence of self, and therefore their minds are wholly free of sorrow. For it is owing to the fact that ordinary beings entertain wrong concepts (imputing a self to that which is without a self) that their minds are tormented. And because they act negatively, killing, stealing, and so on, they are subject to physical pain.

[verse 28] Wherever Bodhisattvas find themselves, they are exempt from physical pain and mental distress. Since they accumulate merit by practicing generosity and the other paramitas, they have a sense of physical well-being; and since they realize the absence of self, their minds are in bliss.

Consequently, although they remain in the three worlds of samsara for the sake of beings, they are not stained in the slightest degree by its defects and sorrows. What indeed could dismay the Bodhisattvas, the compassionate offspring of the Buddha? There is nothing that can make them downcast.

[verse 29] Furthermore, by the power of their bodhichitta, the former sins (causes of suffering) of the Bodhisattvas are totally consumed and purified, as was shown in verses 13 and 14 in the first chapter. And as it is said in verse 19 of the same chapter, their practice of the paramitas increases at every instant, thereby accumulating and perfecting their merit, which is as vast as the ocean and is the cause of their happiness. This is why it is said that they surpass the Shravakas in their antidotes to negativity and in the accumulation of merit.

[verse 30] For the reasons explained above, how could those who desire good for themselves and who distinguish defects from qualities feel dejected and adopt a defeatist attitude while they are mounted on the excellent horse of bodhichitta, which banishes all mental sorrow and weariness of body, and confers the ability to progress upon a blissful path toward a blissful goal that abides in neither of the extremes of existence and of peace? [verse 31] Even so, we may still consider ourselves unequal to the task of accomplishing the welfare of all beings. But, for example, just as the son of a chakravartin, who turns the wheel of power, is able to establish others in virtue by relying on his four armies, in the same way, the Buddha, who turns the wheel of Dharma, has given to his Bodhisattva children four forces also, so that they too can accomplish the welfare of beings. These four forces are aspiration, steadfastness, joyfulness, and relinquishment (the ability to let go or desist). The latter three derive from the first, namely, aspiration, which is their root. Aspiration is based on fear of suffering (the result of negative action), and it is to be cultivated through reflecting on the benefits of liberation and the advantages of aspiring to this.

2. IMPLEMENTING THE FAVORABLE CONDITIONS FOR DILIGENCE

3. A BRIEF EXPLANATION

[verse 32] As we have just said, it is through the four forces of aspiration (a keen interest in the Dharma), self-confidence or steadfastness (whereby one does not go back on what one has begun), joyfulness (whereby one takes pleasure in what one is doing), and relinquishment (when this is called for), that we will be able to discard the three kinds of laziness and enhance our diligence. These four forces must in turn be supplemented by two kinds of strength: first, the earnest implementation of the principle of adopting and rejecting and, second, the control of one's body and mind.

3. A DETAILED EXPLANATION

4. SUMMONING THE FOUR REMEDIAL FORCES

5. THE FORCE OF ASPIRATION

[verse 33] Shantideva decides that since he cultivates bodhichitta, he will himself bring unbounded evils, the afflictions of himself and all other beings to nothing. For the purposes of abandoning any of these obscurations, he must now apply his diligence, even if each of the eighty-four thousand defilements and other faults takes many, indeed an ocean of, kalpas to exhaust. [verse 34] And yet, he reflects that in the interests of such a great enterprise, he does not find within himself even the slightest degree of diligent enterprise. Seeing that he himself must be destined to boundless sufferings in the future, he asks himself why his heart does not burst asunder. [Using this rhetorical device,] he shows how necessary it is for people to free themselves from faults.

[verse 35] In the same spirit, he says that he himself must now acquire all the innumerable spiritual qualities related to the path and result, both for himself and others, even if a single one of them (such as the different kinds of preternatural vision and knowledge) takes countless ages to attain. [verse 36] And once again he reflects that he has never possessed the kind of endeavor necessary for achieving even a fragment of such qualities. How strange it is, he comments ironically, to squander this human life with its freedoms and advantages, which he has managed to achieve by the power of his karma, even though it is so rare!

[verse 37] It may be thought that his behavior has not been entirely meaningless and that at least he has managed to accomplish some virtue. But, Shantideva asks, what virtue has he ever accomplished? He has never made offerings to the Buddhas, whether in reality or through the power of his imagination. No pleasant feasts or services have been provided for the sangha through his well-intended donations. Neither has he ever done anything for the Buddha's Doctrine in the way of teaching and studying the Tripitaka or the practice of the three trainings of the path. And alas, the wishes of the destitute, the hungry, and the naked have been left unsatisfied—he has never provided them with anything substantial in the way of material aid. He has not given them anything, not even so much as a cup of tea or buttermilk. On the contrary, he has treated them with scorn. [verse 38] No protection from fear, he says, has he ever given to those in terror of their lives (by saving and ransoming them and so on). Neither has he ever comforted the wretched (who were ignorant of what to do and what not to do) with the gift of Dharma by teaching them well and bringing them to an understanding of the principle of correct conduct. His only accomplishment has been the pain he caused his mother when she carried him in her womb and when she gave him birth (at which point both she and he almost died of pain). He has utterly failed to achieve the potential of the human life that he has obtained, endowed with freedoms and advantages.

[verse 39] Shantideva concludes, therefore, that his poverty in virtue comes from his failure, both in the past and present, to aspire to the sublime Dharma, with regard to which he has been as uninterested as a dog confronted with a pile of grass. But what kind of person is it that wants happiness and yet forsakes all aspiration to the sacred Doctrine? [verse 40] Aspiration to the sacred Dharma, the Buddha has said, is the root of every virtue, whereby high rebirth and the definitive excellence of buddhahood is achieved. As it is said in the *Sagaramatiparipriccha-sutra*, "Aspiration is the root of every virtue." And we find also in *The Appearance of Manjushri's Buddhafield*,

> Everything depends upon conditions,
> And lies within the root of eager aspiration.
> Whatever prayers a person makes,
> Results in kind are surely to be reaped.

Consequently, it is those who have the keenest interest in the Dharma who will turn out to be the best practitioners. Average interest and aspiration make for an average practitioner; lesser interest will result in a practitioner of lesser capacity. Thus aspiration and interest are of capital importance, and since it is difficult to have this from the very beginning, it is necessary to cultivate it in the mind.

But nowadays people disparage themselves and doubt their ability to observe the discipline, to receive the teachings, and to reflect and meditate on them. This is how they bring themselves to ruin. We should never allow this to happen. We should not be always downward-looking like a dog on the roof of a house. Instead, we should be like a bird perched on the ground beside the house, constantly looking up. By learning how to observe the discipline, and by receiving, reflecting, and meditating on the teachings, we will gain in happiness and we will progress. To be sure, if from the very outset we had every good quality and were wholly free of defilement, there would be no point in the Dharma's being taught. But this is obviously not the case.

The root of aspiration or keen interest in the Dharma is a constant reflection and confident meditation on the fully ripened effects of positive and negative actions—knowing that these same effects are indelible and must be experienced either as happiness or as misery. [verse 41] Indeed, every physical discomfort experienced as a result of illness, heat, and cold, together with all the anxieties and sufferings of the mind, all the various perils of death, of being killed and wounded, and the pain of being separated from what one wants and of encountering what one does not want—in brief, all the sufferings of this and future lives—do not [ultimately] derive from wicked people and their cruel treatment. The cause of all of them is our own negative behavior. In making this point, Shantideva gives a general indication of the karmic law of cause and effect.

[verse 42] In particular, statements about the results of "mixed" actions (which display both good and bad aspects) are not just empty words. If our intentions and corresponding actions are wholesome, then no matter where we go (or where we are born), the merit of the virtue accomplished in the past will offer us its fully ripened fruit, namely, an abundance of happiness and good qualities. This is illustrated by the story of Prince Punyabala, who, taking up residence in a poor man's dwelling, discovered a great and inexhaustible treasure there. [verse 43] On the other hand, if we do evil in our quest for satisfaction, then no matter where we go, wherever we are born, the sharp knives of misery (the ripened effects of former evils) will cut us down and destroy us.

With regard to "mixed" actions, there are four possible permutations in which propelling and completing actions relate to each other.[165] (1) When positive propelling action is complemented by positive completing action, the result will be birth in the higher destinies in happy and comfortable conditions. (2) When both propelling and completing actions are negative, they give rise to birth in the hell realms where suffering is the only form of existence. (3) When virtuous propelling action causes one to be born in the divine realms but is completed by nonvirtuous completing action, one will be deprived of the advantages that normally accompany such a state and one will have to suffer. Finally, (4) when a negative propelling action is accompanied by positive completing action, one's destiny will be as that narrated in the story of Dzabo'i Pumo or, for example, like that of an animal that has the enjoyment of a happy and fortunate life. A nonvirtuous propelling action may result in the ephemeral hells. But if the completing action is both positive and negative (as in the case of a butcher who takes the vow not to kill during the night or a person who vows to abstain from sexual misconduct during the day), the beings in question will have to experience a corresponding alternation of happiness and suffering by day and by night in the ephemeral hells. Such a situation is described in the story of Shrona.[166] Likewise, if, as a result of positive propelling action, one is born in a human form, and if this is complemented by actions that are both positive and negative, one will have to undergo a variety of experiences of both joy and sorrow, as for instance, in the earlier and later stages of one's life.

In short, it should be understood that though one may have been born in a fortunate realm, all the experiences of happiness and suffering in one's very lifetime are the effects of virtuous and nonvirtuous acts, the same being also true of the happiness and suffering of those born in the lower realms. The effects of one's actions must all be experienced; they do not fade away and disappear.

[verse 44] The result of exclusively positive action, unadulterated with even mild negativities, will result in birth in the pure lands such as Sukhavati. In such places, the actual locus of birth is far superior to a hot womb, cramped and malodorous. For in the pure lands, one dwells in bliss within the heart of a many-colored lotus flower, spacious, fragrant, and cool to the touch. All the splendor of one's body and senses will grow and come to maturity, nourished by the nectar of the Dharma expressed by the sweet voice of the Buddha—which is indeed a form of nourishment superior to any sustenance provided by a mother and her impure mucus. Moreover, the way of being born [in Sukhavati] is also superior to the kind of parturition that exists in our world, which, on account of the narrowness of the birth canal is as painful as being dragged through an iron keyhole. The rays emanating from the Buddha will cause the lotus petals to open, and one will miraculously emerge from the fully blossoming flower, equipped with a beautiful body endowed with the major and minor marks of buddhahood. Subsequently, one will live in the presence of the Buddha Amitabha and other enlightened beings—a manner of dwelling far superior to the foul tenements of ordinary beings. And nourished by the Dharma, one will become a fortunate child of the Sugatas. All this will be the result of perfect virtue.

[verse 45] On the other hand, the result of evil action for which one has no remorse is to be devastated by suffering, the skin of one's sensitive and tender body flayed off with the blazing knives of the creatures of the Lord of Death, his terrifying workers, who pour over and into one's body liquid bronze melted in fires as dreadful as the conflagration at the end of time. And pierced by incandescent swords and knives, one's flesh will be dismembered into a hundred parts that fall upon the white-hot ground of iron. Such experience of endless terrible suffering is due to negative karma.

[verse 46] Therefore it is through having confidence in the principle of karmic cause and effect that we will abandon negative actions and aspire and tend exclusively to virtue by means of keen and focused interest. We must steep ourselves in this understanding of the principle of adopting and rejecting.

5. THE FORCE OF STEADFASTNESS

6. A GENERAL EXPLANATION

In the sixth chapter of the *Avatamsaka*, which describes the dedication of Vajradhvaja (one of the ten beings called Vajra who, coming from the ten directions, all appeared in the presence of the Buddha Vairochana) we find the following text:

> Devaputra, when the sun rises, it is not dismayed by the fact that some men are blind nor by the mountain shadows that it is unable to dispel. No, it sheds light on all that can be illuminated. In the same way, when Bodhisattvas appear for the sake of beings, they are not dismayed by the fact that some are wild and hostile. They bring to maturity and liberate all those who are capable of liberation.

It is therefore with this kind of courage, as described in the *Vajradhvaja-sutra*, that we must cultivate an assured confidence and determination, telling ourselves that we will bring to completion whatever positive action we have begun for the sake of others.

[verse 47] First, as Shantideva says, we must take stock of our resources (in both spiritual and temporal terms) and begin or hold back according to whether we can or cannot complete the given action. For if we are unable, it is better not to begin at all. Once we have begun, however, we must never turn back from what we have promised.

[verse 48] The reason for this is that if we act in this way (dropping our studies, for example, or abandoning our practice in retreat), the effect similar to the cause will be the habitual tendency (in this and future lives) to fail to complete the good deeds we have begun. The proliferating effect of the breaking of our pledge to virtuous practice will make for an increase in negativity. As for the fully ripened effect, the result will be an increase in suffering. And if, before finishing the action we have begun, we embark upon something else, the result will be that we will fail to complete both the earlier and the later actions. And at the time of harvest, the fruit will be meager.

[verse 49] Therefore we must apply or cultivate a sense of courageous self-confidence[167] with respect to three things: the action, the affliction, and our ability. First, we must decide that we ourselves will accomplish the task. Second, we must tell ourselves that we will not succumb to defiled emotion. Third, we must assure ourselves that we are able to do it, reflecting that we are indeed able to discard all faults and accomplish every excellent quality. However, this sense of courageous self-worth is not to be cultivated in the preparatory stages. It is for the time when we are already engaged in the task and have started to flag and become weary of it.

6. An explanation of specific points

7. Cultivating a feeling of self-confidence with regard to the task

Consider the following example, which is also taken from the *Avatamsaka:*

> The outer palace of the sun, O Devaputra, which is material, has no choice but to do its work of illuminating the four continents all by itself. It is unobstructed by cloud, dust, or wind, and it sheds its light impartially over everything. And although all beings place their hope in it, the sun for its part has no need

to rely on anything. In the same way, I, a Bodhisattva skilled in emptiness and the means of great compassion, will bring to maturity and liberation all beings, whose number is as limitless as space itself. And I will do this by myself alone! I shall be impeded by none of the faults or defects of beings, wild and barbarous as they are. I will become the great and unknown friend of every being. Though they may place their hopes in me, I do not place my hopes in them.

It is the cultivation of this kind of determination and courage that constitutes the feeling of self-confidence with regard to the task.

[verse 50] Overwhelmed by their afflictions, worldly beings, whose deeds and wishes are constantly at war with each other, are unable even to secure their own happiness in this present life. Therefore, Shantideva reflects, they are unable to secure the happiness of all beings, as he, a Bodhisattva, is able to do. This indeed will be his chosen task. He will labor for the sake of the happiness of himself and others.

[verse 51] When others give themselves to low activities (confounding their enemies, protecting their friends, and indulging in farming and trade), how, Shantideva asks, can he connive as their companion? Such a course of action would be quite inappropriate. Instead, he should practice the six paramitas of the way of the Bodhisattvas.

Alternatively, Shantideva's words could be interpreted as meaning that, when others are engaged in the mundane activities of making hay, chopping wood, carrying loads, and so on, how can he idly stand by? It is not at all correct. On the contrary, he should give help to people in everything that does not involve negative action—just as Dromtönpa carried the luggage of an old tantrika and the Indian master Padampa Sangye did the same for the yellow-bearded acharya.

But whichever interpretation we follow, we should not have the pride of thinking that our actions make us superior to others. To rid ourselves of such ordinary conceit is the best of Bodhisattva practices.

7. Cultivating a feeling of self-confidence with regard to one's abilities

[verse 52] When they find a dead snake, even crows behave like eagles soaring in the sky, and they contemptuously devour it. In the same way, if we have a very low estimate of ourselves and our abilities—in other words, if our antidote is of little strength—we will [like the dead snake] be vulnerable to injury even on the part of small misdemeanors, which will be able to harm us by driving us down into the lower realms as though they were much more serious downfalls. [verse 53] Because of their weak determination, people like us think that they are unable to practice virtue and to avoid sin. And being discouraged, they abandon every effort in this direction. As a result, they never get the better of their miserable condition whether in this or future lives.

But those who stand their ground, proudly resolved, with determination and diligent perseverance—confessing what is to be confessed with a firm promise of amendment—cannot be defeated even by serious root downfalls. The latter will be powerless to send them to the lower realms. As it is said in the *Mahaguhyaupayakaushalya-sutra:* "Bodhisattvas who are wise in emptiness and skilled in the methods of compassion will not be defeated even by serious downfalls, just like holders of the vidya-mantras, who are able to deliver themselves as they wish from the fetters of the five enchantments."

[verse 54] And so, Shantideva cries, with a steadfast heart confident in his abilities, he will get the better of his failings, the downfalls that are to be discarded. For if he allows himself to be defeated by his own weaknesses, his wish to attain buddhahood, to gain victory over all the defilements in the three worlds, is laughable indeed. [verse 55] And so, he says, he will be the victor over all the defilements of the three worlds. Against him, no afflictions shall prevail. For he is the offspring of the Conqueror, the Lion among men, who has gained the victory over the four demons and has acquired the power of the four fearlessnesses. He will therefore maintain a self-assured confidence in his ability, thanks to which no defiled emotion will be able to get the better of him.

[verse 56] We may well wonder why it is taught here that we should cultivate this sense of pride and self-worth when pride is something that we had been told to abandon at an earlier stage. Indeed beings in the three worlds who are ruined by their pride and arrogance are defiled and miserable creatures. They are in fact completely devoid of the self-confidence that Bodhisattvas have in respect of their abilities. To be sure, if they had *this* kind of self-confidence, which is an antidote, they would not fall beneath the power of their enemy: the kind of pride that is an affliction. For people who are proud in the ordinary sense of the word have fallen into the power of their enemy—the kind of pride that is a defilement.

[verse 57] What fault is involved when one falls into the power of pride? When the mind is puffed up with arrogance, it draws beings down to the states of misery or, failing this, destroys any happiness and joy of the human condition should this be gained. For one will take rebirth as a slave or a servant, wholly dependent on the gifts of others for one's sustenance. Alternatively, one will be born as stupid as a pig, not knowing what to adopt and what to reject. Or again, one will have an unsightly appearance, looking as ugly as a toad, or emaciated and weak. [verse 58] And even if one is not actually harmed, one will be despised like an old dog, the butt and laughingstock of everyone. Those whose minds are puffed up with conceit—those "ascetics" who are able to live without tasting the food of the sublime Dharma—*they* are the ones who are the real objects of contempt. Although they are unable to cultivate true Bodhisattva pride, if they are numbered among the stable ones (those who have self-confidence regarding their ability), then, Shantideva exclaims, whom shall we call wretched?

[verse 59] The offspring of the Conqueror, who maintain a stable self-confidence (the antidote that overturns the enemy of afflictive pride) are the ones who are truly proud [in the positive sense] and worthy of praise. For they are heroes who have vanquished their foe, the pride that is a defilement. Those who have true self-confidence in their ability overwhelm completely the mighty force that holds the three worlds in its power—the thought of "I." And thus, according to their wish, they are able to offer to beings the perfect fruit of buddhahood. It is in this way that Shantideva praises the qualities of a healthy sense of self-worth that is the antidote [to pride].

7. CULTIVATING A SENSE OF SELF-CONFIDENCE WITH REGARD TO THE AFFLICTIVE EMOTIONS

[verse 60] When one keeps the company of attractive people, desire will grow; when one is with hateful people, anger develops. When therefore we find ourselves in dangerous situations in which there are abundant stimulants for the afflictions, we should cultivate the antidotes to them with a proportionate intensity and we should stand up to them in a thousand ways. For example, just as a lion cannot be injured by a fox, we should ensure that our minds are proof against the onslaught of the afflictions. It is said that the best practitioners use as the path the very object that gives rise to the afflictions. Average practitioners apply the antidotes and hold their ground. By contrast, practitioners of a more basic capacity must abandon such objects and retreat.

[verse 61] However difficult may be the circumstances in which they find themselves, even when their lives are threatened, people will instinctively protect their eyes, their most cherished possession. In the same way, and regardless of the dangers, we must protect ourselves from falling into the power of the afflictions of desire and anger. [verse 62] Therefore, we may be burned to death or decapitated with a sword (this is of comparatively minor importance), but at no time must we allow ourselves to bow and scrape before our enemies, our defilements. From the very first, we must take an earnest and determined pledge never to allow ourselves to be stained by defiled emotion. In every circumstance of time and place, we shall only act properly, and never in a manner that is inappropriate.

5. THE FORCE OF JOY

[verse 63] Small children delight in their games, and they do not expect any reward for what they do whether now or in the life to come. They want only the simple joy of play, and they never have enough of it. This is exactly how Bodhisattvas should be in whatever they do for the sake of others—acts of generosity or any of the other paramitas. They ought not to expect any reward for what they do. Indeed, they should be devoted to their tasks with ever greater intensity. They should never be satisfied, but take the most intense pleasure and exhilaration from what they do.

[verse 64] In a bid for happiness and contentment, worldly people toil strenuously in their work of farming or commerce. But success is very far from certain. For how can they gain happiness if they act negatively, if they fail to perform the virtuous deeds of the Bodhisattvas, such as generosity and discipline, from which happiness derives? Unhappiness is their destiny in this and future lives.

[verse 65] There is little profit and indeed great danger in the enjoyment of the five objects of pleasure (forms and so forth). Indeed, it is like licking honey on the edge of an extremely sharp razor. We are attached to the transient pleasure that comes from the coincidence of an object and its corresponding consciousness. We have a powerful craving for such gratification and enjoy it again and again. It is like drinking salty water; we never have enough of it.

But if we can never have enough of pleasure, how can we ever have enough of the Bodhisattva's tasks? For they are like nectar, are of the greatest profit, and are completely without danger. They cause us to accumulate wisdom and merit and bring us to the fully ripened effect of human and celestial happiness in higher realms and thence to the ultimate result of buddhahood, the state of peace in which every pain and suffering subsides. We ought never to be satisfied.

[verse 66] Therefore, with a view to completing whatever aspect of the Bodhisattva's activities we have undertaken, we ought to be like elephants in the noontime sun in summer, when they are tormented by heat and thirst and catch sight of a cool lake. They throw themselves into the water with the greatest pleasure and without a moment's hesitation. In just the same way, for the sake of ourselves and others, we should give ourselves joyfully to the practice of generosity and other virtues.

5. The force of relinquishment

[verse 67] If our strength is impaired by weakness or fatigue (due to exhaustion or illness) and we are unable to accomplish some activity, we should resolve to lay it aside for the time being, the better to resume it at some later stage. And when the task we intended and have begun is brought to completion, we should not rest on our laurels, thinking that we have done enough. Instead we should relinquish all tasks that have been accomplished and look forward eagerly to doing even greater things.

4. Cultivating the two strengths

5. The strength of earnest practice

[verse 68] With regard to the earnest practice of carefulness, it is just as when seasoned fighters, confronting the swords of their enemies on the line of battle, avoid the weapons of their adversaries and crush them down instead. In the same way, we must dodge the sharp weapons of the defilements and overcome and vanquish these foes so that they do not harm us.

[verse 69] When it comes to the earnest practice of mindfulness, it is as when a soldier drops his sword in battle. He quickly snatches it up again for fear of being killed. In the same way, if the weapon of mindfulness is lost and if, carried away by inattention, we forget the antidote, we must quickly recover and strive to implement it, fearful of falling under the power of the afflictions and the ensuing infernal destiny.

[verse 70] When one is struck by a poisoned arrow, the venom, carried on the bloodstream, seeps through the body with fatal effects. In just the same way, when the senses are carried away toward their objects and when even a small affliction gets its chance to attack our minds, greater afflictions are able to spread through the mind and destroy the life of the happy destinies.

[verse 71] Let us conduct ourselves therefore like a man walking with a jar brimming with oil, threatened by a swordsman with death if he spills a single drop! Such a person will be terrified and will walk with the greatest care. It is thus that those who have entered the door of the Dharma and who keep the vows should hold themselves—in great fear of the hells and the three worlds of samsara. They should bind themselves in body, speech, and mind with mindfulness, vigilant introspection, and carefulness, without ever falling into the power of the afflictions. Here, it has been said that one should, in addition, consider the story of Katyayana.

[verse 72] Even minor faults can be productive of great harm. Therefore just as a beautiful woman with her hair on fire will race to put it out or a nervous man will jump with fright on finding a snake coiled in his lap, if we sink into lethargy and sleepiness (in the evening or early morning), we should get up from our seats at once and shake them off. We should make a promise to ourselves that we will do this. For example, when the great translator Rinchen Zangpo was in strict retreat for seven years, he established three boundaries for himself—outer, inner, and intermediate—and he enjoined the dakinis and the dharmapalas as follows. If (for the outer boundary) a single defiled emotion were to arise in his mind; if (for the intermediate boundary) a single selfish thought were to arise; and if (for the inner boundary) a single dualistic thought were to appear, the dakinis and dharmapalas were to take away his heart and life.

It is said that it is of great importance to make firm promises and to be determined accordingly. [verse 73] In the midst of such efforts, on the occasions that we fail, we must reprove and chide ourselves in all manner of ways. We must lengthily reflect that, by whatever means necessary, such faults shall never occur again. And we should strive in amending them.

[verse 74] At all times, over the months and years, and in any situation, we should ask ourselves how we can acquire the habitual attitude of mindfulness, whereby we never forget to focus on virtue within our minds. Thinking only of the causes or methods of cultivating it, we should long for, and strive in, appropriate actions—all the ways that help us nourish and increase mindfulness and introspection within ourselves: meeting with spiritual masters, doing retreat, going on pilgrimages, and all such conducive practices. According to Sherab Jungne,[168] the strength of earnest practice [as discussed above] means the sincere implementation of the instructions received from the teacher.

5. THE STRENGTH OF CONTROLLING BODY, SPEECH, AND MIND

[verse 75] By every means then, before embarking on any of our virtuous works and in order to be able to complete them all, we must reflect on the precepts to be implemented. And we should keep in mind the teachings described above, which show how we are to rely on carefulness. Then with a light heart we should apply ourselves to the task in hand swiftly and with pleasure.

[verse 76] This is necessary because, just as flax wafts readily back and forth, moved by the power of the wind, likewise our body, speech, and mind are inevitably influenced when we take pleasure in virtue. It is thus that every good action, undertaken with enthusiasm, will be perfectly achieved.

Here ends the seventh chapter from the *Bodhicharyavatara*, on diligence.

· 8 ·

MEDITATIVE
CONCENTRATION

*Whereby Precious Relative
Bodhichitta Is Intensified*

1. A BRIEF EXPLANATION OF HOW THIS CHAPTER IS RELATED TO THE PREVIOUS ONES

[verse 1] It is written in the *Shikshasamucchaya:*

> Cultivate forbearance, seek the teachings,
> Then in the forest take up your abode.
> In meditative equipoise exert yourself,
> And contemplate repulsiveness and other things.

As it is stated in verse 74 of the previous chapter, it is necessary to rely on a spiritual teacher: to listen to his or her instructions, to reflect, and then to meditate, on them. And Maitreya, the regent of the Buddha, also says in the *Sutralankara* that if it were unnecessary to hear and study the teachings, the Tripitaka and all the doctrines of the Conqueror would be pointless. If there were no need to meditate upon the meaning of what one has heard, then the meditation of all the holy beings who have appeared in the past would likewise have been in vain. This however is not the case. It is first by listening to the teachings that we should make a concerted effort to discover what we should practice or meditate upon; then we should steep oneself in it. Therefore, as was stated earlier, we must cultivate diligence, eating with moderation and reducing the measure of our sleep. Then we should one-pointedly concentrate on the object of meditation, narrowly focusing our minds and not allowing ourselves to be distracted by other things.

What happens if we fail to concentrate? A person whose mind is slack and left to drift to the objects of the six consciousnesses is like a scrap of food caught between the fangs of demons, namely, the defilements of attachment and hatred. It is certain that people who leave their minds to their own devices will lose whatever spiritual qualities they may have. The essence of liberation will be destroyed, and suffering will be the only outcome.

1. A FULL EXPLANATION OF CONDITIONS CONDUCIVE TO MEDITATIVE CONCENTRATION

2. A BRIEF SUMMARY

[verse 2] How are we to rid ourselves of distraction? We must renounce the company of many people and retreat far from the bustle of worldly affairs. Giving up all hankering for the objects of our desires, we should keep ourselves far from thoughts related to the events of the past, present, and future. It is by such means that all manner of outer and inner distractions are prevented from manifesting.

If we want to give up the afflictions, we *must* give up distractions, and in order to do this, we must have recourse to solitude, which means to distance ourselves from two kinds of object. On the physical level, we must relinquish all attachment to the affairs and meaningless doings of the world. On the mental level, we must completely put a stop to the mind's wandering toward the objects of the senses, and we should train ourselves in concentration. And for this, it is necessary to be alone. For the company of even one person will result in obstacles to concentration. If we really want to train in concentration, we must stay in solitude, alone, and without our friends.

2. A DETAILED EXPLANATION

3. RELINQUISHING THE WORLD

4. WHY THE WORLD SHOULD BE ABANDONED

[verse 3] It is because of attachment to our loved ones and because of our desire for property, and so on, that we do not give up—that we cannot give up—the distracting activities of worldly life. Therefore someone who is wise, who has managed to relinquish attachment and desire, and who has received and reflects on the teachings on what to do and what not to do should practice as follows. [verse 4] It is said in the *Dharmasangiti-sutra*, "When the mind is placed in meditative equipoise, one can see things perfectly, as they are." Accordingly, when the states of movement and stillness in the mind have been brought under control, the mind remains one-pointedly in the state characterized by the bliss that arises from its perfect flexibility. That is, it dwells in the "all-sufficing preparatory stage"[169] to the first samadhi and so on. This is the concentration of calm abiding or shamatha. When this is united with penetrative insight or vipashyana, the wisdom that understands the ultimate mode of being of phenomena, the afflictive states will be utterly banished, together with their seeds and habitual tendencies.

Knowing this, we should first pursue, or rather accomplish, through the application of many methods, the calm abiding of the mind. This concentration of calm abiding, which is the cause or basis of penetrative insight, is achieved by those who renounce attachment to the world (in the sense both of possessions and of other beings), who dwell in solitude, and who train in concentration with unfeigned joy. No one else can manage it. The unfailing way to engage gradually in the perfect path has been described by Vasubandhu, the second Buddha:

> Observe the discipline. Listen and reflect upon the teachings.
> Then apply yourself to meditation.

And he also said, "Wisdom is both the cause and the effect of concentration." The protector Nagarjuna has likewise declared:

> Where there is no wisdom, neither is there concentration;
> Where there is no concentration, wisdom there is none.
> All those endowed with both will quaff
> The ocean of existence in a single drop.

And in the *Purnaparipriccha-sutra* it is said:

If thus you wish to rid yourself of the afflictions,
Rid yourself of all your goods.
Once rid of them, remain in perfect solitude
And meditate on emptiness.

4. GIVING UP ATTACHMENT TO BEINGS

[verse 5] Because no one is permanent and everlasting, people find themselves in a situation in which, being impermanent themselves, they are strongly attached to what is also ephemeral, namely, their relatives and friends. It is not wise to be attached in this way because those who have such longings will [inevitably] lose the happiness of seeing those they love—and this is a separation that lasts not just for a few moments, but for thousands of lives. [verse 6] Even when they are only temporarily separated from their beloved companions, they have no happiness of mind. Brooding upon their situation, they are disturbed and are incapable of remaining in a balanced, concentrated state. And even if they do meet and see their friends, they still find no satisfaction. For as before, they are made unhappy by their attachment and longing. As it is written in the *Lalitavishtara-sutra*:

Taking pleasure in the things you want,
Like drinking salty water, quenches no desire.

[verse 7] When we long and crave for other beings (friends and relatives), a veil is cast upon the perfect truth and we fail to see it. The wholesome sense of disillusionment and sadness that we once possessed with regard to the sorrows of samsara melts away and does not return. And finally, when those who are dear to us abandon us or die, we are left with an agony of suffering. [verse 8] For our thoughts are all for them, our longed-for friends, and thus our lives pass by in vain. No virtue is accomplished, and our lives are spent in negativity and pain. All our families and friends fade and pass; nevertheless, the attachment that we feel for them undermines all practice of the Dharma, the means whereby the unsurpassable state of immutability or indestructibility is attained.

[verse 9] [In Tibetan,] the word "child" (*byis pa*) is used in three senses, depending on whether it describes a condition contrasted with older people,

with Aryas (the noble ones), or with those who are wise and learned.[170] In the ninth verse, the word is used in the second and particularly the third senses, the point being that, if we act childishly—physically, verbally, and mentally like ordinary, foolish beings—it is certain that we shall fall. We shall be reborn in the lower realms.

Why associate with foolish beings who behave like children, when they lead us into states of desire and a lack of contentment with what we have? We become disinclined to study or to spurn defilement, and we cut ourselves off from the lineage of the Aryas—those who rely on the ragged robe, on little food, and on solitude. Having few desires, the latter are satisfied with little; and they take delight in study and in ridding themselves of defilement. It is thus that our present and future existences are brought to ruin by consorting with childish people.

[verse 10] Such associates have no constancy of mind, and are always in search of something new. They are loving friends at one moment and bitter enemies the next. When you try to urge them to virtue, the source of happiness, they get irritated and reject it. If you are rich in Dharma and ordinary possessions (things at which friends ought normally to rejoice), they are resentful and jealous. No matter what you do, it is hard to please ordinary people.

[verse 11] If, with the best of intentions, you tell them to practice the Dharma—something that will do them good both in this and future lives—not only do they refuse to listen, but they lose their tempers. They say that they *can't*, and anyway they have no time. All they do is dissuade you from the right course (the practice of Dharma) by talking a great deal and creating all sorts of obstacles. If you turn a deaf ear to what they say, they get angry, which will only bring them down to the lower realms.

[verse 12] When in the company of their peers, childish people are jealous. They cannot stand anyone better than themselves. They vie and compete with their equals, and they arrogantly ignore or poke fun at those who are below them. If they are praised, they become conceited and pretentious. If they hear unpleasant references to their own defects, they seethe with rage. What good was ever to be had from consorting with such childish people?

[verse 13] If we are not Aryas, we are childish (that is, ordinary) beings. And if we consort with other childish beings, every kind of vice is sure to follow. Whether directly or indirectly, there will be self-aggrandizement and contempt for others. There will be talk about "the good things of samsara." We will find ourselves protecting the people we find attractive and getting the better of those we dislike. We will get involved in business and farming, discussing horses and livestock, provisions, clothing, and other commodities. Even chance meetings at the corner of the street can elicit nonvirtuous behavior, cold looks, and harsh expressions. [verse 14] Only an increase of negativity, only the ruin of this and future lives can be the result of such connections. Relationships with such people bring us no benefit either now or in the future, and we in turn are incapable of doing any good to them. [verse 15] We should therefore intend to avoid the company of childish friends, relatives, and the other intimates whom we like, and we should aspire to stay in solitude, alone and far away from them. There is a saying that goes:

> The love of our relations is a sign of the celestial demon.
> Meeting our dear friends is the demon who cuts down our
> virtuous deeds.
> Talking is the treasure-house of sin, the door of faults and
> downfalls.

And according to another saying, "In lonely, unfrequented places, all one's works are virtuous." Reflecting thus on the defects resulting from associating with friends and on the good qualities of resorting to solitude, we should take to heart what Milarepa said:

> When I'm sick, there's no one who will fret for me;
> When I die, there's no one who will weep.
> If in this mountain solitude I die,
> The wishes of this yogi will have been fulfilled!

If it happens that we meet friends and relatives while in the solitude of the mountains, we should greet them merrily—that is, with pleasant speech and other gestures just for that one occasion, without inviting any kind of lasting relationship whether of affection or resentment. We should keep on terms of pleasant courtesy, free from either attachment or aversion.

It is said in the *Uposatha of Vishvabhukra* (the third in the sequence of the seven Buddhas):

Like a bee that does not harm
The blossom's scent or hue
But sips the nectar and departs:
That's how the Sage goes into town.

[verse 16] As the text says, if there is a need to visit a village, whether in search of alms (our necessities in terms of food and clothes) or in order to read the scriptures and perform ceremonies, we should be like bees that can take the nectar from the flower without disturbing its color or perfume and fly away again without attachment. We should take only a few possessions in the way of food and clothing and only what is consonant with the Dharma, treating those who help us like first-time acquaintances, without encouraging familiarity, the source of both attachment and aversion.

Longchenpa, the omniscient lord of Dharma, has said:

In towns or monasteries, lonely places, forest groves,
Wherever you may be, seek not for friends.
Whoever you are with, keep to yourself.
No attachment, no resentment: That's the counsel of my
    heart.

That is surely a piece of advice we should follow. But what usually happens nowadays is that lamas act as though their benefactors were their private property. And benefactors do the same with regard to the lamas whom they sponsor. How can they possibly be of benefit to beings and the Doctrine? What we need to do is to give up the eight worldly concerns and actions motivated by attachment and anger. For these will destroy us in this and future lives. We need to establish ourselves firmly in solitude, alone and without company! It has been said that Shantideva's words "Take only what will serve the practice of the Dharma" can also be interpreted as referring to the essence of the teachings received from one's teacher.

4. GIVING UP ATTACHMENT TO WORLDLY GAIN

[verse 17] We may think, "I'm rich; I have a horse, money, things to enjoy myself with. What's more, I'm well regarded. People look up to me; I have followers and benefactors who appreciate me." But if we nourish this kind of complacency in our lives (grabbing whatever we can lay our hands on:

the offerings of the faithful, the money given for performing ceremonies for the dead and so forth), later on, after we ourselves are dead, we will experience all the fears and sufferings of the lower realms in our later lives. We ought to reflect about the life story of Lama Tanakchen from Tsang[171] and conduct ourselves prudently and with care.

As a general principle, the Buddha taught that monastic religious property may be used by noble beings on the path of no-more-learning as though it were their own property. Those who are still on the path of learning may regard it as something gifted to them. Ordinary beings who are nevertheless endowed with the qualities of knowledge and freedom [from defilement] may use it as beneficiaries of something granted by dispensation. On the other hand, when other beings, who are without wisdom and liable to indolence (but who observe nevertheless the monastic discipline) avail themselves of it, it is as though they were contracting a karmic debt. Finally, in the case of those who are degenerate in their discipline, it is as if they were swallowing incandescent balls of iron.

[verse 18] Shantideva upbraids his own mind, saying that it is besotted and fettered with ego-clinging, it thinks in terms of "I" and "you," and it strays to the objects of the senses. Whatever his mind craves, especially meat and alcohol, women, tobacco, provisions offered by the faithful, wealth offered on behalf of the dead—it is all extremely negative. He implies that the more one craves it, the greater the fault. For if, in this life, one drinks a hundred bowls of tea or a hundred bowls of beer belonging to the monastic order, it will all turn to suffering in the next life, when it will be multiplied a thousandfold (for every bowl drunk, one will have to swallow a thousand bowls of molten bronze). One will have to suffer in the lives to come, much as one is obliged to pay off old letters of credit. However small may be the cause, the result will be great. Such is the inconceivable principle of causes and their ripened effects.

[verse 19] This being so, a wise person, aware of what is to be implemented and what is to be avoided, craves neither possessions nor position. For it is from such cravings that fear and anguish arise in this and future lives. And anyway, all that people wish for—wealth, honor, and so on—will, by its very nature, fade away to nothing. This is certain. We should fix this truth in our minds: Nothing is stable and abiding. [verse 20] For indeed, we may well gain a wealth of riches and enjoy a good reputation and pleasant renown. But in the end, who is to say where we will have to go, with all the baggage of our money and fame? The outcome is far from certain!

[verse 21] What reason do we have to feel pleased when people praise us, given that there are always others who criticize us disagreeably and hold us in contempt? Their criticism dampens whatever pleasure we might feel. Conversely, if pleasant appreciation does come our way, why be despondent at the criticisms of others? The appreciation that others might show to us makes us feel less downcast.

[verse 22] It could perhaps be argued that we ought to try to please everyone and make them happy. As a result, absolutely no one will blame us; everyone will praise us. But beings have accumulated various karmas, and consequently they have various aspirations and interests. Not even the perfect Buddha, free as he was from every defect and endowed with every excellence, was able to please everyone! He failed to satisfy Bharadaja and the brahmin's daughter Gochali, the six non-Buddhist teachers, as well as Devadatta and Sunakshatra. This being so, it is hardly necessary to point out that pitiable creatures like ourselves will be powerless to please everyone. Therefore, we should give up any desire to be on pleasant terms with the world—we should abandon our fixation on the eight worldly concerns and our desire for the company of childish beings. We should leave human companionship behind and remain in solitude.

[verse 23] The poor and weak, who have nothing, are usually an object of contempt. People regard them as miserable and without merit, unable even to make their living as servants. By contrast, although it would be consistent for such people to praise the rich, they do not do so. Instead they criticize the wealthy who are fortunate and have lots of attendants, and say unpleasant things to them—asking sarcastic questions about whether they will be able to take their possessions with them to their next lives or whether they will try to bribe the Lord of Death with them, and wondering what they will do with all that they have! Logically, such people ought to praise the poor. But they do not; they revile them instead. What joy can possibly come from keeping company with such individuals, people who are completely perverse and who are so difficult to please and to be with?

[verse 24] What is the reason for avoiding the company of childish beings? Unless they have their way in everything, they are not happy. They are unwilling to give even food and drink to others unless it is in their own interest, whether now or in the future. Shantideva advises us to shy away from making friends with such people who are interested solely in their own advantage. This indeed is what the Tathagata has said, as we find in the text entitled *Engaging in the Objects of All the Sugatas:*

No joy will come to you
From company with savage beasts.
Likewise, in the company of childish beings,
No happiness will come to you.

Similarly, it is written in the *Samadhiraja-sutra:*

However long you dance attendance on the childish,
You will get no friendship in return; they will think ill of you.
Once they grasp the nature of such childish folk,
The wise and prudent shun their company.

There are many other quotations to the same effect.

4. ONCE ONE HAS RELINQUISHED ALL ATTACHMENTS, ONE SHOULD RELY ON THE EXCELLENT QUALITIES OF SOLITUDE

[verse 25] We should, [as practitioners,] aspire to live in solitary places away from the society of human beings, in the mountains or in pleasant forests (the dwelling place of so many learned and accomplished beings) where we will have only birds and animals for company. We should aim to live among the trees, where there is no jarring dissension, no flattery, no criticism, no scorn, and where, however long we stay, we need not worry about irritating our excellent and easygoing companions. "When," Shantideva exclaims, "might I make my dwelling there amid that pleasant company?"

[verse 26] When might we too be able to settle in deserted places, caves, or empty shrines that are the property of no one or under pleasant trees—places that are the heart's delight? When will we be definitively free from backward glances and second thoughts about the future? When will we be also free from anticipation and the making of plans for more than a day ahead, or else a month, or at worst, a year, without attachment for our dwelling place, our bodies, or possessions? [verse 27] When might we be able to live alone in solitary regions, unowned and therefore undisputed by anyone, in the bosom of nature that is wide, delightful, and unconfined, which we can enjoy freely and where we can wander and remain at will, being released from all dependency, free from all sense of ownership and consequent attachment? [verse 28] When might we be able to live alone, with only a clay begging bowl and a few possessions of no value, dressed in cotton rags found on the rubbish heap and unwanted by anyone else—without the need to hide either ourselves or our belongings for fear of thieves and predators, unafraid of being seen or harmed?

[verse 29] And specifically with regard to our state of mind, although we are not living in a charnel ground, we might well nourish the aspiration that, on our occasional visits to such places, we might be able to regard our own living bodies as the equal of the corpses lying there, recently dead or old and decomposed, as well as all the skeletons—remembering that our bodies too are subject to destruction in just the same way. This is how we should reflect on impermanence and upon the unclean nature of our bodies, and develop a determination to free ourselves from samsara.

When we look at corpses, blue and rotting, we should reflect that they were once owned and cherished, and that, like our own bodies now, they were unable to bear with heat, cold, and disease. We should consider that the corpses are like our own bodies; they are exactly the same kind of thing. And we need to remember that, however alive they may seem now, however much we cherish them, and however much they are sensitive to illness and the extremes of heat and cold, our bodies are at no time different in nature from the corpses that we see. We should call to mind that our bodies are just the same as the corpses—and we should meditate and become accustomed to this idea.

[verse 30] We should also reflect and meditate on the fact that this body of ours, which now seems so alive, will die and rot. It will give out such a stench that even jackals and wolves (which normally devour meat regardless of whether it is clean or filthy) will not even come near, much less anyone else. That is our body's destiny; and it will not be long in coming. [verse 31] This body of ours, which now seems so whole and entire, which was born from our mother's womb—this flesh and bone that life has knit together—will fall apart. When we die, it will disintegrate.

This being so, there is no need to add that [in human relationships] friend will depart from friend, relation from relation. We should indeed remember that everything that is now united will finally separate. [verse 32] We are born alone. Alone we come into the world, and when we die, we will go forth alone. The root of all the sufferings of the three worlds of samsara lies in birth and death. No one is able to share in the sufferings we feel when we are born and when we die—none of our intimate companions are able to experience it and take it upon them. We are the only ones to feel it. Therefore of what avail are our relatives and friends—who create obstacles to our virtuous practice of ethical discipline, to our learning and study, and to the approach and accomplishment phases of our practice in retreat? Such relationships are by no means indispensable.

[verse 33] Like travelers on a long journey, who from time to time halt along the way and take lodging in inns and guest houses, only to leave again and continue on their road, beings on the pathways of the world (ignorant of whence they have come and of whither they will go) all halt and seize upon the lodging of their birth. Those who now have been born into the human state are attached to their condition and do not want to leave it and go elsewhere. But whether they like it or not, the Lord of Death will soon be upon them, and he will take them to the next life, unwilling but powerless to resist. At that moment, as the *Rajavavadaka-sutra* has described, [verse 34] worldly folk (their family and friends) will all cry out, "My poor father! My poor mother!" and their eyes will fill with tears. They will tear their hair in sorrow, as the body is carried by four men from the house to the charnel ground.

Shantideva resolves that, until that moment comes, he will go away into the forest far from human company and devote his efforts to virtuous practice, the one thing that will be of help at the moment of death. [verse 35] There, "with no befriending or begrudging," he says, he will stay in solitude. Because his family considers him as someone already dead, they have ceased to harbor any expectations in his regard. This being so, his death will be a source of pain and grief to none. [verse 36] Moreover, if he stays alone in solitude, there will be no one, no Dharma friends with him to be upset and mourn his passing, and he himself will not be troubled by their pain. In such solitude, there will be no one to distract him from the thought of the Buddha and the Dharma and from performing the practice at the time of death. Consequently, he will die in peace, in a virtuous state of mind. As it is said in the sutra:

> Since you live a good and blameless life,
> And are grown used to virtuous deeds,
> When death arrives, you will not suffer,
> For it will be like fleeing from a burning house.

[verse 37] Solitude has so many advantages. Shantideva reflects that in the beautiful, gleaming forest, there is no need to care about housekeeping, no need to think about flattering important people or protecting the lowly. He will have few worries. He will have ease of body and happiness of mind. Indeed, solitude confers its own blessing, namely, the fact that the distractions of body, speech, and mind naturally subside. There, he says, he will remain alone forever.

[verse 38] Abandoning all other aspirations and wishes and all unvirtuous and even neutral states of mind that focus on this present life and are concerned with self-enrichment, the gaining of religious offerings, the overcoming of enemies, or the protecting of friends, Shantideva resolves to watch his mind and bring it under control. This will be his only concern. He will strive in the profound meditation of the union of shamatha and vipashyana: the former to still his mind in the even state of calm abiding, the latter to subdue it with penetrative insight.

3. GIVING UP WANDERING THOUGHTS

4. A BRIEF EXPOSITION

In general, there are many teachings for the discarding of wandering thoughts. Indeed, the entire *Bodhicharyavatara* is devoted to it. The patience chapter deals with the specific remedy for anger and the wisdom chapter expounds the antidote to ignorance. The present chapter on meditative concentration sets forth the antidote to desire and attachment.

[verse 39] In this and any other world (in other words, in this and future lives), desire for lovers, for possessions, and so on, is the fertile parent of all suffering. On account of a woman or material gain, a man may be killed by others, imprisoned and bound with iron chains, his limbs wounded and cut with swords. As the saying goes, "Joyful though the act may be, the price is paid in tears"—paid, in other words, in the next life, in the experience of the boundless pains of the hell realms and the states of pretas and animals.

4. A DETAILED EXPLANATION

5. ABANDONING ONE'S CRAVING FOR A LOVER

6. THE DIFFICULTIES MEN GO TO IN ORDER TO ACQUIRE A WOMAN

[verse 40] In order to possess a woman, a man may make use of numerous go-betweens, both male and female, with many invitations for the prize, avoiding in the quest no sin—not even the slaying of parents—no breach of vows and samayas, no actions that might ruin his reputation. For the destruction of vows in this life results in widespread disgrace in the eyes of others. Vow-breakers are despised by humans and spirits alike. Nevertheless, such a person will give no consideration to these difficulties, eagerly ready even to put up with hunger and thirst. [verse 41] He cheerfully takes appalling risks, making himself the target of physical attack and bringing suffering on himself in this and future lives. For he could be killed and then could burn in the fires of hell.

It is hardly necessary to say that none of the food, clothes, accoutrements, goods, and wealth; none of the offerings made generally by the faithful or those made on behalf of the dead (which he has accumulated with such greed and avarice) will be offered to the Three Jewels or used for religious purposes: the making of paintings and other representations of the enlightened body, speech, and mind. None of it will be offered in charity. The person in question will not even feed or clothe himself properly. All will be squandered in gifts for his lady-friend, for the sake of the bliss of that uttermost embrace of what in truth [verse 42] is nothing but a skeleton, a heap of bones!

For if her body is dissected, it is no more than the three hundred and sixty bones [of the human skeleton] knit together. That is all it is. In itself, it is nothing pleasant, nothing desirable. What is so enjoyable about it? For the "body" is merely imputed on the basis of a gathering of parts; it has no independent being. And since it does not exist as such, there is no truly existent personal self.

Alternatively these words may be interpreted as meaning that "since the body of this woman is not mine, it is not mine to control. Since it is another's, it is not mine." How is it that one lusts and craves for such a thing? Why not instead go further, and push on to the state that is beyond suffering?

For it is as though one is faced with a choice. If one wishes for the state beyond suffering, one has to give up desire for a lover, for without this, obstacles are created to the three trainings of the path, and nirvana cannot be achieved. It is through the perfect observance of discipline, the basis of all excellent qualities, that outer and inner cravings must be abandoned. Otherwise, concentration, namely, the calm abiding of shamatha will not arise, and without this, the penetrative insight of vipashyana will not occur.

If, moreover, one does not posses the union of shamatha and vipashyana, it will be impossible to discard completely the afflictions present even in the Peak of Existence, and one will be unable to pass beyond suffering.

6. A REFLECTION ON THE UNCLEAN NATURE OF THE HUMAN BODY

[verse 43] Wishing to lay eyes for the first time upon his spouse, what pains a man will go to in order to be able to lift her face as she looks modestly down—her face, which whether looked upon or not, before she became a bride, was always carefully concealed, veiled as in the tradition of Mathura! [verse 44] As Shantideva now imagines, this same face by which the lover was tormented and which he had so longed to see, is here now in the charnel ground, nakedly exposed with no veil to cover it. For the vultures have done their work. "What!" exclaims Shantideva, now that he has seen her. "Is the lover so frightened? Is he running away?" [verse 45] The woman, says Shantideva, whom the jealous lover guarded so possessively, selfishly hiding her from other men—why should her body not be protected now, when it has become the food of graveyard birds? If he will not protect it in the charnel ground, he ought not to be so selfish and protective of it now.

[verse 46] Just consider, Shantideva says, this mass of human flesh, which the lustful man regards as a clean and lovely object of desire (but which nonetheless is soon to be the food of carrion beasts: vultures and jackals), which he decks with flowers and the scent of sandalwood, with jewels, precious bracelets and other ornaments—adorning something that in truth is but the food of others. "Why do people do this kind of thing?" Shantideva asks. It does not make sense.

[verse 47] For the lover should look again—at the dreadful skull and bones in the charnel ground, inert and dead. What is he so scared of? Why was he not afraid of them when they were walking around, propelled by the ghostly presence of the breath and the afflictive emotions of the mind, like a risen corpse? He ought to have been more afraid than lustful! [verse 48] He loved her body once, when it was clothed and adorned. Why does he not want it now that it is naked and thrown in the charnel ground? Logically, he ought to want and desire it. If he were to reply that he does not desire this naked corpse because it is unclean, why did he embrace it when it was all bedecked and covered? For the fact is that it was as unclean then as it is now.

[verse 49] What if he were to say that he took delight in the saliva of his mistress? In truth, her excrement and her saliva come from a single source. Both derive from her food. Why then does the ignorant and lustful lover not enjoy her excrement, finding it disgusting, while at the same time he delights to taste her saliva as though it were a honeyed nectar?

[verse 50] Perhaps he says that it is the softness of her touch that pleases him. Softness of touch, however, is also supplied by cotton wool, yet the lover has no desire for it and takes no delight in pleasant pillows, telling himself that cotton wool derives from something unclean. But the lustful lover is all mixed up. He fails to recognize the uncleanness of his mistress's body for what it is and claims it does not emit an evil stench. [verse 51] In their desire, lustful people are confused. Thinking only of their lovers, who are unclean by very nature, they crossly find fault with cotton pillows (though they are soft and smooth) just because they cannot copulate with them! They are attached not to the softness of touch, but to impurity.

[verse 52] For if they deny that they are attracted to filth, how can they coddle on their laps a human body, no more than a cage of bones tied fast with sinews and plastered over with the mud of flesh? [verse 53] A lover's own body is itself full of filth. It contains the thirty-six unclean substances, such as spittle, mucus, excrement, and urine, and he or she wallows in it constantly. And in addition to this, the lover still craves for another sack of filth, the filth of a partner's body, which also has the nature of the thirty-six impurities. Why on earth is it so desirable? It does not make sense.

[verse 54] Lovers could argue that they have no attraction for cotton wool; it is the skin and flesh of their partners that they love to touch and look at. But if this is so, Shantideva replies, why do they not delight to touch the flesh of their partners' corpses, when, devoid of mind, they are abandoned in the charnel ground in their natural condition?

[verse 55] Perhaps the lovers will object that they do not want them any more because their partners' minds have departed; indeed, it is rather in their minds that they delight. To which Shantideva retorts that the lovers are physically unable to touch or see the minds that they desire. Conversely, their partners' bodies, which they can touch and see, are not at all the minds that they claim to want. Why therefore do lovers indulge in copulation, looking at and touching bodies that have nothing to do with the minds [that they supposedly want]? It can only mean that the lovers are completely confused.

[verse 56] The failure to understand the unclean nature of a lover's body, which is concealed for the time being, is not perhaps so strange. But the failure to appreciate the obviously filthy nature of one's own body is very strange indeed. It is both stupid and laughable.

[verse 57] Lovers might proclaim that they are in love with the beauty of their partners' skin. But in that case, why do they overlook the color and loveliness of the fresh, young lotus blossoms opened in the sunshine of a cloudless sky and instead allow themselves to be entranced by a bag of dirt, their minds engrossed by masses of filth? This is surely illogical.

[verse 58] Shantideva demonstrates by stages [for the benefit of the putative lover] that, in having the nature of both a cause and an effect, the body of a partner is both the cause and effect of impurities. When clothing or the surfaces of things are fouled with filthy substances, excrement, urine, and so on, one shrinks from touching them. But the body of the beloved is the cause of such substances. Why therefore should the lover desire to touch it? [verse 59] The body of the beloved is also the outcome of unclean substances. Lovers may consider that they are not attached to, and have no desire to handle, filthy things like excrement and urine. But the bodies of their partners have arisen from an impure source, their mother's womb, and they were engendered from an unclean seed: the ovum and semen of their parents. Why then do lovers clasp to their bosoms the bodies of their partners, the products of such foulness? [verse 60] They are, by their very nature, both the cause and effect of impurity.

As Shantideva remarks, people feel no attraction for the tiny, fetid worms that appear in excrement. Why then do they lust after a human form, which has also arisen from numerous unclean sources and is replete with impurity: flesh, blood, excrement, urine, and so on? [verse 61] Such clinging is perverted. Not only do lovers feel no disgust toward their own impurity, but they—whose bodies are themselves sacks of foul substances—thirst for even more of it. They yearn for others' sacks of impurity: the bodies of their partners. There is something extremely contemptible in this!

[verse 62] A thing that defiles something pure is, for that very reason, itself impure. When pure and pleasant substances like camphor, saffron, sugarcane, rice, and delicious aromatic herbs are placed in the mouth and then spat out, the clear floor is rendered filthy. What need is there to mention the human body, by which these clean substances are made impure?

[verse 63] If still we doubt the filthiness of the body, in both its aspects of cause and effect—though it is very plain for all to see—we should go to the charnel grounds and observe the corpses abandoned there, rotting, devoured by worms, fetid and disgusting. [verse 64] If we were to peel away the skin from the corpses abandoned there, seeing the revolting, stinking blood, intestines, excremental discharges, and so on, we would feel great horror and repulsion. We are perfectly aware of this. Yet how is it that we are still not apprehensive of this body? How can we still crave and desire it without ever being satisfied?

[verse 65] A man may declare that he is attracted by the sweet smell of his mistress's body. But the delightful scent, which seems so pleasant, derives from what her body has been anointed with. It is the perfume of sandalwood and musk; it is not the scent of the body itself. How therefore can it be said that the lover desires his mistress's body owing to a perfume that in fact belongs to something else? [verse 66] If a man is attached only to a scent, it would surely make more sense to refrain from longing for a woman's body, which, left to itself, gives off unpleasant odors. Yet worldly people lust for what is not to the purpose.

What point is there in applying the sweet perfume of sandalwood to an impure body? [verse 67] For given that the sweet fragrance derives from the sandal with which the body is anointed, what perfume can possibly arise from a female form, which of itself is unclean and malodorous? How is it that the smell of something extraneous excites longing for something that is impure and ill-smelling—a woman's body? [verse 68] For if a woman's body is not at all washed and kept clean; if it is left untended, with lanky hair; long, overgrown nails; dirty, stained teeth that reek with decomposing sediment— what a disgusting horror it is! This naked body is as frightful as a ghost!

[verse 69] Moreover, why go to such excessive trouble to clean and groom this body, the object of our attachment? It is like cleaning and polishing the very weapon—sword or whatever else—with which we are to be wounded. Clinging in ignorance to their bodies—identifying something that is without a self as "I" and "mine" and taking as pure something that is impure—people lavish care upon themselves, bathing and preening.

As they drink down the intoxicating waters of desire, their minds are driven wild. The entire surface of the earth is engulfed in madness. Beings are indeed pitiful. The earth is filled with those who strive exclusively for their own ends, taking care of those they love, combating those they hate, doing the utmost to secure wealth and renown. When the Bodhisattvas, offspring of the Conqueror, behold them—high or low, powerful or weak, or just ordinary people—behaving as though they were completely insane, their hearts are filled with sorrow and they weep with compassion. It is like when the Bodhisattva Keshawa came skillfully to the assistance of a certain woman whose husband had died. They had loved each other with a deep and mutual love. She went almost mad with sorrow, adorning her husband's corpse until it looked like his living ghost.

[verse 70] We are reluctant to visit and look at the charnel grounds where there is nothing but human corpses and skeletons. We feel fear and revulsion. Why then do we take so much pleasure in the cities of the living dead, inhabited by skeletons that live and move, moved and animated by the mind and breath?

6. A REFLECTION ON THE MANY INJURIES THAT RESULT FROM ATTACHMENT

[verse 71] Moreover, a woman, unclean as she may be by nature, is not to be acquired free of charge. In the most expensive situation, gold and silver must be paid. Lower down the scale, it is a question of horses or livestock, or finally whatever a man has. The work involved in earning the necessary sums and all that is needed for banquets, clothes, jewelry, food, and so on, bring only an increase in negative actions: vexation and fatigue in this life and the agony of burning, hellish torment in the next.

[verse 72] Small boys are unable to accumulate wealth, and so they cannot enjoy the kind of pleasures that derive from ownership. When they grow into young men, how are they to enjoy the pleasure of having a wife? They must spend their entire time traveling around earning their living, accumulating, and protecting their wealth through farming or commerce. And when they are old, what pleasure can they get from the enjoyment of their desire? There is no time for it in the first case, no ability in the second!

[verse 73] There are some miserable people who have much desire but who spend their entire days working. From the early morning they plough the fields, cut the hay, shear their sheep. It is already night when they go home, worn out by the day's work; and broken with fatigue, they sleep the slumbers of a corpse. Then as soon as they awake, back they go to work. Their lives are a continuous hardship.

[verse 74] Others are obliged to go abroad on long travels for the sake of trade or banditry and are exhausted by the hardships they encounter. They are wayfarers far from home. Weary in mind and body, they long for their wives, their children, and friends but do not see them for a year or for years on end. No need to say that they are unable to satisfy their desires.

[verse 75] Some people, wishing to help their daughters, give them to others because they are ignorant of how else to benefit them. They wish happiness and contentment for them, but their daughters never get it. In other households, without family ties, they are obliged to perform worthless labors, without leisure by day or rest at night. Propelled by their negative karma as by the wind, their various negative actions and evil gossip bring them only suffering, destroying them in this and future lives.

[verse 76] Some, servants and others, sell their own bodies into the service of others, considering only their wages. No longer free, they are completely and permanently enslaved by their masters. And when the slave girls, their wives, give birth, they must do so wherever they happen to be, under a tree, in the wilderness, in a cave in the earth, or among the rocks—all alone without their family.

[verse 77] Foolish men, ensnared by their attachments to the objects of the senses, wanting wealth and comforts, make their living as robbers, thieves, soldiers, and so on. They decide to make their fortune in the wars, even though they fear for their lives. In order to be successful and to get the better of their opponents, they pay protection money to wicked and cruel bosses and submit to them. They live in fear and become their slaves.

[verse 78] Having robbed and stolen because of their attachment to the objects of the senses, some have their bodies slashed by weapons, others are impaled on pointed stakes, others are wounded by being run through with the lance, still others are put to death by fire. They suffer in this and future lives.

Because its visual consciousness is attached to a certain form, a butterfly is burnt in a flame; because its ears are drawn to sound, a deer is killed by a poisonous arrow;[172] because its nose loves the scent, a bee is trapped inside a flower; because its tongue is attached to taste, a fish is caught on a hook; and because its sense of touch is attached to certain sensations, an elephant gets trapped in mud. We ought to reflect on the drawbacks of the objects of desire and rid ourselves of attachment to them.

5. Giving up attachment to wealth and possessions

[verse 79] First of all, there is the trouble of accumulating the property that previously one did not have. Then there is the trouble of protecting it from damage. Finally, there is the trouble that comes when it is destroyed by thieves and burglars. In order to amass and protect their property, their horses and possessions, all members of society of whatever class—kings, lamas, or ministers—must get up early and go to bed late. They must be constantly vigilant day and night, enduring all the discomforts of heat and cold, hunger and thirst. They have to put up with fatigue and to neglect their bodies' needs, and they are tormented by every sort of discomfort.

If you want to acquire a horse, you have first to go through all the difficulties of getting a horse. Then you have the trouble of being a horse keeper. Without leisure by day or rest by night, you become the horse's servant. Finally, when the horse dies or is captured by an enemy or a thief, you weep and beat your breast. Such are the sufferings of horse ownership. All belongings—sheep, money, and the rest—bring difficulties that their owners are forced to contend with. You must acknowledge that, in the beginning, middle, and end, possessions are the ruin of this and future lives. For it is the cause from which all sufferings and pains derive. People who are distracted by their love of riches never have the time to practice the three trainings of the path. They never have the chance to free themselves from the sorrows of the three realms of existence.

In the first place, people who crave wealth and are attached to it do not belong in the ranks of the Aryas, noble beings who have few desires, are free of attachment, and are content with little. In the second place, because they do not relinquish their love of objects of desire, such people are unable even to reach the preparatory stage of meditative concentration. And without such a preparation, penetrative insight cannot arise, for there is no foundation for it. Finally, for as long as they thirst for objects of desire, such people will continue to take birth in samsara, just as they have done in the past. They will never be free from the sufferings of existence. Remember the story of the man long ago who had three gold vessels to which he was attached. When he died, he was reborn for several lives afterward as a snake that lived coiled in those selfsame pots. As it is said in the *Suhrillekha:*

> We suffer in proportion to the property we own
> And those with little wants have little pains.
> The headaches that afflict the naga kings
> Are equal to the heads possessed by them.

[verse 80] As it has been explained, people with many desires must suffer much, and all for very little joy. At the very most, there is the single instant of pleasure when consciousness meets the object of desire. Such people are like oxen pulling a hay cart. They chew a mouthful of grass, and then the wheels of the cart jolt and they are wrenched with pain.

[verse 81] These paltry enjoyments of food and shelter, that even dumb cattle are able to get for themselves, are not so rare. They are easily acquired but at the cost of how much mischief! For the sake of them, those tormented by their evil karma, destroy their precious human existence, so difficult to find and endowed with freedoms and advantages, together with all the perfect qualities needed for the accomplishment of buddhahood. As it is said in the *Shishyalekha* by Chandragomin:

> Human beings with great strength of heart
> Alone are able to achieve the path and teachings of the
>   Sugatas.
> The gods and nagas find them not, nor demigods;
> Garudas, vidyadharas, kinnaras, and uragas do not encounter
>   them.[173]

People who are completely distracted, who do not listen to explanations of the Tripitaka, who do not embrace the three trainings or practice a sadhana, who do not pray or engage in good works waste their entire lives and make their freedoms and advantages meaningless. The Buddhas and Bodhisattvas think of them with pity.

[verse 82] The happiness of mind that is based on objects of desire is unstable. It is transient and sure to end. For whatever is born will die; whatever comes together will separate; whatever is gathered will be exhausted; whatever is high will be brought low. Yet, for the sake of such pleasures, we nurture [only] the people we like and destroy those we hate; we engage in agriculture and commerce; we gather and use the gifts of the faithful and the offerings made for the sake of the dead. As a result of the negativities committed in all such activities, we cannot but fall into the hells and other lower realms in our next lives. Such activities are not much use to us either now or in the future! All our unending labors in samsara, all the hardships we undergo to obtain our wants, bring us only sorrow and travail.

[verse 83] If, however, we were to practice the ways of the Bodhisattvas, buddhahood itself could be attained with just a millionth part of the pointless hardships and fatigue [that we usually undergo]. To be sure, the pains taken by those who crave the objects of desire are greater and more protracted than any encountered in the practice of the Bodhisattva path, and yet they do not lead to enlightenment. [verse 84] If we consult our own advantage, we might well reflect upon the horrors of the states of sorrow (the realms of hell and the condition of pretas and of beasts), all of which are the end result of craving for objects of desire. None of our present adversities (such as being struck by weapons, killed with poison, burned in fire, falling into ravines, or being beaten by enemies) is to be compared with such attachment. For such adversities can only result in our death; they do not in themselves project us into the lower realms.

5. A REFLECTION ON THE EXCELLENCE OF SOLITUDE

[verse 85] And so, Shantideva says, depressed and revolted by our craving for sexual pleasure and riches, which are worse than poison, let us now rejoice in the excellence of solitude—of places where all strife for the sake of companions and possessions, and all the afflictions of attachment and aversion come to an end. It is through the blessed effect of such empty and solitary regions that every distraction ceases of its own accord.

In the peace and stillness of the pleasant and verdant forest, [verse 86] Bodhisattvas, fortunate in possessing the supreme Dharma, dwell in vast and pleasant abodes, formed of smooth, massive rock and cooled by the moon's rays more refreshing than the balm of sandalwood. They are far better-off than even great and opulent kings dwelling in their sandalwood palaces, cooled by jeweled fans. For, troubled neither by the bustle of people by day nor by commotion at night, they live in the quiet serenity of the woods wafted by gentle, cooling zephyrs. And whereas a king may journey throughout his realm, pondering how he might further its welfare, the Bodhisattvas pace here and there intent exclusively on bringing good to an infinity of beings. It is thus that in this and future lives, only happiness will come to them.

[verse 87] And therefore, says Shantideva, may we linger as long as we may wish—months and years—in pleasant caves, beneath the beautiful trees, in abandoned dwellings no longer claimed by anyone. May we give up the troubles that come from the preoccupation of houses and possessions of our own. May we live in freedom, unconfined by cares, with no need to curry favor with those in high position or to protect friends and those lower down the social scale—hoping for advantage and fearing adversity. [verse 88] To enjoy such liberty of action, the freedom to go or rest according to our wish, unspoiled by attachments to home, companions, and possessions, loosed from every bond and tie whether to high or low, friend or foe—a life of such contentment and such bliss, even the god Indra would be pressed to find!

To the extent that we have wealth, contentment is unknown to us and we are tormented by desire. But to the extent that we have contentment, we possess all the riches of happiness. As it is said in the *Suhrillekha*:

> Of every kind of wealth, contentment is supreme:
> This the Teacher of both gods and humankind has taught.
> Therefore be content. If so you are,
> You may have nothing but are rich indeed!

In this section, which deals with the gathering of the conditions conducive to meditative concentration, the excellence of solitude is alluded to on two [separate] occasions. There is no mistake in this. The first mention is made to inspire us with a delight in solitude and to make us want to go and stay there. Later, however, when, after taking up residence, we feel unable or unwilling to stay—owing to insufficient provisions or because of a longing for companionship—it might be helpful to remind ourselves of the qualities of solitude, so much praised by the Buddhas and Bodhisattvas. The repetition is to encourage us to remain firmly and joyfully in such a place.

1. MEDITATIVE CONCENTRATION ON BODHICHITTA

2. A SHORT EXPOSITION THAT LINKS THE SUBJECT TO THE PREVIOUS TEACHING

[verse 89] Shantideva sums up by saying that we should reflect again and again, from the various points of view that he has explained, on the advantages of having no distractions on the outer level, no movements of thought on the inner level, and no self-centered attitudes on the secret level. We should reflect also on the advantages of solitude of body, speech, and mind, remembering that they are all the causes of perfect and perpetual happiness in this and future lives. With this understanding, we should completely pacify our thoughts, our desire and clinging to outer and inner things, and we should meditate on bodhichitta.

Broadly speaking, by training ourselves in the preparatory stage (characterized by a basic, peaceful serenity) of the first samadhi, the samadhi itself will manifest. In this context, it is through meditation, by discarding the faults of attachment and desire for outer things and inner [emotional] states, and by adopting the positive qualities of detachment, that the actual samadhi will be accomplished. Failing that, its authentic preparatory stage will be perfected, and our bodies and minds will be rendered fit for wholesome action. With bodies and minds well-prepared, whatever we meditate on, be it bodhichitta or something else, all will be well-accomplished.

It should not be thought that samadhi (or meditative stability or concentration) is a state of "unknowing" or mental blankness. Samadhi or shamatha (calm abiding) means to possess full control over one's mind, regardless of whether it is allowed to move or made to remain still. When it is allowed to move, it will engage in every kind of virtuous object of focus. When it is made to rest, it will remain as immovable as Mount Meru.

2. A DETAILED EXPLANATION ON HOW TO TRAIN IN MEDITATIVE CONCENTRATION ON BODHICHITTA

3. EQUALIZING SELF AND OTHER

4. A BRIEF EXPLANATION

[verse 90] Two things are to be practiced on the level of relative bodhichitta: meditation on the equality of self and other and meditation on the exchange of self and other. Without training in the former, the latter is impossible. This is why Shantideva says that we should first meditate strenuously on the equality of self and other; for without it, a perfectly pure altruistic attitude cannot arise.

All beings, ourselves included, are in exactly the same predicament of wanting to be happy and not wanting to suffer. For this reason we must vigorously train in ways to develop the intention to protect others as much as ourselves, creating happiness and dispelling suffering. We may think that this is impossible, but it isn't.

Although they have no ultimate grounds for doing so, all beings think in terms of "I" and "mine." Because of this, they have a conception of "other," fixated on as something alien—though this too has no basis in reality. Aside from being merely mental imputations, "I" and "other" are totally unreal. They are both illusory. Moreover, when the nonexistence of "I" is realized, the notion of "other" also disappears, for the simple reason that "other" is only posited in relation to the thought of "I." Just as it is impossible to cut the sky in two with a knife, when the space-like quality of egolessness is realized, it is no longer possible to make a separation between "I" and "other," and there arises an attitude of wanting to protect others as oneself and of taking them as one's own. As it is said, "Whoever casts aside the ordinary, trivial view of self, will discover the profound meaning of great 'Selfhood.'"[174]

Thus, for the realization of the equality of "I" and "other," it is essential to grasp that "I" and "other" are merely labels without any basis in reality. This vital point of egolessness is difficult to understand, difficult even for a person of high intelligence. Thus, as the teachings say, it is of great importance that egolessness be clearly demonstrated and assimilated.

4. A detailed explanation

5. How to meditate on equality

[verse 91] The way to reflect upon equality is as follows. We can distinguish the various parts of our bodies: hands, feet, head, inner organs, and so on. Nevertheless, in a moment of danger, we protect them all, not wanting any of them to be hurt, considering that they all form a single body. We think, "This is my body," and we cling to it and protect it as a whole, regarding it as a single entity. In the same way, the whole aggregate of beings in the six realms, who in their different joys and sorrows are all like us in wanting to be happy and not wanting to suffer, should be identified as a single entity, our "I." We should protect them from suffering in just the same way as we now protect ourselves.

Suppose we were to ask someone how many bodies he had. "What are you talking about?" he would reply, "I have nothing but this one body!" "Well," we continue, "are there many bodies that you should take care of?" "No," he will say, "I take care only of this one body of mine." This is what he may say, but the fact is that, when he talks about his "body," he is doing no more than applying a name to a collection of different items. The word "body" does not at all refer to a single indivisible whole. In other words, there is no reason why the name "body" should be attached here [to these items] and why it is inappropriate to attach it elsewhere. The word "body" is fastened, without ultimate justification, to what is merely a heap of component items.

It is the mind that says "my body," and it is on the basis of this idea of a single entity that it is possible to impute the notions of "I," "mine," and all the rest. To claim, moreover, that it is reasonable to attach the name "I" to this aggregate and not to another is quite unfounded. Consequently, it is taught that the name "I" can be applied to the whole collection of suffering beings. It is possible for the mind to think, "They are myself." And if, having identified them in this way, it habituates itself to such an orientation, the idea of "I" with regard to other sentient beings will in fact arise, with the result that one will come to care for them as much as one now cares for oneself.

[verse 92] But how is it possible for such an attitude to arise, given that others do not feel my pain and I do not feel theirs? The root text may be interpreted as meaning that, while these sufferings of mine have no effect upon the bodies of other living beings, they are nevertheless the sufferings of my "I." They are unbearable to me because I cling to them as mine. [verse 93] Although the pains of others do not actually befall me, because I am a Bodhisattva and consider others as myself, their pains are mine as well and are therefore unbearable to me.

How is it that when suffering comes to me, the pain affects only myself and leaves others untouched? Regarding my present incarnation, just as from beginningless time until now, my mind entered amid the generative substances of my parents as they came together. Subsequently, there arose what I now identify as "my body." And it is precisely because I seize on it as myself that I am unable to tolerate its being injured. But within suffering itself, there is no separation between "my suffering" and "another's suffering." Therefore, although another's pain does not actually afflict me now, if that other is identified as "I" or "mine," his or her suffering becomes unbearable to me also.[175]

Maitriyogin, a disciple of the Lord Atisha, did indeed feel the suffering of other beings as his own.[176] This was the experience of one who had attained the Bodhisattva grounds of realization. However, even on the level of ordinary people, we can take the example of a mother who would rather die than that her dear child should fall sick. Because she identifies with her baby, the child's suffering is actually unbearable for *her*. Other people who do not identify with the child are, for this very reason, unaffected by its pain. If they did identify with it, the child's suffering would be intolerable for them as well.

Moreover, a long period of habituation is not necessary for this kind of experience to occur. Take the example of a horse that is being put up for sale. Right up to the moment when the deal is struck, if the horse lacks grass or water, or if it is ill, or if it has any other discomfort—all this will be unbearable for its owner, while it will not at all affect the client. But as soon as the transaction takes place, it is the buyer who will be unable to stand the horse's suffering, while the seller will be completely indifferent. Within the horse itself, however, there is no basis whatever for the distinction "this man's horse" or "that man's horse." It is identified as being this man's or that man's according to how it is labeled by thought.

In the same way, there is not the slightest reason for saying that the notion of "I" must be applied to me and not to another. "I" and "other" are no more than a matter of conceptual labeling. The "I" of myself is "other" for someone else, and what is "other" for myself is "I" for another. The notions of "here" and "there" are simply points of view, designated by the mind in dependence on each other. There is no such thing as an absolute "here" or an absolute "there." In just the same way, there is no absolute "I" and no absolute "other." It is just a matter of imputation. And so, on account of this crucial point, the Dharma teaches that when "I" is ascribed to others, namely, sentient beings, the attitude of accepting and taking them as one's own will naturally arise.

This is how Buddhas and Bodhisattvas claim sentient beings as their own selves in the way explained above, so that even the slightest pain of others is for them as if their entire body were on fire. And they do not have the slightest hesitation in doing so, just as when the Buddha claimed as his own the swan that Devadatta had shot down with an arrow.[177] Similarly, Machig[178] said that in the centuries after her, perverted practitioners of chö would with violent means subjugate the wealth-gods, ghosts, and demons, whom she had taken with the crook of her compassion—meaning by this that she had taken these gods and spirits to herself as beings whom she cherished.

As we have said, taking sentient beings as one's own does not require lengthy training. For example, if you tell someone that you will give him an old horse, no sooner are the words out of your mouth than the other person has already appropriated the horse and cannot bear it if the horse is in distress. Still, it might be thought that, because one has drifted into such bad mental habits, the thought of taking others as oneself will never arise. But the Lord Buddha has said that in all the world, he never saw anything easier to educate than the mind itself, once it is set on the right path and steps are taken to subjugate it. On the other hand, he also said that there is nothing more difficult to govern than an untrained mind. Therefore, if we do not let our minds stray onto wrong paths but instead train them, it is perfectly possible to bring them into submission. Conversely, if we fail to subdue our minds, it will be impossible for us to overcome anything else. This is why the teachings say that we should strive to subdue our minds.

[verse 94] Shantideva's justification for the necessity of eliminating suffering is presented in the form of a probative argument.[179] His thesis is that he will eliminate all the sufferings of others, that is, the sufferings that will not bring them any ultimate benefit. His reason is that their suffering does them no good, and, by way of example, he says that he will remove it just as he removes his own discomforts of hunger, thirst, and so on. By a similar procedure, he says that he will benefit others and make them happy because they are living beings, and, once again by way of example, he will do this in the same way that he attends to the comfort of his own body. [verse 95] Since there is not the slightest difference between ourselves and others (in that all want to be happy), what reason could we possibly have for not working for the happiness of others? It does not make sense that we should work only in our own interest. [verse 96] In the same way, there is not the slightest difference between ourselves and others in that no one wants to experience suffering. Therefore what reason do we have for failing to protect others from suffering? It does not make sense that we should strive only to protect ourselves.

[verse 97] Now suppose someone were to object, saying, "Yes, I am affected by my own suffering, and therefore I have to protect myself. But when suffering happens to someone else, nothing at that moment is actually hurting me; therefore another's suffering is not something I have to protect myself from." But major and obvious sufferings (from the sufferings of the next life in the hell realms to the pains that will come tomorrow or next month) or the more subtle kinds of suffering occurring from moment to moment—all such discomforts great or small (due to lack of food, clothing, or whatever) *are located in the future*. They are not actually harming us in the present moment. If these future pains are not tormenting us now, what do we have to protect ourselves from? It makes no sense to do so. [verse 98] But we may think that these sufferings are not the same as those of other beings. For even though such sufferings are not affecting us now, we protect ourselves nevertheless because we will experience them in the future. But to cling, on the gross level, to the aggregates of this life and the next life as constituting a single entity, and to cling also, on the subtle level, to the aggregates of one instant and the next as being the same thing is a mistaken conception, nothing more.

When we reflect about our present and future lives in the light of such arguments, [we can see that] the entity that dies and passes out of life is not the same as that which is born in the succeeding existence. Conversely, that which takes birth in the next life, wherever that may be, is not the same thing as that which has perished in the previous existence. The length of time spent in the human world is the result of past karma. When this is exhausted as the final moment of the human consciousness ends, it creates the immediate cause [of the new life], while the karma that brings about birth in a hell realm, or whatever, constitutes the cooperative cause. Wherever people are subsequently born, whether in hell or elsewhere, they have at death a human body, whereas at birth, they will have the body of a hell being and so on. In other words, the previous consciousness now terminated is that of a human, while at the moment of the later birth, the consciousness is that of a hell being. The two are thus distinct. When the mind and body of a human come to an end, the mind and body of the following life come into being. It is not that there is a movement or transmigration of something from a former to a subsequent state. As it is said:

> Like recitation, flame, and looking glass,
> Or seal or lens, seed, sound, astringent taste,
> The aggregates continue in their seamless course,
> Yet nothing is transferred, and this the wise should know.

When, for example, one uses a lamp to light another lamp, the later flame cannot be lit without dependence on the first; but at the same time, the first flame does not pass into the second one.

If the earlier entity is terminated, however, and the later one arises in such a way that the two are quite separate, it will be objected that, in that case, the effect of former actions is necessarily lost, while (in the course of the subsequent existence) karmic effects will be encountered that have not been accumulated. But this is not so. Phenomenal appearances—which arise ineluctably through the interdependence of causal conditions—cannot withstand analysis, they lie beyond the scope of both the eternalist and nihilist positions. The assertion that karmic effects are not lost is a special feature of the Buddhist teachings. It lies within the exclusive purview of an omniscient mind and it is thus to be accepted through reliance on the word of the Conqueror. As it is said:

> What arises in dependence on another
> Is not at all that thing itself—
> But neither is it something else:
> There is no break; there is no permanence.

All we have are relatively imputed terms. Being neither identical nor different, [earlier and later moments of consciousness] appear. Consciousness manifests in different ways according to karma, whether good or bad. But in itself, it consists of moments of mere knowing, clear and cognizant, arising uninterruptedly in like kind.[180] The notions of permanence or discontinuity do not apply to it. Thus the results of karma are not lost and one never encounters karmic effects that have not been accumulated.

If, on a more subtle level, one considers the momentary nature of phenomena, everything in the outer or inner sphere consists of point-instants. The earlier moment ceases, and the later one supervenes, so that the one is distinct from the other. Likewise, when the karma for remaining in the human state provides the circumstances and the final moment of consciousness [in that state] provides the cause, the following moment of consciousness comes to birth and arises in like kind. But the two moments are separate.

[verse 99] An opponent might object that it is those who suffer who should protect themselves when they are injured; it is not for others to do so. But the pain the foot feels when it is pierced by a thorn is not felt by the hand. So what reason does the hand have for protecting it? It does not make sense.

[verse 100] Such protective acts may not be logical, the opponent will continue. Nevertheless, because people are habituated to self-clinging, they are mentally orientated in such a way that, in the present life, they protectively provide for their future existence and their body's limbs look after each other. To this, Shantideva replies that the inadmissible clinging to "I" and "other," (or—alternatively interpreted—that which is inadmissible to oneself and others, namely, suffering) should be discarded as much as possible. For it is a delusion.

[verse 101] Again the opponent will say that although previous and subsequent existences do not constitute a single entity, they do form a continuum. Although the hand and the foot are separate, nevertheless, they form a single composite. That is why the one protects the other.

But Shantideva replies that what the opponent calls a single continuum or a composite are illusions. A continuum is nothing more than the coming together of many instants, nothing else—in the same way that the many beads of a chaplet are identified as the single string or continuum of a mala. As for a composite, this is just a gathering, as when many armed men grouped together are called an "army." An army is a figment; it is just an imputation or name and does not exist as such.

This is the best way to establish the personal No-Self. Aside from the self believed to be single, permanent, and independent, all assumptions of "I" or "self" are associated with a continuum or gathering. Since the latter are not established, the self is shown to be nonexistent. Since continua and gatherings have no existence in themselves, there is no "experiencer" of the suffering, no personal self to possess the pain. Who "owns" it? No one.

[verse 102] If there is no subject, no "experiencer" of the suffering felt, then there is no means of distinguishing between "I" and "other." For if there is no "I," no "other" can be posited in contrast with it. Since neither of them exists, there is no basis for a distinction, and therefore no difference between our pain and another's pain. For this reason, it is illogical to protect ourselves from suffering and not to protect others from it. In view of this, it is demonstrated that, since suffering is something to be dispelled, the sufferings of others are to be dispelled along with our own—for the simple reason that pain is pain. What grounds are there for getting rid only of our own suffering and not that of others? It would be a great delusion to think there were.

[verse 103] Some might object that if there is no self to feel or appropriate the pain, it surely follows that suffering is harmful to no one. In that case, why dispel the sufferings of beings? For what is there to be dispelled, and who is there to dispel it? There is nothing to get rid of.

One cannot argue like this. On the ultimate level this is the case. But on the relative level, we do feel suffering as something to be got rid of, and it follows that the suffering of others is to be removed also. Conversely, if the suffering of others is something that is not to be removed, it follows in similar measure that our own suffering should not be removed either. To remove it would be logically inconsistent.

5. ANSWERING OBJECTIONS TO THE EQUALIZATION OF SELF AND OTHER

[verse 104] It could be argued that when we consider the sufferings of others, compassion induces in us the feeling of great and unbearable sorrow. Given therefore that all sorrow is to be removed, what is the purpose of generating the pain of compassion, whether in oneself or in others? In answer to this, it should be urged that we only need to think about the suffering of beings in hell. How could the "smart of our compassion" be considered intense compared with such agony?

[verse 105] And even though one may suffer [by virtue of compassion], it is as when a wound is inflicted on the body for the purposes of curing a disease. If it is by the single pain of a compassionate person that the many sufferings of other beings are removed, then loving persons must surely foster such pain both in themselves and other practitioners!

[verse 106] The sorrow of compassion is therefore something to be cultivated. It was thus that the Bodhisattva Supushpachandra, clairvoyantly aware that the king would kill him, did not turn away. In order to remove the suffering of many other beings, he himself did not shy away from pain. On the contrary, he earnestly embraced it. The story is recounted in the Samadhiraja-sutra. At a time when the Doctrine of an earlier Buddha, Ratnapadmachandra, was in decline, the monk Supushpachandra lived together with a host of seven thousand Bodhisattvas in the forest called Samantabhadra. He was gifted with second sight, and he knew that if he were to go and teach in the jeweled palace of the king Viradatta, many millions of beings would gain high rebirth or liberation in the state of a non-returner. None of this would happen if he failed to go. On the other hand, he knew that if he went, the king would kill him. And so he went to the palace and fasted for seven days. At night, he circumambulated a stupa that contained relics consisting of the fingernails of one of the Buddhas, and during the day, he taught the Dharma in all the villages around. He placed an inconceivable number of beings in the higher realms and in the level of nonreturners. After he died, killed on the orders of the king by Udayana the executioner, the king himself repented, built a stupa for Supushpachandra's bones, and made offerings before it.

5. THE BENEFITS OF SUCH A PRACTICE

[verse 107] Shantideva remarks that those who have grown used to the view of the equality of self and other, whose happiness it is to soothe the pain of others, will venture for their sake even into the Hell of Unrelenting Pain with the joy and delight of swans that sweep down happily on to a beautiful lake adorned with lotuses. [verse 108] Some people might say that those who belong to the Shravaka lineage have no need [in the interest of gaining such joy] to enter the hell realms. For when they practice in order to attain liberation and enlightenment, they obtain it swiftly and experience an intense happiness whereby all suffering is pacified.

But, asks Shantideva [ironically], is the ocean-like immensity of joy, that comes when all beings without end are freed from all their pains, not enough for him? Why ever should he wish for his own liberation? What use has he for the desire for only his own liberation? What use has he for such an insipid happiness? All the commentaries interpret the text here as meaning that the kind of liberation that lacks the flavor of altruism is pointless. As it is said in the *Shikshasamucchaya*, "What use have I for such insipid liberation?"

[verse 109] On the other hand, the task of bringing benefit to other beings in a manner that is free of all self-centeredness should not be a cause of pride and self-congratulation. Such altruistic labors are themselves their own reward, says Shantideva. He has no expectation of being rewarded in a future life.

4. SUMMARY

[verse 110] Shantideva sums up by saying that since he and others are equal without any difference between them, it follows that, just as he defends himself against even the slightest criticism and false accusation, in the same way, he will now cultivate and habituate himself to compassion and an attitude of benevolence: wishing to protect others and to care for them.

3. The exchange of self and other

4. A brief explanation of this practice by stating the reason for it

[verse 111] People will say that it is impossible to consider other beings as oneself, that such a mental attitude will never happen. But it will. In respect of ourselves, the drops of semen and blood belonging to our parents are things completely alien and do not have the slightest existence as things belonging to us that could serve as the basis of either liberation or deluded [samsaric] existence. Nevertheless, it is through sheer force of habit that we have come to have a sense of "I" in relation to them. [verse 112] Since we are able to identify as our bodies and minds things that are devoid of such an "I-identity," why should it be difficult to identify the bodies of other people (which are also of the nature of the generative substances of their parents) as "I" and grow used to such a perspective? And vice versa, why, as a result of habituation, should it be difficult for us to think of this body of ours as though it belonged to someone else?

[verse 113] The holy beings have criticized the fault of self-clinging and the selfish, self-cherishing attitude that is the source of sufferings in this and future lives. And they have praised the endless, ocean-like qualities that give rise to happiness and well-being—a state that derives from loving others with selfless altruism. In view of this, Shantideva says, he will lay aside all self-love and gladly strive to acquire the habit of adopting others and considering them as himself.

The exchange of self and other as explained in the texts is not like the one practiced by yogis. Thus though there are four ways of effecting the exchange of self and other (the exchange of the self-cherishing itself, the exchange of the body as the ground of imputation of the self, the exchange of happiness and suffering, and the exchange of negative and positive actions), in Shantideva's text only the first three topics are mentioned.

4. A detailed explanation of this practice

5. The general way of exchanging self and other

6. Taking the place of others with enthusiasm

[verse 114] Again, it could be asked how all beings, so many and various as they are, could be considered as oneself. In answer to this, we could use the following example. We distinguish the many parts of our bodies, our arms, and so forth. Nevertheless, all these members are considered a single body. In the same way, in taking beings as ourselves, why should we not consider them—all the beings of the six realms: gods, humans, nagas, and so forth—as limbs and members of a living whole? We ought to do so, according to the reasoning just given.

[verse 115] It might be thought that such a state of mind could never arise. However, within our present form (which is the fully grown effect of the generative substances of our parents and which, in itself, is devoid of any "I" acting as the basis of either liberation or delusion in samsara), the sense of self has naturally arisen. It has done so on account of a long propensity to self-clinging, the result of which is that, when the body is at ease, there is the feeling, "*I* am comfortable," and when the body is wounded, it is as if "*I* am in pain." Why, therefore, as a result of long habituation to the apprehension of the bodies of others as being ourselves, should the state of mind of thinking, "They are myself," be impossible?

[verse 116] What will be the outcome if we train ourselves in this way? To begin with, when we work for the sake of others, we will have no boastful sense of self-congratulation. It will be just as when we feed ourselves; we won't expect reward or recognition! [verse 117] Similarly, just as we defend ourselves from anything unpleasant that might arise (disagreeable words, false accusations), we will grow used to an attitude of compassion and protectiveness toward others.

[verse 118] It is necessary to protect others even from small injuries. The compassionate Lord Avalokita wished to dispel the great dangers and fears of beings in the three realms of samsara, right down to the worries someone might feel when standing in front of a large group of people. Therefore, after he generated bodhichitta aiming at the attainment of buddhahood, he blessed his own name by the power of prayer, concentration, and wisdom, and prayed that the mere remembrance of it would protect all beings from their fears. Quoted in the *Gandavyuha-sutra*, he said, "May every fear and danger, such as being burned in great fire and being carried away by water, be brought to nothing just by the mere remembrance of my name.... By recalling my name three times, may everyone be released from fear and anguish when in the midst of many people."

[verse 119] We should rid ourselves of all apprehension, thinking that, although its benefits are great, the exchange is just too difficult for us. We should not allow ourselves to be deterred by hardships; we should not turn away from something just because it is difficult. It will become easy by dint of training. With the passage of time, and thanks to gradual habituation, the thought that we might gladly take upon ourselves the sufferings of others, exchanging our position for theirs—an idea that at the outset we were afraid even to hear about—will become so second nature to us that we will be miserable without it. We will feel deprived at the prospect of being unable to work for the good of others. It is as when there are people who at first seem so terrible to us that we are frightened even by the sound of their name. But when we get to know them and get used to them, we may end up actually liking them and would miss them if they were not there! [verse 120] Therefore, those who wish quickly to become a refuge from suffering both for themselves and for others should practice and embrace the sacred mystery: the exchange of self and other. It is a secret because it lies beyond the possibilities of the Shravakas and others.

6. Getting rid of self-cherishing

[verse 121] Because of our attachment to our bodies, we are terrified by even little things like bees and meat flies, let alone things that are really terrifying. This body of ours is the occasion of so much fear both now and in our future existences! What intelligent person would not resent it as the worst of enemies? It would make more sense to hate it instead of being so attached to it!

[verse 122] For the sake of food and clothing, wishing to relieve our bodies' discomforts of hunger and thirst, heat and cold, we kill fish, birds and deer and cattle, and we rob and steal from others, lying in wait for them along the road. [verse 123] For the sake of wealth and position, some extremely misguided people will even go so far as to kill their parents, like King Ajatashatru, who slew his father, and Udayana, who murdered his mother. Likewise, some people embezzle and secretly appropriate the goods dedicated to the Three Jewels and do business with them. Having accumulated such terrible karma, they will have to suffer unbearable agony, burned in the blazing fires of the Hell of Unrelenting Pain.

[verse 124] What prudent people are there then, who, wishing to be happy, take delight in their bodies, lavishing all their care, food, clothes, and resources on them—loving and protecting the very thing that is the source of present and future suffering? Such behavior is completely wrong-headed. Shantideva says this precisely to dissuade us from identifying and cherishing our bodies as ourselves.

6. The defects of considering oneself as important; the excellence that derives from considering others as important

[verse 125] "If I give this, what will there be left for me? If I give away my food, clothes, and property to others, what shall I have to eat, wear, and use?" Such self-concern, such a self-centered attitude is the way of demons. For it is through being avaricious and tightfisted that we will be reborn as pretas and flesh-devouring spirits.

"If I keep this, what will there be left to give? If I hang on to my food, clothes, and wealth, what will I have to give to others?" Such a concern for others and such acts of generosity are the source of great happiness and joy in this and future lives. It is the excellent way of the Buddhas and Bodhisattvas who are masters of generosity. It is the spiritual tradition of the enlightened ones.

This principle is illustrated by the following tale. Once upon a time, in the country of King Brahmadana, no rain fell for twelve years. The whole population was fed from the royal treasury. Finally, the king even took the bushel of barley that had been set aside for himself and offered it to a Pratyekabuddha. As a result, the latter miraculously produced rain, so that the famine came to an end.

[verse 126] Shantideva goes on to say that, if, for the sake of escaping from suffering and in order to gain our advantage, we physically harm someone else or destroy their possessions, we will later have to suffer in the realms of hell. On the other hand, if, for the sake of dispelling the suffering of others and bringing them to happiness, we harm our own bodies and possessions, we will inherit every excellence. In the immediate term, we will achieve rebirth in the higher realms, and ultimately we will attain buddhahood. This is how it was for the Buddha our Teacher. It was by giving away his body and all he possessed that he achieved enlightenment.

[verse 127] Wanting to be the best, wanting to be the most beautiful and the most important, wanting to be served and to be richer than others—all this will lead in the next life to birth in the lower realms. It will give rise to an inferior condition, to an unattractive physical appearance, to stupidity, and so on. Our whole orientation should be turned around and all such concerns should be applied to others. If we want *them* to have the best, the realms of bliss will be our destiny. We will be born kings of divine and human realms, with every excellence and honor.

[verse 128] But if we enslave others to our own interest, we will have to experience the miserable, painful condition of servitude in our next lives. For example, it was said that the six-year-long pregnancy of Drakzinma was the fully ripened effect of forcing someone to carry a pitcher full of water in one of her previous existences. If on the other hand we labor for others as though we were their servants, we will enjoy mastery and leadership in our next lives. We will be prosperous and happy, attended by good servants and helpers.

[verse 129] In brief, as Shantideva says, all the joy the world contains both now and in the future has come from wishing happiness for others. All the misery the world contains both now and in the future has come from wanting pleasure for oneself.

[verse 130] There is no need for lengthy commentary. In sum, ordinary (childish) beings think only of themselves. Without resting day or night, they work exclusively in their own interest. The only result they reap from this is suffering both now and in the hereafter. The compassionate Buddhas and Bodhisattvas, on the other hand, are free from selfish concerns and work for the good of others alone. In this and future lives therefore they know only happiness, for they perfectly accomplish their own and others' benefit. Just look at the difference between the Buddhas and beings! And ridding ourselves of selfishness, let us work exclusively for the benefit of others.

[verse 131] If we do not make this perfect exchange, if we fail to give our happiness to others and fail to take their sufferings on ourselves, not only will we not gain perfect buddhahood, but even in samsara we will have no joy, either in the divine realms or even in the human state. [verse 132] If we do not work for the good of others, changing places with them, we will fail to achieve even the goals of our present existence, let alone those of our future lives. When dishonest servants, wanting only their own advantage without hardship, refuse to work for their employers, and when tightfisted masters fail to reward their servants with money and clothing, the worldly aims of both parties are left undone. What kind of exchange should they practice? If the servant does not give up the pleasures of inactivity and if the master does not give up the pleasure of not paying wages and if they do not gladly assume the discomfort of work on the one hand and payment on the other—in other words, if they fail to make the exchange, the needs and goals of life will never be accomplished.

[verse 133] By failing to discriminate correctly between the causes of happiness and misery, we cast away so much of the former. For we forsake the practice of exchange, the cause of every joy both "seen and unseen" (that is, in this and future existences), and we inflict pain and sorrow on others. It is thus that, in our confusion, we bring upon ourselves unbearable suffering both now and in our future lives.

6. The actual practice of exchange. Why it is necessary

[verse 134] All the aggression and violence in the world and all the fear that there is (of enemies, evil forces, poisonous snakes, and so on), together with all the sufferings of birth, sickness, old age, and death, whether now or in our lives to come—everything comes from self-clinging, from our attachment to our nonexistent "I." What, Shantideva exclaims, are we to do with this great demon, this ego-clinging, which prevents us from escaping from the great ocean of suffering of the three worlds of samsara and which will destroy us now and in the hereafter? The three so-called rudras— which are the roots of samsaric existence—are the three kinds of ego-clinging, associated with thought, word, and deed. Ego-clinging is the mighty demon of the three worlds; it is the source of all evil spirits and deadly influences.

[verse 135] We cannot avoid adversity and suffering if we do not completely rid ourselves of ego-clinging, of our clinging to "I." If we do not keep away from fire, we will not escape from being burned. As it is said:

Having "I," we know of "other."
From "I" and "other," clinging and aversion manifest.
And it is from these two, so closely linked,
That every evil, every sin appears.

[verse 136] Since ego-clinging is thus the root of every ill in this and future lives, it follows that in order to free ourselves and everyone else from pain and suffering, we must give away ourselves to others; we must cherish others in the same way that we now cherish ourselves. Every effort must be put into this training.

[verse 137] Once we have made this exchange, it follows that from that moment on, we are "beneath the rule of others." This is what we must tell ourselves; this is how we should inform our minds. We must resolve that from now on, concern for the benefit of all beings will take the place of the self-centered thoughts that we formerly had. [verse 138] Our sight and all our other powers, our ears, our hands, our feet, and so on, with which we see, hear, and move—all are now the property of others. It would now be incorrect to use them for ourselves. And how much more incorrect (through physical aggression or angry looks) would it be to use these faculties against the very ones who are now their owners.

[verse 139] It is thus that living beings must be our chief concern. Everything beneficial we find that our body possesses (food, clothing, and other commodities) will be seized and handed over to those who do not have them, exclusively for their use and service. As it is said, if we dread giving away even a little quantity of something, we must develop the confident courage to surrender an entire load of it. We should take the food from our very mouths and give it to others. This is how we should crush down our craving and attachment with regard to such material goods. It is said that we should give them all away.

5. TRAINING IN THE PRACTICE OF EXCHANGE, WITH REGARD TO SPECIFIC ANTIDOTES

6. BRIEF EXPLANATION

[verse 140] When you perform the meditation of exchange, take other beings, whether inferiors, superiors, or equals and consider them as yourself, putting yourself in their position. When you have changed places, meditate without allowing any other thought to come in the way. Put yourself in the position of someone worse off than you and allow yourself to feel envy. Then put yourself in the position of someone on the same level and soak yourself in a sense of competitiveness and rivalry. Finally, taking the place of someone better-off, allow yourself to feel pride and condescension.

6. A DETAILED EXPLANATION

7. THE PRACTICE OF ENVY FROM THE POINT OF VIEW OF SOMEONE LESS WELL-OFF

In each of these three meditations [following Shantideva's lead], whenever the text says "he" or "this person," the reference is to your own "I" (now regarded as another person). When the text says "you," it is referring to this other person (better-off, equal, or worse off in relation to yourself) with whom you have now identified.[181] You must now systematically generate the antidotes to pride, rivalry, and jealousy. The reason for doing this is that as soon as even the slightest virtue appears in the mind stream, these three defilements follow in its wake. They are like demons that sap one's integrity—which explains the importance given to their antidotes.

Now, of the eight worldly concerns, honor, possessions, adulation, and happiness are the things that make you proud. So perform the exchange, placing yourself in the position of someone contemptible, someone despised, a beggar or a tramp. Imagine that you become the poor person and that the poor person becomes you.

Now allow yourself to feel that person's envy. [verse 141] Looking up at your former self (your ego, now regarded as someone else), someone talented, think how happy "he" must be, praised and respected by all and sundry. You, on the other hand, are nothing, nobody, a complete down-and-out, despised and utterly miserable. The person you are looking at is rich, has plenty to eat, clothes to wear, money to spend—while you have nothing. He is respected for being learned, talented, well-disciplined. You, on the other hand, are dismissed as a fool. He enjoys a wealth of every comfort and happiness; you by contrast are a pauper, your mind weighed down with worries, your body racked with disease, suffering, and the discomforts of heat and cold. [verse 142] You have to work like a slave, digging, harvesting grass—while he can just sit back with nothing to do. As these thoughts pass through your mind, feel your envy. He even has servants and a private horse, on whom he inflicts a great deal of discomfort and suffering. He is not even aware that they are in distress, and there he is, oh so comfortable. And as if that weren't enough, he gets angry and lashes out, whipping and beating them. Put yourself in the position of his poor victims and take their suffering on yourself. If you manage to do this, it is said that you will come to recognize their sorrows. Compassion for them will grow, and you will stop hurting them.

Once again, reflect that he is talented and belongs to a good family. He is wealthy and surrounded by friends. You, on the other hand, are a complete nobody, well-known to be good at nothing. [verse 143] But, even though you have nothing to show for yourself, you might well ask *him* what reason he has for being so arrogant. After all, the existence or non-existence of good qualities, and the concepts of high and low are all relative. There are no absolute values. Even people who are low-down like you can be found to have something good about them, relatively speaking. Compared with someone with even greater talent, *he* is not so great. Compared with someone even more disfavored, feeble with age, lame, blind, and so forth, you are much better-off. After all, you can still walk on your own two feet; you can still see with your eyes; you are not yet crippled with age. You have at least something.

This verse, which begins, "What! A nobody without distinction!" could be understood in a different sense, namely, that you have it in you to acquire all the excellence of training, since you have all the qualities of the utterly pure tathagatagarbha, the essence of buddhahood, implicit in your nature. Thus you are far from being bereft of good qualities.

[verse 144] If he retorts that you are despicable because your discipline and understanding are a disgrace or because you have no resources and so forth, this is not because you are either evil in yourself or simply inept; it is because your afflictions of desire, ignorance, avarice, and so on, are so powerful that you are helpless. And so you should retort, saying:

> All right, if you're such a great and wonderful Bodhisattva, you should help me as much as you can; you should encourage and remedy the poor condition of my discipline, view, and resources. If you *do* help me, I am even prepared to accept punishment from you—harsh words and beating—just like a child at school learning to read and write who has to take a beating from the teacher.

> [verse 145] But the fact is that you, the great Bodhisattva, are doing nothing for me; you don't even give me a scrap of food or something to drink. So why are you passing yourself off as someone so great? You have no right to look down on me, no right to behave so scornfully to me and people like me. And anyway, even if you *did* have any genuine virtues, if you can't give me any relief or help, what use are they to me? They're to-

tally irrelevant. [verse 146] After all, if you *are* a Bodhisattva but can stand by without the slightest intention of helping or saving me and those like me—who, through the power of evil karma, are on our way to the lower realms, like falling into the mouth of a ferocious beast—if you have no compassion, you are yourself guilty of something completely unspeakable! And not only do you not acknowledge this, but you are all the time passing yourself off as someone wonderful. The fact is, however, that you have no qualities at all. In your arrogance, you want to put yourself on the same level as the real Bodhisattvas, those beings who are truly skilled and who in their compassion really do carry the burdens of others. Your behavior is totally outrageous!

This is how to meditate on envy and resentment as the chief antidote to pride. By appreciating the suffering involved in being a poor and insignificant person, without talents or honor, you come to realize how wrong it is to be arrogant and scornful. It dawns on you how unpleasant it is for people in a humble position when you are proud and supercilious toward them. You should stop behaving like this and begin to treat people with respect, providing them with sustenance and clothing, and working to help them in practical ways.

7. The practice of jealous rivalry from the point of view of an equal

Next you should make the exchange taking the place of someone similar to, or slightly better than, yourself—someone with whom you feel competitive, whether in religious or worldly affairs. [verse 147] Tell yourself that, however good he is in terms of reputation and wealth, you will do better. Whatever possessions he has, and whatever respect he has in other people's eyes, you will deprive him of them, whether in religious disputation or even by fighting—and you will make sure you get them all for yourself.

[verse 148] In every way possible, you will advertise far and wide your own spiritual and material gifts, while hushing up whatever talents he has, so that no one will ever see or hear about them. [verse 149] At the same time you will cover up whatever faults you have, hiding them from the public gaze, while at the same time gossiping about all the shortcomings of your rival, making quite sure that everyone knows about them. Under the impression that you are beyond reproach, lots of people will congratulate you, while for him, it will be just the opposite. From now on, you will be the wealthy one, the center of attention. For him, there will be nothing. [verse 150] For a long time, and with intense satisfaction, you will gloat over the penalties he will have to suffer for breaking his vows of religion or because he has misbehaved in worldly life. You will make him an object of scorn and derision, and, in public gatherings, you will make him despicable in the eyes of others, digging out and exposing all his secret sins.

By using a spirit of rivalry in this way as an antidote to jealousy, you will come to recognize your own faults in being competitive with others. Then you will stop behaving like this and instead do whatever you can to help your rivals with presents and honors.

7. THE PRACTICE OF PRIDE FROM THE POINT OF VIEW OF SOMEONE BETTER-OFF

Now imagine yourself in the position of someone who is better-off, who looks down on you with pride and derision. [verse 151] [And from this vantage point,] think that it has come to your notice that he, this tiresome nonentity, is trying to put himself on a par with *you*. But what comparison could anyone possibly make between you and him—whether in learning or intelligence, in good looks, social class, wealth, or possessions? The whole idea is absurd. It's like comparing the earth with the sky! [verse 152] Hearing everyone talking about your talents, about all your learning, and so on, saying how it sets you apart from such an abject individual—all this is extremely gratifying. The thrill of it is so intense that your skin is covered with goose pimples. You should really enjoy the feeling!

[verse 153] If, through his own hard work and despite the obstacles he has to contend with, he manages to make some headway, you agree that, so long as he abases himself and works subserviently according to your instructions, this low-down wretch will get no more than the merest necessities in return: food to fill his stomach and enough clothes on his back to keep out the wind. But as for any extras, you, being the stronger, will confiscate them and deprive him of them. [verse 154] Every kind of pleasure that this inferior might have you will undermine, and, in addition, you will constantly attack him, piling on all kinds of unpleasantness.

But why are you being so vicious? Because of all the many hundreds of times that this person [your own ego] has harmed you while you were wandering in samsara. Or again, this verse could be explained as meaning that you will wear away the satisfaction of this self-cherishing mentality and constantly undermine it, because this self-centered attitude has brought you suffering so many hundreds of times in the hells and other places of samsara. This is how Shantideva shows the fault of not being rid of pride.

In this way, use this meditation on pride as the principal antidote to jealous resentment. When people who are superior to you behave proudly and insult you with their overweening attitude, you will think to yourself, "Why are these people being so arrogant and offensive?" But instead of being envious and resentful, change places with them. Using the meditation on pride, place yourself in that position of superiority, and ask yourself whether you have the same feelings of pride and condescension. And if you find that you too are proud and condescending and have scorn and contempt for those lower down than yourself, you will be able to look at those who are now behaving arrogantly toward *you* and think, "Well, yes, I can see why they feel the way they do." And so you will serve them respectfully, avoiding attitudes of rivalry and contention.

Sakya Pandita, Manjushri in person, said in his *Explanation of the Sage's Thought:*[182]

> Place the person you do not like in the low position that you now occupy, and imagine yourself in the present high condition of your enemy or some other important person. Meditate on the envy that your enemy feels from his lowly position toward you who are so superior. What will be the fruit of such a meditation? You will think, "Since meditating on myself in a high position and on someone else in a low position and on the envy the latter feels toward me produces so much suffering, how can it be right to envy others?" And in this way your envy will naturally subside.
>
> Likewise, when you meditate on competitiveness and rivalry toward an equal, put yourself in the place of the person you do not like and consider that he or she has your position. And consider that your enemy competes with you in every possible way. When the meditation is finished, you will think that since so much discomfort comes to you when you meditate on yourself

as your enemy and on others as harming you and competing with you, you must stop harming others and competing against them. In this way, the spirit of jealous rivalry with naturally subside.

When you meditate on pride, imagine yourself in a lower position than the one you now occupy, and put someone inferior in your present position. This other person will act arrogantly toward you (now in the lower place) because of the difference in social status, qualities, knowledge, and so on. It is said that when you have finished this meditation on how others are arrogant toward you and how much pain this creates for you, you will see how wrong it is to act arrogantly toward others, and your pride will naturally subside.

It is excellent to meditate in this way. It is also excellent to put such a meditation into practice as described above. When we experience pride, rivalry, or envy, we should recall the appropriate meditation as an antidote and use it as a means to rid ourselves of our defilements. Moreover, it has been said that it is permissible to meditate using whatever method seems easiest.

5. How to act once the meditative exchange of self and other has been made

6. An instruction on the gentle way

[verse 155] From this point onward, Shantideva resumes the more usual distinction between self and other.[183] He addresses his own mind saying that from beginningless time, it has only ever wished to work for its own benefit, and for this reason, it has had to endure the great agonies of hell and the other lower realms for countless kalpas. The great weariness of all its fruitless labors has only resulted in great and protracted misery, the sufferings of [infernal] heat and cold and so on. And he observes that this ought to be a matter of intense regret.

[verse 156] He tells his mind that it should be convinced that all self-centered action results in suffering, whether now or in the future, and that it should now begin instead to work enthusiastically only for the good of beings, by means of the practice of exchange. The Buddha has declared that working for the welfare of others will result in great happiness in all one's lives; and the words of the omniscient Buddha are utterly certain and never deceive. Moreover, as one works for the benefit of others, and as, in due course, one gradually attains the grounds of realization, one will perceive the excellent qualities that derive from such actions; they will become manifest.

[verse 157] Continuing to address his own mind, Shantideva observes that, if in earlier existences it had undertaken such a practice, performing the exchange of self and other, it would now be experiencing a state of bliss like the Buddhas Shakyamuni or Amitabha, who are the objects of offering of the three worlds. He would possess a body adorned with the major and minor marks of buddhahood; he would have speech as melodious as that of Brahma and an omniscient mind, together with every perfection. He would no longer be in samsara, as he is at present, controlled by negative emotion, tormented by suffering in the present moment, and with no surety that he will escape from falling into the lower realms in his next life. It is thus that Shantideva instructs us about the resulting profit or danger of having either an altruistic or egotistic attitude.

[verse 158] Shantideva addresses again his own mind. It has identified drops of his parents' generative substances, which are devoid of "I" or self, and has clung to them as though it were itself. Now it must make every effort in taking sentient beings as its "self." This verse brings to a conclusion the teaching on exchange.

[verse 159] The omniscient Longchenpa illustrated the use of the word "spy" in this verse by saying, "When you are cutting felt, a dog will not spy on you."[184] Shantideva considers that when, in the past, he looked upon the belongings—food, clothing, and goods—of other people, he tried various ploys in the hope of manipulating them into giving him what they had—just like a dog watching people eating meat in the hope of getting some. But from now on, he says, he will instead spy on his own belongings as though through other people's eyes. And to help others, he will despoil himself of all that he has, giving it away to those who have nothing. He reflects that, in the past, he used to be envious of others. From now on he will be envious of himself.

As a disciple of the compassionate Buddha, he wears the red and yellow robes as a mark of the Buddha's blessing. And he follows in the Buddha's footsteps and correctly trains himself. Therefore he is himself a refuge for beings, the object of their homage and respect. He does not harm them at all, but only brings them benefit. [verse 160] Therefore, he is indeed perfectly happy in this and future lives, while others suffer now and in the hereafter through their bad behavior. He is in an eminent position, since others pay him homage and are respectful, whereas others are in a lowly position and are subject at all times to the payment of taxes and other duties. At all times, he has lots of people to look after him, whereas other people have no one to care for them and are harmed by many. This is not right, Shantideva reflects. He ought to be jealous of himself!

[verse 161] In the past, he injured others while trying to secure satisfaction for himself. But henceforth, his happiness and the enjoyment of possessions—all this he will give away. Whatever he has in terms of food and clothing he will give away to those who have nothing, in a bid to make them happy. In return, he will embrace their sorrows. He will take on himself the poverty that they are now suffering. In the past, he says, he constantly found fault with others. Now, having understood the way of the Bodhisattvas, he will not use his knowledge as a searchlight to inspect the shortcomings of others. Instead he will use it as a mirror with which to examine his own faults. Questioning all his actions of thought, word, and deed, he will repeatedly examine them and repudiate his own shortcomings.

[verse 162] In the past, he concealed his faults and shifted the blame to others. Now, he will act like the Bodhisattvas of the past (who would take the place of guilty criminals about to be executed). When others are at fault, whether their crimes are great or small, he will take the blame upon himself. As for his own sins, he says that he will not hide them but confess them, however slight, declaring them in the presence of many people. He will proclaim whatever faults he has, confessing them to the Buddhas and Bodhisattvas, promising never to commit them again.

[verse 163] In the past, he despised others and praised himself. Now, he will magnify the fame and excellence of others, allowing them to outshine him totally. Henceforth, he says, he will never make use of others as his servants; instead he will be a humble servant to them. He will at all times devote himself to the securing of their welfare.

[verse 164] This baneful ego is *by nature* full of faults, whatever rare talents it has (successful activities, learning, intelligence, meditative practice in retreat) are purely accidental. We should keep quiet about them, almost as if they were stolen goods, so that no one knows about them. We should never make use of them as a means to improve our situation. As the Buddha advised his disciples, "Do not advertise your good qualities; do not conceal your faults."

[verse 165] In short, we should make the wish that all the damage we have done from time without beginning in trying to get advantage for ourselves in the way of fame, possessions, and so on, at others' cost (through theft and so forth) should descend entirely on us. May we be injured, and may others benefit. In brief, as it has been said, we must purify our karmic debts and repay what we owe.

[verse 166] We should not strut around the place like proud and insolent children, so arrogant and overbearing. Instead, we should behave like newly wedded brides, demure and nervous of behaving in an impolite and headstrong manner. Let us be restrained; let our sense powers be kept well under control! In other words, without any kind of self-seeking, but with the intention of benefiting others, we should, [like the bride,] keep our eyes lowered. That is to say, we should observe a correct behavior of body, speech, and mind, whether we are sitting still or moving around. We must take care as to what we should do and how we should remain, avoiding the twenty-seven entrances into wrong action.

[verse 167] In other words, we must strive in the discipline of accumulating virtuous qualities, remain in the discipline of bringing benefit to others, and observe perfectly the discipline of avoiding any kind of negativity. And when we fail, we must use our minds to bring our bodies to heel. The mind too must be curbed with antidotes. It is as when the master of discipline exhorts the monastic community to strict observance, saying, "You must do this; you must do that. If you disobey, you will be punished!" In the same way, if, because of bad physical and mental habits, our minds transgress the rules of proper conduct, they must be subdued with antidotes. For example, if we find that we cannot give up a single evening meal, we must discipline ourselves by not eating for a whole week!

6. AN INSTRUCTION ON THE SEVERE WAY

7. TREATING THE MIND SEVERELY

[verse 168] [Shantideva continues to upbraid his mind.] Despite the fact that it has been so lengthily advised on what it should do and what it should refrain from doing (by being shown the advantages and defects that ensue), if, he says, his self-cherishing mind continues to follow its old behavioral patterns, it is indeed deserving of severe treatment through the forceful application of antidotes. For it is in his mind that all the faults and evils of this and future lives have their root. They do not arise in the body, for this is a material thing and has no such faults.

[verse 169] How is it that all faults are based on the mind? As Shantideva observes, it is through its self-centeredness, that his self-cherishing mind has guided him on wrong paths and brought him harm—in former times when he failed to appreciate the mind's defects. All that is in the past. Now that he has seen the faults of his mind and understood the Bodhisattva way, he realizes all the defects of his mind's selfishness and will now subject it to his own rule. It will have no escape, Shantideva says. He will bring his mind down with all its haughty insolence and all its self-seeking desire for profit, respect, and the like.

[verse 170] But although he speaks like this, the thought still lingers that self-interest is necessary and that he should still work in his own interest. He resolves, nonetheless, to throw all such thoughts away. Now that his mind has been handed over to others (through the practice of exchange), it is henceforth in their power. Therefore, he cries, it should stop complaining and should be of service!

[verse 171] But then, it might be asked, why should he give himself to others? The reason is that, if, out of self-interest, he becomes inattentive and fails to subject his self-cherishing mind to others, this same mind will betray *him*; it will certainly hand him over to the dreadful guardians and workmen of hell and send him into terrible suffering. [verse 172] For this is how his self-cherishing mind has betrayed him countless times in the past. It has delivered him to the janitors of hell to be boiled and scorched in interminable suffering for countless kalpas on end. With deep resentment, Shantideva recalls the harm his mind has done to him and decides that he will crush its selfish schemes.

[verse 173] For so it is, he reflects. If he desires permanent contentment and happiness, he must never strive to please himself or work for egotistical goals. Instead, he must work joyfully for the good of others. Likewise if he would like to be protected from suffering, he must strive always to be the guardian of others, never of himself.

7. TREATING THE BODY SEVERELY

[verse 174] To the extent that this human body is cherished and cosseted, protected from every discomfort and pampered with sweet and delicious food, soft, warm clothes, and the rest, to that very degree it becomes more sensitive than the flesh of infants, more peevish than ghosts and spirits. We become irritable; we feel that nothing is as it should be. And great suffering is the outcome.

[verse 175] We might well think that there is nothing wrong in satisfying our wants, if we have the wherewithal to do so. But the fact is that the earth itself and all it contains (people, possessions, amusements, and so on) are powerless to satisfy those who have fallen into this state of querulous and exaggerated sensitivity. For who can provide them with all that they crave? Take for example King Mandhata. He had power over the four continents and even shared the throne of Indra. But still he was not satisfied and at length fell from his position.

[verse 176] Such people crave beyond hope and suffer the misery of exhaustion or of the afflictions of desire and aversion. Their minds are invaded by evil schemes, owing to which they resent even holy beings and steal the possessions of the Three Jewels. By contrast, holy beings have free, untrammeled hearts, neither hoping nor craving for the delights of the senses, of friends and possessions. For them there is no end of perfect bliss.

[verse 177] Consequently, Shantideva resolves that he will give no rein to the increase of his body's wants, no occasion for acquisitiveness even on the level of food and clothing. He will have no admiration for beautiful clothes and precious things hard to obtain; instead he will be content with whatever comes his way. In the beginning, such items are easily obtained. In the middle term, they are easy to retain and are beneficial to enjoy, since there are coveted by no one. Finally, when they are destroyed, their loss occasions neither suffering nor regret, for such conditions can easily be found again. In short, the best things are those that are obtained without difficulty and toward which, at the moment of loss (at death for instance), one will feel no attachment.

As it is said in the *Suhrillekha:*

> Of every kind of wealth, contentment is supreme:
> This the Teacher of both gods and humankind has taught.
> Therefore be content. If so you are,
> You may have nothing but are rich indeed.

Contentment is the wealth of all the Aryas. If we are without it and instead have strong attachments and cravings, it will be as history narrates: A monk who was attached to his begging bowl was reborn as a snake; a monk attached to his Dharma robe took rebirth as a spirit; and a child who was attached to its woollen garment was reborn as a preta with the [same kind of] garment.

[verse 178] But even if we are not attached to our possessions, why should we not cherish our bodies? The fact is that, though we nurture and protect our bodies, in the end, when we die, they will be burned in the fire and reduced to ashes. And even now, while we are alive, this body of ours is material, inanimate, inert, moved only through the force of the mind and breath. (Alternatively, this expression could be understood to mean that the body is inert when it is dead; it is unable to shift for itself and must be carried away by others.) How is it possible that we regard as ourselves this ghastly, frightening body composed of so many filthy substances? [verse 179] Whether it be alive or dead, of what possible use to the mind is this unclean and putrescent machine? If we fail to use it for the Dharma, what difference is there between it and a clod of earth or a log of wood? None at all. So why, asks Shantideva, does his mind not rid itself of such a pretence, imagining that "This is me; this is my body"?

[verse 180] In order to provide for the needs of just his body (to provide it with food, clothing, and other goods), he has [in the past] worked on the land or as a trader or used religious property or exploited living beings. In addition to being pointless from the point of view of achieving liberation, such a situation has been the occasion of accumulating many causes of suffering, the devastation of both this and subsequent lives. To what end is all his wanting (attachment to what is near, aversion for what is not)—all in the name of something that is like a rotting tree stump? Why does he cling to it; why does he protect it so?

[verse 181] For indeed, whether he protects and pampers it now, while it is alive, with food and clothing, or whether it is devoured by carrion birds after death, the body in itself is inert. It is not pleased when it is pampered; it is not grieved when it is devoured. Why then does he give so much love to something that is completely unaware of being helped or harmed? [verse 182] Resentment when reviled, pleasure when admired—neither of these things does the body feel. So why, Shantideva asks, does he tire himself out for the sake of the body, by craving approval and hating to be scorned?

[verse 183] It might be argued that it is not because he is attached to his body that he protects it. It is because other people, his friends, appreciate it. But, he reflects, [if his mind protects his body because of *their* appreciation,] since all beings, even worms, appreciate their bodies, why does he not like their bodies as much as his? He ought to do so and to care for them as if they belonged to him. The point here (as already explained in the section on the equalizing of oneself and others) is that since there is no real difference between oneself and others, neither are there any grounds for making a distinction between one's own body and the bodies of others.

[verse 184] Since, Shantideva reflects, it is inappropriate to cling to his body out of selfish concern, he will instead give it away without the slightest attachment, for the great benefit of others, as their servant and utensil. And however many may be its blemishes (for it is filled with filth and its maintenance is the occasion of much wrongdoing), nevertheless, he resolves, he will use and protect it as a necessary implement, much as blacksmiths or carpenters might employ their tools. As it is said:

> Misused, this body is a stone for sinking in samsara's depths.
> Well-used, this body is a boat that sails to liberation.
> This body is the slave of evil or of good.

Although this body is possessed of many defects, it is also the indispensable tool for virtue. Therefore let us employ the body for its proper purpose.

2. An injunction to practice meditative concentration

[verse 185] In order to rid oneself of afflictive emotions and thoughts, it is important to let the mind settle in meditative equipoise. Therefore, Shantideva says, he has had enough of all his childish ways (all the activities of ordinary life: protecting those he likes; beating down those he hates; trading; farming; gathering possessions, respect, fame, and so on)! All of it is useless! From now on, he will follow in the footsteps of the wise, the Buddhas and Bodhisattvas. Since he has made the pledge to follow their example, he will call to mind their advice on carefulness with regard to thought, word, and deed, and will carefully fulfill all the precepts that are to be implemented. And he will avoid everything that militates against concentration: somnolence and mental dullness; all excitement and grief; all desire and attachment; anger; and doubt. He will strive to free himself of these five factors whereby concentration is dulled.

[verse 186] As described in the life stories of the great and compassionate Bodhisattvas, the Buddha's heirs, who trained themselves in this concentration, Shantideva pledges himself to do likewise. And he will, he says, generate the courage to do so. For if he fails to strive for this both day and night, when, he asks, will he ever free himself from the sufferings of samsara? When will there ever be an end to it? Saying this, he pledges himself to unremitting effort.

[verse 187] The gaining of liberation is something for which we must strive. Therefore Shantideva says that, in order to remove the two obscuring veils, together with the habitual tendencies associated with them, he will turn himself from the mistaken path (of holding apparent phenomena as truly real). He will continuously rest his mind in a state of meditative equipoise, in perfect concentration (the fusion of mental stillness and penetrative insight) upon the dharmadhatu, the authentic and ultimate object of meditation.

Here ends the eighth chapter of the *Bodhicharyavatara,* on meditative concentration.

◆ 9 ◆

WISDOM

Whereby Precious Ultimate
Bodhichitta Is Intensified

1. BRIEF EXPOSITION

[verse 1] If each of the six perfections (generosity and so forth, as explained above) is regarded as being based on the perfection preceding it, it follows that the cultivation of the perfection of wisdom is founded on that of concentration. In the present text, however, we will follow the interpretation of the Lord Manjughosha our teacher.[185] Accordingly, the Buddha, the great enlightened Sage, expounded "all these branches of the Doctrine," that is, all skillful methods, which are contained in the five preceding perfections from generosity to concentration, for the sake of, or as auxiliaries to, the attainment of wisdom. This wisdom is the principal aspect of the extraordinary path and is the direct cause of omniscience; it removes the two kinds of obscuration and actualizes ultimate primordial wisdom[186] endowed with twofold knowledge.[187] It is as when a king arms himself for war. He is surrounded by the four divisions of his army, which go with him like auxiliaries and help him to attain his goals. In the *Prajnaparamita-sutra* in a hundred thousand verses, it is also written that, "Just as all the rivers that empty into the Ganges are carried along thereby to the great ocean, likewise the paramitas, when seized by wisdom, will lead to omniscience." And in *Ratnagunasanchayagatha* it is said that:

Blind from birth, without a guide,
The teeming multitudes know not which path to take.
How can they reach the town?
When wisdom is not there, the five perfections are deprived
    of sight.
Unguided, they are powerless to reach enlightenment.
Yet when they are caught up and seized by wisdom,
They gain their sight and thus assume their name.

This is explained at length in the greater, medium, and shorter *Prajnaparamita-sutras*, the meaning of which in brief is to proclaim wisdom as the main and indispensable aspect of the path, thus revealing its great importance. Likewise, the expressions "branches" and "for the sake of," used in the root text, are meant to imply that wisdom itself is the main factor.

In the digest of the *Ashtasahasrika*, the *Prajnaparamita-sutra* in eight thousand verses, it is said that:

The wisdom paramita is nondual primal wisdom,
Tathagata, buddhahood itself.
And to the texts and path that have this as their goal,
The name of "wisdom paramita" also is applied.

This means that in order to attain the perfection of wisdom, which is the fruit, it is necessary to hear and reflect correctly upon the Prajnaparamita texts. Then experience must be gained in the supreme method, the Prajnaparamita path, in such a way, however, that wisdom and skillful means are never separated. It is therefore said that all who wish to have the complete end of all the sufferings of existence, both for themselves and others, must diligently cultivate the wisdom that realizes suchness. As it is said in the *Bodhichittavivarana*, when emptiness is realized,

The minds of yogis
Used to emptiness
Are turned with ease and joy
Toward the benefit of others.

This same text also speaks of "emptiness with the essence of compassion," referring to the fact that, as the Buddhas and Bodhisattvas have proclaimed, the realization of emptiness occurs simultaneously with the birth of compassion. And out of compassion, emptiness is taught to others, so that all the sufferings of oneself and others may be brought to nothing.

1. DETAILED EXPLANATION

2. WISDOM ESTABLISHED BY MEANS OF THE VIEW

3. AN OUTLINE OF THE TWO TRUTHS

4. DISTINGUISHING THE TWO TRUTHS

[verse 2] All phenomena, of both samsara and nirvana, have two modes. There is the "appearing mode," the mere appearance of things, in all their multiplicity. This is the relative truth. Then there is the "abiding mode," the way these things really are, their emptiness. This is the ultimate truth.

These two aspects are, on their respective levels, incontrovertible, and this is why they are regarded as two *truths*. It is incorrect to say that the two truths are distinct on the ultimate level or that they are one and the same on the relative level. Both these claims are invalidated by four unwanted consequences.[188] In fact, as it is said in the *Sandhinirmochana-sutra*, the two truths should be understood as being neither identical nor distinct.

4. DEFINITION OF THE TWO TRUTHS

It follows from what has just been said that the way of being of things, their ultimate truth—since it is free from all ontological extremes of existence, nonexistence, both existence and nonexistence, and neither existence nor nonexistence—is not the object of the ordinary mind. Indeed the intellect that thinks that things exist or do not exist and the language that speaks in these terms are said to be relative ("all-concealing") and not ultimate. It should therefore be understood that the ultimate truth transcends the ordinary mind and cannot be expressed in thought or word. By contrast, the relative truth is defined as the deluded mind and its object.

Briefly, from the point of view of the ultimate mode of being, the two truths are not cut off and separated from each other with existence referring to the relative truth and nonexistence referring to the ultimate. For the scriptures say, "Form is emptiness; emptiness is form. Emptiness is none other than form; and form is none other than emptiness." This being so, the dharmadhatu, the union of appearance and emptiness, is beyond the four, eight, and thirty-two extremes of misconception. It is inexpressible in thought and word. It is mind-transcending primordial wisdom, self-cognizing awareness. It is the perfection of wisdom, Prajnaparamita, the actual ultimate truth in itself. On the other hand, whatever the ordinary mind conceives and whatever language expresses: All such things, which thus become the object of thought and word, if examined, are found to be nonexistent. They are empty like mirages and it is never possible for them to withstand analysis. Therefore the Lord Buddha has said in one of the sutras:

> If the ultimate truth, Devaputra, were to become the object of body, speech, or mind, it could not be accounted ultimate; it would be relative. The ultimate truth, O Devaputra, transcends all expression; it is utterly unoriginate and has no cessation; it is utterly beyond signifier and signified, the knower and the known. Insofar as it is not even the object of primordial wisdom, which is omniscient and altogether supreme, it is the ultimate truth itself.

Now when it is said that the dharmata (or ultimate nature) is not an object of knowledge, this means that since the dharmata transcends all conceptual constructs, it is not *conceivable*. Indeed, how could something that is neither subject nor object and is totally devoid of characteristics be properly called an object of knowledge? As it has been said:

> People say, "I see a space."
> They certainly express themselves in words like these.
> But how can space be seen? Examine what this means.
> In such a way, the Buddha spoke of "seeing" the dharmata.
> No other image can express such vision.

But though this is the case, when speaking in ordinary terms of how Aryas rest in meditation, it is quite all right to speak in terms of subject and object, and to consider the dharmadhatu as an object of knowledge. For as it has been said in the *Madhyamakavatara:*

Suchness is unborn, and mind itself is also free from birth;
And when the mind is tuned to this, it is as though it knows
    the ultimate reality.
For since you say that consciousness cognizes when it takes
    the aspect of a thing,
It's right for us to speak in such a way.[189]

Again, given that the basis for the division into two truths consists of phenomena as objects of knowledge, the ultimate truth in this context is referred to as an object of knowledge; this assertion is made from the standpoint of exclusion. This does not conflict with the earlier contention that the ultimate truth is not an object of knowledge—an assertion made from the standpoint of detection.[190] For one should have recourse to the intended meaning of the teachings.

4. CONCERNING THOSE WHO ESTABLISH THE TWO TRUTHS

[verse 3] With regard to the understanding of the two truths, one finds two classes or groups of worldly people. There are (Buddhist) yogis who are as yet worldly beings[191] but who possess the qualities of shamatha and vipashyana; and there are ordinary worldly people who are without these qualities. And within the category of ordinary people, there are those who are disinclined to philosophical investigation and those who are not. The former are people who believe implicitly that their "I" is an unchanging reality. They regard their bodies as single, unitary wholes, and their minds as permanent entities. The latter are philosophers expounding non-Buddhist tenets, which, though they are very numerous, may all be subsumed under the two headings of eternalism and nihilism. To assert the existence of an eternal self and primal substance is an example of eternalism. To deny the existence of past and future lives and the karmic law of cause and effect is what we refer to as nihilism. All such theories, however, are successively refuted by the worldly yogis of the Buddhist tradition, who teach that bodies are aggregates of parts and not whole and single entities, and that the mind is impermanent, a process of constant change. The arguments that disprove the theories of eternalism and nihilism will be explained in due course.

Buddhist yogis who are still worldly beings, are, for their part, classified according to four distinct schools of tenets. The first is that of the Vaibhashikas (a Shravaka school). They accept the existence of external objects but reject the idea that consciousness can know itself. Their system has many distinctive features, for example the assertion of the five bases of knowledge objects, the existence of the past, present, and future as real (substantial) entities, and the belief that, apart from the simultaneous cognition by the senses of external things, the mind knows neither objects nor itself.[192]

The Vaibhashika way of positing the two truths is as follows. It is said in the *Abhidharmakosha* that:

> When objects are destroyed or mentally dissected,
> There is nothing left of them for mind to recognize.
> Such things are relative, like water
> Or like vessels. All else is ultimate.

The meaning of this is that physical objects may be crushed and destroyed, for instance with a hammer, whereas things like visual consciousness may be dissected by mental analysis [to the point of being no longer understood as such]. Gross objects like these, which can be crushed or dissipated, have a relative existence. By contrast, the smallest constituent of material form, namely, the infinitesimal partless particle, and the shortest constituent of consciousness, namely, the indivisible moment—neither of which can be destroyed or split—are held to have ultimate existence. These ideas are held in common by both the Vaibhashikas and the Sautrantikas.

The Sautrantikas[193] (the second Shravaka school of tenets) assert the existence of the external object and the self-knowing mind. Their distinctive tenets are that extramental objects are concealed by the mental objects,[194] that nonassociated conditioning factors[195] are mere names, and that nirvana is a nonthing (without real existence). Nonassociated conditioning factors and nirvana are for them mere imputations. They assert that the mind is both self-knowing and object-knowing.

And within the context of the two truths, when the Sautrantikas refer to the relative, they [make a further distinction and] say, as detailed in the *Pramanavarttika:*

> Everything that's functional
> Is here ascribed an ultimate existence;
> The rest exists but relatively.
> The one, we say, is specific, the other general in character.

In other words, all specifically characterized phenomena (both mind and matter) that are functional or causally effective are defined as ultimate; all that is not causally effective and is generally characterized is relative. For the Sautrantikas, "specifically characterized" (*rang mtshan*), "thing" (*dngos po*), "impermanent" (*mi rtag pa*), "functional or causally effective" (*don byed nus pa*), and "ultimate" (*don dam*) all have the same meaning. By contrast "generally characterized" (*spyi mtshan*), "nonthing" (*dngos med*), "permanent" (*rtag pa*), "nonfunctional or causally ineffective" (*don byed mi nus pa*), and "relative" (*kun rdzob*) are likewise synonyms. Some of these expressions, which seem to be in agreement with Vaibhashika terminology, in fact undermine the latter's tenets. Both schools affirm, however, that the indivisible particles of matter and instants of consciousness are the ultimate truth; and in this they are refuted by the Chittamatrins, who constitute the third school of tenets.

The Chittamatrins reject the existence of outer objects but affirm the ultimate reality of self-cognizing consciousness. They disprove the theory of the Vaibhashikas and Sautrantikas concerning the ultimate existence of the infinitesimal partless particle with arguments such as that of the venerable Vasubandhu:

> If six particles are joined to one,
> This partless one acquires six parts.
> If these six particles all coincide,
> Then even heaps become a single particle.

If one particle is in contact with six other particles, above, below, and in the four directions, the question is: Does the central particle have parts or not? If it has parts, the so-called partless particle is divided into six. If it has no parts, then however many particles we assemble, the result will only ever be a single partless particle, and even gross aggregations like mountains would be reduced to a single particle. The particles could never produce extended objects, and phenomena could not exist. It is thus that Vasubandhu refutes the theory of indivisible particles.

The Chittamatrins also reject the view that the inward mental perceiver, that is, the indivisible moment of consciousness, is an ultimate truth. For the question is: In the mental activity of cognizing the syllables OM AH HUNG, do the two successive instants of consciousness which know OM and AH have contact with each other or not? If there is no contact between them and they are separated by unconsciousness, it follows that there is no link between successive instants of knowing, and therefore no such thing as a continuation of awareness. If, however, there is contact between moments of consciousness, the question is whether these moments have segments, some of which touch while others do not? If there are such segments, this means that the instant of consciousness that knows OM has a first part that does not touch the consciousness of AH, and a second part that does. And likewise, there is a first part of the consciousness of AH that touches the consciousness of OM, and a second part that does not. Thus, four parts are accounted for altogether. In other words, there is a proliferation and therefore no such thing as an indivisible instant. Again, if the instants do not have parts, of which some meet and some do not, then all instants become identical, and one ends up with such faults as asserting an immutable consciousness that is not divided into earlier and later moments.

Consequently, the Chittamatrins say that whatever seems to be an external object, in fact, appears only in the mind and exists nowhere else. All phenomena are therefore said to be mind, like the horses and oxen one sees in a dream. As for the mind itself, only self-knowing, self-illuminating consciousness, devoid of the duality of subject and object, is posited as ultimate.

In this tradition, the two truths are posited in the following way. All objects of knowledge are accounted for within three natures: imputed, dependent, and completely existent. "Imputed" refers to phenomena that appear according to a separation of subject and object. This is relative truth. "Dependent" refers to nondual consciousness beyond subject and object. This, according to the way it appears [in mental events or factors (*sems byung*)], is relative. According to the way it is in itself, however, it is the "subject ultimate" (*chos can don dam*). "Completely existent" indicates the ultimate truth pure and simple. The Chittamatrins consequently attribute true existence to the self-knowing mind, and this position is refuted by the arguments of the Madhyamikas, as will be shown in due course.

Madhyamaka[196] constitutes the fourth school and attributes ultimate reality neither to external objects nor to the self-cognizing mind. The Madhyamikas say that all knowable phenomena are, in their very nature, beyond conceptual construction; they are the union of the two truths; they are equal. For this reason, Madhyamaka is supreme and enormously superior to other tenet systems. According to the acuity with which the two truths are investigated, the Madhyamikas are divided into two subgroups: the Svatantrikas and the Prasangikas.

Madhyamaka has two ways of positing the two truths. The first is in terms of an examination of the ultimate status [of phenomena]. According to this method, the way phenomena appear is their relative truth; the way they actually are is their ultimate truth. The second method is in terms of an examination of the relative status, the way phenomena appear. When subject and object appear in such a way that there is a discrepancy between the way they appear and the way they really are, this is the relative truth. By contrast, when subject and object appear in accordance to the way they actually are, this is the ultimate truth.

The faults of the lower tenet systems may be summarized as follows. The two Shravaka schools, Vaibhashika and Sautrantika, have two main defects. With regard to the relative level, they are self-concerned. As for the ultimate level, they attribute an absolute reality to the partless material particle and the indivisible instant of consciousness. The Chittamatrins say that the self-knowing, self-illuminating mind is the ultimate truth. Finally, the Svatantrika Madhyamikas insist on separating the two truths.

[verse 4] So it is that, through varying degrees of insight into the status of phenomena, there are, even within the ranks of Buddhist practitioners, those who are refuted and overmastered by others of successively elevated view. For in proportion as their insight into the nature of things becomes more acute, those equipped with valid cognition are able to refute inferior theories and not otherwise. In just the same way, as realization increases on the five paths and ten grounds, and their qualities are acquired, lower realizations and qualities are superseded.

3. REFUTATION OF OBJECTIONS TO THE TWO TRUTHS

4. REFUTATION OF OBJECTIONS WITH REGARD TO THE GROUND, THE TWO TRUTHS

5. REFUTATION OF THE OBJECTIONS OF ORDINARY PEOPLE

How are Buddhist practitioners able to disprove the point of view of ordinary people? It could be argued that, since ordinary people perceive origination and so forth as realities and are convinced of this (whereas the Buddhists reject such a view), there is no shared ground on which one side might invalidate the other. One says that all things lack true existence, the other that all things have it. There is nevertheless an example of something that both sides accept to be illusory and not real. The example in question is that of mirages or dreams, which, though they appear, are not in fact truly existent [in the way they seem]. Thus it may be demonstrated to ordinary people that, just as objects appear in mirages or dreams without actually existing, in the same way, all things, material form and so on, appear without really existing. By contrast, there is no commonly held example that could be used to show that something appears and also exists truly. It is for this reason that worldly people can never prove to Buddhist practitioners that phenomena truly exist.

At this point the objection may be made that, if all phenomena were unreal and illusory like mirages, what would be the point of training on the path with such activities as generosity and so on? It is completely unnecessary, like exhausting oneself trying to buy the mirage of a horse! The answer is that, although phenomena are found, on investigation, to be nonexistent, one must, for the sake of necessity (in other words, in order to achieve the goal), follow the path without subjecting it to analysis. And the attainment of the goal is necessary for the simple reason that, through the power of interdependent origination, the appearances of samsara and nirvana, though illusory, are inescapable.[197] Until the dualistic fixation on subject and object is dispersed in the expanse of suchness, these same appearances will continue without interruption to affect living beings—to help or harm them as the case may be. It is as a means to dispel the sufferings of ourselves and others, and to acquire benefit and happiness, that we persevere on this path—not because we believe in its real existence or in the reality of its result. It is like emanating a phantom army in order to deliver people from their [illusory] enemies or like trying to wake up someone who is suffering in his sleep.

But if the perception of things is the same for both Buddhist thinkers and ordinary people, what is there to disagree about? Actually, the disagreement is not about the existence or nonexistence of phenomenal *appearance*. No Madhyamika would ever deny the way things appear. [verse 5] The point at issue is that, when ordinary people perceive objects, they believe that they exist in just the way that they appear: perfectly real and absolutely existent. They do not have the insight of Buddhist yogis, who understand that though objects appear, they are like mirages and do not exist truly. This is the point on which they disagree.

5. REFUTATION OF THE OBJECTIONS OF THE SHRAVAKAS

The Shravakas object that if all is emptiness and without basis, this runs contrary to the fact that there are forms and other things that impinge upon our sight and the other senses. [verse 6] To this the Madhyamikas reply that to claim that form and other sense objects exist because they are perceived is the unexamined assumption of worldly people; it is just the common consensus. When such things are examined, however, they are not established by valid cognition. For, as will be explained, they can be disproved by investigating whether the sense faculties contact their objects or not. The assertion that material forms and so forth are truly existent is as deceptive as the worldly opinion that the human body is pure and permanent, whereas in reality it is impure and transient.

It could also be objected that forms and other things must exist truly, since the Buddha affirmed the existence of the aggregates, elements, and the sense fields, and defined the aggregates as momentary. But in this case, Buddha was speaking on the level of expedient meaning; his real intention was only implied.[198] [verse 7] Thinking only of the mode of appearance— his purpose being to lead the worldly (as yet unable to understand emptiness) gradually onto the path of the authentic Middle Way—the universal protector, the perfect Buddha, taught that things like forms exist. But on the ultimate level, the aggregates and so on, have no such momentary being because, on investigation, they are not established, either in the singular or plural;[199] they are without origin or cessation.

The Shravakas say, however, that if momentariness is not the ultimate truth, it follows that, since it is a contradiction to posit it as the relative, it cannot be accounted for within the two truths. Both reason and the authority of the scriptures show how momentariness cannot be posited as the relative truth. For, given that the relative is defined as that which is commonly perceptible to all, it follows that momentariness should be perceived even by ordinary people. Since this is not the case, momentariness is not the relative. Finally, did not the Lord himself say that to see momentariness is to see the true mode of being of phenomena?

In reply to this, we might say that the ordinary minds of worldly people are deceived by the illusion created by the arising of a series of different entities that seem the same; they are unaware that objects like pots are momentary. But yogis who contemplate the mode of being of the conventional level see and ascertain the momentary nature of phenomena—which is therefore relative for them.[200] [verse 8] Consequently, the objection mentioned above that momentariness is not accounted for in either of the two truths is resolved. In relation to ordinary people, who conceive of things as permanent and unchanging, the insight of yogis into momentariness represents a kind of ultimate nature within the boundaries of the conventional. Otherwise, if there were no difference between the way yogis and ordinary people understand the way things are on the relative level, it would follow that clear insight into the impurity of the human body by one who meditates on ugliness could be invalidated by ordinary people, who perceive it as pure—since the understanding of the nature of things of both parties would be on a level. Thus, while the insight of yogis into the body's impurity invalidates the ordinary perception of the body's purity, that insight cannot itself be invalidated.

But if, the Shravakas will say, all phenomena are unreal and mere illusions, then the Buddha himself is an illusion too. That being so, how could merit be gained from making offerings to him? [verse 9] The answer to this is that illusory offerings made to the illusory Buddha give rise to illusory merit, in the same way that the Shravakas consider real merit to be accumulated by making real offerings to a real Buddha. The only difference lies in the respective reality or nonreality of the merit (and of the Buddha); it does not lie in the arising or nonarising of such merit.

Again, how, if beings are like illusions, could they be reborn after death? They ought to be like the horses and oxen of a magical display, which, once they disappear, are not reborn elsewhere. [verse 10] The fact is, however, that as long as the ingredients, the magic spell, and so on, are assembled, the illusory display of the horse or ox will continue to manifest. In the same way, as long as the conditions of karma and defiled emotion are present, beings will continue to be reborn. Whether or not beings or illusions manifest depends on the presence or absence of the full complement of their causes; it does not depend on whether they are truly existent or not. But even if this is the case, it could still be argued that since samsara is beginningless and endless, sentient beings last for a very long time. This is not so with magical illusions, which cannot therefore be compared with them. No one is saying, however, that beings or magical displays are similar in all respects—duration, for example. Both may be short or long; they are said to be similar only because, although they appear, they are empty of true existence. How can true existence be attributed to sentient beings merely on account of their long duration? Indeed it cannot. Otherwise it would follow that, because some illusions last a long time and some beings last only a brief moment, true existence is to be ascribed to the former but not to the latter.

Again, if beings are illusory, it might be objected that, just as with positive or negative acts done to people encountered in magical apparitions, no merit is to be gained by giving them food and clothing, and likewise no sin is involved in killing them or harming them in some other way. [verse 11] To this it must be pointed out that even if one has the intention to help or kill an illusory man [created in a magical display], and even if one does actually proceed to slay or injure him, because no mind is present in this phantom being that could experience phantom happiness or sorrow based on such events, it follows that, aside from the subjective fault of intending an evil action, the sin of actual murder, and so on, is not committed. But in the case of sentient beings who possess minds (albeit illusory), merit and sin do arise on the basis of the good or evil done to them. In sum, the difference between living beings and magical apparitions lies in the presence or absence of a mind. There is no difference between them from the point of view of their ontological status (their real existence or illusoriness).

But then it will be argued that it is because beings have minds that they cannot be compared with magical apparitions: Their ontological status is different. But though sentient beings possess minds, these minds are themselves like illusions—how could they be truly existent? [verse 12] Because there is nothing in an incantation, or in the material ingredients for a magical display, that has the power to bring minds into existence, no illusory mind manifests. By contrast, the cause of sentient beings does have that power. One cannot say, however, that a thing is real just because it is produced by something able to produce a mind, nor can we say that a thing is not real when this capacity it lacking. A multiplicity of causes gives rise to a corresponding multiplicity of illusions. [verse 13] Nowhere in the universe is there a single cause able to produce the whole ensemble of extramental and intramental effects. From different causes, different effects appear; but they are not different [from each other] according to real existence or illusoriness. It is like apparitions of horses and oxen produced by magic. You might make a difference between them according to whether or not they have horns, but not according to whether they are real or illusory.

Those who hold that nirvana is a real entity (the Vaibhashikas) take issue with the Madhyamikas, who deny that things exist inherently. They say that the Madhyamikas believe that, on the ultimate level, all the phenomena of samsara are intrinsically nirvana and that relative truth is samsara endowed with the characteristics of birth, aging, sickness, and death. If this is so, they say, then because samsara and nirvana have a common basis, [verse 14] it follows that even if the level of buddhahood is attained, it must revert back to samsara. In other words, the exhaustion of samsara does not result in the attainment of buddhahood because [the Madhyamikas have said that] nirvana is actually samsara. Therefore what, they ask, is the point of practicing as a Bodhisattva in order to attain buddhahood? It is completely futile!

According to the Madhyamikas, this is not so; for there is a difference between nirvana that is the utterly pure nature [of phenomena] and nirvana that is freedom from adventitious defilements. [verse 15] If the stream of causes that result in different phenomena is not severed, there will be no cessation either of samsara or of magical appearances. But if the continuum of causes is interrupted, their effects will not manifest even on the relative level. And if they do not manifest on the relative level, there is no need to talk about [their manifesting on] the ultimate level. Therefore, for those who, through the wisdom of realizing the absence of self, uproot ignorance together with its seeds, there is no returning to samsara, for there is no further cause for it. The Buddha's birth in this world was not a samsaric event. It was through the strength of primordial wisdom and the cooperating conditions of his aspirations and concentrations that the Buddha displayed deeds that were like a magical illusion, while never once stirring from the dharmadhatu.

5. Refutation of the Objections of the Chittamatrins

The True Aspectarians, a subdivision of the Chittamatra school,[201] say that all things, which appear to be real—whether in the outer or inner sphere—are like optical illusions or dreams. They have no reality outside the mind. Our perception of a physical environment, mental states, and other beings is due to the ripening of various specific habitual tendencies. Therefore, even though external things do not exist, the mind itself does; and even in dreams, it experiences objects, such as color. How, they ask, can the Madhyamikas say that external objects are mere illusions and do not exist and then say that the deluded mind itself does not exist either? For if it has no existence, what is it (since there is no mind) that observes the illusory object?

The Madhyamikas respond with the same argument. [verse 16] If, they say, the Chittamatrins assert that the illusory object has no reality, then, even if they claim that the mind itself exists, what is it that could be perceived? For if either of the two poles, subject or object, is lacking, it is impossible for perception to occur. The Chittamatrins reply, however, that, according to their theory, things are not held to be completely nonexistent. They are like objects, horses or oxen, for example, seen in dreams. Instead of a material object, the mind perceives a mental object in its place. This apprehended aspect is apparently an exterior thing but is in fact the mind itself, not something extramental.

[verse 17] The problem here, as the Madhyamikas point out, is that if the perceived illusory object is the mind, what object is seen by what subject? If the two are identical, no seeing can take place. And why? The Lord Buddha, the guardian of the whole world, has himself said that the mind cannot see the mind. [verse 18] Indeed, just as the sword's edge cannot cut itself, just as the finger tip cannot touch itself, just as an acrobat cannot climb on his own shoulders, likewise the mind cannot see itself. As it is said in the *Ratnachudaparipriccha-sutra*, "It is thus: Just as the blade cannot cut itself and the finger tip cannot touch itself, even so the mind itself cannot see the mind." The crucial point here is that as long as the mind is established as truly existent, it is partless and one; and this undermines the notion that it could be divided twofold into a seen object and a seeing subject. If something appears as an object, it cannot be the subject; and if something does not appear as an object, it cannot be apprehended as one. Therefore to say that the mind is self-knowing on the ultimate level is just words; it has no truth.[202]

But why, the Chittamatrins contend, should the mind *not* know itself? It is, after all, no different from a flame, which sheds light on pots and other things and perfectly illuminates itself at the same time without relying on any other source of radiance. But to say that a flame "illuminates itself" is simply a conventional expression; it is not strictly true. [verse 19] A flame in fact has no need of illumination, for, since there is no darkness in a flame, what is there to be illuminated? If it were possible to illuminate something even when there is nothing to be lit up, the absurd conclusion would follow that a flame could illuminate even the sun and moon! Furthermore, if a flame is the object of its own illuminating, the same could be said, mutatis mutandis, of darkness, in other words, that darkness obscures itself. Consequently, if an object, such as a pot, were placed in the dark, it would be the darkness itself that could not be seen, whereas the pot itself would remain visible!

The Chittamatrins object, however, that in the context they are discussing, the illuminator and that which is illuminated are not two separate things. The flame illuminates itself by its very nature just as a lapis lazuli is blue in and of itself. A distinction can be made, they say, in the way that things are blue. There is a blue color that arises in dependence on external factors, as when a white crystal becomes blue by being placed on a blue cloth. On the other hand, there is a blue color, the blueness of which exists independently of any extraneous agency, as in the case of a lapis lazuli, which is blue by nature. [verse 20] In the same way, it may be understood that there are agents of illumination and objects that are illuminated [which are separate and interdependent], as in the case of visual consciousness and a visible form. On the other hand, there is also a consciousness that is by *nature* self-aware and self-illuminating, and here there is no mutual dependence between a distinct illuminator and a distinct object illuminated.

The example employed here by the Chittamatrins is inapplicable. It is false to say that lapis lazuli is blue independently of other factors. It appears blue due to an accumulation of extraneous causes and conditions; it is impossible to claim that at some point, and independently of extrinsic causal factors, it produced its own blueness. It is a mistake to say that blueness is self-producing.

[verse 21] Their intended meaning is also untenable. When it is said that "the flame is self-illuminating," this is understood and expressed in terms of an "other-knowing mind" distinct from the flame itself.[203] But in the case of the expression "the mind illuminates, [i.e., knows,] itself," what is the status of the mind conceiving and expressing this? Is that which knows the mind to be self-illuminating identical with that mind or is it some other mind, some other knower? To state the first of these alternatives is clearly unacceptable here, since this is precisely the subject of investigation [between Madhyamikas and Chittamatrins] and it is not established. If, on the other hand, another knower is needed, different from the first consciousness, we will find ourselves with an infinite regression of knowers with the result that knowledge becomes impossible.

Moreover, if such moments of knowing [in this infinite stream of know-ers] are not simultaneous, there can be no knowledge of past objects, [or knowledge moments], which have ceased to be; or of future ones, which have not yet occurred. On the other hand, if they are simultaneous, they must be independent of each other, with the result that, once again, knowl-edge is impossible. [verse 22] Therefore, if the consciousness (that is, the dependent reality) is not seen by anything—whether by itself or by a consciousness distinct from it—it is meaningless to examine whether it is illuminating or non-illuminating. To talk about the characteristics of something which is never perceived is as futile as discussing the grace and posture of a barren woman's daughter. It is completely meaningless.

The Chittamatrins claim, however, that though they are unable to prove it on the basis of valid perception, nevertheless, the self-knowing mind is demonstrated inferentially. [verse 23] If, they say, the mind does not know or experience itself, then, being without self-knowledge or self-experience in the past, how could it remember anything at a later stage? Memory in-deed would be impossible; it would be like having a result without a cause. Consequently, how is it that, when the blue object experienced in the past is remembered, the subject that experienced it (the apprehending con-sciousness) is also recalled?

The Madhyamikas reply that the fact that the mind can now remember that it experienced blue is not evidence that, in the past, it knew or experi-enced itself perceiving blue. The mind's present memory of itself experi-encing blue [in the past] derives from the earlier perception of a blue thing and from the fact that (in every experience) subject and object are always interdependent. (Indeed, one never finds a subjective consciousness of blueness divorced from blue objects.) By the same token, when one re-members a blue thing experienced in the past, there occurs also the recol-lection of the subject that perceived the blue. But this is not a matter of some independent consciousness apprehending blue separate from the blue thing formerly experienced. This is illustrated by the example of the venom of the water rat. Suppose in winter one were bitten by a poisonous water rat. One would, at that moment, be aware that one had been bitten, but not that one had been poisoned. It is only later, at the sound of spring thunder, that the venom begins to act and one realizes that one had been poisoned at the same time as being bitten. In other words, there occurs a newly arisen consciousness whereby one thinks that one was poisoned in the past.[204]

[verse 24] The Chittamatrins go on to object that if it is true that those who have achieved great concentration in the practice of shamatha are able to see the minds of others, how is it that the mind cannot know something as close to it as itself? The mind must be self-cognizing! If one can see a hair at a distance, they say, one can surely see a rope close by! But there is nothing certain in this. The situation is rather like that of a certain eye ointment prepared with magical incantations and so on. When this is applied to the eyes, one can see things at a great distance or perceive things like treasure vases hidden under the earth. But one cannot see the ointment itself, which is of course very close to the eye.

But, the Chittamatrins say, if the mind is not self-illuminating and self-knowing, consciousness of other things is impossible. All conventionalities seen with the eyes and heard with the ears, and all mental cognitions, would be prevented. For they are all necessarily based on the mind's clarity and self-cognition. They are impossible otherwise. [verse 25] The Madhyamikas answer that they are not refuting experiences such as sight, hearing, and understanding, which appear to have a satisfactory existence provided they are not subjected to analysis. For it is impossible to deny them, and there is no need to do so. What, then, are the Madhyamikas attacking? The cause of suffering: the belief and clinging to the *true existence* of all things. In this context, "things" are explained as referring to conventionalities validly perceived through sight, hearing, or the mind. And here, "sight" refers to sense perceptions generally; "hearing" refers to reports from other sources; and "mind" refers to the process of inference.

[verse 26] The view of the False Aspectarians, who also belong to the Chittamatra school, is as follows.²⁰⁵ They say that illusion-like objects, which appear to be external to the mind, are not distinct extramental things: The extramental object therefore does not exist. But in answer to the question of whether these objects, which are not different from the mind (for it is the mind appearing in their guise), are one with the mind, the False Aspectarians consider that they are not. For if [the illusory outer objects] were identical with the mind, this would undermine the latter's oneness and partlessness. They say therefore that the external object is just like a mirage hanging in space—a groundless appearance—and that the mind is by nature free from all aspects. It is like a sphere of pure crystal. And they claim that this resolves any possible flaw in their position.

But the Madhyamikas reply that if the Chittamatrins hold the mind to be really existent, how can the aspect or object not be different from it? For they have said that aspects are unreal, while they believe that the mind is real, and between real and unreal there is no common ground. They may be frightened by this objection into admitting that aspects are not different from the mind. But in that case, the Madhyamikas say, if the mind is identical with unreal aspects, it follows that it is unreal as well.

But if the mind were unreal, the Chittamatrins reply, it could not be a perceiving agent. [verse 27] The Madhyamaka reply to this is that, in just the same way as an object, though unreal and illusory, is said by them to be perceived by the mind, likewise the mind, though unreal and illusory, may act as a perceiver of objects. This argument has just been used for purposes of refutation; now it is being used to serve as a proof.

The Chittamatrins also say that samsara is supported by dependent reality, the really existing mind. If the situation were otherwise, if the mind were not truly existent, samsara would simply be nothing, like empty space. It would be impossible for the appearances of samsara to arise, for they would be without anything to support them. It would be like having a pot without clay or a cloth without yarn. But if samsara is real, the Madhyamikas ask, is it identical with the mind, or different from it? If it is identical, it is impossible to escape from it. On the other hand, if it is different from the mind, this is inconsistent with the Chittamatra position (which is why they say it is unreal). [verse 28] But if samsara is like this, if it is unreal, it is causally ineffective. Therefore, even though it is supported by a truly existent mind, how can one be either imprisoned in it or freed from it? One cannot hold a rabbit's horn in one's hand and dig with it. An unreal thing cannot be supported by anything. If it could, it would become a thing, part of the sequence of cause and effect.

The Tibetan expression *dngos med* [translated as "nonthing," "nonexistence," "unreal," or "untrue"] is used in two different senses. On the one hand, it is used to refer to what has no existence at all, even conventionally. On the other hand, it denotes things that are untrue in the sense of being like mirages. This is how Madhyamikas reply to those who believe in true existence, who, through not understanding that things may very well appear without truly existing, think that the "absence of true existence" means utter nothingness.

Since there can never be any connection between a truly existing mind and something that is unreal, it follows that the self-knowing, self-illuminating mind propounded by the Chittamatrins is solitary and completely isolated. [verse 29] But if the mind is without a perceived object, it is empty also of a perceiving subject. Now according to the Chittamatrins, when the "emptiness of subject and object" is actualized, ultimate reality manifests. So [according to their argument] this must mean that all beings are Buddhas from the very beginning, without needing to endeavor on the path. In which case, what is the point of elaborating a philosophical system saying that everything is mind? By affirming that all is mind, the Chittamatrins say that objects do not exist separate from the mind, and they claim to establish that ultimate reality is voidness of the subject-object dichotomy. Even so, what is the use of such a system, given that both these assertions (that of refuting dualistic appearance and that of establishing nonduality) have become superfluous? If therefore one asserts that mental aspects do not exist, it follows that the appearances of samsara are groundless, with the result that all experience becomes impossible.

4. REFUTATION OF OBJECTIONS WITH REGARD TO THE PATH, THAT IS, EMPTINESS

[verse 30] Even if it is known that all phenomena exist in the manner of an illusion, how could this understanding repel afflictive emotion such as desire? For it might be argued that a magician who produces the illusory appearance of a beautiful woman might himself feel desire for her, even though he has himself created her and knows that she is an apparition.

[verse 31] The reason for this is that the creator of the illusory woman has not eradicated the habitual patterns in himself of afflictive emotions (in this case desire) toward phenomena such as women. And so, when the creator of the apparition sees the woman, because his familiarity with the antidote to the passions, namely, emptiness, is extremely weak, how can he possibly resist the affliction of lust? There is no understanding of emptiness in his mind to counteract his fixation on real existence and the substantiality of things. If, on the other hand, he realized that the women encountered in his ordinary experience are not at all real, he would not feel any interest in an illusory one nor have any hope to have an involvement with her.

The root of craving is thought born from conceptual elaboration. Now [the realization of] emptiness gradually eliminates such thought-elaboration and leads to the destruction of both types of ignorance: all-labeling ignorance and coemergent ignorance. Finally, the mind itself assumes the nature of the antidote. It becomes like the mandala of the sun, without a trace of darkness, so that even the subtlest seeds of such ignorance are eliminated, never to return.

It may be objected here that since belief in the reality of phenomena and the conviction of the truth of emptiness both lie within the purview of conceptuality, it follows that, come what may, we are caught in the web of thoughts—like elephants washing themselves in mud. How can we ever put a stop to conceptual activity?

[verse 32] The answer is that when people cultivate the habit of considering all phenomena as empty of inherent existence (an attitude that runs contrary to fixation), they are ridding themselves of the ingrained belief in the reality of things. At the same time, by using the argument of dependent origination, they will also conclude that even the conviction in the unreality of phenomena is merely one thought supplanting another, and that it cannot in itself be the true mode of being of phenomena. Meditating on the fact that both the reality and unreality of things are completely lacking in true existence, they will finally overcome even their clinging to emptiness or nonexistence. As it is said, "Existence and nonexistence both are inexistent. The Bodhisattva who knows this is free indeed from samsara." And Nagarjuna says in his *Lokatitastava*:

> That conceptualization might be relinquished,
> You have taught the ambrosia of voidness;
> And whatever clinging there might be to this,
> That indeed you have yourself discarded.

Given, however, that the real existence of phenomena is disproved, how is it possible, some people ask, to refute the nonexistence of phenomena as well? When the nonexistence of something is refuted, its existence returns. For denial of nonexistence is the assertion of existence, and the reality of a thing is the contrary of its unreality.

The fact is that we have the habit, from time without beginning, of taking phenomena as truly existent; for this reason we must establish, and accustom ourselves to, their nonexistence. For indeed, if we do not understand that phenomena lack inherent existence, the moment of certainty as to their ultimate nature beyond all ontological extremes will never come to us. Nevertheless, mere nonexistence is not the ultimate mode of being.

[verse 33] When things, such as material forms, are examined and analyzed, nothing at all is found. One discovers that the object under investigation, on the relative plane, has no existence, no origin, and so forth from its own side. At that point, the nonexistence (*dngos med*) of that object (posited in relation to its real existence) is thus deprived of all support (since there is nothing there), and consequently, there is no way in which it can present itself as a conceptual target to the mind. It is just like the son of a barren woman: If he is not born, it is impossible to conceive of his dying. This is to say that nonexistence is posited only on the basis of a supposed existence. It is not an independent entity in its own right.

[verse 34] Therefore, when neither the thing (to be negated) nor the nonexistence of the thing (the negation thereof) are present to the mind, no alternatives for true existence remain (in terms of being both existent and nonexistent or neither existent nor nonexistent). Consequently, the mind has no other object to fix on, no ideas like "It is empty" or "It is not empty." All conceptual activity is brought to complete stillness. This is a state of equality, which is like the abyss of space. There is no name for it; it is beyond thought and explanation, perfectly revealed only by self-cognizing awareness wisdom. It is said in *The Praise to the Mother*:

> No name, no thought, no explanation is there for the Wisdom
>   that has Gone Beyond;
> Unceasing and unborn, the very character of space.
> It is the sphere of awareness-wisdom self-cognizing:
> To this, the mother of the Buddhas past, present, and to come,
>   I bow.

And in the *Mulamadhyamaka-karika*, it is said:

> It is not known through other sources, it is peace;
> And not through mind's construction can it be constructed;
> Free of thought, it is beyond distinctions:
> This describes the character of suchness.

And again we find, "Since this is the ultimate mode of being, Bodhisattvas who entertain the notion 'The aggregates are empty' are enmeshed in ideas of characteristics. They have no faith in the unborn nature [of phenomena]." And:

The Buddhas say that voidness
Is the banishment of all assertion;
Those who "have a view" of voidness,
Are barred, they say, from its accomplishment.

4. REFUTATION OF OBJECTIONS WITH REGARD TO THE FRUIT, THAT IS, THE BENEFIT OF OTHERS

When the level of buddhahood is attained, all discursive thought dissolves into the expanse of emptiness, and as a consequence, the concept of endeavoring for the sake of others cannot occur. How then is it possible to work for the benefit of beings?

[verse 35] It is just as with the wish-fulfilling jewel or the tree of miracles, which, while not having the intention to benefit anyone, nevertheless perfectly satisfy the hopes of those who pray before them. In just the same way, through the power of their former aspirations, Buddhas appear in forms appropriate to the needs of beings and constantly deploy their activity for the happiness and good of all, setting forth the Doctrine and so on. One who has attained the ultimate nirvana, wherein all efforts made along the path of training are completely stilled, and which never diverges from the dharmadhatu, has no concept of endeavor, and yet activity occurs for the welfare of beings. This, as we have said, is illustrated by the wishing jewel and other things, as well as eight further examples such as the reflection of Indra.[206]

It could of course be objected that if, at the present moment, a Buddha does not strive to accomplish the benefit of a given being through any specific miraculous work, how could such a thing come about through aspirations made in the past? But why should it not be so? [verse 36] The case is no different from that of the brahmin Shangku who once accomplished the magical enchantment of the garuda.[207] Because of the power infused into them by the brahmin's mantra and concentration, the sacred objects, such as the shrines or images of the garuda, which he made of earth and stone, had, for all who saw them, the capacity to counteract any ailment caused by the nagas and so on. And for a long time after the brahmin had passed away, these objects manifestly retained the power to counteract poison and evil influences. In the same way, why should the welfare of beings not be accomplished now without any effort being made, through an impetus set in motion beforehand?

[verse 37] A similar thing may be said for the supreme Bodhisattvas, who, in accordance with their tremendous exploits in the twofold accumulation directed at enlightenment, achieve the sacred object of enlightenment, that is, the level of buddhahood. Although such Bodhisattvas pass beyond suffering into the dharmadhatu, which abides in neither extreme, and although all their labors and dualistic mental activity now completely subside, they nevertheless effect the temporary and ultimate welfare of other beings.

An objection is raised at this point with regard to the making of offerings. The merit accruing from an offering depends on the interaction of one who offers and of someone else who consciously accepts the oblation. [verse 38] But if the Buddhas do not have thoughts or intentions, how can something offered to them give rise to merit? Of course, if nothing results from making offerings to inanimate objects, it must follow that nothing will be gained from making offerings to the relics of the Tathagatas or to stupas. Nevertheless, it is asserted repeatedly in scriptures such as the *Maitreyamahasimhanada-sutra* that the merit arising from making offerings to a living Buddha and the merit of offering to his or her mortal remains, or to stupas containing them, after such a Buddha has passed into nirvana, are one and the same. As it has been said:

> Offerings made to me today,
> And those made in the future to my relics:
> Both have equal merit and the same result.

[verse 39] Therefore, regardless of whether one considers (as Madhyamikas do) that the Buddhas themselves and the merit gained from making offerings to them are just illusions on the level of relative truth, or whether one believes (as do those who raised this objection) that both exist truly in an ultimate sense, the merit gained from making such offerings is extremely great. There is scriptural authority for this assertion. To repeat, just as the making of offerings to a truly existent Buddha is productive of merit, in the same way, illusion-like merits arise from making offerings to a Buddha devoid of true existence. Both positions, in fact, have the support of scripture.

3. Proofs of the supremacy of the Mahayana

4. The Mahayana is the Buddha's teaching

There are in general four kinds of Shravaka: those who are emanations, those who will attain great enlightenment, those who are only journeying toward peace, and the so-called sendhavas, who have much intellectual pride.[208] The latter two claim to see or realize the truth, though they do not, and are strongly attached to their theories. [verse 40] They say, for example, that the direct vision and assimilation of the sixteen aspects of the four noble truths[209] (such as impermanence) is sufficient to achieve complete freedom, the fruit of arhatship. Since this is the case, what use is there, they ask, in realizing that all phenomena are empty, without inherent existence?

It is, of course, in the Mahayana that the emptiness of all phenomena is expounded, and it is out of fear, in fact, that the Shravakas reject it. They have no understanding of this teaching on emptiness, and yet they argue against it, claiming that they realize the No-Self of the individual person. Their objection is however futile. If the emptiness of phenomena is rejected, there remains no possible antidote able to uproot completely the afflictive emotions. This is why the scriptures, such as the *Prajnaparamita-sutra*, say that without following the path whereby emptiness is realized, liberation, namely, the three kinds of enlightenment[210] cannot be attained. For it is said that for those who retain a belief in the reality of things, liberation in any of the three types of enlightenment is impossible. As a matter of fact, even the attainment of the Shravakas and Pratyekabuddhas cannot be reached without relying on emptiness, namely, the perfection of wisdom, which in consequence is referred to as the mother of the four kinds of noble beings or Aryas.

But the Shravakas do not accept the authority of the Mahayana scriptures just cited. They do not accept these scriptures as the pure word of the Buddha, but consider that they are writings composed, after the Buddha had passed into nirvana, by mere intellectuals under the influence of Mara, and that therefore no reliance can be placed in them.

[verse 41] Given that the Shravakas do not accept the Mahayana as the genuine teaching of the Buddha, the question how they prove the authenticity of their own scriptures should now be asked. The Shravakas say that their canon derives from the four texts of Vinaya, one section of Sutra and so forth, and it includes seven sections of Abhidharma. The authenticity of these scriptures, they say, is demonstrated by the fact that they are accepted by both parties—meaning that there is no disagreement on the matter.

What exactly is meant by the expression "both parties"? The Shravakas must either intend themselves and some other group, or else they must be referring to two other authorities entirely separate from themselves. Let us begin by considering the first of these alternatives. The Shravakas themselves do not possess an innate certainty that the Tripitaka of the Shravakayana constitutes the Buddha's word. So they cannot appeal to a commonly held opinion of "both parties." On what grounds, therefore, do they claim their scriptures to be authentic? Since there is no intrinsic link between the teachings and the Shravakas, it is impossible for these scriptures to be established for them a priori as authoritative.

[verse 42] The Shravakas accept this, but they say, nevertheless, that there is good reason for trusting in their scriptures. First, they say, the Buddha expounded the Doctrine. Subsequently, his words were compiled by the Arhats and elucidated in their commentaries, and finally the Doctrine was passed down by the teachers of the lineage. Reasoning proves that their tradition does not contravene any of the three criteria for examining the doctrine;[211] it is therefore a teaching that reveals the pure path. These facts, they say, show that their doctrine of the four sections of Vinaya and so on, is indeed the authentic teaching of the Buddha.

This is all very well, but the Mahayana disposes of exactly the same arguments to establish its own credibility. In the first place, the Buddha set forth the teachings. These were subsequently compiled by Manjushri, Maitreya, and others. Maitreya and Nagarjuna elucidated them with commentaries, and they were handed down by a lineage of teachers in whom we can have total confidence. Again, they do not offend against the three criteria for examining teachings and will be accepted by anyone who is intelligent and honest. This is all perfectly demonstrable, and these teachings may thus be established to the satisfaction of followers both of the Mahayana and Shravakayana.

In the second case, if by "both parties" the Shravakas mean that the common assertion of any two parties is sufficient to demonstrate the truth of a position, it follows also that the non-Buddhist doctrines, such as the four Vedas and so on, are also true. For they are believed in by many more than two individuals!

[verse 43] All the same, it might be argued that whereas, among Buddhists, there is no debate about the validity of the Shravakayana, the Mahayana *is* disputed, and this is enough to discredit it. But a doctrine is not disproved merely by the fact of its being objected to. If that were the case, then since the Buddhadharma in general is disputed by non-Buddhists, and since the different Buddhist schools (each with their specific tenets based on a particular aspect of the teachings, not to mention the eighteen Shravaka schools) all argue amongst themselves, it follows that the Shravakas should reject their own system of teachings as well.

[verse 44] The root of the perfect doctrine is the perfect monk, but to be a perfect monk is not an easy matter. It is said that five categories of men receive the designation of monk. There are those who are simply called "monk," those whose vows are degenerate, those who are just the recipients of alms, those who are fully ordained, and those who have abandoned negative emotions. Of these, the first three are only nominally monks. The latter two are the best kind, and it is they who are the root of the doctrine. Of these, the supreme monk in the ultimate sense is the one who has abandoned negative emotion.

It is difficult (for the Shravakas) to achieve such a status, because it is impossible for them to realize the truth that brings about the elimination of negative emotion. For, as they themselves admit, they do not possess an understanding of emptiness, the true nature of phenomena. The state of the fully ordained monk also presents difficulties. This is inevitable since it is a subject of controversy, and the Shravakas have already said that all controversial subjects are to be rejected. By the same token, the four sections of the Vinaya scriptures should be discarded as well.

But why, the Shravakas ask, should they not to be considered as monks who have abandoned negative emotions? After all, even if they are lacking in the view of emptiness, they do have a complete understanding of the four noble truths. The reason given in reply is that the realization of impermanence and the other aspects of the four truths are not in fact the most important aspects of the path. What is crucial however is the wisdom of No-Self that completely eradicates afflictive emotion. This alone is the perfect remedy. Therefore, those who reject the doctrine of emptiness and whose minds are still engrossed in concepts will have difficulty in attaining nirvana. For without the complete destruction of clinging to self, there is no way to overcome afflictive emotion; and it is only through the realization of the emptiness of phenomena that clinging to self is uprooted. No other way is possible. Moreover, if the habitual tendency to assume the true existence of phenomena has not been eliminated, then even if it is temporarily suppressed by means of certain concentrations, it will later reassert itself—as will be explained—in much the same way as when one emerges from a meditative absorption of nonperception. Consequently, there is no other way of overcoming afflictive emotion than the realization of the truth. And by "truth" is meant the perfect comprehension of emptiness: the understanding that the self, the conceived object of the innate process of ego-clinging, does not exist inherently.

The Shravakas of course are in perfect agreement about the need to realize No-Self, but they do not consider No-Self and emptiness to be the same. For them, emptiness means the denial of phenomenal existence like material form; it is a frightening, nihilistic notion. By contrast, the recognition of the nonexistence of the personal self (which has never at any time existed) constitutes for them the perfect view in accordance with the true nature of things.

As a matter of fact, there is no difference at all between these two assertions of emptiness: that of the personal No-Self and that of the phenomenal No-Self. Personal No-Self means that the person is merely an imputation on the basis of the aggregates; it has no objective existence from its own side. Similarly, phenomenal No-Self means that even aggregates like a body, for example, or a pot, are imputed on the basis of their assembled parts. They are empty of themselves. The only difference between these two emptinesses lies in the thing considered to be empty. The understanding of the phenomenal No-Self undermines clinging to phenomena in general, while the realization of the personal No-Self acts against the root of samsara. Aside from this, there is no difference between these two modes of emptiness.

The Shravakas, on the other hand, claim that the difference between the personal and the phenomenal No-Self is very considerable. They say too that [the realization of] the phenomenal No-Self (or emptiness) is unnecessary: Liberation is attained merely through the realization of the personal No-Self. This means that, for them, existent phenomena are not empty, whereas the personal self, which has never at any time existed, is as unreal as a rabbit's horns. They consequently have no use for the belief in the phenomenal No-Self. And so they debate, without realizing that a personal self imputed in dependence on the aggregates is in fact the very same thing [as the phenomenal self].

If one considers the matter carefully, it will be seen that the absence of a personal self and the absence of phenomenal self are of one taste. [These absences are] simply the emptiness of phenomena that are interdependently imputed. There is absolutely no difference between them. In view of this, the Shravakas and Pratyekabuddhas do indeed possess a realization of phenomenal No-Self or emptiness. This is evident from the fact that, if they were without such a realization, they would be unable to overcome afflictive emotion. It is necessary to understand that the emptiness of the person (its lack of inherent existence) is just a case of the phenomenal No-Self or emptiness. The primordial wisdom, therefore, which realizes the phenomenal No-Self, may be regarded as the general term, while the wisdom that realizes the No-Self of persons may be taken as a specific instance, a lesser category. Conversely, the belief in the self of phenomena corresponds to ignorance generally, whereas the belief in the personal self is a particular case of this. It is like the relationship between the genus tree and the species juniper.

From the belief in the personal self, emotional obscurations like avarice arise. From the belief in the phenomenal self derive the cognitive obscurations, namely, the concepts of the three spheres.[212] It should thus be understood that whereas the Bodhisattvas, who realize the two types of No-Self, have a wisdom that overcomes both kinds of obscuration, those on the Shravaka path only manage to eradicate afflictive emotion.

Yet again, the Shravakas say that afflictive emotions are eliminated through the realization of the four truths and that nirvana is thus attained, in the same way as a fire goes out when the wood has been consumed. It has however been proved that it is impossible to behold the (ultimate) truth without the realization of emptiness. And the position of the Shravakas exhibits a further drawback in that the realization of personal No-Self leads only to the elimination of the emotions and therefore not to ultimate liberation. [verse 45] The Shravakas contend that by simply overcoming afflictive emotion, one is liberated from all sufferings. This would mean that as soon as all negative emotion has been eradicated and arhatship attained, liberation from suffering should occur. For the Shravakas say that there is no more bondage. If this is indeed their position, it is apparently contradicted by the examples of the noble Arhats, the great Maudgalyayana and Kubja the Small, who though they were free from negative emotion, nevertheless suffered from the maturation of past karma. [verse 46] The Shravakas get around this difficulty by saying that even though the effects of karma were observable in their continued physical existence, propelled as it was by former karmas and emotions, nevertheless, since all craving, which is the cause for the taking of subsequent existences, was extinguished, it may be affirmed with certainty that they could never take another rebirth.

The Madhyamikas also hold that the Shravaka and Pratyekabuddha

Arhats are no longer subject to rebirth resulting from karma and emotions. They deny however that they remain in the peace of nirvana like extinguished flames, as the Shravakas believe. On the contrary, they have all the causes unhindered for the appearance of a subtle mental body. And why? Because, although Arhats do not have afflictive craving engendered by clinging to self, they do have a nonafflictive ignorance—as the Shravakas themselves admit—on account of which, the knowledge of objects is impeded through the effects of time and space.[213] Likewise, there is no point in denying that they have a nonafflictive craving. For since they have not overcome the cause, namely, ignorance, they cannot in any way be immune to its effect. [verse 47] Craving arises from feelings, and even Arhats have feelings. This is an inevitable conclusion, since all the causes are complete. On account of their propensity to ignorance, and by virtue of the pure actions performed under the influence of this—and because they are not beyond the transference at death into inconceivable mental bodies—Arhats are not completely liberated. The continuum of subtle aggregates is not severed and it remains for them to enter the Mahayana. All this is because they have not meditated, to the point of perfect realization, on the No-Self of phenomena; and therefore they have not eradicated the extremely subtle defilements that are to be abandoned.

Yet, the Shravakas ask, when Arhats die, how could the continuum of their aggregates *not* be terminated, with the result that they do attain the peace of nirvana? After all, the causes of rebirth are lacking; they are like lamps, the oil of which is all consumed. The answer the Madhyamikas would give is that such Arhats do not take rebirth in the world since the causes of reappearance in samsara, namely, negative emotions, are no longer present. Nevertheless, since they do not have a perfect realization of emptiness (the lack of inherent existence of phenomena), their minds are still oriented toward conceptuality and are attached to ideas such as "Samsara is to be abandoned" and "Nirvana is to be sought." They are not in a state of perfect peace free from conceptuality.

[verse 48] As a result, their minds, which do not have a realization of emptiness free from all extremes, and still conceive of existence and nonexistence, come to rest for a time in the expanse of cessation—only to manifest and take birth again later on. For their minds' latent propensity for ignorance, as well as their pure activity, continue to act as causes for the propulsion of their mental bodies. Because they have not gained a perfect realization of emptiness (the antidote through which all concepts vanish), they remain, as it were, in a condition similar to the absorption of nonperception or else in a state produced by this, namely, the condition of the insensate gods. Therefore, those who wish to go totally beyond sorrow should meditate on emptiness, for, without it, it is impossible to transcend suffering either temporarily or ultimately. With regard to the fact that, in the case just mentioned, ultimate nirvana is not attained, the *Saddharmapundarika-sutra* has this to say:

> Thus you say that you have passed beyond all pain,
> But from the sorrows of samsara only are you free.
> You have not yet transcended every misery;
> The Buddha's highest vehicle you should now pursue.

And in the *Uttaratantra-shastra,* it is also said:

> Until the state of buddhahood is gained,
> The state beyond all sorrow is not reached;
> Likewise with its light and beams removed,
> The sun alone we could not see.

And again, in the *Bodhichittavivarana* we find:

> The Arhat Shravakas,
> Till the Buddhas call them,
> Rest in wisdom bodies,
> Drunk on concentration.

> Roused, they take on various forms,
> And work with love for beings' sake,
> Merit and wisdom gathered in,
> They reach the awakening of buddhahood.

[verse 49] We will now consider other objections raised by the Shravakas against the authenticity of the Mahayana scriptures. They say that the teachings on higher mental training are found in the sutras; that those that deal with training in discipline are found in the Vinaya; and that there is no contradiction between those that expound the training in wisdom and the authentic Abhidharma. All these teachings, they say, must be accepted as the Buddha's word. But since the Mahayana propounds the emptiness of phenomena, it runs counter to these same three trainings. This goes to show that, taken as a whole, the Mahayana cannot be the authentic teaching of Buddha.

But is it not believed that most of the Mahayana scriptures are similar to their own sutras? They may claim that some of the Mahayana sutras teach that it is possible to avoid the fruition of even the five sins of immediate effect; that some speak about an everlasting sambhogakaya; that others assert that it is unnecessary to abandon samsara; while others say that forms and so on, do not exist. All this is considered incompatible with the scriptures of the Shravakayana. But such objections are logically inconsistent. [verse 50] If it is claimed that the existence of a single sutra, expounding an uncommon subject peculiar to the Mahayana, and which is consequently not found in the scriptures of the Shravakayana, is sufficient to invalidate the *whole* body of Mahayana doctrine as being the Buddha's word, why should the converse also not be true? Why should a single text in agreement with the sutras of the Shravakayana not be enough to prove the whole of the Mahayana as the authentic teaching of the Buddha? They do not have to be all similar to the collections of teachings of the Shravakayana. In point of fact, thinking of their compatibility with the three trainings, we may say that the Mahayana provides a much more extensive treatment on this subject than does the Shravakayana. As it is said in the *Sutralankara:*

> Mahayana harmonizes with the Sutras
> And it is in tune with the Vinaya;
> Being profound and vast,
> It does not contradict the truth of things.

Again, the Shravakas object to the *Prajnaparamita-sutras.* If they were the authentic teaching of the Buddha, they should have been understood by Mahakashyapa and the like and handed down by them through an uninterrupted lineage. This is not the case; therefore the *Prajnaparamita-sutras* are not genuine.

[verse 51] The fact is that the Shravakas themselves do not understand a subject the depths of which even the great Mahakashyapa and others could not fathom; this is the reason why they contend that these scriptures are inauthentic. But who would accept this as a valid reason for rejecting them? It is a well-known fact that the Mahayana is hard to understand because of its profundity. It is also possible to interpret Shantideva as meaning that the argument is weak because the Shravakas are not in a position to know whether Mahakashyapa and his confreres understood the Prajnaparamita or not.

It should be noted that some authorities have questioned the authorship of verses 49 to 51.

4. PROOFS THAT THE THEORY AND PRACTICE OF EMPTINESS ARE THE REAL SOLUTION

The objection may be made that if one were to realize emptiness, one would not remain in samsara and would not therefore endeavor in respect of the path and fruit. [verse 52] Although, from the point of view of the ultimate, there is no such thing as suffering, beings suffer because their minds are stultified by delusion. It is for the sake of such beings that those who realize the emptiness and mirage-like appearance of phenomena dwell in the world—which they neither crave nor fear, being freed from these two extremes. Though they abide in the world, they are untainted by its defects, like lotuses that grow in the mud. Now the ability to live in the world in such a way is indeed the fruit of realizing emptiness. On the other hand, it is precisely through not understanding the equality of samsara and nirvana that a mind sees faults in samsara and advantages in nirvana and leans exclusively toward the latter. [verse 53] It is therefore a mistake to find fault with the view of emptiness. Rather than being troubled by doubts, one should meditate upon it correctly.

[verse 54] To be sure, emptiness is the only corrective for the darkness of the emotional obscurations (the principal obstacle to liberation) and of the cognitive obscurations (which obstruct omniscience). Therefore, those who wish swiftly to rid themselves of these two obscuring veils and thus attain omniscience should by all means meditate on emptiness.

It might be thought that people do not meditate on emptiness because they are afraid of it. [verse 55] Of course, one would be right to fear something that causes suffering in this or future lives, but since emptiness brings about the complete pacification of all suffering, how can it be a cause for fear? There is nothing to be afraid of! [verse 56] If there existed a self, susceptible to fear, then of course anything frightening could alarm it. But since there is no self, who is there to be afraid? No one at all. Fear is inappropriate. Faintheartedness therefore should be cast aside. Let us be quick to meditate on emptiness!

2. Wisdom experienced by means of meditation

3. Meditation on the absence of self in individuals

4. Meditation on the emptiness of the coemergent self

On the basis of the five mental and physical aggregates there occurs the thought "I am." This "I" or self, which is identified with the "five perishable aggregates," and which, in the absence of critical analysis, is assumed to exist, must be found somewhere among those five aggregates. No one would say that it was somewhere else.

Now through the application of wisdom, the mode of existence of this self may be investigated along the following lines. [verse 57] It may be inquired whether the self or "I" is the same as, or different from, one's thirty-two teeth (for example)—whether taken individually or as the whole set together. If it is identical, it follows that the self is inanimate, impermanent, and thirty-two in number, and also that it ceases to exist when one's teeth fall out—which is, of course, absurd! On the other hand, if the self is regarded as distinct from the teeth, it is also absurd to say that *I* am ill when my teeth ache. Moreover, what one refers to as a set of teeth is not something different from the teeth themselves, and it, [the set,] does not exist as such. Therefore it cannot constitute the self.

The same kind of argument may be applied in the case of the body's twenty-one thousand hairs or its twenty nails. They are not the self. Neither is the self the three hundred and sixty bones of the skeleton. It is not the blood, nor any of the watery substances in the form of nasal mucus or phlegm. It is neither lymph nor rotten blood in the form of pus. [verse 58] The self is not the outer or inner fats, nor the perspiration of the body. The lungs are not the self; neither is the liver, nor the heart nor any of the body's inner organs. It is not the body's excrement, the feces or urine. [verse 59] The flesh and skin are not the self; the body's warmth and respiration are not the self; neither are the body's cavities, for instance the ears.

All these elements consist of many separate components, arising from infinitesimal particles. And all are impermanent. Neither individually, nor in the aggregate, can they constitute the self, for this would be in conflict with the very definition of a self. By the same token, the six types of consciousness, for example that of vision, cannot ever constitute the self, for they are a multiplicity and are impermanent.

A discussion of this matter is to be found in the *Pitaputrasamagamasutra*. The elements of earth and water account for the body's constitution, from teeth to skin; the element of fire accounts for the body's warmth. Then there is the element of wind and that of space, corresponding to the body's cavities, together with the element of consciousness. When these six elements come together, a personal identity is imputed to them and is the object of fixation. And yet the "I" as such has no real existence of its own.

The situation is comparable to what might happen in the gathering twilight when one cannot see very clearly. One sees a striped rope and thinks that it is a snake—a conviction that will remain unshaken for as long as the circumstantial conditions persist. Applying this example to the question in hand, the rope corresponds to the aggregates, the gathering twilight and unclear eyesight refer to the ignorance that gives rise to delusion, while the conviction that there is a snake corresponds to the belief in a self-identity. To pursue the analogy, one may try to locate the snake, reaching out in the gloom with one's hand, but even though one's hand does not encounter anything, it is difficult to shake off one's feeling that the snake is there, and one is filled with dread. In just the same way, one can examine the entire body, asking whether the head is the self, or the hand, and so on, only to find that they are not. Nevertheless one might still be quite unsure as to the nonexistence of the self. This only shows that the investigation has not penetrated to the crucial point. Now if a bright lamp were to be set up in the dark house, illuminating the whole place, no snake would be seen, but only a rope, and one would realize one's mistake. One would see that there was no snake, and one's earlier conviction would naturally subside. In just the same way, if this hesitant questioning is supplanted by a firm conviction that the self which is grasped at as the personal identity of the five aggregates is nothing but a mere imputation, and if one becomes accustomed to this, the absence of self will be clearly seen.

To this end, we have been told to examine where this sense of "I" arises, where it abides, and where it subsides. In accordance with this instruction, we should make a thorough investigation and should then simply rest in the state of finding nothing. When we are unable to continue with this, we should proceed with the analytical meditation described earlier. These two kinds of meditation should be practiced alternately. The first counteracts excited mental activity, while the second is an antidote for dullness and torpor.

4. MEDITATION ON THE EMPTINESS OF THE IMPUTED SELF

5. REFUTATION OF THE BELIEF IN A SELF THAT IS CONSCIOUS

The Samkhya school accounts for all objects of knowledge in terms of twenty-five principles. The self, according to their theory, is the purusha, which is conscious and experiences, or "tastes," the flux of manifestation. It is not, however, the creator of it. It is a real, eternal entity, disassociated from the three gunas, or universal constituents, and it is nonactive. All objects of its experience arise from prakriti, the primal substance. This is the name used when the three universal constituents are in a state of equilibrium. These constituents are rajas, corresponding to pain; sattva, corresponding to pleasure; and tamas, corresponding to neutrality. This prakriti is the cause of the twenty-three modulations in the same way as clay is the material cause of a pot. From this manifests the intellect, which the Samkhyas call the "great principle." From this, there arises the threefold sense of self, thence the five elementary principles, five elements, and eleven faculties. Both prakriti (the primal substance) and purusha (the self) are deemed permanent. Everything else is impermanent. Further, while the Samkhyas believe that the self is conscious, the Vaisheshikas and others hold the contrary opinion, that the self is unconscious. Now, if these two antithetical positions are refuted, all other [intermediary] positions will be disproved at the same time.

A self that is conscious and (as the Samkhyas say) permanent by nature does not exist. [verse 60] If the consciousness that perceives a sound is permanent, it must perceive sound all the time—for the Samkhyas believe that the consciousness in any given moment of audition is permanent. They reply that, although sound is not constantly perceived, this does not mean that consciousness is impermanent; it only means that it no longer has sound as its object. But if there is no object of cognition (in this case sound), what is consciousness aware of; what is it conscious of? What reason can there be for claiming that consciousness knows this or that object?

It does not make sense. [verse 61] For if the Samkhyas say that something that is not conscious of an object is still conscious, the absurd consequence follows that even a stick can be conscious (of sounds and so forth). For it is still conscious even though it is not conscious of anything. To be sure, when there is no object like sound present, there is certainly no consciousness that is conscious of it. Consciousness depends upon whatever objects it is conscious of. It is not possible for something to be a consciousness without its being a consciousness of something.

The Samkhyas do not consider this a problem. [verse 62] They say that the consciousness which perceives sound earlier on can perfectly well perceive something else, say a shape, at a later stage. Consciousness is permanent; there is simply a difference of focus on individual knowledge objects.

But if the consciousness that previously was perceiving sound is permanent, how is it that when it later perceives a form or something else, it does not still perceive sound, since it has not discarded the (permanent) nature which it had before? When the Samkhyas reply that this is because the sound is not present, the Madhyamikas respond as previously: If the object is absent, the consciousness of the object is also absent. [verse 63] Furthermore, how can a consciousness that perceives sound change into a consciousness that perceives form? The two are essentially different. This argument militates against the idea that consciousness is both a permanent and single true reality. (It should not be thought, on the other hand, that the perception of sound in a single continuum of consciousness precludes the perception of form. For the simultaneous experience of several different nonconceptual perceptions is perfectly possible.)

The Samkhyas say, however, that just as a single man can be both a father and a son at the same time, likewise objects like sound and form do not exclude each other. From the point of view of modulation in prakriti, all form, if considered under the aspect of its nature, *is* the same as sound; for this nature is one and the same in both cases. Thus, when form is perceived, even though there is no perception of sound-modulation, nevertheless there is a perception of sound's nature. This avoids (so the Samkhyas say) the unwanted consequence that auditive consciousness is impermanent.

The example that the Samkhyas give is invalid. When one says that a man is both father and son, one is merely attaching labels to him on the basis of two distinct relationships. He cannot, in any absolute sense, and *by nature*, be both father and son. If by nature he is truly existent as father, it is impossible for him ever to assume the condition of being a son, since in that case, fatherhood takes precedence over sonship. On the other hand, if *by nature* he is truly existent as a son, it is impossible for him to become a father, because it is impossible for [the truly existent state of] sonship to precede [a later] state of fatherhood. This whole matter is simply one of labeling. As such, we have certainly no intention of refuting it, and in any case it does not prove what the Samkhyas want it to prove.[214]

[verse 64] If the man is simultaneously both father and son in an absolute sense, it follows that these (attributes) must exist in the three gunas, since the Samkhyas do not accept any absolute other than these. But the nature of sattva, rajas, and tamas (pleasure, pain, and neutrality) is neither "son" nor "father." If all modulations have such a nature, in respect of whom, ultimately speaking, can the man be posited as son, and in respect of whom can he be posited as father? Indeed, it is incorrect to posit him as the one or the other.

[So much for the example that the Samkhyas use.] Now for the meaning, which is also invalid. If the apprehension of a visible form exists in the nature of the perception of sound, this ought to be obvious and clearly observed. But we have never yet observed the consciousness of form to have the nature of perceiving sound. In other words, no one has ever experienced a visual form with the properties of sound.

The Samkhyas reply that even though the perception of form as having the nature of the perception of sound is not a matter of experience, the nature of consciousness is nevertheless *one*. [verse 65] They say that it is just as when a dancer dresses in the costume of a god in the morning and as a demon in the afternoon; likewise, the earlier consciousness of sound appears later in the aspect of a consciousness of form, and thereby sees. But the consequence of this is that the previous sound consciousness is impermanent, because the earlier aspect is lost and another one is assumed. If consciousness assumes a new aspect, which is dissimilar from the first but is nevertheless considered to be one with it and not different (even though the two aspects appear quite separately), then, as Shantideva sardonically remarks, this is a kind of identity unknown anywhere in the world and is something that has never been seen before!

Things are said to be one or identical when they cannot, by their nature, be separated. They are said to be different when they can be so separated. So Shantideva is saying that to assert as one or identical what can clearly be seen to belong to two different categories is plainly contradictory. If things are seen to be distinct but are still one and the same, the absurd consequence follows that everything must be a single whole. Thus it cannot be that a dancer is [really] different at various moments (namely, when he assumes different guises) but stays the same ultimately speaking. If this is claimed, the same investigation may be applied as previously.[215]

[verse 66] The Samkhyas go on to say that the variously appearing forms of consciousness, such as consciousness qualified by sound, are no more than deceptive appearances, contingent upon circumstances. They do not exist truly. It is just as when a white crystal ball becomes iridescent; the color is not truly existent in the nature of the crystal.

Although it is acceptable to say that the different types of consciousness qualified according to an object (as in the case of auditive consciousness) do not truly exist, Shantideva asks whether the Samkhyas can tell him something about this *truly existent* consciousness of theirs. They reply that it is just consciousness, unqualified by any object. It is a single entity of consciousness that is present in all [specific] conscious experiences, past or future.

But if this is the case, it follows that all beings are one, for this mere, unqualified consciousness is necessarily present in the mind streams of everyone. [verse 67] Moreover, the conscious self (purusha), as well as the twenty-four unconscious principles (prakriti and so on), would, by the same argument, have to be identical. For they are all alike in simply existing. On that level, there is no difference between them.

Finally, the Samkhyas say that various and specific types of consciousness, the hearing of sounds, the seeing of objects, and so forth, are untrue and deceptive and therefore have no true existence as separate things. But once one has totally discounted all specificity (of experience), what remains of this mere consciousness, which is supposedly real, single, universal, and, as it were, the general foundation? There is nothing left of it.

5. REFUTATION OF THE BELIEF IN A SELF THAT IS UNCONSCIOUS

The Naiyayikas believe that the self is, like space, all-pervading and permanent. This being so, it is unconscious, for if it were conscious it would be impermanent and nonpervasive. For the Naiyayikas therefore, the self is unconscious and inanimate. When, however, it is joined with consciousness, this self supposedly identifies experiences (happiness and so on) as its own and clings to them. [verse 68] But that which is mindless cannot, for that very reason, be the self. After all, even if they were to claim that a self which is similar to a jug or a piece of cloth could perpetrate an action and therefore be the basis of happiness or suffering, things that are unconscious could never actually experience happiness.

The Naiyayikas say, however, that although the self is not of the same nature as the mind, it is concomitant [or in partnership] with it; and due to the mind's power, it cognizes objects. But this completely undermines the assertion that the self is unconscious and unaware of objects. For the self thus comes to acquire the awareness of something. By the same token, it also becomes impermanent. [verse 69] In any case, if it is claimed that the self is immutable and permanent, what object-cognizing effect could the consciousness produce in it? Obviously none. Consciousness cannot cause an immutable self to pass from one state to another, any more than one can make the sky blue by using paint! Their statement that the unconscious and inanimate thing, which, like space, is free from all activity, is the self is no more than a dogmatic claim. Alas, so much for the intelligence of the Naiyayikas!

5. Answers to Objections Concerning the Nonexistence of the Self

6. The Nonexistence of the Self is Not Incompatible with the Principle of Cause and Effect

[verse 70] Those who believe in the existence of the self object that if, as the Madhyamikas say, the self does not exist, this contradicts the assertion that causal actions of good and evil are unconfusedly linked with their resultant experiences of happiness and suffering. For if there is no possible passage of the self, or agent of actions, to future lives, there is nothing that might experience the results of actions. Since [the five aggregates] arise and cease moment by moment and the agent vanishes the instant after the action is accomplished, it is impossible for such an agent to be affected by the maturation of the act. And since no maturation is experienced, and since it is impossible for the results of one person's actions to ripen upon another, who is there to undergo the karmic result?

[verse 71] In their reply, the Madhyamikas employ the same kind of reasoning, pointing out that they and their opponents both accept that the aggregates which form the basis of an action and the aggregates which underlie the experience of its fruit are different from each other. On the other hand, a permanent self, separate from the aggregates on both occasions, would necessarily be unconscious and unchanging; and being unchanging, it would be inert or actionless. This, the Madhyamikas say, is a matter of simple logic and is as valid for their opponents as for themselves. Both parties must therefore abandon this kind of argumentation; it is nonsense to say that the relationship of cause and effect is invalid only for the Madhyamikas.[216] The latter, however, go on to say that, whereas in their tradition they are able to resolve this difficulty, their opponents are unable to do so. For, they say, the Buddha, their Teacher, has said: "The result, O monks, of an action once performed does not affect inanimate elements such as earth and so forth. It ripens on the aggregates, elements, and sense powers that are assumed by a consciousness." The result that ripens on the doer of an action is thus posited in terms of a single mental continuum.

[verse 72] For it is impossible to find an effect, the substantial cause of which has not ceased and is still present, for effects must manifest *from* causes. According to an alternative explanation, it has been said that it is impossible to find the performance of a causal action occurring in the same moment as the experience of its result, any more than a father and his son can be born simultaneously. Thus, at the time when the effect occurs, the cause has necessarily ceased. Nevertheless, by the ineluctable force of interdependence, it is certain that the effect will happen. Furthermore, this effect ripens wherever the causal conditions are all complete—in the mind stream of a specific person and not elsewhere. It is just as when seeds are sown in the earth. They spring up from the soil, not from rock. It is due to the fact that there is a single stream (one uninterrupted, homogeneous continuity) of the five aggregates, that the perpetrator of an act and the one who enjoys the result are said to be one and the same—which is, of course, the opinion that people commonly hold.

The question may be asked whether this mental continuum does not in fact constitute a single self. It does not. "Continuum" is just a label. Like a garland, it does not actually exist as such. And it is easy to see that the aged and youthful bodies of a single life, and likewise earlier and later births, are not the same. [verse 73] With regard to the mind, it is said that past and future mental states do not make up the self, for the simple reason that, the former having elapsed and the latter having not yet occurred, they do not exist. The possibility of their being the self is thus excluded. But suppose that one were to consider the present thought, occurring now, to be the self. This would mean that when this thought passes, the self does likewise. In any case, those who believe that the self exists claim that it passes from the past to the present and from the present to the future, which means that the self cannot be identified with the present mental state. It is said in the *Madhyamakavatara:*

> Qualities ascribed to Maitreya and to Upagupta
> Are distinct and cannot be assigned to one continuum.
> Phenomena that differ by their varying particulars,
> Do not compose a single continuity.[217]

Thus the theory that the mental continuum is the self is refuted. [verse 74] It is just as when one cuts open a banana tree, which is full of sap but is hollow and without any firmness or body to it. Gradually cutting through the fibers, one finds nothing substantial, and eventually the tree disintegrates. So too, if one searches analytically, one will find that the self has no reality, no ultimate existence.

6. THE NONEXISTENCE OF THE SELF IS NOT INCOMPATIBLE WITH COMPASSION

[verse 75] If there are no selves or living beings, on whom do the Bodhisattvas focus when they meditate on compassion? There is nothing to act as an object! In reply to this question, the Madhyamikas say that, on the ultimate level, there is neither an object nor an agent of compassion. "Migrating beings are never ceasing and are never born," as will be explained later. If the state of mind beyond all reference is not perfected, compassion does not become completely pure and limitless. This is indeed the case.

All the same, for beings, who impute a self upon the aggregates and become fixated on it, it is undeniable that on the level of appearance, happiness and sorrow invariably arise. There is therefore a need to liberate beings into the expanse of nonabiding nirvana whereby the continuum of dream-like appearances of suffering is severed. This is why we take the vow to liberate them.

And yet these beings, whose burden we assume, have no existence in an ultimate sense. They exist only insofar as they are imputed as selves, through the force of ignorance. Consequently, although the Bodhisattvas realize No-Self, they take as the object of their compassion all beings who do not have this realization and who incessantly and pointlessly experience the appearances of suffering, through their belief in selfhood.

Likewise, the Bodhisattvas have no regard for their own welfare. They see that others suffer meaninglessly, and the attitude of cherishing them more than themselves naturally arises in their minds. They perceive that the suffering of beings is like a deep sleep and that they are able to wake them from it.

6. A DEMONSTRATION THAT THE SELF AS LABEL IS NOT REFUTED

[verse 76] If beings do not exist, it might be asked, who is it that attains buddhahood, and on account of whom is all the effort made? Surely, it will be urged, there is no sense in taking a vow to attain such a goal. The Madhyamaka answer to this is: Yes, on the ultimate level, this is perfectly true. The person who attains such a result, the beings on account of whom the result is gained, and the result that is to be attained—not one of them has true existence in itself. Neither, on the ultimate level, is there any difference between going beyond suffering and not doing so. But in the perception of beings all these things do exist. As we have just said, they are affirmed in ignorance. It is through our ignorant belief in the self that all that pertains to samsara, karmas and afflictive emotions—and likewise the opposite, all that belongs to perfect purity—is produced. For what we call nirvana (literally, going beyond suffering) is nothing other than the exhaustion of the deluded mind's thoughts. As the *Sutralankara* says, "Liberation is but the elimination of error."

For one who, through ignorance, is enmeshed in dualistic mental patterns, samsara incontestably appears. And because of this, nirvana, the reverse of samsara, also exists. It is rather like a man oppressed by malignant spirits. He lives in the same kind of place as ordinary people, but he suffers because he sees demonic shapes and things that others do not perceive—and yet all the while he is in a perfectly wholesome and pleasant environment. In an ultimate sense, neither samsara nor the peace of nirvana has true existence. It is for this very reason that such things as bondage in samsara and liberation from it are possible; if they had real existence, neither could actually occur. This is a key point, which should be fully assimilated.

But why then, it will be asked, should we train on the path, why hope to gain what is unobtainable—surely every kind of confusion is to be dispelled? The answer to this is that, although on the ultimate level there is nothing to obtain, on the level of appearance, there is. For the sake of dissipating the sorrows of existence, and until the attainment of buddhahood, when ultimate reality appears directly, the ignorance of thinking on the relative level that nonabiding nirvana is something that can be attained should not be shunned. For it is on this basis that suffering will be removed. In the end, when one is free from every kind of dualistic concept, even the subtlest cognitive veils (arising from the firm belief in samsara and nirvana) are drawn aside.

This indeed is the level of buddhahood. But at the present moment, this is not possible for us. For us, the two truths are not in union—which is why the way things appear to us never corresponds to their true mode of existence. It therefore stands to reason that, in terms of phenomenal appearance, we should train ourselves with a view to gaining a result. It is true, we have to overcome the discrepancy between the appearance of, and the true nature of, phenomena, but for the time being we are unable. On the other hand, when this discrepancy is utterly eliminated, ultimate reality, where there is nothing to be obtained—and also nothing to be abandoned—will manifest. But until that happens, it is impossible to rid ourselves of the expectation and wish for the goal.

But that being so, why do we have to remove our ignorance regarding the self? In reply to this objection, it must be said that the two cases are not the same. The mind that seeks to obtain the fruit of enlightenment will extinguish suffering and will also put an end to itself, like wood from which fire springs and which is consumed thereby. [verse 77] The cause of all the sufferings of samsara is ego-clinging—the pride of thinking, "I am," which is fed and enlarged by the ignorance of actively believing in the existence of a personal self. The ignorance that ascribes existence to the nonexistent self is what is to be overcome. Once it is dispelled, there will be no more clinging to self, and once that has been eliminated, there will be no further birth, no further turning, in samsara.

It will be argued that just as it is impossible to turn the mind away from the merely designated self, in the same way it is wholly impossible for the mind to overcome [the belief in] the inherently existent self. After all, our natures have been imbued with it from time without beginning.

Once again, these two cases are not the same.[218] The sense of self that is just a label arises through the power of interdependence, and it is impossible for reasoning to prove that it does not appear in the experience of ordinary people. Moreover, there is no need to do so. On the other hand, belief in the inherently existing self may be annihilated by a mind that meditates on No-Self and realizes the nature of phenomena, just as darkness is scattered by the presence of light. This has the backing of perfectly coherent logic as well as reality itself. The view of self is a temporary deviation of the mind away from the nature of things and is due to extrinsic circumstances. Through the application of scriptural authority and reasoning, this aberration is overthrown. The mind thus penetrates the nature of phenomena, and since this is also the nature of the mind, the nature of things and the nature of the mind can never be separated. It is said in the *Pramanavarttika*, "The nature of the mind is luminous clarity; all stains are adventitious."

To sum up therefore, belief in selfhood is the root of samsaric existence. As long as this is not eliminated, no matter what practices one undertakes, whether austerities or meditation, one cannot get beyond samsara. Consequently, it has been said that those graced with good fortune who wish for liberation should constantly make their practice a remedy to self-clinging.

3. Meditation on the Absence of Self in Phenomena

4. Close Mindfulness of the Body

5. Examination of the Body in General

[verse 78] What we call "the body" is a mere imputation; it does not exist inherently. Our reason for saying this is that if a body, which is apprehended as a single (partless) whole complete with all its sense faculties, existed as such, it would have to be present in its members, for example the hand. But the various body parts, the foot, the shins and calves, are not the body. The thighs and hips, the waist and loins, the belly, back, chest and arms, and so on and so forth—none of these is the body. As Shantideva says [verse 79]: The body is not ribs or hands, armpits, shoulders, bowels or entrails such as lungs and heart. It is not the head and it is not the throat. What is the "body," then, in all of this? None of these different elements in fact conforms to the actual definition of the whole body. Indeed, they appear to be related to each other, but like body parts scattered on a charnel ground, they do not make up a single whole. How could any member, left to itself, constitute the body? Moreover, a hand may be amputated, but the body is still considered to remain. What, therefore, is this so-called body, this aggregate of many parts? In itself, it is nothing.

Here it will be objected that, granted that the individual parts are not the body, the body nevertheless is a reality and is present throughout its parts. It should be pointed out, however, that if this is so, it means either that one "body" with all its parts is present throughout our whole anatomy or that an entire body is present in each of our physical parts (thus implying a multiplicity of bodies). [verse 80] If it is meant that the parts of the "body" coincide with the physical parts, hands and so forth, this means that the body's parts correspond to the physical members in which it is present. But if we examine to see where this body, whole and entire, is actually located, checking off each part one by one, no single, pervasive body is found. [verse 81] If, on the other hand, an entire body, complete with all its parts, subsists in the hand and all the other members, this means that there are as many bodies as there are bodily parts. But this is impossible, since we cling to the body as a single whole.

[verse 82] Therefore, since there is no body, or rather since no body appears, when we search for it analytically within the outer and inner fields of the sense faculties, how can the body be said to exist in its parts? Obviously, it cannot. Finally, since there is no ground of imputation for the body, other than its parts, how can it be said to exist at all? It cannot. The root verse 78, beginning with the words "What we call the body . . ." shows that the body is not one with its parts. Root verse 80, which starts "If the 'body' . . ." indicates that the body is not something different from its interrelated parts.

[verse 83] Consequently, although the body does not exist as such, it is through ignorance that the idea "body" occurs to the mind on the basis of the assemblage of physical parts. Aside from being a mere label, the "body" has in fact no existence. It is just as when a pile of stones is mistaken for a man, on account of the similarity of its appearance. [verse 84] As long as the conditions are fulfilled with regard to a specific shape, the body will continue to appear as a man or a woman. But when these conditions are not complete, it will not do so, as when a change of sex occurs or during the development of an unborn child or when the body is cremated and only ashes are left. In just the same way, as long as the circumstances for the imputation of the body are found (that is, the interconnected physical parts), a body will appear. But in themselves these parts are not the body; they are just pieces of flesh and bone.

5. Specific examination of physical parts

But even if the body does not exist, can we not still say that its limbs, the arms and so on, which we can see before our very eyes, really exist? [verse 85] No, just as the body itself does not exist truly, likewise the hand is simply a collection of fingers and so on, and is merely ascribed to the assembly of its parts. It does not exist as such. The fingers also are themselves assemblages of joints, and they too are therefore without true existence; and the joints in turn are divided into their separate sides and are therefore composite, not single units. [verse 86] Again, these parts may be progressively subdivided, from the comparatively gross down to the most subtle particles, and even the tiniest particle may be split sixfold—above, below, and in the four directions. Ultimately, not one truly existent fragment can be found in any of these directional segments; even the fragments themselves disappear. Thus, if all apparent forms, for example the hand, are assessed by dissecting them in this way, going from comparatively gross to more subtle fragments, down to the directional segments of the infinitesimal particle, they are seen to be empty, like space; they have no existence as physical forms. Even the infinitesimal particle does not exist.

5. The need for relinquishing attachment to one's body

[verse 87] On investigation of its true mode of being, how could anyone cling to this physical form, which is so like a dream, appearing but devoid of inherent existence? It does not make sense to cling to it! Since the body is thus without inherent existence, what is the status of its particular character as man or woman? Neither category has ultimate existence.

Just as one analyzes one's own body, so too should one analyze the bodies of other living beings, as well as other phenomena in the outer universe, such as mountains and continents, arriving at the firm conviction that they are like space, without inherent existence. Once this has been understood, and when all dualistic clinging to one's body and the bodies of others has been rejected, all that manifests in the postmeditative state should be regarded as illusory—appearing but without inherent existence. And when meditating, one should rest in the natural state, spacious and free from conceptual activity. As it is said in the sutras, "Whoever, O Manjushri, sees that his body is like space is applying to his body the close mindfulness of the body."

4. CLOSE MINDFULNESS OF THE FEELINGS

5. EXAMINATION OF THE NATURE OF THE FEELINGS

[verse 88] If the feelings of suffering in the mind stream are ultimately and by nature real, how is it that they do not prevent the occurrence of happiness? For they ought to stop happiness from ever arising, whereas obviously they do not do so definitively. The same would also apply in the case of an ultimately real happiness with regard to suffering, and there is no need to discuss it separately. Feelings are thereby shown to be without true existence in the mind. The text goes on to prove that, in respect of the external world, feelings such as pleasure are not inherent in outer objects either. If a beautiful form or a sweet taste and so on, are intrinsically pleasurable, how is it that delicious food or an interesting sight do not make people happy when, for instance, they are in agony over the death of their child or when they are out of their minds with fear? If in pleasant tastes and other phenomena, pleasure were intrinsically present, it would have to be felt, like the heat of fire. But this is obviously not the case.

[verse 89] Again, it might be thought that discomfort is present in the mind but that it may be overwhelmed by a particularly powerful sense of inner joy and therefore not experienced, in exactly the same way as the stars are outshone by the sun. But how can something that is not at all experienced be a feeling—lacking, as it does, any such qualification?

[verse 90] Even if this last point is conceded, however, it could still be argued that when a powerful sense of pleasure supervenes, it is not that pain is not experienced at all, but that it is present in a very subtle form and therefore it is not recognized or felt, just as when a tiny drop of brine falls into a large quantity of molasses. But it is impossible for a subtle form of pain and a powerful sense of pleasure to coexist within a single mind stream. If it were, it ought to be possible for them to be felt at the same time, whereas this never happens. And since it was contended earlier that the powerful, gross aspect of pain may be suppressed by feelings of pleasure, how is it that the subtle aspect is not dispelled likewise, in the face of such a powerful antidote, as when something cold touches a surface that is totally suffused with a fierce heat?

Perhaps it could be said that the subtle pain does, nevertheless, exist, but that it is prevented from acting like pain. It is transformed by the powerful sense of bliss into a sensation of mere pleasurableness; it is experienced as a sort of subtle pleasure. It nevertheless remains what it is, like a clear crystal stained with vermilion, which looks red but is still a clear crystal underneath. To this it must be said that the subtle pain classified as mere pleasurableness is a form of pleasure; it is not pain at all. What purpose is served by calling it "pain"? And what difference is there in a mere pleasurableness that is pain experienced as subtle pleasure and a mere pleasurableness that is a subtler form of pleasure? What is the point of racking one's brains to find such nonexistent distinctions, like trying to tie knots in the sky! These examples are themselves incoherent, yet they have been adduced as proofs. But what can they prove? Nothing at all!

[verse 91] Again, one might think that when the antithesis of pain, namely, a powerful sense of pleasure arises, pain is not experienced because its causes are not all present. But in that case, if the word "feeling" is attributed to something that has no reality, surely this is a clear case of merely conceptual imputation. For according to circumstances as they arise by turns, one can see that, when the mind experiences pleasure, there is no pain; when pain is experienced, there is no pleasure. Therefore to consider that so-called pleasure and pain exist in and of themselves and to strive purposely to gain the one and avoid the other is delusion. Aside from the imputation of pleasure and pain by the mind itself, there is no such thing as self-subsistent pleasure and pain, whether inside the mind or outside it. This can be exemplified by the effect of melted butter on a hungry person as compared with someone who is sick and nauseous, or the effect of a heap of manure on a person obsessed with cleanliness as compared with a pig, or the effect of a woman on a lustful man as compared with one who is meditating on the body's impurities. Pleasure, and so on, arise by virtue of the subject's thought; there is no such thing as a sensation that is intrinsically pleasant or otherwise.

[verse 92] For this reason, the remedy for clinging to pleasure and other feelings as though they were real and the delusory chain of thoughts connected therewith (wanting this, not wanting that) is the meditation that examines and shows that feelings have no inherent existence in themselves. Apart from this meditation, there is no other antidote to grasping at the supposed reality of feelings—something that convulses the world with a kind of collective insanity. The contemplation or meditation on the unreality of feelings, arising from such a rich field of analysis, is the food enjoyed by yogis. Just as food satisfies and nourishes the body, likewise yogis, through the experience of pleasure free from desire, nourish the body of the qualities of realization.

Since feelings are the root of craving and constitute the main grounds for all disagreements and quarrels, it has been said that it is of vital importance to come to a clear-cut conviction that they are without any inherent existence, and to become accustomed to this. Whether one performs analytical or resting meditation as described above, the most important thing in the beginning is to acquire wisdom through listening to the teachings. It has been said that among the disciples of Buddha Shakyamuni, those who realized the truth were the ones who had imbibed the teachings of the preceding Buddha Kashyapa. In the future, therefore, when the Buddha Maitreya appears, those who listen to the teachings now will be born as the first of his followers and will see the truth.

5. EXAMINATION OF THE CAUSE OF THE FEELINGS

[verse 93] A physical sense faculty and its physical object such as form are either separated by space, or they are not so separated. If they are separated, how can contact take place? If they are not conjoined, they do not meet, but are like two mountains, one in the east and one in the west. On the other hand, if there is no gap between the faculty and the object, the two become one. In that case, what faculty encounters what object? It would be meaningless to say, for example, that the eye is in contact with itself.

But could it not be argued that the faculty and the object simply touch each other, like the palms of one's hands joining? No, the contact is only apparent and not real, merely attributed by thought. The reason for this is that a sense organ and a physical object do not have omnidirectional contact. If contact is made from the front, no contact is made from behind. According to this kind of analysis, particles that are separated from each other by other particles cannot be said to touch.

On the other hand, it might be thought perhaps that infinitesimal particles, unseparated by other particles, of the faculty and the object, should meet. [verse 94] Yet, the infinitesimal atomic particle of the sense faculty cannot penetrate the infinitesimal atomic particle of the object. Since they are partless, they lack all dimension with which to accommodate any kind of joining or intermingling. In relation to each other, they enjoy a status of perfect parity. On the other hand, if the two particles touch on one side only, but do not have contact throughout, they cannot be partless.

Leaving aside the particles that do not have contact, and considering those particles that do, if they were to have contact in all their parts, they must mutually interpenetrate and fuse into one. They do not however interpenetrate since neither of them has the volume that would enable them to do so. If there is no interpenetration, the particles do not intermingle. If there is no intermingling, there is no contact. For if two partless entities meet, they must have uniform contact in every direction; contact from only one side is impossible. [verse 95] How, therefore, is it acceptable to speak of contact between partless entities? It is impossible for them to have contact either from one side or from all sides. And so, Shantideva demands rhetorically, if ever contact has been observed between partless entities, let it be demonstrated and it will be established. He knows, of course, that such a demonstration is impossible.

Thus, with regard to the so-called union of object, sense power, and consciousness, Shantideva has demonstrated that the sense power and the object do not meet. [verse 96] If, however, it is contended that there is, nevertheless, contact between the mind and objects, he replies that it is unacceptable to speak of a meeting between a physical thing and the mind, which is incorporeal. One might just as well say that one could touch the sky with one's hand or meet with the child of a barren woman. Of course, it will be said that it is inappropriate to cite such examples with regard to the mind, because the mind exists. It is not inappropriate, however, because the point at issue is the possibility of contact [between a material] and an immaterial thing. Even so, given that there is no meeting or touching, surely there must be some sort of convergence of object, sense power, and consciousness? But no, even this putative "gathering" is unreal, as was shown in the earlier investigations, for example in verse 85, "Likewise, since it is a group of fingers . . ."

[verse 97] Therefore, if there is no contact acting as cause, from where do feelings result? Feelings themselves have no existence on the ultimate level, and if that is so, what sense is there in exhausting ourselves in demanding pleasure and turning away from pain? The pleasures that people desire and work for are nonexistent. It is the same with suffering. Therefore, what suffering is tormenting whom? It is just the delusion of the mind, and the mind is itself illusory.

5. EXAMINATION OF THE RESULT OF THE FEELINGS

If craving arises constantly in all sentient beings, how could feeling, which is its cause, be nonexistent? The answer is that craving too is no more than a delusion; it is not real. [verse 98] That which feels, namely, the mind and the self, and that which it experiences, namely, the feeling, have no inherent existence at all. When it is realized that that which feels and that which is felt are both without true existence, how could the result of feeling, namely, craving, *not* be averted, since its cause is removed?

5. EXAMINATION OF THE FEELING SUBJECT

If both the feelings and the one who feels do not exist, how is it possible to admit such perceptions as sight and hearing? [verse 99] By mentioning sight with regard to form and tactility with regard to physical contact, which are the first and last of the sense feelings, the root verse indicates the whole range of sensory experience: sight, sound, smell, and so on. None of them has true existence; they appear like dreams and mirages; they are simply our unexamined designations. They are mere appearances without true existence. Ultimately there is nothing to be found.

The question could be asked whether feeling and the conscious experiencer of it are simultaneous or not. Let us consider simultaneity first. If the conscious experiencer and the feeling itself were to occur at one and the same time, with the one coming neither before nor after the other, it would be impossible for the mind to observe the feeling. If distinct entities occur at exactly the same time, without the one preceding the other, they must both be completely independent of each other. Being different, they are unconnected. Therefore experience is impossible.

But what if they are not simultaneous, but rather the feeling comes first and consciousness later; what if the mind assumes the aspect of the feeling [and is thus able to experience it]? [verse 100] If a feeling precedes and the consciousness of it follows, it must be admitted that when the consciousness arises, the feeling is no longer present: It is just a recollection. Now all thoughts of things past are memories, and what is past does not exist in the present moment, and cannot, now, be really and clearly experienced. Feeling thus becomes impossible. If we examine the memory of something in the past, we find something that is deceptive. For what is past no longer abides as an object in the present. The consciousness of the past moment—the subject when the feeling was being experienced—is now no more; it can no longer experience anything. And logic proves that the feeling cannot be experienced by the present and future moments of consciousness. Consequently, the past feeling can now be experienced only as memory; the present feeling cannot be experienced; and the future is not yet here and so obviously cannot be felt by the present consciousness.

Neither can it be right to say that feeling is "self-feeling," since it is contradictory to say that a sensation acts on itself. This argument is similar to the refutation of the self-knowing mind. [verse 101] On the other hand, as we have just explained, the consciousness that is distinct from the feelings cannot experience them either. That which experiences the feelings, the agent of sensation, has no true existence. Thus, such feelings are devoid of intrinsic reality. How then can this agent of experience, self-less and like a mirage or dream-vision, composed of a collection of aggregates, be affected by a feeling designated as "suffering" but which has no inherent existence? In truth, such an agent can neither be helped nor harmed.

4. CLOSE MINDFULNESS OF THE MIND

5. THE MIND IS WITHOUT INHERENT EXISTENCE

[verse 102] No matter where we look for the mind, we cannot find it. It is not located in the six organs of sense, like the eyes, nor in the six objects of sense: form and so on. Neither is it somewhere in between these two poles of experience. The mind cannot be located somewhere inside the torso, nor within the body's outer limbs; and it cannot be found elsewhere. [verse 103] Whatever is body is not mind. But while the mind is not to be found separate from a body, as it were in exterior objects, neither does it mingle and merge with the body. But since it can have no independent existence, not even slightly, apart from the body, the root verse says, "Beings by their nature are beyond the reach of suffering." As it is said in the *Ratnakuta,* "The mind is not within; the mind is not without; neither is it both. You cannot point to it." And later, "The mind, O Kashyapa—even all the Buddhas have never seen it! They do not see it and they never shall!" And as the *Prajnaparamita-sutra* in eight thousand verses says, "The mind indeed is not a 'mind'; the nature of the mind is lucent clarity."

5. THE MIND IS UNBORN

[verse 104] If the mind, for example a visual consciousness, exists prior to its object of cognition (in this case a visible form), in respect of what object is this consciousness produced? For at that earlier moment, no object had presented itself, with the result that no subject could be generated. If, on the other hand, the consciousness and the object of cognition arise simultaneously, once again, in respect of what object is consciousness produced? If there is no consciousness present, a perceptual condition does not occur, and so it is unable to generate the consciousness. For if a perceptual condition has arisen, there must have already been a consciousness present, perceiving it. It is thus inappropriate to say that the object is the origin of that consciousness, since both terms are in that case (causally) unrelated.

[verse 105] If, however, consciousness arises subsequent to its object, again, from what does it arise, since the object of its perception has ceased to be? Does the object that has ceased continue to exist or not? If it still exists, it has not yet ceased and thus becomes simultaneous with the perceiving consciousness. If, on the contrary, something derives from it even though it does not exist, then we would have to say that a plant can arise from a burnt seed or that even a rabbit's horns can give rise to a visual consciousness!

4. CLOSE MINDFULNESS OF PHENOMENA

5. ACTUAL CLOSE MINDFULNESS OF PHENOMENA

As we have just explained, the way in which phenomena, whether compounded or uncompounded, arise is beyond our conceptual grasp. Phenomena do not come into being before, after, or simultaneously with their cause; they do not arise from themselves nor from something else nor from both nor from neither. They are without origin; and what is without origin can have no abiding or cessation. Indeed, as it has been said:

Do not cease to be and do not come to be.
They have no ending and they are not permanent.
They do not come; they do not go.
They are not different; they are not the same.

5. REFUTATION OF OBJECTIONS

6. ELIMINATING THE OBJECTION THAT THE TWO TRUTHS ARE UNTENABLE

[verse 106] It will be objected that if phenomena never arise or subside, and so on, the relative truth—which is itself characterized by origin and cessation, coming and going—collapses. And if the relative truth is not asserted, the ultimate cannot be retained either. What then happens to the two truths? They are reduced to one.

To this it must be said that the system of the two truths is propounded solely for didactic purposes, as an entry to the path. On the ultimate level, the division into two truths has no place. There is only the inconceivable dharmadhatu, pure suchness, the ultimate mode of being. As it is written in the sutra:

> There is but one truth, absence of all origin,
> But some will crow about there being four.
> Yet in the essence of enlightenment,
> Not one is found, why speak of four?

But whereas on the ultimate level, the two truths are not posited, on the relative level, they are. For there is certainly a difference between the way things are and the way they appear; and this corresponds to two truths as was declared earlier.[219]

It may be objected that if, of the two truths thus posited, the specifically characterized things of the relative do not exist, the so-called relative is necessarily posited by something other than it, namely, by the mind. Being so posited, [the relative] occurs in the mind, which means that beings will never pass beyond suffering. For as long as beings last, their minds last; as long as their minds last, the mind-posited relative truth also lasts.[220] Therefore nirvana, in which all dualistic conceptions of object and subject are exhausted, will never occur.

[verse 107] The answer to this is that these appearances of the relative, the continuum of which is insuperable, are what occurs through the thought-elaboration of individual sentient beings (which is "other" in the sense given above). They are like optical illusions, dreams, and so on. But this is not the relative that appears to someone who has passed beyond suffering.

This being so, it is not because others have dualistic conceptions that one cannot go beyond suffering, and conversely beings do not all attain the state of nonduality simply because the dualistic clinging of one individual vanishes into the space of dharmata. During sleep, objects appear like wild beasts, rivers, and so on, posited through the power of thought. They are not specifically characterized things. The appearances occurring during sleep cease in the experience of each individual who wakes. And though such things may continue to appear to those who are still asleep, they can have no effect upon those who have awakened. It is said in the *Madhyamakavatara:*

> Both when we are awake and when we are not roused
> From sleep, these three appear to be;[221]
> These same three melt away when from our dreams we stir,
> And so it is when waking from the sleep of nescience.[222]

If, after the attainment of buddhahood in the expanse beyond suffering (when even the subtle traces of dualistic perception disappear), the relative conceptions of origination and so forth were still to occur, this would mean that one was still caught up in the relative—in other words, mental elaborations dependent on oneself.[223] But this is not how it is. All the elaborations of the relative level cease to exist and this is therefore the state beyond suffering. Again the *Madhyamakavatara* says:

> The tinder of phenomena is all consumed,
> And this is peace, the dharmakaya of the Conquerors;
> There is no origin and no cessation.
> The mind is stopped, the kaya manifests.[224]

Just as when the firewood is all consumed and the fire goes out, every idea of origin, and so on, subsides; all movements of the mind and mental factors are arrested without exception. This is the dharmadhatu. In this ineffable union of appearance and emptiness, like water mingled with water, the self-arisen primal wisdom beyond all ontological extremes sees all objects of knowledge, and yet it is itself completely nonconceptual. For it should be understood that when the activity of the mind and its mental factors come to rest without any further movement, ultimate primordial wisdom manifests. When self-arisen wisdom appears, the [ordinary] mind ceases. If, bemused by ordinary opinions, we were to think that the discursive mind cannot come to a halt, or that if it could, then (as with an extinguished fire) no wisdom would ensue, this would be a great disparagement of the Buddha. This fault is to be avoided through the cultivation of certainty concerning the profound meaning.

6. Refutation of the Objection that Phenomena are Inaccessible to Reasoned Analysis

[verse 108] It could be objected that if knower and known are both by nature empty, it does not make sense to analyze them. The answer is that, although the subject (the mind) and the object to be analyzed are empty by their nature, they are said to be mutually dependent. And since all analysis is conducted on the basis of the conventionalities of the common consensus in which things seem real as long as they are not subjected to close investigation, the analysis of them is quite tenable.

6. Refutation of the Objection that Analysis Must Result in an Infinite Regress

[verse 109] In order to understand that *all* imputed phenomena are without true existence, the investigation or systematic examination made to show that all objects are by their nature unreal may itself be examined. But if so, it will be objected that the investigation cannot be the object of its own investigating. A first investigation must be examined [by a second and so on]; and in this way, the analysis must lead to an infinite regress.

[verse 110] In reply to this, Shantideva says that when phenomena are investigated and are found to be without true existence, and when it is ascertained with certainty that they cannot be characterized as produced or unproduced, analysis itself ceases to have an identifiable object or basis. When there is no longer any object or basis to act as a target, no analyzing subject will arise to focus on it. All concepts are stilled, and the analysis itself subsides like ripples on the water. This is called the "natural nirvana in the state of dharmata."

2. MISCONCEPTIONS DISPELLED THROUGH REASONING

3. A REFUTATION OF THE ARGUMENT OF THOSE WHO BELIEVE IN TRUE EXISTENCE

[verse 111] The belief in the true existence of both object and consciousness, as put forward in substantialist philosophies, is very difficult to maintain, since it cannot be established by valid cognition. The proponents of such philosophies will of course say that consciousness is established as a valid cognizer and that therefore the very fact that, as valid cognizer, it observes things as existing is enough to establish that they do in fact exist. In reply to such an objection, however, the question need only be asked: On what grounds is consciousness itself said to be truly existent? It cannot, of itself, establish its own existence on the ultimate level, and if another consciousness is needed to do so, we find ourselves with an infinite regress. On the other hand, there is no other proof.

[verse 112] It could be argued perhaps that the existence of consciousness is established by the fact that it perceives truly existent objects. But in that case, what proof is there of the existence of the cognized object? If it is again said that the proof is consciousness, in other words, that object and consciousness both prove the existence of each other, then obviously the two are without inherent existence; they exist only through mutual interdependence, just like the relative concepts of shortness and length. In other words, it is impossible to use either term as proof of the other; [the argument is circular]. [verse 113] Ultimately speaking, neither of the two has true existence; it is just as in the absence of a son, one cannot talk about there being a father, since the grounds for positing fatherhood are absent. Likewise, if there is no father, where would the son come from (for he would have no cause)? Consequently, both are untenable. When no son exists, no father can be posited as having preceded him. And likewise in the context of consciousness and objects of consciousness—whichever of the two is to be proven—if one of them (the son according to our example) is not established, the other (a father) cannot exist prior to it in the past to serve as proof. In the end, neither of the two [consciousness and objects] has real existence.

[verse 114] Those who raised the objection continue by saying that they do not claim that the two terms mutually prove each other. Rather it is just as when a shoot is produced from a seed: The existence of the seed is understood from the presence of the plant. In the same way, consciousness, which is the effect arising from the object of cognition, itself demonstrates the existence of the object. Unfortunately, this example is inadequate. For it is not the case that the existence of the seed is understood simply by virtue of the plant. [verse 115] It is our minds, different from the shoot, that infer that the shoot (the result), was preceded by a seed (the cause). It does this by separately considering seeds and plants and ascertaining the causal relationship between them. If, however, a causal relationship has not been previously ascertained, [the existence of the seed] is not revealed simply by observing the plant. What therefore proves the real existence of consciousness, in other words, the very thing that is in turn taken as evidence for the existence of the cognized object? On the ultimate level, it cannot be established by a self-knowing consciousness, nor by an other-knowing consciousness.

It may be seen from this that it is extremely difficult to render conventional reality tenable from the point of view of those who hold to real existence. On the other hand, this is highly acceptable for those who say that [true existence] is just an imputation.

3. An exposition of the proofs of those who uphold the doctrine of emptiness

4. Investigation of the cause: the diamond splinters argument

5. Refutation of the belief in uncaused origination

Philosophical schools, such as that of the Charvakas, argue that just as no one made the sharpness of a thorn or the brilliant hue of the peacock's tail, likewise, so they say, the universe has simply "happened" by itself. [verse 116] But it is a matter of everyday perception that all results are seen to be produced by causes; it is impossible to find something that arises uncaused. Here, the term perception is being used in a general sense and it covers the notion of inference.

It could perhaps be argued that the whole variety of items of which a lotus is composed: the stem, the size and number of the petals, and so on, are not to be found in the lotus's cause, and that therefore it is unacceptable to say that its various aspects have each a cause of their own. But in reply to this it should be pointed out that if a result were really present in its cause, a causal relationship could hardly be said to exist between them. On the other hand, it is evident that a lotus does not grow without dependence upon its seed; one can see that it grows out of the grain. This being so, it is a variety in the cause that produces a variety in the result. In other words, as the verse says, a variety in the result proves that there was a division or variety of potency within the cause.

[verse 117] But who or what, it may be asked, has so arranged that there is this variety in the cause? The answer is that there is no extraneous agency. The seed itself cannot arise in the absence of its own cause; its own variety arises from yet an earlier causal variety. But again, if there can be a variety of potentialities in a cause, how is it that only a seed of barley can give rise to the barley plant, and not a seed of rice? Actually, it is not that a given barley grain contains distinct capacities as it were in and of itself. It is through the power of previous causes that the grain is brought forth as something that generates according to its own kind. This is simply the nature of things, which no one can alter.

An alternative reading would be to ask why different causes can produce different effects. The answer is that they manifest owing to their respective earlier causes; and this, once again, is simply the nature of things. It follows, therefore, that what arises without a cause must either be eternal or else nonexistent; whereas phenomena are established as being caused, since they are observed sporadically in one situation or another.

5. REFUTATION OF THE BELIEF IN OTHER-PRODUCTION

6. REFUTATION OF THE BELIEF IN PRODUCTION FROM A PERMANENT CAUSE

Extraneous production may be discussed according to whether the supposed cause is impermanent or eternal. The first of these alternatives has already been dealt with; we will therefore consider the second. Those who believe in Ishvara say that he is the Lord, all-knowing, eternal, and self-arising. He is divine, pure and worshipful, permanent [immutable], one, and, in the movements of his mind, he is the maker of everything. Possessed of these five attributes, he has created the universe by his premeditated will.

[verse 118] If an almighty deity is said to be the cause of beings, it is incumbent upon those who make this assertion to define his nature.[225] It will be said, perhaps, that he is the great elements: earth, air, fire, and water. Let us admit this [for the sake of argument]. Since all things come into being on the basis of these elements, the latter may be regarded as the (material) cause of the former. This is in fact the Buddhist position also; the only difference is in the name. What they call "God," we Buddhists refer to as the elements. And since people can name things as they wish, why go to the trouble of proving the existence of God? It does not make sense. Or again, why, Shantideva asks, should we weary ourselves with questions of mere terminology? He, for his part, will not do so.

[verse 119] The theists have said, however, that God is eternal, one, and worthy of veneration, whereas the elements are multiple and transient. Moreover, the latter are without any movement of mind; neither are they divinities to be revered, for they may be trampled underfoot and are not objects of veneration. They are also impure. The theists therefore cannot mean that the elements are God for they attribute to him characteristics that are inconsistent with them. [verse 120] Perhaps they will say that he is space. But this cannot be right either, since space is inert or devoid of creative movement; it is unable to produce anything. In any case, the idea that space is the same as purusha or the self has already been refuted.[226]

The use of such images, the theists will say, does not in fact weaken their position, since, viewed from the side of creatures, the divine nature is inconceivable. But if God is beyond understanding, so is his creative role. If he is inconceivable, what is to be gained by calling him creator? Assertions must be based on reflection and knowledge. If God is utterly unknowable, who can say that he is the creator? [verse 121] Moreover, if the cause, the creator, is unknown, how can we say that creation is willed by him? It is in knowing both the "creator" and the "created" that the causal relationship between them is to be ascertained and expressed. If this were not so, it would follow that even a barren woman's son could be the creator.

But what is the created work of this almighty deity? Does he create the permanent self and so on, or the transient states of consciousness? In the first case, the theists may say that God creates the self. But do they not also say that the self and the particles of the physical elements (the created effects) are eternal, just like God? If so, how is the attribution of eternity to both cause and effect consistent with their relationship of creator and created? For such a cause is without creative function and such a result is without the character of being created. [verse 122] In the second case it could be argued that a consciousness of blue arises through the perceptual circumstance of a blue object and so on. And from time without beginning, the feelings of joy and sorrow, arising again and again in the mind stream, do so on the basis of preceding actions. This being so, what, the root verse asks, has God created? There cannot be any effects produced by him.

If God, the cause, is beginningless, then, given that he is an immediate cause of unobstructed power, how is it that his created effects could have beginnings? For if this thesis is true, it is impossible to assert that these effects arise only at a given moment and not before. They would have to exist from all time, for it does not make sense for them to be perceptible only momentarily; and the absurd consequence follows that the men and women living today have existed from all eternity.

[verse 123] In reply to this, the theists may defend themselves saying that God creates the universe in stages, and that there are times when he brings forth some things and not others. But granted that they are all God's creation, how is it that they are not all produced constantly and at once? For if the cause of the whole of creation is God and God alone, and if God is dependent on no other conditional circumstances, the cause for creation in its entirety is present constantly, and therefore the whole of it ought to be created simultaneously.

On the other hand it might be argued that God does in fact depend on various cooperative conditions. But even if that were the case, how is it that these conditions are not entirely present all the time? If it is true that there is nothing that God has not made, it is impossible to claim that what God creates depends also on some cause other than himself. [verse 124] And if he does indeed depend on other conditions, it follows that the cause of creation is rather the coincidence of cause and conditions; it is not God. For this means in effect that when cause and conditions are present, God cannot but bring forth the effects, and conversely, when the cause and conditions do not converge, God is powerless to create. [verse 125] Furthermore, granted that God is dependent on the convergence of cause and conditions, if he is thereby constrained against his will to bring about the suffering of others, it is clear that he is subject to an extraneous power.

And even if he creates according to his pleasure, he is dependent on his wishes and is once again constrained by something else, for he is caught on the hook of his desire. Finally, even if we were to accept that God is the creator of the world, in what does his omnipotent divinity consist? For if he is accounted the maker of objects, he is necessarily impermanent; if he is permanent, this can only mean that he is without causal effectiveness.

[verse 126] Finally, the Mimamsaka theory, that the [material] cause of the universe is the infinitesimal and permanent particle, was disposed of above with the argument that particles may be directionally divided. There is no need to discuss it separately here.

5. Refutation of the belief in self-production

6. Refutation of the primal substance

A primal substance that is the cause of the world and is characterized in five points as being eternal, one, devoid of consciousness, invisible to ordinary sight, and universally creative is propounded by the Samkhya school, which classifies all phenomena into twenty-five principles. [verse 127] The nature of this primal matter, or prakriti, is defined as the equilibrium of the three universal constituents, or gunas: sattva (pleasure), rajas (pain), and tamas (neutrality). Prakriti is the cause of all manifestation and is thus referred to as "primal." For the Samkhyas say that, when its constituent elements fall into a state of imbalance, the modulation [or appearance] of the whole multiplicity of the world is set in motion.

[verse 128] It is inconsistent to say that the primal substance is truly one and then say that its nature is threefold. If it has three elements, it is not *one*. There can be no such thing, therefore, as a primal cause that is both one and permanent. Likewise, the three universal constituents have no real existence in themselves either. For each constituent is again divisible into three. In other words, there is rajas of rajas, sattva of rajas, and tamas of rajas, and so on. Otherwise they would be more fundamental than the primal substance itself. [verse 129] Now if these three causal constituents are nonexistent, the theory of such things as "sound modulation" arising from them becomes, as the root text says, extremely far-fetched. In other words, these modulations must also be nonexistent. [To talk about them] is like talking about [clay] pots not made of clay.

Moreover, if it can be validly established that feelings fall within the mental sphere, it is obviously impossible for pleasure, and so on, to be located in inanimate things like clothing. [verse 130] The Samkhyas may object, however, that their position is tenable because inanimate objects like sounds or clothing do in fact give rise to pleasure, pain, or indifference. But did not Shantideva examine phenomena such as clothes and show them to be nonexistent, at the time that he refuted the existence of bodies?

The Samkhyas should understand too that from the relative point of view, they undermine their own position. For they claim that the cause of woollen cloth is the gunas, pleasure and so forth, and then go on to say that the effect of woollen cloth is pleasure also. In other words, pleasure is made out to be both the cause and the result of cloth. This is ridiculous. It is like saying that a man is both the father and son of the same person. If it is protested that there are different kinds of pleasure, then this militates against the single nature of pleasure and is manifestly at variance with what is perceived. [verse 131] Woollen cloth has certainly never been seen to arise from pleasure and the like, while on the other hand, it is true that things like blankets or garlands of sandal flowers may be seen to give rise to pleasure. But given that things like cloth have no real existence even on the level of the infinitesimal particles, the feelings of pleasure and so on that arise from them cannot exist separately on their own.

But pleasure, the Samkhyas say, is not necessarily dependent on such things as cloth, it is the eternal nature of the primal substance. If that is so, however, it follows that pleasure must be perceived constantly and cannot be averted, for this observable pleasure cannot diverge from its previous nature. Pleasure, on the other hand, is not at all permanently perceived, and thus the assertion of the Samkhyas is untenable. They insist however, that although the gunas have a permanent existence, they have a particular feature of being sometimes manifest and sometimes not. Thus, they say, it does not inevitably follow that they should be constantly detectable. The answer to this is that if pleasure and suchlike were not at all manifest, they would be beyond all knowledge, and it would be inappropriate to speak of their existence. The Samkhyas do not indeed claim this. [verse 132] But if pleasure and so forth are manifest intermittently, the question is: Why are they not the object of constant perception? For the Samkhyas claim that pleasure and the other gunas are perceptible—they pervade the object of perception and dwell constantly in it. The gunas should therefore be as obvious as a lighted lamp before one's very eyes.

In fact, the Samkhyas make a distinction, saying that if pleasure and the rest, in a gross apparent form, become more subtle, they exist in a state of nonmanifest potentiality and cannot be perceived. But it is a contradiction to say that pleasure and so forth, defined as one and permanent, have opposite states of grossness and subtlety. How can they possibly be both? [verse 133] The Samkhyas may try to defend themselves by saying that a preceding state of grossness may be cast off and a new state of subtlety assumed. But a pleasure that can become gross or subtle is demonstrably impermanent. And if the Samkhyas assert that pleasure and the other gunas, when manifest, can throw off a preceding state and enter into another, why do they not also attribute impermanence to *all* of the twenty-five principles? For it is never possible for all of them to be observed with the same mode of appearance. The Samkhyas may say that, whether gross or subtle, the actual nature of pleasure is never lost, and therefore its permanent character is not impaired. To this it must be said that pleasure and its character of grossness are either two different things or the same. If they are different, it follows that when its grossness subsides, the pleasure itself does not subside and is still manifest, and should therefore continue to be felt. [verse 134] If, on the other hand, it is said that this gross aspect is not different from the pleasure but is actually the same thing, the impermanence of pleasure is clearly and certainly established.

6. THE ACTUAL REFUTATION OF SELF-PRODUCTION: THE MAIN ARGUMENT

The Samkhyas argue that when the guna of pleasure ceases to manifest, it abides hidden, in a potential state, within the expanse of prakriti, the primal substance. When it reappears later, it is merely the manifestation of what was already there. For if it did not preexist in any sense, it would be incorrect to speak of its coming into being. It would be like a rabbit's horns being produced from clay. Therefore whatever becomes manifest must have existed until that moment, according to its own nature, within the sphere of the primal substance. This amounts to saying that the cause and the result coexist.

[verse 135] But the question must be asked, If all results are contemporaneous with their causes, why is it that they are not constantly perceptible? The Samkhyas reply that it is simply because these results are not, at a given moment, apparent to consciousness. Later on they become so, just like a pot in a darkened room becomes visible in the light of a lamp.

In speaking like this, the Samkhyas are undermining their own main thesis. Although they do not mean, and do not say, that manifestation is absent at the time of the cause and that it arises newly, what they have just said in fact comes to this. And if manifestation does occur at the time of the cause, they cannot assert a distinction between manifestation and non-manifestation; and it follows that there must be manifestation from the very beginning. The position of the Samkhyas is both self-contradictory and irrational. For if, for the Samkhyas, the result is truly manifest in the cause, it follows that when they eat their food, they eat their excrement! [verse 136] Moreover, with the money that they use to purchase their clothing made of fine cotton, let them rather buy cotton seeds from which the fabric comes and wear those! That, says Shantideva, is how they might substantiate their doctrine!

The Samkhyas insist, however, that the result coexists in the cause but that ordinary people do not perceive this because their eyes are dimmed by the darkness of stupidity. [verse 137] But [Shantideva replies] this is said by the Samkhya teachers, who claim to have a knowledge of the truth (that the result is already present in the cause). Well then, since this knowledge of the truth exists in the minds of ordinary people, how is it that they do not see it as well (for the cause for it is complete)? How is it that they do not? If we follow the theory of the Samkhyas, a conscious knowledge of reality, being a result, should be present in all sentient beings. But even supposing that people accepted the proposition of the Samkhyas that the result is present in the cause, who was ever seen to consume filth when they ate or to show an interest in cotton seeds when they were buying material for their clothes? The fact is that no one has ever under any circumstances been observed to live according to the Samkhya description of reality, which collapses as a result.

The Samkhyas will perhaps retort that the perceptions of ordinary people have no validity and therefore do not constitute a refutation. But in that case, the manifestations, which have the nature of results and which ordinary people perceive, must be unreal and not true. If they are unreal, to say that these results were present in their causes because they manifested later is meaningless.

[verse 138] The Samkhyas tax the Madhyamikas with the following question. If, because an agent of assessment is deceptive, an object of assessment is not established, and if, as the Madhyamikas say, the assessing consciousness is not a valid (that is, an ultimately valid) cognition, does it not follow that a tenet system assessed by such a consciousness is also deceptive? Consequently, when such an analytical cognition (which is deceptive) makes an assessment saying that, ultimately, on the level of suchness, all is emptiness, and when such emptiness is meditated upon, does not this become an untenable position, for the reason just given?

[verse 139] The answer is that Madhyamikas have not, in fact, elaborated any system of tenets based on the true existence of a specifically locatable object called "emptiness," regarded as something established by valid cognition. The reason is that, without referring to or basing oneself on a pot or some other actual thing, it is never possible to conceive of a "nonpot" or "nonexistent pot," [a nonthing or nonexistent thing,] as if this were a separate entity. For this reason, the emptiness of the pot, in the sense of the nonexistent pot, is a lesser, approximate form of emptiness. For it is just the clearing away or refutation of its existence aspect.[227] Therefore the Madhyamikas say that because things are deceptive or unreal *in themselves*, their nonexistence is also clearly and certainly unreal also.[228]

Well then, say the Samkhyas, what is the point of meditating, telling oneself that phenomena do not exist, given that both their existence and their nonexistence are equally false and unreal? The Madhyamikas reply that it is our clinging to the inherent existence of phenomena, a habit acquired from time without beginning, that is, at the moment, binding us to samsara. The antidote to this is quite simply to acquire the habit of considering phenomena to be without inherent existence. But both their existence or nonexistence are equally unreal. [verse 140] It is just as when people suffer when they dream that they have a child which then dies. In the dream, the thought of the death supplants the thought that the child was alive, yet the thought of the child's death is itself unreal. Two sticks which, when rubbed together, produce a fire, are themselves burned up in the blaze. Just so, the dense forest of all conceptual bearings, which posit phenomena as existent and nonexistent, will be totally consumed by the fires of the wisdom of ascertaining that all phenomena are without true existence. To abide in that primal wisdom in which all concepts have subsided is the Great Madhyamaka, the Great Middle Way, free from all assertion. It is written in the *Mulamadhyamaka-karika:*

> What is called "existence" is but clinging to things'
>   permanence;
> And "nonexistence" is the view of nothingness.
> And thus the wise and learned do not rest
> In either "This thing is" or "It is not."

5. CONCLUSION OF THE ARGUMENT

[verse 141] On the basis of the reasons and analytical methods given above, we can see that things do not exist uncaused and also that they do not proceed from an eternal cause. Just like shoots burgeoning from their seeds, all inanimate phenomena arise in dependence on their own causes and conditions; and all animate phenomena arise dependently in a continuous chain, from ignorance down to old age and death. Nevertheless, none of these resultant phenomena coexist in their own causes and conditions, either one by one or in the aggregate. Causal elements taken one by one, are unable to produce effects, and a combination of such elements is not the slightest bit different from these individual elements. For example, a flint stone, steel, and tinder taken individually are unable to produce a flame, and a combination of them, being no different from the said elements, is equally unproductive. This does not mean, however, that the effect arises from causes other than these or that it has coexisted in these causes from the outset.

[verse 142] It does not mean that, when the result appears, it *arises* from something other than its own causes and conditions. Neither does it mean that the result *abides* in the present, produced in dependence upon its causes but nevertheless different from them by nature. Furthermore, when it *subsides*, it does not depart hence and go elsewhere. This is why it is said that all phenomena are by nature empty of their causes.

In this context, the expression "causes taken one by one" refers to the refutation of origination from self and from other. The expression "in the aggregate" indicates the refutation of origination from both [and neither]. This is also explained as the refutation of the four theories of production.

4. INVESTIGATION OF THE NATURE: THE GREAT INTERDEPENDENCE ARGUMENT

[verse 143] Outer and inner entities, which the ignorant accept as real, appear but are without true existence. How are they different from mirages? They are not at all different. We need only investigate the horses and oxen of a magical illusion and then the things produced from causes, considering where they come from, where they abide, and where they go to when they subside. We will find that both have an equal status.

[verse 144] Be that as it may, if a resultant effect comes about through the convergence of productive causes, its appearance and the perception of it occur on account of those causes, or through their power. If, on the other hand, the causes are not present, the effect does not appear and is not to be seen. Therefore how can real, objective existence be attributed to what is in fact like a reflection, a figment put together from causes and conditions?

It should be understood that interdependent origination involves none of the extreme positions implied in terms like permanence, annihilation, arising and subsiding, existence and nonexistence. It accords, rather, with the eight examples of illusoriness.[229] As it is written in the sutra, Whatever is produced from causal conditions is not produced; it does not have the nature of a produced thing. Dependence on conditions is the same as emptiness, and those who understand emptiness are careful [in their actions]. The master Nagarjuna said:

> But for what originates dependently,
> There are no phenomena;
> There are no phenomena, therefore,
> That are not empty.

4. Investigation of the Result: the argument that refutes the origination of the existent and the nonexistent effect

[verse 145] When an investigation is made into resultant effects, is a produced effect found to exist or not to exist? If the resultant thing is truly an entity, or rather, if it exists inherently, what need is there for a cause? A relationship of cause and effect cannot properly be ascribed to it. On the other hand, if it were said that the [previously] nonexistent result is produced by a cause, one could reply by asking why a cause is necessary for a result, the nature of which is nonexistence? Generally speaking, what does not exist has no cause. It just abides in its essence of nonbeing. It might perhaps be thought, however, that, even if mere nonbeing is not produced by causes, it is nevertheless through causes that a nonexistent effect is made into an existent thing. This, however, is impossible.

[verse 146] Even if millions of causes were to join forces, they could never make a "nonexistent thing" (something intrinsically nonexistent) pass into existence. In exactly the same way, however many causes there are, they are unable to impart existence to a rabbit's horns. Nonexistence can never act as the basis of anything. The reason why there can be no passage from "nonexistent thing" into "existent thing" is that a transformation in which the character of nonexistence is not discarded and a transformation in which it is discarded are both untenable. In the first place, how can a nonexistent thing be at the same time an existent thing? Both notions invalidate each other; there is just nothing. In the second place, it is through the removal of its nonexistence that the nonexistent thing is transformed into an existent one, but what can this newly existent thing be? Nothing is possible.

[verse 147] Thus, what is defined as nonexistent cannot, throughout its nonexistence, be a real thing. When can such a thing be said to come into existence? The answer is that it never can. For as long as there is no assumption of existence, there is no relinquishing of nonexistence. [verse 148] If there is no laying aside of the character of nonexistence, there is no possible occasion for coming into existence. Therefore how can one ever speak of a nonexistent thing becoming an existent thing? Clearly, it is impossible. Conversely, just as a nonexistent thing does not become an existent thing, likewise an existent thing does not become a nonexistent thing. Once again, since both terms are mutually exclusive, one can apply the same kind of reasoning as has just been used.

[verse 149] If, on the other hand, an existent thing could become a nonexistent thing, it follows that it would possess the nature of both existence and nonexistence simultaneously. This is why, according to ultimate reality, there is no such thing as cessation and why things have no true existence. And this in turn is the reason why, throughout the three times, beings are never born and never pass away. [verse 150] Thus all beings who appear in the various dimensions of existence manifest and yet have no reality; they are like the visions of a dream. When subjected to reasoned analysis, we find that, just like the banana tree, they are devoid of an underlying essence able to withstand analysis. Therefore, on the ultimate level, there is no difference between attaining nirvana and not attaining it, because where there is no bondage, there is no liberation. For at all times, there is nothing but the state of perfect equality. The *Mulamadhyamaka-karika* says:

> Between these two is not the slightest,
> Not the subtlest, distinction.

Although there are different ways of classifying the Madhyamaka arguments, in the present text, they establish that all phenomena, which appear to exist in the manner of cause, result, and nature, are the three doors of liberation. The examination of causes shows that they are (1) devoid of all conceptual characteristics; [in other words, there are no causes]. As regards the nature of phenomena, analysis shows that this is (2) emptiness. And as for the results, analysis reveals that they are (3) beyond expectancy.

2. The benefits of realizing emptiness

3. The equivalence of the eight worldly concerns

[verse 151] Since all things, such as food and clothing, are empty by their nature, what is there for us to gain or lose? Nothing at all. What praise and honor, what insults and humiliation can be heaped on us and by whom? Again, none. [verse 152] Examine the causes for the experience of joy and sadness. They are found to lack inherent existence. What, then, is there that could be unpleasant in being slandered? What is there that could be delightful in being celebrated? Nothing at all. Let us cast aside all discrimination with regard to these eight worldly concerns and place our minds in meditation on profound emptiness. As Nagarjuna says in his *Suhrillekha*:

> Regard as equal, you who know the world,
> All gain and loss, all joy and pain,
> All good and ill repute, all praise and blame:
> These eight mundane concerns are not the worthy objects of
>   your mind.

If an examination is made on the level of ultimate truth, the question arises: Who is the person craving and what is it that is craved? Neither has inherent existence. [verse 153] Since this world of living beings, if we consider well, has no real existence, who can ever be said to die who lives therein? Who will ever be born in the next life, and who was ever born in the past? Who, moreover, are our friends, and who our dear relations? [verse 154] Let those who, like the wise master Shantideva, investigate the nature of things fully understand that all phenomena are like space and elude the conceptual categories of "is" and "is not." Let them regard as equal the eight mundane concerns.

3. The effortless display of great compassion

The glorious master Atisha has said that when emptiness is realized, all sin and nonvirtue come to an end and great compassion arises. Emptiness possesses the essence of compassion. Therefore, when emptiness is realized, it is in the nature of things that great compassion manifests.

Not realizing that phenomena are empty and that their mode of being lies beyond all conceptuality, ordinary beings take as real what is unreal: They attribute existence to what is nonexistent and selfhood to what is not a self. Therein lies their delusion. They long for happiness, but they are ignorant of how to attain it. They struggle against all that seems hostile, and love and cling to what appears as friendly. [verse 155] Thus they are troubled in body and mind. In situations of joy and pleasure, they distract themselves physically and mentally with dancing and song. But when adversity befalls them, when death occurs or the loss of livestock, or when they fail to get what they want, they suffer. High and low, strong and weak, rich and poor, for friends and family, for wealth and pleasures—all that is desired—everyone strives and competes with someone else. They slash each other with swords and stab each other with spears. Their possessions, ill-gotten through the sins of body, speech, and mind, are the source of lives of great toil and sorrow, both now and in the future. People pass their time, their minds completely taken in by the senseless pleasures of life.

[verse 156] Through the kindness of religious teachers, the Buddhas and Bodhisattvas, beings occasionally perform a little virtue such as observing the eight-precept upavasa vow and so on. Because of this, they are fortunate in their migrations, appearing again and again in the many states of high rebirth in the various universes. There they live, enjoying all the pleasures they desire. But because they fail to practice virtue and instead commit evil actions, they fall, at death, into hell or other of the three lower destinies, and for a long time they suffer unbearable pains. High and low, through states of joy and sorrow—such are the unpredictable wanderings of sentient beings. [verse 157] Within the three realms of existence, every evil thought of attachment, hatred, stupidity, craving, and so on, will precipitate beings into infernal and other states of loss—into many chasmic abysses of dreadful woe. In such a world, no learning and understanding of reality (the means of liberation) is to be found. Instead, on account of an intense clinging to self with respect to outer and inner phenomena, there arises something quite different: the false conviction in permanence and true existence. In such a situation, the understanding of emptiness free of all conceptual construction is the very antithesis of such mistaken clinging to the true existence of things. Indeed, the study and realization of suchness or profound emptiness is something quite different in this world. It is like a light shining in an immense darkness.

But now, through the kindness of the compassionate Teacher and his Bodhisattva children, profound doctrines such as the teaching on voidness are expounded and listened to. But perhaps we grow despondent and think to ourselves, "How will someone like me ever be able to understand and realize a teaching like this chapter on the perfection of wisdom, which expounds the teachings on emptiness?" If so, we should understand that we have fallen prey to the "fear of emptiness" (however undaunted we may be by enemies and negative forces). Moreover, it has been said that when people nowadays show no interest in hearing and studying the texts that expound the doctrine of emptiness, and have no grasp of them, this is a sign that emptiness is something to which, in their previous lives, they have never turned their minds.

On the other hand, it has been said that if, when we hear the teachings on emptiness, our minds become elated, and if, through our strength of faith, our eyes fill with tears and our skin stands up in gooseflesh, this is a sign that we already possess a propensity for study and reflection instilled in us in our earlier existences. And it is said too that even though we may not gain realization in this life, if nonetheless we turn our minds to the profound doctrine of emptiness, listening to the teachings and reflecting and meditating on them, it is certain that in our subsequent lives we will hear such teachings again and attain realization. This view is confirmed by the *Yogacharachatushataka:*

> Even though we do not, in this life transcend—
> Through understanding suchness—every sorrow,
> It is, like any action, certain that, in later lives,
> We will without travail attain this goal.

In times gone by, Kubja the Small and Lekyong fell victim to terrible suffering on account of strongly negative karmic residues. Nevertheless, when they encountered the Buddha, they realized the truth and attained arhatship simply through hearing his teachings. The scriptures say that this was through the karma of having become learned in the teachings on the aggregates, elements, and sense fields at the time of the Buddha Kashyapa.

On the other hand, when it comes to emptiness, people who are dull and narrow never even wonder whether phenomena are empty or not. Had they the slightest doubt about it, samsaric existence would fall to shreds for them. As it is said:

> Due to little merit, not the slightest doubt
> Will rise against phenomena.
> Let the slightest doubt arise,
> And this existence falls to shreds.

Consequently, at this time, when we have come upon this profound teaching on emptiness, we should give meaning to this encounter, by listening, reflecting, and meditating with joyful hearts.

[verse 158] In this realm of existence, in which the light of suchness does not shine, afflicted by unexampled difficulties, beings languish for ages in a vast ocean of unbearable suffering, stretching beyond the limits of space and time. There, as we have just explained, they are oppressed and beaten down by the strength of their karma and negative emotions. They are feeble in their ability to practice virtue. For even if a good intention surfaces in their minds, the proper support for wholesome activity, namely, a human existence endowed with freedoms and advantages, is short-lived, and they have not the leisure for the practice of virtue.

[verse 159] Throughout their short lives, beings spend their time hoping for longevity, caring for their bodies in all sorts of ways, taking different remedies and cures to maintain a healthy constitution. Then there are others who lack the necessities of food, drink, and so on; they are hungry and destitute and must labor wearily for their livelihood. They spend half their lives in the stupefaction of sleep. Outside and in, they are assailed by different troubles. They abandon themselves to futile behavior in the company of ordinary people whose conduct is no better than that of children. And in their various doings life goes quickly by. It is frittered away, without any virtuous accomplishment to render it significant.

[verse 160] The cause of liberation from samsaric existence, the mind's discernment of the ultimate reality—the No-Self of phenomena, their lack of true existence—all this is extremely difficult to find. The habit of mental wandering of those who dwell in samsara is extremely powerful, like a river in spate. How could there ever be a way to stop it short, all of a sudden?

[verse 161] Not only is it impossible, but there are demons like Devaputra, friends of darkness, who work and labor to cast us down, to cause us to fall into hell and the other evil destinies. For the lord of demons will not tolerate that a Bodhisattva (for a single one will set many hundreds and thousands of beings in the state of enlightenment) should ever receive an earnest or portent of the attainment of buddhahood. And thus, he will throw many obstacles in the Bodhisattva's way. He will take false and lying forms, appearing as a Buddha, a Bodhisattva, or the disciple's teacher, declaring that the disciple has now gained superior qualities. He will denigrate the true Dharma as false, substituting a parody in its place. And he will send his daughters, the mistresses of distraction and stupidity, to create obstacles. As the proverb says, "For profound Dharma, a profound dark demon."

Moreover, there are many false trails, such as eternalist and nihilist views. And if one does not gain certainty, coming to the conclusion that "This is the pure and unmistaken path," by discerning its goal and point of view, it is hard to free oneself from doubts and hesitation. For it is difficult to have all the outer and inner conditions favorable to their removal. Nowadays, people love novelty and thus neglect the ancient texts, excellent and pure though they be, liking only what is new. But among the recent texts, there are some that are genuine and some false, and it is difficult to discern the goal and point of view of a genuine teaching from a false one— it is difficult to have certainty, unclouded by doubt.

And even if a teaching is authentic, if it is practiced with doubt, it will be fruitless and without meaning. It is thus hard to have a true discernment. It is hard to overcome distraction. Moreover, if because of doubts and so forth, one dies without ever discovering the light of the Doctrine, [verse 162] it will be extremely hard to find the freedoms of the human state again and to encounter the enlightened beings present in this world. It will be difficult to find time to practice their teachings wholeheartedly and so be able to turn back the flood of desire and the other negative emotions.

[verse 163] "Alas!" says Shantideva. With love and great regret, he laments that in this state of samsara, beings go continuously from sorrow to sorrow. Given their various kinds of suffering, they live in great torment. In their ignorance they are unable to understand what they should do and what they should not do. They are not aware that they are foundering in suffering; they cherish and cling to this existence. Alas, how can one not lament at the thought of their being carried away on the flood of sorrow? [verse 164] There are some people, for example, who wish for the sensation of coolness and bathe themselves repeatedly. Afterward, they are discomforted by the cold and wish to be warm again. Thereupon they apply heat to themselves until they are tormented by the searing temperatures and have to bathe again. They thus torture themselves through this alternation of heat and cold, but, blinded by their desires, they claim that all is well and that they are perfectly happy!

[verse 165] So it is that people live "happily," abandoning themselves to carefree pleasures, as if the terrible hardships of old age and death will never come to them. But old age will befall them first of all, with incurable sickness in its train, and then at last the implacable Lord of Death will come upon them to kill them. And once again they will have to undergo the unbearable pains of falling into the lower realms.

[verse 166] Destitute of insight into the meaning of suchness, and taking suffering for happiness, beings are tormented in the fires of misery in the three worlds of samsara. When, asks Shantideva, will he be able to extinguish this fire with a rain of happiness that issues from the clouds of his unlimited accumulation of merit? When indeed will such a heavy downpour of all good things supply beings with all that they desire (wealth and comfort, clothing, places of rest, and so on), satisfying their every want and removing the misery of their poverty? And it is with thoughts like these that we should aim for the temporal happiness of beings.

[verse 167] And again in Shantideva's words, with a view to the state of definite goodness, when will we too understand and assimilate the profound emptiness of all phenomena, the state free of all conceptual constructs—the voidness of the three spheres? For, to the extent that we understand it, we will, with joy and reverence for the welfare of living beings, bring our store of merit to fulfillment. When will we too have a direct experience of the suchness of all things, the union of appearance and emptiness—equality itself free from all concepts? And when might we too be able to set this doctrine forth—the medicine for beings poisoned by their clinging to the true existence of things and brought to ruin in the three worlds of samsara? O may this come to pass!

When we reflect like this, great compassion is brought to birth. And when we see that phenomena are indeed devoid of true existence, we will be engulfed by such a strength of great compassion that we will never abandon living beings who circle in samsara through their fixated belief in true existence. In sum, the birth in the mind of great compassion and love for others, and complete indifference to the eight worldly concerns, will naturally occur, as this text has explained.

If those, therefore, who wish for fortunate destinies in samsara and the definite goodness of nirvana practice wholesome ways such as generosity, ethical discipline, and meditation, they will certainly reap great benefit thereby. But greater than these is the wisdom of realizing profound emptiness beyond all conceptual elaborations, the deep and final remedy for the two kinds of obscuration. In order to generate it, we must strive in proper study and reflection. As it is said in the *Uttaratantra-shastra:*

> Thus it is by giving that all wealth will be produced;
> Perfect ethics lead to high rebirth, while meditation rids you
>   of defilement.
> But the veils, emotional and cognitive, are both removed by
>   wisdom.
> Therefore wisdom is supreme. Its cause is study of this
>   teaching.

Here ends the ninth chapter of the *Bodhicharyavatara*, on wisdom.

PART FOUR

Dedication of the Resulting Merit
for the Benefit of Others

· 10 ·

DEDICATION

*Whereby the Merit of Striving
in the Way of the Bodhisattva
Is Pledged to the Welfare of Others*

1. A BRIEF EXPOSITION

The welfare of beings secured by the Buddhas and Bodhisattvas arises proportionately in accordance with the latter's foregoing attitude of bodhichitta and prayers of aspiration. As it is said:

> If the wishing gem, the two accumulations,
> Is not well polished with good aspirations,
> The needed, wished for, fruit will not arise.
> So finish all your works with dedication.

Dedication and prayers of aspiration are crucially important. According to our tradition, the difference between dedication and aspiration should be understood in the following way. Dedication consists in pledging one's positive actions to perfect enlightenment for the sake of beings. By contrast, a prayer of aspiration is just the wish that beings themselves attain enlightenment; it is not connected with the performance of wholesome deeds.

Failure to dedicate virtuous action to the good of others is a fault:

> Not to dedicate or to dedicate awry,
> To brag to others or to have regrets:
> Four things that lay your virtue waste.

As for the benefits of dedication, it is said:

> Dedication is the path of never-ending merit
> For virtue is augmented and transformed thereby.

Accordingly, without the dedication of the roots of virtue, virtue comes to nothing, for there are many causes for its destruction, such as the occurrence of anger. By contrast, when virtue is dedicated to the attainment of enlightenment, it is as when drops of water fall into the ocean; they will remain for as long as the ocean lasts. Virtue dedicated to the attainment of buddhahood will not be spent until enlightenment is gained. Indeed, it will increase and actually take us there. It is said in the *Akshayamati-sutra:*

> As, in the great sea, drops of water fall,
> And will not dry until the sea itself runs dry,
> The virtue that to buddhahood is pledged
> Is not consumed till buddhahood is gained.

Dedication causes an increase in the effects of positive action commensurable with the aggregate of beings, and this is as vast as space. Dedication transforms virtue into the cause of great enlightenment or buddhahood, in the same way that a skilled goldsmith can fashion fine gold into ornaments and other things of small and medium worth or into images of the Buddhas and their diadems: things of great value.

When dedication is associated with a wisdom unstained by the concepts of the three spheres, it is said to be uncontaminated. If it is not so associated, it is regarded as contaminated. Now the omniscient Lord of Dharma (Longchenpa) has said that to dedicate positive action and to "seal" it only afterward with emptiness is tantamount to a nihilistic view. It does not constitute a dedication free from the concepts of the three spheres. Therefore it is important to make the dedication in a manner that is free from these three concepts: the agent who dedicates, the virtue dedicated, and the object on account of which the dedication is made (all of which lack real existence even though they appear).

If, however, one is unable to make such a dedication, one should think that one will dedicate one's virtue "in the way that the Bhagavan Buddhas and others like Manjushri and Samantabhadra did." To this end, one should recite texts like the "Confession of Downfalls," the "Prayer of Good Action," and the "Confession to the Sugatas" from the *Confession Tantra,* together with prayers of dedication such as the one beginning "Just as the hero Manjushri . . ." All learned authorities agree that this kind of dedication is in harmony with uncontaminated dedication, which is free from the concepts of the three spheres. To proceed like this is thus a key point of great importance.

When one is dedicating virtue or merit and making prayers of aspiration, one should do so in a way that is consonant with that of noble beings who have seen the truth and whose discipline is utterly pure. It has been said however that failure to make one's own dedication and prayers of aspiration (leaving it for others to do) is a mistake. For one must be aware of the virtue to be dedicated and must dedicate it consciously.

Once in the past, the people of Vaishali had wealth and prosperity comparable to that of the gods in the Heaven of the Thirty-three. They sent an invitation to the Lord Buddha and his disciples, saying that they would offer them the midday meal on the following day. Now there were certain pretas who had previously been the parents of the people of Vaishali. They had been very avaricious at that time, on account of which they had been reborn in their present state. They came to the Buddha and asked him to dedicate the merit of the food offering that would be made on the morrow for their benefit. When the Buddha asked them the reason for making such a dedication, they replied that they had once been the parents of people at Vaishali. So the Buddha told them to be present at Vaishali the following day and said that the offering would be dedicated for them. To this, the pretas replied that they were full of shame and dared not appear.

"How is it," the Buddha asked, "that you are ashamed of the evil forms that you have now received but were not ashamed of the evil acts that caused them? If you come to Vaishali, the merit will be dedicated for you. But it will not be dedicated for you if you do not come."

So the pretas agreed to attend. But when they appeared, the people of Vaishali were terrified. The Buddha explained to them that the pretas had formerly been their parents, that avarice had been the cause of their taking such a birth, and that they had come because they wanted the merit of the offering to be dedicated for their benefit. When the Buddha asked the people of Vaishali whether they would be willing to dedicate the merit to them, they replied that they were indeed willing. It is thus that we should dedicate our positive actions, our roots of virtue in full awareness of the actions that we have accomplished.

On the other hand, it is said that when aspirations and prayers for protection are made by people whose tantric samaya has declined, they will have an evil effect. For example, when such people pray or make wishes for longevity, this actually results in a shortening of life. All their prayers for protection turn into curses and sorcery. And as it has been said, we might well wonder about the aspirations made by such people for their own sake!

[verse 1] As the witnesses of our dedication, we should invite all the Buddhas and Bodhisattvas of the three times and the ten directions, imagining that they are seated in the space in front of us. Alternatively, we might call upon the Buddhas to testify to our dedication by reciting verses like these:[230]

> By my strength of confidence in their enlightened deeds,
> I imagine clearly the Victorious Buddhas here before me.

And:

> On each and every particle,
> Buddhas as many as the particles themselves
> Are seated in the midst of Bodhisattva heirs.
> And so I think the whole of space
> Is filled with the Victorious Ones.

Regarding the agent of the dedication, originally this was Shantideva. Now it is ourselves. As to what is dedicated, it is all the virtue, first, of Shantideva's intention to implement the Bodhisattva practices, followed by his actual development of bodhichitta and the virtuous practice itself, namely, his training in the six paramitas. As for ourselves, we dedicate the virtue that has resulted from engaging in the conduct of the Bodhisattvas by means of any of the ten activities of Dharma such as composition, the making of offerings, and the distribution of alms.

In the past, Shantideva dedicated all positive actions past, present, and future related to the Bodhisattva conduct, in a way that was free of the concepts of the three spheres. But although, as a result, he dedicated even the virtuous actions performed by ourselves, it is nevertheless said that we, for our part, should dedicate our own virtue, mingling it with his—just as we might mix a drop of water with the great ocean. In brief, we should gather together all the virtue accumulated in the three times both by ourselves and others, and considering that it is represented by the merit of our present striving in the way of the Bodhisattva, we should dedicate it.

The object of such a dedication is the entire aggregate of beings, as vast as space. We should wish that they all attain perfect buddhahood. We should pray that they develop an attitude turned toward supreme enlightenment and that they engage correctly in the paramitas, namely, the practice of generosity and the other Bodhisattva practices. Great enlightenment cannot occur in the absence of its proper cause. To dedicate virtue to the attainment of the *result,* namely, enlightenment, or to dedicate virtue (as in the *Bodhicharyavatara*) to the practice that is the *cause* of great enlightenment comes to the same thing.

The dedication should be linked with aspiration, heartfelt longing, commitment, and prayer. Aspiration is the wish, "May all beings adopt the conduct of the Bodhisattvas, virtuous in the beginning, middle, and end. May they be happy! Let there be no fighting or quarreling among them." Heartfelt longing makes us cry, "How wonderful if beings were happy!" The commitment is the resolution, "I myself will bring them happiness." Prayer is the supplication, "May the lama and the Three Jewels bless me that I be able to accomplish this task!" Thinking and speaking thus, we should imagine that our teachers, together with the Buddhas and Bodhisattvas, are present in front of us expressing their consent melodiously with such words as "Let it be! Let this come about!" And we should consider that all beings are imbued with happiness.

We should likewise aspire, long, resolve, and pray that all beings be free from suffering, and we should think that our action receives the consent of our enlightened witnesses. And we should proceed in the same way for all the four immeasurable attitudes. As it is said in the *Sutralankara:*

> Compassion is considered bodhichitta's root.
> And love is the very sinew of compassion.

It is just as when a tree absorbs water through its roots and grows in leaf and branch. If we cultivate loving-kindness toward beings, compassion will arise and we will wish to free them from their suffering. Compassion will bring about the growth of bodhichitta both relative and ultimate. On the other hand, if bodhichitta is lacking, it will be as the glorious Saraha has said in one of his songs of realization:

> The view of emptiness without compassion:
> This is not the supreme path.

Therefore it is said that the most important thing here is to apply the practice of loving-kindness and compassion in the case of all the topics mentioned in this chapter on dedication, whether or not such an attitude and its referent are specifically evoked. Meditation on loving-kindness is more excellent in its effects than even the act of making offerings to all the Buddhas. Moreover, it brings forth the eight qualities of love, as we find exemplified in the story of the ancient king Maitribala who by his meditation on love was able to prevent five demon brothers from causing harm to the world's inhabitants.

Through meditation on compassion, the authentic, profound view will manifest in the mind, just as it did in the case of the teacher Dharmarakshita. In addition, all evil actions, which hinder the arising in the mind of the perfect view and other qualities, will be purified, and one will behold one's yidam deity, just as Asanga did. It is said that in the past, when King Mahaprabha used to meditate on compassion, no one in our world experienced anger. Once when the deeds of the Kadampa masters were being recounted to Dromtönpa—of how Potowa would often teach the Dharma to many thousands of people; of how Gonpapa would only meditate in the uninhabited wilderness; of how Puchungwa would make many representations of the Buddha's body, speech, and mind; and finally of how Khampalungpa used to go only to valleys where the rivers had run dry and weep—Dromtönpa joined his hands at the mention of Khampalungpa and praised him exceedingly. For, he said, there is nothing greater than compassion.

If one meditates alternately on loving-kindness and compassion, they mutually remove the obstacles peculiar to each. For by meditating on love, the mind can become excessively exhilarated, whereas by meditating on compassion it is possible for the mind to become downcast and despairing. It is said that the meditation on loving-kindness and compassion can, in the best case, preserve all the world's inhabitants from harm. Then to a less exalted degree, one can, with such meditation, protect the people of one's homeland. Finally, at the very least, one is able to protect oneself from harm and aggression.

1. A DETAILED TEACHING

2. DEDICATION OF VIRTUE AS THE CAUSE OF HAPPINESS AND OF BENEFIT FOR OTHERS

3. DEDICATION OF VIRTUE IN ORDER TO FREE THE WEAK FROM SUFFERING

4. GENERAL DEDICATION OF VIRTUE IN ORDER TO RID THE THREE WORLDS OF THE SORROWS WITH WHICH THEY ARE FILLED

[verse 2] There are three kinds of suffering. The dedication of our virtue in order to free beings from the suffering of suffering [suffering in the ordinary sense of the word] consists in the wish that, by the virtue or merit of our practice of the Bodhisattva way—namely, through study, reflection, and meditation on it—all beings, to the farthest reaches of the ten directions, who are tormented by the consequences of their evil actions, whether physically through the diseases of wind, bile, and phlegm, or mentally, through depression, insanity, and so on, be freed instantly, here and now. It is thus that we should meditate on compassion, wishing that beings be free from sorrow and its causes. As for meditation on loving-kindness (the wish that beings have joy and the causes of joy), this is the desire that all should gain an ocean-like abundance of physical and mental well-being, and happiness in all its perfection.

[verse 3] Similarly, dedication with a view to liberating beings from the suffering of change consists in the wish that, by the power of our virtue, all the world's inhabitants who have, for the time being, great prosperity, strength of body, and happiness of mind, should never lose their good fortune for as long as they remain in samsara. This is how to meditate on loving-kindness and compassion.

As for all-pervading suffering in the making, this will be with us for as long as our physical and mental aggregates are defiled. Dedication with a view to freeing beings from this kind of suffering consists in the wish that the unbounded multitude of beings existing in every dimension of space, be free from all-pervading suffering in the making and attain the vast, unceasing bliss of the immaculate nonabiding nirvana of the Bodhisattvas. This again is how to meditate on loving-kindness and compassion.

By reflecting that all suffering arises from its proper cause, namely, negative action, we will acquire confident faith in the karmic principle of cause and effect. Understanding that wherever we are born in samsara, high or low, there is nowhere beyond the reach of sorrow, we will feel revulsion for samsaric existence and will be determined to free ourselves from it. And when we consider that of all those who are tormented by suffering, there is not one who has not been our father or our mother, a keen willingness to help others will arise in us. And so it is that the paths of beings of the three scopes are all contained in this practice.

4. DEDICATION OF VIRTUE IN ORDER TO FREE BEINGS FROM THEIR PARTICULAR SUFFERINGS SUCH AS THOSE OF THE THREE LOWER REALMS

[verse 4] When we dedicate virtue to the deliverance of hell beings from their sufferings, we should think as follows. In all the universal systems lying in the ten directions, evil actions are perpetrated because of anger and the other defilements. Their karmic effect is the unbounded pain of heat and cold, and such torments as being cut and dismembered in the various realms of hell. We should make the wish that, by the strength of our positive actions, the outer environment as experienced by all the denizens of hell be completely purified and become like the western pure field of Sukhavati, where even the words "pain" and "suffering" have no existence, and where all is made of precious substances, where everything is spacious and mild. Let all the beings that dwell in hell be purified; may Yama, the Lord of Death, become the Buddha Amitabha, and may his workers become the Buddha's eight close sons, Avalokiteshvara, Vajrapani, and the rest. And may the dwellers in the hells be transformed into practitioners of the Mahayana: Bodhisattvas adorned with the major and minor marks of enlightenment. May they have perfect happiness and joy; and without travail, may they receive whatever they wish.

[verse 5] May all those who do evil, impelled by the power of their anger, abandon their wickedness, and may they truly perform the practice that will bring about their birth in Sukhavati: the visualization of Buddha

Amitabha and the recitation of his name. This is how we should meditate on compassion and loving-kindness (wishing that beings be freed from suffering and its causes, and that they be endowed with happiness and the causes of the same).

In brief, we should meditate, taking upon ourselves the heat and cold and all the other sufferings of the hell realms. We should confess the evil actions that we ourselves have perpetrated (for these are the causes of hell) and we should resolve never to commit them again. Recognizing the fact that all those who have been born in hell were once our own parents, we should meditate on compassion for them, praying to the Buddhas and Bodhisattvas and invoking their assistance. Likewise, we should meditate on loving-kindness and compassion, as previously explained, for all who are committing negative actions—actions that will bring them to birth in the hell realms—and we should recite prayers of good wishes for them.

Actions such as denying clothing to one's parents and others, and stealing the silken name coverings of sacred texts will result in births in the cold hells. The ground and surrounding landscape of these is just snow mountains and glaciers. Blizzards rage. There is no light, either of sun or moon, and all is enveloped in thick darkness. The beings that inhabit such realms have extremely sensitive skins, and the slightest contact is unbearable for them. They are naked and in terrible pain. Suffering gradually increases in intensity from the highest of the hell realms down to the lowest. In the Hell of Blisters, the dreadful cold causes swellings to appear on the bodies of the beings there. In the Hell of Burst Blisters, these swellings burst open and become wounds. Then there is the Hell of Lamentation, a place where the beings utter terrible cries. In the Hell of Groaning, their voices are broken, and only a long drawn out moaning escapes from their mouths. In the Hell of Chattering Teeth, the jaws of beings snap and chatter incessantly. In the Hell of Utpala-Wounds, their skin turns blue and splits apart, forming patterns like the four petals of an utpala flower. Then in the Lotus-Wound Hell, raw red flesh erupts through the bluish skin and breaks into eight fragments like [the petals of] red lotuses. In the Great Lotus-Wound Hell, the red flesh becomes black and splits open into patterns of a hundred, a thousand, or even more fragments like the petals of a lotus. And in the gaping fissures, masses of iron-beaked worms burrow into the flesh and devour it. Such is the endless pain of the denizens of hell.

The duration of life in the hell realms can be imagined in the following way. Take a basket containing eighty koshala[231] measures of sesame. The length of life in the Hell of Blisters is equivalent to the time it would take to empty such a container by removing one seed every hundred years. In the Hell of Burst Blisters and so on, the lifespan of beings born there is multiplied by twenty for each successive hell. We should feel compassion for their poor inhabitants and wish that they be freed from their dreadful torments of cold, and we should wish that, thanks to the strength of our merit, pleasant warmth and the rays of the sun melt the mountains of snow and the icy glaciers and that the infernal regions become like celestial realms, where the inhabitants enjoy the deep pleasure of gentle warmth.

The hot hells are the result of defilements like hatred. Their ground and all their surroundings are composed of burning iron. With tongues of blazing flame and crackling sparks, the fire of the Reviving Hell is hotter than the conflagration that will destroy the world [at the end of time]. And all the subsequent hells in descending order become increasingly hot, whether by seven or four times. And there in the midst of the fire, beings have, on account of their actions, very large bodies. For example, it is said in the *Saddharmasmrityupasthana-sutra* that those who have perpetrated the five sins of immediate effect will have bodies five leagues in height. The *Mahaparinirvana-sutra* says that those who have committed the eight sins of immediate effect will have bodies eighty thousand leagues tall. In the *Ratnolka-sutra* it is said that tongues that have criticized the Mahayana will be three leagues in length. The flesh of all such beings will be extremely tender and will find the slightest contact unbearable.

In the Reviving Hell, beings have sharp weapons in their hands with which they wound each other, and when they are overwhelmed and fall unconscious, a voice will come from the sky shouting, "Revive!"—or else a cold wind will blow—and they will come to their senses. And once again, they will experience the same suffering as before. The beings of the Black Line Hell are horribly tormented by the guards of hell, who use blazing saws to cut along black lines (eight, sixteen, and so on) that have been traced upon their bodies. Beings in the Hell of Crushing suffer by being crushed together between great mountains of iron or between cliffs that have the form of the heads of sheep or other animals, or else in mortars of iron. Beings in the Hell of Screaming suffer from being burned in red-hot iron houses that have no doors. In the Hell of Great Screaming, the doorless, burning iron houses in which beings are enclosed have walls of double thickness. Beings in the Hell of Heat are impaled on white-hot metal spikes that enter through their anuses and emerge through the crowns of their heads. Their mouths, nostrils, and every pore of their bodies are suffused with fire. In the Hell of Great Heat, the body is impaled on blazing metal spears and tridents from the anus and the soles of the feet to the crown of the head and the shoulders. In all the openings of the sense organs, fire is blazing, and the body is enveloped in sheets of incandescent metal. In the Hell of Unrelenting Pain, upon the ground of burning metal, there is such a terrible conflagration that there is no distinguishing the bodies of beings from the blaze itself. There is just a mass of fire, in which the beings are subject to tremendous torment. The sound of their lamentation is the only evidence of their presence; their pain is beyond all measurement.

Concerning the duration of life in the hot hells, it should be remembered that one day experienced by the gods in the Heaven of the Four Great Kings corresponds to fifty human days, and these gods can live for five hundred years according to their reckoning. The span of life in the four higher celestial realms increases twofold at each stage. Therefore in the Heaven of Mastery over the Magical Creations of Others, six thousand one hundred human years corresponds to a single of their celestial days, and these gods can live for sixteen thousand years according to their reckoning. Using this as a basis, we may calculate that one day in Reviving Hell corresponds to the lifespan of beings in the Heaven of the Four Great Kings; and the beings in hell live for five hundred years according to their own reckoning. Then, stage by stage, the lifespan of hell beings increases until the Hell of Heat, where one of their days corresponds to the entire lifespan of the gods of the Heaven of Mastery over the Magical Creations of Others. And the beings in this hell can live for sixteen thousand of their years. In the Hell of Great Heat, life lasts for half an intermediate kalpa, while in the Hell of Unrelenting Pain, the span of life corresponds to one intermediate kalpa.[232] And throughout that entire time, the beings in the hell realms experience intense suffering and unending pain. We should form the wish that the great and massing clouds formed by the bodhichitta and aspiration prayers of the Bodhisattvas gather in the sky and rain down streams of every possible perfection, bringing coolness, removing all the pain of the beings there and filling them with tender joy.

[verse 6] Around the hell realms there are the sixteen neighboring hells: the Pit of Fiery Embers, the Swamp of Rotting Corpses, the Plain of Razors, the Sword-leafed Forest, and the Shalmali Trees. From the point of

view of the weapons found there, the last three resemble each other and are therefore counted as one region. Finally, there is the River of Burning Ashes. This makes four hells surrounding all the eight hot hells in the four directions [with a fourfold group for each of the directions], thus making a total of sixteen neighboring hells.

When beings are finally freed from the fire of their hellish state, they see in the distance a blue-green forest. They hurry into the coolness of its shade, only to be confronted by red-haired hounds that chase and devour them. And the sharp double-edged blades of the knife-like leaves lacerate their bodies causing horrible pain. This is the dreadful sword-leafed forest. We should form the wish that by the strength of our virtue, these hell realms become like the wonderful gardens of Indra surrounding the blissful city Fair to See in the Heaven of the Thirty-three. To the east there is the Grove of Sundry Trees, to the south, the Grove of Mingled Pleasures, to the west, the Grove of Happiness, and so on. And we should pray that the beings therein find perfect comfort and happiness.

Then there is Shalmari—the Hill of Shalma—so called because of the shalmali trees that grow on it. This is the product mainly of sexual misconduct and similar faults. The trunks of these trees are covered with iron thorns sixteen inches long, and all around them are red-coated dogs big as mountains and barking like thunder. Their fangs, as they snarl, are like snow mountains; their tongues dart like red lightning; their tails are sharp saws. They chase the beings among the trees so that their bodies are torn open by the thorns, and then they devour them from head to foot. At the summit of the hill, the beings see visions of those whom in the past they had desired, and who now seem to call to them. They hasten up the hill, only to have their eyes gouged and their tongues torn out by crows and vultures. They are engulfed in pain. When they reach the summit, they are met by men and women of iron who squeeze them in a terrible embrace so that their heart and lungs are forced out through their mouths. These monsters mangle and chew their heads so that their gray brains spurt out on both sides of their mouths. [Having endured this experience,] the beings hear their former lovers calling them from the bottom of the hill, and once again the same torment is repeated. We should meditate on compassion (wishing that these creatures be freed from suffering) and on loving-kindness (wishing that the shalmali trees turn into celestial wish-fulfilling trees satisfying every need and desire in harmony with the Dharma, and that this hellish region becomes a place of every perfection).

Similarly, when—mainly as a result of former craving—the beings in hell see a river, they rush toward it, only to suffer on finding that it transforms into a swamp of decomposing corpses. Mainly as a result of anger, they rush toward what seems to be a deep shadow and are tormented when it becomes a pit of glowing embers. We should have the wish that these beings be delivered from all such pains and that they should find themselves in places that are pleasant, limpid, and cool, suffused with perfumes and the tastes of the five medicinal substances.

In the ephemeral hells, beings suffer by identifying themselves with doors, pillars, ovens, ropes, and so on. We should pray that they be free from their sufferings and endowed with every happiness. [verse 7] May all the abodes of hell be transformed into places of ravishing beauty, where every kind of waterbird (wild ducks blue and red, geese and swans white as conch and yellow as gold, with beautiful plumage and sweet song) disport themselves, in playful dance and joyous flight. May beautiful lakes of water endowed with eight qualities, adorned with lotus and utpala, blossoms of every hue and fragrance, transform the regions of hell into joyful places of exquisite loveliness.

[verse 8] To abandon the Dharma and to commit any of the five sins of immediate effect are causes of the Hell of Unrelenting Pain. The beings there are burned in masses of fiery coals on grounds of blazing, incandescent metal. The beings' bodies are indistinguishable from the fire itself. They scream in agony, and as soon as they see the slightest opening in the blaze, they run away only to be caught by blazing tongs. Their heads are smashed with hammers and molten bronze is poured into their mouths. And again they are burned in masses of fiery coals. In their pain is concentrated all the sufferings of the seven other hot hells. We should have the wish that these beings be freed from their sufferings—that the blazing conflagrations become heaps of wishing jewels, satisfying every need and desire, and that the denizens of hell come to fulfillment and bliss. May the ground of the hot hells, composed of burning, fiery metal, be changed into pavements of myriad-hued crystal. May they be as smooth to the touch as panjalika silk, even and yielding. May all the beings there be contented and happy.

May the beings who are gathered and crushed between the cliffs shaped like the heads of animals (the sheep, goats, and wild animals that they have slain and the lice that they have crushed with their nails), who are lamenting loudly, their bodies broken and bleeding—may they all be free from pain! May the mountains that crush them become heaps of gems, with vast and jeweled palaces, on whose terraces goddesses present offerings that delight the senses and are enveloping the palaces, outside and in, with cloud-like masses of gifts. In the center of such palaces, upon lion thrones encrusted with jewels, the blessed Buddhas, the Tathagatas, set forth the teachings to vast retinues of Bodhisattvas. May beings be happy, may they make reverential offerings to those who dwell within the palaces, and may they listen to their teachings!

[verse 9] May those who, as a result of their evil speech, criticism and scornful words, or as a result of quarreling or throwing things while eating or drinking in the monastic assembly, must suffer a hail of lava and a rain of glowing embers or burning stones and blazing swords that fall upon them—may they all be released from their sufferings. Henceforth, may they be happy beneath a shower of beautiful flowers.

It is said that once upon a time there were about five hundred monks living in a beautiful monastery in a pleasant wood. When the hour of the midday meals arrived, a gong would sound, and the five hundred monks, arrayed in their Dharma robes and patched shawls of full ordination, would come together in the assembly hall with their begging bowls, their water bottles, and their staffs. Suddenly, the hall would transform into a house of fire, and the monastic bowls and accoutrements turned into weapons, blazing and sharp. And the monks would fight with each other and have to suffer. When the hour of noon was past, everything would return to normal. It is said that this was the result of arguing and disputes in the past that occurred when they were eating the food offered by the faithful. We should therefore be very careful not to quarrel and throw things when we are in the monastic assembly.

Those who die in wars and murderous conflicts are reborn in the Reviving Hell. They perceive each other as enemies, and whatever they take in their hands turns into swords and other weapons with which they strike each other. They perish and are again revived, and thus they suffer endlessly. We should wish that they be freed from their pain and that in an instant they may transform into youthful gods and goddesses, who take delight in each other, playfully casting beautiful flowers at each other.

[verse 10] Those who kill animals that live in water, those who act with perverted [sexual] desire for young children, and those who, through deceitful commerce, take the belongings of the sangha for themselves are born in Vaitarani, the unfordable river of fiery ashes. Here, they might see children, boys and girls, carried along in the blue water, sometimes just their black-haired heads, sometimes just their hands emerging from the stream. "Take us out!" they cry. But when the beings born there decide to enter the water to take them, or when they want to go and fetch the property of the sangha that they can see on the other side of the river, or again when they take to the water in order to kill the fish or water otters, the river transforms into a stream of burning ash, deep and unfordable. Their bodies sink into blazing fire and are all consumed. Sometimes, the waves, rising skyward, lift the bodies up and then throw them against sharp triangular rocks on the riverbed, so that they are broken in pieces and devoured by the very same fish and otters [that they were trying to catch]. Along the shore are diamond-beaked crows that gouge their eyes out of their sockets, tear out their tongues, and open their intestines. The boiling water scalds their flesh and completely destroys it so that these beings are reduced to skeletons white as kunda flowers. The waves project them out of the water and as soon as the wind blows on them, they regain a human form; and, as before, they suffer unbounded pain. We should wish that by the power of our virtue, all such beings be freed from their suffering and that they obtain a celestial existence and dwell in joy and bliss, bathing and at play with young, beautiful goddesses on the beaches of gold and silver sand, adorned with every kind of flower, that lie along the banks of Mandakini, the softly flowing celestial stream. It is thus that we must dedicate our virtue and make prayers of aspiration that "through our own power" the sufferings of the hells be brought to nothing.

[verse 11] We also dedicate our virtue and we make prayers of aspiration that "through the power of others" (that is, the Bodhisattvas, the lords of the three lineages) the pains of hell be assuaged. And we consider that by the power of our having previously received an empowerment of Vajrapani, meditated on him, and recited his mantra, his perfect, illusory manifestation will be suddenly visible to those in hell. Then, as Shantideva says, the hell beings will wonder what it is that causes the headlong, panic-stricken flight of the evil henchmen of the Lord of Death, with heads of tigers, leopards, crows, and vultures. When the light of compassion scatters the great darkness cast by the thick smoke arising from the burning flesh, blood, and marrow—a darkness so dense that one is unable to see even the bending and stretching of one's own limbs—and when the prisoners of hell feel the physical and mental relief brought by this light, they will wonder what holy being it is that has such amazing power. They will lift their eyes and there in the sky, in a mass of fire, they will clearly see the Bodhisattva, the glorious Lord of Secrets, shining in a splendor of light, and holding a vajra in his hand, the sign that he has been empowered by all the Buddhas. Then may those who in the past had made images of Vajrapani, who meditated on him, and received his empowerment at the moment of their deaths recognize him and feel great happiness. By the power of the great faith that will arise in them may their past evils be cleansed. And in the company of Vajrapani, may they go to his buddhafield of Willow Trees, to enjoy forever great and stainless bliss. At this very moment we should request an empowerment of any of the Buddha's eight close sons (such as the lords of the three lineages), and, taking him as our yidam deity, we should strive in the meditation and recitation of his mantra, making offerings, and giving praises.

What hell being will not feel joy on seeing the Buddhas and the great Bodhisattvas, Vajrapani, Manjushri, Avalokiteshvara, and so on? Only an evil spirit would fail to do so. When reflecting on the pains suffered in the realms of hell, it is surely impossible not to wish for the appearance of the Buddha's eight close sons in such a place. Indeed, it has been said that the failure to do so is proof that one is as ignorant as a bird's egg, extremely stupid and as mindless as a rock!

[verse 12] Likewise in the way just described, through our having previously received an empowerment of Avalokiteshvara, meditated on him, and recited his mantra, may all the beings in hell behold a rain of sweet-scented flowers drenched with perfume falling from the sky, which with a gentle swishing sound immediately extinguishes the seething flood of infernal lava. May these beings be immediately filled with the kind of happiness that they have never before experienced. And wondering by whose power it has happened, may they look up and clearly see the Lord of Great Compassion, seated on a lotus throne, himself adorned with lotuses, with lotus-like eyes and holding a lotus in his hand, from whose mouth resounds the sublime and sovereign words of the six-syllable mantra. May those who in the past have made images of him, who have meditated on him and recited the six-syllable mantra recognize him and have great joy. By the power of the extraordinary faith that will arise in them, may their former evils and defilements be cleansed, and in the company of the noble Avalokiteshvara, may they go to his buddhafield of Potala Mountain to enjoy great and immaculate bliss forever.

[verse 13] By the power of having once received an empowerment of

Manjughosha, of having meditated on him, and of having recited his mantra, may the beings in hell now behold him. May their attitudes of hatred dissolve, and with thoughts of love may they encourage each other saying, "Friends, put away your dread of hellish realms. There is no need to be afraid. Come, make haste! Here before us is the sublime Manjughosha. By his power we are freed from the sufferings of being hacked and cut in pieces. He will make us happy and bring joy to our hearts. He is the Bodhisattva who by many methods protects the beings of the lower realms from their sorrows. He is the Bodhisattva in whose mind has arisen great compassion and love beyond all reference. He is Manjushri, the youth of sixteen years, whose hair is tied in five locks (one is bound up on the top of his head and adorned with a jewel, while the others are arranged above and below, to left and right). For who is it who comes to put to flight all fears of hell, if not Manjughosha, brilliant with the splendor of the major and minor marks of his enlightenment?

[verse 14] The beings in hell call out, telling each other to gaze upon the hundreds of gods, Brahma, Indra, and others, who constantly bow down in reverence to Manjughosha, lowering their diadems to the level of his lotus feet, making different offerings to him. Alternatively, the text could be interpreted here as meaning that hundreds of divine beings actually offer their diadems to Manjughosha's lotus feet. A great rain of flowers falls down upon his head, accompanied by the praises of the Buddhas and Bodhisattvas, and because of his great compassion and love for beings in their endless suffering, his beautiful eyes are moist with tears. In marvelous many-storied pavilions, thousands of divine maidens sing tuneful songs in praise of his body, speech, mind, qualities, and activities. And we should wish that, as soon as the denizens of hell tell each other to look, they immediately perceive all these visions of Manjughosha and are extremely happy. Let them sing and be glad, enjoying perfect and immaculate bliss!

[verse 15] So it is that Shantideva prays that, thanks to the virtue accumulated through the study and explanation of this text, the beings in hell encounter Samantabhadra, Akashagarbha, Maitreya, Kshitigarbha, Sarvanivaranavishkambhin, and others—and that, free from defilement, they listen to the teachings of these Bodhisattvas. Alternatively, the verse could be understood as expressing the wish that, through the bodhichitta and aspirations of the Bodhisattva who is free from defilements, namely, Sarvanivaranavishkambhin, and others, the beings in the hot hells may see a cool and fragrant rain that brings them bodily relief falling from the clouds, which are massing in the sky, and that they may soon secure the great joy and happiness of high rebirth in samsara and the definitive excellence of buddhahood.

[verse 16] To feel antipathy for the exposition and study of the Dharma, to repudiate and deride it, produces rebirth as an animal, of which there are two kinds: those dwelling in the depths of the ocean and those that live scattered over the face of the earth. The animals that live in the ocean range from enormous fishes and sea monsters hardly smaller than Mount Meru itself down to organisms that are like the tip of a hair. They are of all sizes and are numerous like the fermenting grains that fill a barrel of beer. They are ignorant and without intelligence. All the great fish gulp down great quantities of the small, while many of the small will burrow into the bodies of the larger ones, feeding on them or living on them as parasites. Animals are prey to uninterrupted suffering. Upon the nagas there falls a rain of hot sand, and they are devoured by eagles and other birds.

The animals scattered over the surface of the earth inhabit both the human and celestial realms. There are wild animals that have no owner, such as birds and ferocious carnivorous beasts that kill and devour each other. Hawks and cats eat small birds, while the birds prey in turn on insects and the like. They are helplessly slaughtered with guns, traps, and nets for the sake of their meat, their skin, and their bones. They are in torment, for they are in a state of constant fear. Then there are animals like horses and pack animals, which are domesticated by human beings. They are ridden or milked or made to carry heavy loads. They are castrated, their muzzles are pierced, and they are enslaved and constantly tormented.

According to the *Suryagarbha-sutra*, the duration of their life may be as short as an instant or as long as an intermediate kalpa. Animals are completely confused and ignorant of the kind of behavior to adopt or forsake; and without the fortune of being illuminated by the sublime Dharma, they kill and devour each other. We should pray that they be forever delivered from their fear and pain, and that they attain a human existence in which they will have contact with the Dharma. We should wish that they be endowed with intelligence both inborn and acquired, that they have the good fortune of listening to the exposition of the Tripitaka, and that they practice with joy the three trainings of the path. In the immediate term, may they gain high rebirth in samsara, and ultimately may they come to the state of buddhahood. As we have seen above, we should make these wishes with aspiration and longing, commitment and prayer; and give voice to them in verbal expression.

Coveting the provisions and wealth of others and being tightfisted with one's own produces rebirth as a preta, with outer, inner, or specific obscurations. The *Suryagarbha-sutra* tells us that the bodies of pretas may be as small as a hand-span or as large as a thousand leagues. As for their dwelling places, there are those that live in the depths [of the earth] and those that move in the sky. As to the former, their principal abode is five hundred leagues below Rajagriha, while their lesser habitations are on the shores of the sea, and in the human and other realms. A particular feature of their suffering is thirst. For many thousands of years, they do not even hear the word "water." Through the torment of such deprivation, their flesh, skin, and blood dry up. Their bodies are emaciated and they are extremely unsightly, looking for example like charred logs of wood. Many unpleasant sounds come from their mouths, and they say things like, "I have nothing; do not give to others." When [in the case of those with enormous bodies] they try to approach something that they might eat or drink, their extremely thin and loose-jointed limbs cannot support their weight. Smoke rises from their bodies that blaze with fire. They are wounded by dogs and birds and are tormented by a rain of burning stones and hot sand. Having seen a river in the distance, they exhaust themselves in trying to reach it, only to be driven away by armed guards. And if the river is unprotected, they find that it dries up [at their approach] becoming a gray and stony channel without a drop of water. Thus their perceptions of rivers are reversed as also is their experience of trees, food and drink, the sun, the moon, and the seasons. These are pretas with outer obscurations.

Then there are the torments of pretas with inner obscurations. Should they come upon a tiny scrap of food, their mouths are as small as the eye of a needle, their throats as narrow as a horsehair. Thus what they find they are unable to ingest, and even if they manage to swallow a little, they are unable to fill themselves, for their stomachs are as vast as an entire country. And even if it were enough to satisfy them, and they were able to swallow it, the food would burst into flames and burn their lungs, their heart, and all their entrails.

Pretas suffering from specific obscurations are for instance those upon whose bodies other pretas are living that have "nested" there and are devouring their hosts—as is described in the stories told by the teachers Jetari and

Shrona, who visited the land of the pretas and who encountered many of them, all suffering in different ways. The pretas fight among themselves, and the pus and blood issuing from their wounds become their and others' only food. Regarding the duration of their lives, it is said in the *Abhidharmakosha* that one human month corresponds to a single day among the pretas, and the latter can live for five hundred years according to their own reckoning. There are also pretas called tsun-lha.[233] When corpses are burned or broken in pieces in a charnel ground, these pretas can perceive from the odor the kind of life the dead people led, and they can assume the latter's appearance and their way of behaving.

What happens after death is described in the sutras. When the Buddha our Teacher went to Vaishali, there was a man called Shakya Gakye. He was mature in years, loved by his family, and widely respected; and many people grieved when he died. When, prompted by this event, the Buddha's father King Shuddhodana asked about the state beyond death, the Buddha answered that, when beings die, they are reborn in different states of existence, high or low, depending on their positive or negative actions. It is not the case that gods are always reborn as gods, humans as humans, and so on. There are also spirits, he said, that feed on odors, who can take the appearance of people after they have passed away. From their fathomless world in the intermediary realm, they can enter into the minds of different kinds of beings at the moment of their death. They appear with the bodies, clothing, ornaments, and behavior of the dead in order to search for sustenance. There are also harmful yakshas, he said, flesh-devouring ghosts, elemental spirits, and others, who assume the form of the dead in order to deceive those who had been close to them. It is also possible to dream of a dead person, owing to a strength of habit acquired from living for a long time with them. But the dead can only go where their karma leads them. They are powerless actually to return to this world. When the living who have left behind make offerings of food and drink, clothes and jewels for the sake of the dead, such a virtuous action, unstained by negativity, will be of help to the dead person. If the dead have not yet taken birth, they will be reborn in the higher realms and even gain liberation. If they have already taken birth, they will have wealth, they will be widely respected, and they will have many advantages. But if beings do not take birth and if they continue to linger in the world of the dead, they are unable to enjoy [actual] offerings of food and drink. When however the dead appear and seem to speak coherently about what might be beneficial or the reverse, this is the activity of the so-called bitsana spirits that live on odors and dwell within the minds of the deceased, the kind of yakshas known as "speech-lovers" and the sarahinita elementals known as "thought-lovers." These are nonhuman beings. They speak like the dead, and they assume their appearance and behavior in order to impersonate them and deceive the living.

This is what the Buddha explained [to his father]. Certain bystanders, Devadatta and others, doubted his word. Then, in order to test the Buddha's omniscience, Devadatta had an immense quantity of trees cut down—sandalwood, chestnut, and others—and had them burned. Marking their ashes so as not to mistake them, he brought them before the Buddha, who identified them all infallibly. It was thus that Devadatta came to believe that the Buddha possessed all-knowing primordial wisdom. And thinking that what the Buddha said about the postmortal states was true, he praised him with the following verses:

> The Blessed Buddha is indeed all knowing.
> The different ashes of these many trees
> Without the evidence of sight or sound
> He has discerned. Thus his words are sure
> Concerning what will happen when we pass from life.

In the same vein, it is told that a man by the name of Shakya journeyed to the great city of Vaishali. From every household, he took a portion of rice chaff. He labeled them, tied them all in a bag, loaded on the back of an elephant as much as it could carry, and came into the presence of the Buddha, who correctly identified them all. It was thus that the man had faith and praised the Buddha, saying:

> The Buddha's eyes see everything.
> Unlike the people of this world, there is no falsity in him.
> Of the households of this town of Vaishali,
> He identified the chaff without mistake.
> Of what becomes of those who pass from life
> The world declares with lying words.
> But what the Buddha says is true.
> To you, who see all things, I make obeisance.

If, at the shore of a river or lake, one fills the hollow of one's right hand with water, reciting over it the mantra of the wisdom lamp (OM JNANA AVALOKITE NAMAH SAMANTA SAPARANA RASMI BHAWA SAMAYA MAHAMANI DURU DURU HRIDAYA JWALANA HUNG) seven times, and if one pours seven such handfuls of water back into the rive or lake, all the pretas seen by the Buddha's eyes will taste divine food and drink. Every preta will be satisfied with seven koshala measures of food and drink. And by drinking such water, all the pretas will be freed from their condition and will be reborn in the happy states of the higher realms. It is said that all who drink this water (men, women, boys, girls, pretas belonging to the animal realm, birds, and water creatures) will have all their negativities and defilements purified, and will proceed on the path of happy destinies. It is also said in the sutras that if one recites just four lines of the Dharma over one's own food and drink, dedicating it for the sake of the pretas, it will also act as sustenance for them. We should therefore implement all such practices with confidence in the undeceiving teachings of the Tathagata.

There are also the spiteful, torma-devouring pretas. When, in this decadent age, a red offering of the flesh of slaughtered animals is presented to the wrathful mandala, the wisdom deities will not approach it at all. But the pretas who move in the air, who love flesh and blood, will be drawn to those who indulge in such practices, and they will mutually assist each other. Through the power of the pretas, such practitioners will have visions of gods and ghosts; they will acquire some measure of clairvoyance and the power of foretelling the future; they will be able to subdue spirits, and their words will have some power. But just as fathers may be deceived by their children and their children tricked by enemies, these practitioners will be beguiled by such ghosts and spirits. For a time, these pretas will behave as friends, removing adverse circumstances and causing favorable conditions to arise. But one false move irritates them, and they become extremely dangerous both to the practitioners and to others. In the long run, sponsors and those who make the offerings will turn against each other, and evil will befall them, ruining their present lives and their lives to come. When people place all their trust in the pretas that move in the air (instead of in the unfailing Three Jewels), when they make them offerings and give them praise, when they take their support as if they were wisdom deities, it is then that the prophecy will indeed have come to pass: "When pretas are considered deities, the time of sorrow for Tibet has come."

The kinds of spirits called tsen, gyalpo, shidre, and so on, which move in the air, are always aggressive toward others, and their actions are violent and evil. As soon as they perish, many fall into the hells or other of the lower realms. Every seventh day, they experience the same pain as that which brought about the circumstances of their death, whether they have been killed by weapons or by something else. Instantly they are reborn, only to die again, again to be reborn. They wish to transfer the suffering of this process to others, and consequently, wherever they go they bring only harm and never anything good. When they return with joy to those who were close to them in the past, the latter suddenly fall victim to all sorts of misfortunes, diseases, mental disturbances, and the rest. People with great spiritual power will subjugate, burn, and assail them [with substances perceived as weapons]. They will be imprisoned in subterranean darkness for half a kalpa. They will be burned in fire rituals or struck by mustard seeds, their bodies shattered into a thousand pieces. The seasons, the sun, and the moon, will act on them in a way contrary to normal, just as with the pretas afflicted with outer obscurations.

We should bear all these things in mind and should remember that ghosts and evil spirits are karmically connected with those whom they harm. As it is said, "The person harmed and the one who harms are causally linked." And without predilection for the devotee who makes the offering and without antagonism toward the evil spirit (for the two are joined by karmic ties), we should consider both equally as the objects of our meditation on compassion. We should abandon all fierce activities performed in the interests of the sick and designed to subjugate and control demons and evil spirits. Instead, we should meditate on loving-kindness, compassion, and bodhichitta. This is a sublime pith instruction that will bring benefit both immediately and in the long-term.

We should pray that, in every universe, all thirty-six kinds of preta (those that suffer from outer, inner, and specific obscurations, the tsun-lha, and other pretas that move in the air) be free from suffering and the causes of suffering. And we should wish that they all enjoy perfect bliss and the satisfaction of all their wishes: food, drink, garments, and ornaments—just as in Uttarakuru, the northern cosmic continent. For there, at the birth of every being, a wish-fulfilling tree sprouts, which, together with the untilled harvest, satisfies their every need. Thanks to this, everyone in Uttarakuru has a life of perfect pleasure and a gentle, virtuous mind, and therefore never indulges in the ten negative actions.

[verse 17] May the noble Avalokiteshvara appear in the land of the pretas. From the ten fingers of his hands and from the toes of his feet—and indeed from every pore of his body—may endless streams of milky nectar flow, sweet to taste and cool to touch. May the throats and mouths of the pretas be enlarged, and may they be satisfied by the nectar perceived as all the food and drink that they desire. And by bathing in this nectar, may they be delivered from the torment of heat and be forever refreshed. In the very instant that they hear the sound of the six-syllable mantra, may they be happy—just as it is said of the Bodhisattva Satisfaction-of-all-Wishes, who came to embody perfectly the meaning of his own name, and was born in Sukhavati.

[verse 18] To be born blind is the residual karmic result of actions such as stealing or extinguishing offering lamps, of obstructing the light of Dharma, of criticizing the Dharma and having wrong ideas about it, of looking askance at sublime beings and at one's own parents, of destroying Dharma books, and of tearing out the eyes of other beings. In all the infinite dimensions of the world, may all who are blind and all those who are performing actions that produce blindness be free from their suffering and its causes. May they instead offer lights and perform other similar actions. May they see perfect forms with perfect eyesight, and with eyes of wisdom, may they see and comprehend phenomena both in their nature and in their multiplicity.

Deafness is the result of such things as interrupting the music played in the presence of the representations of the enlightened body, speech, and mind. May all who are deaf be released from their suffering, and with the clairvoyance of the "divine ear" may they hear sweet sounds all the time.

In the moment of childbirth, both mother and baby are tortured almost to their deaths. The babies are tormented for it is as though they are being forced through a narrow passage as hard as iron. And the mother's bones and joints are dislocated and forced apart. May they all be free from pain! May all women near their time give birth without travail to beautiful, healthy children. May they be in bliss like Queen Mayadevi, who gave birth to Prince Siddhartha beneath a tree in the forest of Lumbini amidst wonderful auspicious signs. Not only did she feel no pain, but her experience was like the perfect bliss of samadhi.

It is said that there are signs that a mother perceives which indicate whether the child she is carrying will have a virtuous or evil life. When Ajatashatru was in the womb of his mother, she felt the urge to devour the flesh of Bimbisara, the child's father. When Shariputra was in the womb of his mother, she was able to dispute successfully with any pandita. When the prince Punyabala was in his mother's womb, all kinds of favorable signs appeared [to her in dreams]. She found herself seated upon a high throne and wanted to teach the Dharma. The baby's father went around ringing a bell, and a crowd had gathered. And from her throne, she recited without timidity verses never said before:

> If merit is accumulated, happiness will come.
> Therefore, human beings, practice virtue!
> Apply yourselves repeatedly,
> Make effort in this very thing.

As soon as she said these words, among the other marvels that also appeared, a voice came from the sky saying, "Well said! Excellently said!" When our own compassionate Teacher was in the womb of his mother Mayadevi she understood a host of teachings, and by feeding the sick or just by touching them, she was able to cure them. And to show her love of solitude, she went away to the forest of Lumbini in order to give birth.

[verse 19] The karmic cause of not having enough to wear, with the result that one is obliged to go naked, is to have stolen the robes from the representations of the enlightened body, speech, and mind or to have stripped one's parents or to have shaken lice out onto the cold ground. May everyone in this predicament be free from suffering. May they be happy and clothed in raiment of divine excellence: fine, light and soft, pleasurable to the touch. Similarly, pilfering someone else's food and sustenance results in the experience of starvation or of rebirth as a dog or a grit-eating pigeon, all of whom are constantly hungry. May those who suffer from hunger have excellent food with a hundred different tastes. May those who suffer from thirst be provided with delicious drink: water endowed with the eight qualities, heavenly ambrosia, and the juice of the three sweet substances.

[verse 20] May those who are poor and destitute (who suffer the result of the residual karma of robbery and stealing) have perfect wealth: gold, silver, horses, and elephants. On the other hand, the poverty of those who wish for many things and are never contented with what they have is even worse than the penury of those who have nothing. An example of this—and it is indeed the worst kind of poverty—is given in the story about a poor but noble man who came upon a precious jewel. He offered it to the

Buddha, our compassionate Teacher, who in turn declared that he would give it to the one who was the poorest in all the world. He then gave it not to some destitute pauper but to King Prasenajit.

May all who are tormented by mental suffering be freed from it. May they have happiness and joy! There are those whose hopes are dashed by their companions and there are those who never seem to succeed in either spiritual or temporal pursuits. All such people eventually despair. May they be successful! May their minds become whole; may they be strong and steadfast and thus able to accomplish everything. May they have courage and perfect self-confidence!

[verse 21] May all the sick in this world, who, as the result of evil action, are tormented by different ailments, especially incurable infections such as the plague, be speedily cured in this very instant from all their afflictions and diseases due to heat and cold. May no one in the world ever suffer from the four hundred and four different kinds of illness, arising through imbalances of the wind-energy, bile, and phlegm.

[verse 22] May all who are afraid, menaced by any of the sixteen great dangers—by evil wraiths, bandits or robbers, flesh-devouring demons, by fire, water, and venomous snakes—have no more fear. May those who are physically chained, and those whose body, speech, and mind are bound by spells, be released from all their bonds. May those who are weak, deprived of power and strength—from high kings down to the tiniest ant—become strong and powerful, but without pride, jealousy, or aggression. May they feel mutual affection and with hearts softened by love; may they be of help to each other.

[verse 23] May merchants and all other travelers, whoever they are and wherever they may be, who set out in pursuit of spiritual or material goals encounter no adversity on their way (such as bandits or diseases that afflict themselves or their animals). May they travel happily on good roads and in pleasant conditions. May they gain without need of toil the spiritual and material purposes (gold or silver and so on) on which they set their hearts and for the sake of which they have gone on their travels. [verse 24] May those who set sail on rivers, or put to sea in ships, be protected from the dangers of sudden storms or monsters of the deep. May they effortlessly accomplish all that they desire (the wish-fulfilling gem and so on). May they come safely to shore and to pleasant reunion with their parents and loved ones, there to pass their time in enjoyment and pleasant conversation.

[verse 25] And may those who wander and have lost their way in the wilderness, in desolate wastes devoid of water, grass, or trees, or else in fearful forests, not knowing where to go, meet with fellow travelers who will show them paths safe from robbers or wild beasts. May they reach their destination without difficulty or fatigue. [verse 26] In lonely places in the wild, filled with venomous serpents, where tigers and leopards prowl, far from the thoroughfares of men, places known to be the lair of cruel nonhuman beings, orcs and wraiths—rocky mountains and jagged cliffs, pathless wastes that are filled with horror—in all such places, may those who are forlorn and destitute, whether young or old, who fall asleep exhausted on their way, completely unconscious and oblivious to their peril, be protected! May they be shielded from the wraiths and flesh-devouring orcs, from spirits that shorten their lives and steal away their radiance, that drain away and sever all their strength of life. May they be guarded from such adversity by protective deities who are on the side of goodness: by the high gods, the seventy-five wardens of the Heaven of the Pure, by the five tutelary deities that are close to human kind, and by the ground lords of those lands!

Even among the wraiths, there are those that have faith in the Buddha's teaching. There is a story that there were once two monks who were traveling together. They were being followed by two flesh-devouring demons, one of whom had faith in the Buddhadharma, whereas the other did not. The latter declared that he would shorten the life of the two monks and steal their radiance. His companion, who had faith, replied that if they spoke some Dharma teaching, he would not allow his companion to attack them, but that he could do so if the contrary proved true.

As the monks continued on their way, they spoke to each other casually and to no great purpose. When they came to a bridge, however, the monks separated and went their different ways, each one telling the other to take care of himself.

"Now I will shorten their life and steal their radiance," said the first demon (who was covered with shaggy hair).

"What are you doing?" said the other. "Did you not hear the Dharma teaching that they gave?"

"But what did they say?"

"When they parted, each one told the other to take care, and there is no doctrine greater than the teaching on carefulness!"

And that was how the demon protected the monks!

[verse 27] May all beings be free from the sufferings implied by the eight conditions in which there is no leisure to practice the Dharma. May they obtain the freedom and excellence of a human existence, and may they be happy! Among those who achieve a human form, there are some whose minds are corrupted by false ideas. They are like upturned vessels. Even if a Buddha were to appear, it would do them no good. If one has no faith in the Three Jewels, no belief in the four truths or in the principle of dependent arising and especially in the karmic law of cause and effect, and if one persists in what should not be done and neglects what should be done, the sole result will be to fall lower and lower into evil destinies.

We should have the wish that such beings be freed from their sufferings and that they be perfectly endowed with [the four kinds of] faith: vivid, yearning, confident, and irreversible. For the eyes of their wisdom have been blinded with regard to what is to be done and what is not to be done. As a result, these ignorant and foolish people have no success even in the profane activities of the present life. It is hardly necessary to say that they fail to understand and accomplish the Dharma. Therefore, may those who are destitute of wisdom be free from the suffering of their stupidity (which prevents them from achieving their own and others' welfare). May they enjoy the fullness of wisdom, both inborn and acquired.

The root of the Mahayana path is compassion for all that lives. When beings lack this, their pitiless intentions and actions bring them ruin in this and future lives. May they be free from such sufferings! May they be endowed with great love and compassion for beings, like loving mothers for their children!

May they refrain from impure and sinful sustenance such as alcohol and meat, and also from the five kinds of wrong livelihood! As it is written in the *Ratnavali:*

> Hypocrisy is to rule one's senses
> For the sake of gain and reputation.
> Wheedling flattery will say sweet things
> For sake of gain and reputation.
>
> Praising other's wealth in hope of getting some
> Is indirectly robbing them.
> Pulling rank for sake of acquisition
> Is to put one's fellow humans down.
> To praise their former generosity (for selfish ends)
> Is "wishing to secure gain from gain."

If one lacks the qualities of realization and liberation, all the offerings received from the faithful and offerings made in order to help the dead are to be considered as explained in the Vinaya written by Sagalha:

> Those upon the path of no-more-learning may enjoy them as
>   their own.
> Those upon the path of learning may enjoy them as a gift.
> Those who meditate and study are allowed the use of them;
>   there is no fault.
> Those engulfed in indolence contract a karmic debt by using
>   them.
> Those whose acts are wanton and undisciplined
> May never use religious goods. For them it is prohibited.

We find also in *The Scalpel of the Heart:*[234]

> When someone who is dissolute takes but a single step
> Toward the use and the enjoyment of monastic wealth,
> Who eats a single mouthful, drinks a single cup,
> Lives wrongly, it is said, and will be born in hell.

May those who consume impure and sinful food rid themselves of it. May they eat the food that comes from an utterly pure livelihood, unstained by negative action. May they be like the birds, satisfied with whatever they find. To behave badly, to despise one's parents, to trade for profit, to slaughter animals and make traffic of their meat, to give scandal to the lay people: All such reprehensible conduct is a disgrace to the Triple Gem. The life of the Doctrine is exchanged for money, the vows are weakened, and the samaya is distorted. Such evil conduct brings destruction to oneself and others. May those who act in this way be freed from it. May they keep their pledges; may they refrain from alcohol; may they not tell lies. May they adhere first and foremost to the sixteen pure principles of human society;[235] may their minds be graced with the seven sublime riches of the Buddha's teaching; may they be grounded in the utterly pure discipline, and, through their perfect and pure conduct (reading, receiving, and studying the teachings, relinquishing defilements, and practicing focused concentration) may they secure great benefit for the Doctrine and beings.

To have remembrance of the series of one's lives is something of the highest moment. For one will thereby be convinced of the karmic principle of cause and effect. And once the seed of bodhichitta is awakened, it will never be forgotten. Therefore wherever they are born, may beings maintain unbroken memory throughout the sequence of their incarnations. Such a thing is illustrated in the story of the prince Kukche or the story of when Shariputra gave a teaching that was heard by a female dog. (When the dog died, it was reborn as a girl who, remembering her previous existence, took monastic ordination and endeavored on the path, thanks to which she attained arhatship.)

[verse 28] When Bodhisattvas achieve the concentration called the "Treasury of Space," five hundred great treasures appear to their right and five hundred to their left. Everything manifests from empty space according to their wish. In the same way, may all beings constantly enjoy immense possessions in harmony with the Dharma. For the sake of their possessions, ordinary people exhaust themselves, guarding their belongings day and night, and fighting among themselves. May they be free from all such quarrels and conflicts. And, delivered from every harm and enmity, may they all have free enjoyment of whatever they wish.

[verse 29] Some beings, among the gods for instance, whose forms are ill-favored and of little splendor, suffer because they are overshadowed and oppressed by the glory of those of beautiful form. Similarly in the human world, lamas and chieftains who are of unsightly appearance and are without presence or dignity are likewise disadvantaged and unhappy. May all of them, gods and humankind, acquire a magnificent and beautiful appearance. The suffering that beings feel because of physical ugliness can be illustrated by the story of the girl Dorjema. May all those who suffer hardship due to the lack of food or clothing, and therefore have emaciated and ill-favored looks, obtain perfect and handsome forms!

[verse 30] May all the women in this world, who are without physical strength, who must bear the many discomforts connected with childbearing and the thirty-two diseases peculiar to women, acquire the strength of masculinity (the physical advantages enjoyed by men). May all those of humble family whose traditional work is very lowly: the slaughtering of horses, the appropriation of gifts that accompany ransom offerings, disposing of corpses, and killing animals—all those who are poor and despised by others—may they be able to leave all this behind. May they acquire wealth and a good social position both in their family and their work. Without succumbing to pride and arrogance, may they have discipline and peace of heart.

[verse 31] By the power of his merit accumulated in the three times, Shantideva again prays that beings, as numerous as the sky is vast, relinquish all their negative actions. May they always act in a perfect and virtuous manner. [verse 32] In particular, as the path of a Bodhisattva comprises both attitude and action, may we likewise never abandon the attitude of the bodhichitta in aspiration and action. May we work for the benefit of others by means of the six transcendent perfections. May we strive in the ways of the Bodhisattvas! Shantideva prays that our friends and helpers, the Buddhas and Bodhisattvas, may hold us all in their compassion and love! May we abandon every kind of demonic behavior. May we avoid all circumstances antagonistic [to the practice]: the bustle of worldly business, distractions, drowsiness and sleep, agitation and quarreling.

The sutras supply many descriptions of the kind of activity associated with demonic forces. Maitreya summarized them in the *Abhisamaya-lankara*. According to him, demonic forces manifest especially against those who make great effort in the practice. For if one endeavors without wisdom, evil forces are able to create obstacles. They come in the guise of one's friends who say that one already has so much knowledge, that one is already endowed with spiritual qualities acquired through past training— surely just a few recitations will suffice! Similarly, difficult relations will arise between teachers and disciples and the Dharma will not be expounded and studied. One will have the presumptuous thought that one's ethical discipline is superior, and one will look down on others. And just as it is said that all pleasures of the senses are the sign of evil forces, in the same vein, clairvoyance, gain, respect, and so on, are also regarded as the work of demons. By contrast, it is said that lazy people are never hindered by demonic forces. For laziness is itself a demon. On the other hand, those who have wisdom are immune to all such demonic hindrances. As it is said in the condensed *Prajnaparamita-sutra:*

> Four causes make it hard for Bodhisattvas, skilled and strong,
> To be diverted and subdued by the four demons:
> Abiding in the view of emptiness, not forsaking beings,
> Acting in accordance with one's pledges, and being graced
>   with the Buddha's blessing.

[verse 33] May beings born in the higher realms have immeasurable longevity. And for as long as they are alive, may they enjoy perfect wealth. May they live constantly in happiness and may they not even hear of untimely death.

[verse 34] The following verses constitute a prayer of aspiration that the world be transformed into a pure land. Shantideva prays that in all the reaches of this universe, on every side and in all directions, may beautiful groves of wish-fulfilling trees abound, providing beings with every amenity and resounding with the sweet sound of the Dharma spoken by the Blessed Buddhas and their Bodhisattva children. [verse 35] May the earth become wholesome everywhere. May it be free from boulders and without chasms and ravines. And instead of being covered with thorns, may it be spacious and beautiful, flat and even like a level palm. May its checkered surface of lapis lazuli shot through with a hundred and one shades of color, be as smooth to the touch as celestial kajalika silk. May the earth abound in all these qualities!

[verse 36] In the monasteries, the Buddhas, Bodhisattvas, and teachers are the principal figures, surrounded by the monks and disciples; in the kingdoms, the kings are surrounded by the their ministers and subjects. In other words, a main figure encircled by a retinue is a "gathering circle" or mandala. In all the assemblies that are gathered around them, may the multitudes of Bodhisattvas in all their excellence (equipped with the material provisions resulting from the strength of their merit and miraculous powers and possessed of all the perfect wealth of Dharma) remove the spiritual and material poverty of their followers. May they spread and consolidate the teaching and study of the Tripitaka and the practice of the three trainings. May they increase and strengthen longevity, merit, influence, and riches, adorning thus the face of the earth with all such good things. May they live for many long years!

[verse 37] Wherever beings can attain enlightenment, that is, in every one of the ten directions, may they constantly hear—in the song of beautiful birds (the king of swans and the king of peacocks), in the sighing of the trees, from shafts of light of sun and moon, and indeed from the sky itself—the sound of the Dharma. This Dharma is profound and vast, and it expresses the four seals (all compounded things are impermanent; all defilements are suffering; all phenomena are empty and without self; and nirvana is peace) and the three doors of perfect liberation (phenomena are empty; they are beyond all attributes; they are beyond all aspiration or expectation).

The benefits that accrue from hearing the Dharma teachings are described in the sutras:

> When, O King, this gong resounds,
> Within this land you will enjoy
> Renown, magnificence, your every wish!
> No terror will there be of adverse foes;
> The crops and harvests will not wilt.
> Buddha's blessing will descend
> Upon this place; the demons will be tamed!
> The hells and all the preta-realms—
> Let no one doubt—will cease to be.
> In Buddha all will have a constant trust;
> In Dharma all will diligently strive.
> The Sangha thus will congregate;
> The learned then will multiply.
> Attachment, anger, ignorance
> Will dwindle and will cease to be.
> When the Dharma drum is struck,
> And when its sound falls on the ears
> Of beings in the four times of the day,
> All those who hear will gain enlightenment.

And it is said also:

> When the gong of the Three Jewels,
> Adored by gods and nagas, and the yakshas,
> Has been struck, the uncouth minds
> Of tirthikas will be subdued.

If such advantages come simply from the resounding of the Dharma drum, the gong, and so on, there is no need to mention the benefits that come from actually hearing the teachings themselves, and from the exposition and study of the Dharma.

[verse 38] May all beings constantly meet with the Buddhas and the Bodhisattvas, the great beings who are their offspring. When they meet them, may they constantly make unbounded clouds of offerings to them either physically or by means of the mind's imagination.

[verse 39] When beings practice pure virtue, the gods are victorious and the asuras are cast down. The powers of purity prevail. May kindly spirits, gods, and nagas who cleave to the side of virtue bring the rains in season so that all the crops and fruit trees come to perfect ripeness, providing thus a good year for the country's people. Likewise may the livestock increase for the nomads. In every land, may there be no disease, no famine, and no war. Let there be nothing but happiness and prosperity. And to that end, may the causes of such effects also flourish, may the spiritual and temporal domains be maintained in peace according to the Dharma, just as during the time of the world-protecting sovereigns and of our three ancestral kings. Thus may the world and the beings that inhabit it prosper and be delivered from all decline.

[verse 40] May the four medicines have perfect therapeutic power.[236] May the chanting of the secret words of power (the secret mantras through which all works are successfully accomplished) be swift in bringing the benefits described. May the evil intentions and actions of spirits that move in space (the elementals, rakshasas, yakshas, flesh-devouring ghouls, spirits, and evil phantoms) be pacified, and may all such entities become loving and compassionate.

[verse 41] In short, let no being ever suffer pain in body or mind. Let no one ever perpetrate evil, which is the cause of suffering, and thus may they never ail or languish. May they be free from fear; may they never have to suffer insults. May their minds be forever free from sorrow. May they be happy and contented and dwell in virtue!

[verse 42] In all temples and monasteries great or small, wherever the scriptures are present, may the Tripitaka be explained, listened to, and reflected upon. May the sutras and the rest be retained in the mind and never forgotten. May they be recited; may they be remembered, and their meaning meditated upon one-pointedly. In brief, in all monasteries, may the activities of the Buddha's followers (the abandonment of defilement, the practice of concentration, learning, and study) flourish and remain for a long time. By contrast, in places of trade and agriculture, where people are enslaved by wealth and tormented by attachment and aversion with respect to each other, and where they are distracted night and day by constant enmity, quarreling, and spiteful grudges—and especially in places where there are conflicts in the sangha—the qualities and experiences of realization can never arise, just as burnt seeds can never produce green shoots. As the scriptures say:

Get thee hence a hundred leagues
From places where contentions spread.

Thus wherever the monastic order finds itself, may the ordained never be divided by demonic forces. May their minds be inclined to virtue; may they bring their discipline in conformity with uposatha, the ritual of purification and restoration of vows, at the full and new moon. May they make their view conform with the uposatha of calm abiding.[237] And in accordance with their wish, may they acquire ever more extraordinary qualities of the path of liberation beyond suffering, which is their goal.

[verse 43] May the monks who wish to school themselves correctly in the three precious trainings find perfect solitude, outer, inner, and secret. And having found it, may they abandon all busy activity and every distraction. With full control over their minds (in allowing them either to move or to remain still), may they acquire the bliss that comes from perfect flexibility of mind and body. May they joyfully practice profound concentration.

[verse 44] May nuns have little difficulty in acquiring their robes and provisions; may they never be quarrelsome and always have undamaged discipline. Peaceful, self-controlled and conscientious, may they remain in the supreme Dharma. In the same way, may all those who, wishing for liberation, have embraced the monastic state be able to uphold at all times and according to their pledge, a pure and unimpaired observance of the discipline whereby the heat of defilement is cooled.

[verse 45] The faults that result from an impaired discipline have been described by the Buddha himself:

One will not listen to the holy teaching,
And what one hears will quickly be forgotten.
Realization of the grounds and paths will not arise.

It was also said:

When discipline is disregarded, one will go to lower realms.
Great learning will be no protection.

And again, as it is said in the *Manjushrimula-tantra*:

Regarding those whose discipline is spoiled,
The Mighty Sage did not declare them able to accomplish
mantra.

May all who spoil their discipline and commit downfalls repair their actions sincerely and with strong remorse, confessing what is to be confessed and resolving not to fail again. At all times, may they purify their negative actions. And having done so, may they never, in the immediate term, be reborn in the lower realms. May they always be born among the higher destinies, and, taking monastic ordination, may they keep their discipline and practice purely and without decline.

[verse 46] The eyes of correct discrimination are open when, as an active karmic effect similar to the cause,[238] people have an unimpaired observance and are learned in the five sciences, especially the inner science of the Tripitaka. They are able to uphold and propagate the precious Doctrine of the Victorious One, the source of all happiness and welfare. Since they are thus on a higher plane than others, may they be honored and respected, and may they effortlessly find whatever they might need: Dharma robes, begging bowl, provisions, and so forth. May they be free of pride with respect to their own qualities and knowledge, and free of jealous rivalry with regard to the qualities of others. May they have neither contempt for other people nor scorn for the doctrines of other schools. May they turn away from all actions that lead to abandoning the Dharma and to the faults of distorted discipline. May their minds be utterly pure and may their reputation for wisdom and pure observance spread in all directions.

[verse 47] May those who have poor discipline, and indeed anyone else, never have to suffer the three lower realms in their lives to come. And without great toil and difficulty, may they attain a human existence endowed with freedoms and advantages (which, from the point of view of liberation, is far better than a divine existence) and quickly attain perfect buddhahood.

3. DEDICATION OF VIRTUE FOR THE SAKE OF PERFECTING THE SUPREME GOAL

[verse 48] May beings, as numerous as the sky is vast, at all times make offerings—both of material things and of their practice—to the Buddhas in the ten directions. And thanks to the Buddhas' blessings, may they attain the inconceivable, endless bliss of the stainless enlightened mind and be forever filled with great happiness.

[verse 49] May all the great Bodhisattvas fulfill their high intention for the sake of beings in exactly the ways that they wish, bringing beings to spiritual maturity and liberation. May beings swiftly receive the assistance and unsurpassed bliss wished for them by the omniscient protectors of beings, the Buddhas and their heirs, the great Bodhisattvas. (This verse is arranged in such a way as to express the agent and the object of the action.)

[verse 50] Pratyekabuddhas gain their enlightenment through their own self-arisen wisdom, whereby they understand the profound truth of dependent arising. Shravakas receive teachings from their holy teachers and then expound them to others. May all be endowed with the happiness that occurs when suffering comes to an end; and may they attain the great bliss of ultimate and perfect buddhahood.

2. DEDICATION OF VIRTUE FOR ONE'S OWN SAKE, THAT IS, AS THE CAUSE OF ENLIGHTENED ACTIVITIES

[verse 51] Here Shantideva formulates the wish that, protected by the kindness of his yidam deity, the noble Manjughosha, he might always, throughout the series of his lives until he reaches Perfect Joy, the first ground of realization, maintain the memory of his previous existences. By such means he will have conviction in the truth of the karmic law of cause and effect and will never forget bodhichitta. He prays that he might "always embrace the perfect discipline of monastic ordination." For whereas to be a householder is the basis of all the faults that bring ruin in this and future lives, to go forth into homelessness is the ground and basis of all excellent qualities and benefits.

In the present age, if one takes and observes just one of the precepts of the Buddha's teaching, one will acquire great merit and benefits. This has been described in the *Samadhiraja-sutra*:

> Those who for as many aeons trillionfold
> As grains upon the Ganga's sandy shore,
> Worship with devoted mind, with food and drink,
> And lamps and flowers, parasols and banners,
> A thousand million Buddhas—
> All are in their merits utterly surpassed

By those who—at this time when sacred Dharma perishes
And when the teaching of the Tathagata wanes—
Will practice day and night a single precept.

This being so, there is no need to speak of the result that will occur when one embraces monastic ordination and observes all the precepts without impairment. One will accomplish perfectly the goals of this and future existences both for oneself and others. The benefits that ensue are inconceivable.

[verse 52] Shantideva prays that he may have a healthy body and live happily, sustained by no more than alms: ordinary, simple fare. And he prays that in every life until he attains buddhahood he might have a proper dwelling place suitable for the practice of virtue—in the outer, inner, and secret solitude of his body, speech, and mind, the need for which has already been explained. Regarding the benefits of solitude, these, once again, are as mentioned in the *Chandrapradipa-sutra*. It is of greater benefit to make seven steps in the direction of a solitary retreat than to make offerings to the Buddhas of the ten directions for as many kalpas as there are grains of sand in the Ganges.

The commentarial tradition speaks of the master Shantideva as a noble being, an Arya. Consequently, the verse "And till, through Manjughosha's perfect kindness, I attain the ground of Perfect Joy . . . ," which is the first level of realization, [does not express his own condition but] is directed at his followers training on the path.

[verse 53] He prays furthermore that, whenever he desires to meet or look upon the face of Manjughosha, adorned as he is with the major and minor marks of enlightenment, and whenever he wants to put to him the slightest question about the Dharma, he may behold him, his protector, clearly and unobstructedly. And he prays that at all times Manjughosha will take care of him and guard him.

[verse 54] In order to accomplish easily the immediate and ultimate goals of beings dwelling in all the world systems that lie in the ten directions and wherever space is to be found, he prays that his every deed should reflect the perfect exploits of the inconceivable emanations of Manjushri's body, speech, and mind: a great flood of Bodhisattva activities for the benefit of others. In brief, he says, "May I be able to practice and behave just like the great eight close sons of the Buddha (Manjushri in his wisdom, Avalokiteshvara in his love, Vajrapani in his power, Samantabhadra in his enlightened deeds, and so on) and the inconceivable emanations of their body, speech, and mind. And it is for this purpose that we too should sincerely dedicate all the roots of our virtue and make prayers of good wishes.

[verse 55] And now, for as long as space endures, and for as long as there are beings to be found, Shantideva prays that, as one who works for the welfare of others, he may continue to remain in order to drive away the sorrows of the world. [verse 56] He prays that all the pains and sorrows of wandering beings should ripen wholly on himself and thus be purified. And thanks to the power of bodhichitta, the twofold accumulation, and the prayers of aspiration of the company of Bodhisattvas, he prays that the infinite multitude of beings might enjoy the perfection of happiness both in the immediate and the ultimate term.

2. Dedication for the propagation and prosperity of the Buddha's Doctrine embodying as it does the twofold goal

[verse 57] The sole supreme remedy that pacifies the pain and suffering in samsara of an infinite number of living beings, the sublime wellspring of every happiness and bliss both now and ultimately is the precious teaching of the Buddha. Speaking of the Buddha's Doctrine, the great pandita, the venerable Vasubandhu has said:

> The Teacher's Doctrine has two aspects:
> Of transmission and of realization.
> The first is held and spoken forth;
> The second is the practice.

Accordingly, holy beings who uphold the Dharma—mindful of the Doctrine and of beings—expound the Dharma of transmission, namely, the Vinaya, the Sutra, and the Abhidharma sections of the Tripitaka. And they practice as well the Dharma of realization, namely, the three higher trainings of the path: discipline, concentration, and wisdom. Their bodies are adorned with the three Dharma robes; their speech is adorned with the teachings of the Tripitaka; their minds are adorned with the three trainings of the path. Possessing the two wheels of explanation and practice of the teachings, they are true upholders of the Dharma. Supported by the wealth and reverence of the benefactors of the Doctrine, who are endowed with perfect faith, generosity, and material means, may the precious teaching of the Buddha, source of every happiness, spread and flourish throughout a vast continuance of time, till the very ending of the world.

It is by thinking in these terms that we should make our dedication, communicating it thus in words of aspiration. Considering how wonderful it would be if the Doctrine were to remain thus, we infuse our wish with longing. Declaring that we will make sure of this, we infuse our wish with resolution. And by imploring the Three Precious Jewels to bless us that we might have the power to bring this about, we infuse our wish with prayer. It is thus that we should make a fourfold wish when dedicating our merit.

In short, any connection whatsoever with the Dharma, the source of happiness, is meaningful. If the precious teaching of the Buddha remains in this world, whoever is linked with it will gain great merit. As it is written in the *Sagaramatiparipriccha-sutra:*

Perfect bodhichitta and upholding of the Dharma,
Accomplishment of Dharma and compassion for all beings:
These four things possess unending excellence—
The Buddha never said that they would end.

Thus we understand that the benefits of upholding the sublime Dharma and the protection of the life of beings are of immeasurable value.

Concerning the merit of generosity practiced in connection with the Dharma, we find in the *Samghata-sutra:*

The one who to my Doctrine gives
No more than just a little thing,
Will have great wealth and many riches
For eighty thousand kalpas.

And the *Samadhiraja-sutra* says that the merits of spiritual discipline will also result in great possessions, and so on, (as shown above) for upward of a million kalpas. The *Mahasamayavaipulya-sutra,* when speaking of the merits that result from meditation, declares that it is more meaningful to practice one session of meditative concentration on the Mahayana than to make the gift of protection of life to all the beings in the three worlds. Such are the benefits of generosity, discipline, and concentration.

If those who wish to attain the higher realms and the definitive goodness of enlightenment engage in these three merit-producing activities, they will indeed secure a great benefit.

But one should make even greater effort in correct study and reflection with a view to cultivating supreme wisdom. For it is through wisdom that one understands profound emptiness beyond all conceptual elaboration, the ultimate remedy that counteracts the two kinds of obscuration. As it is said in the *Uttaratantra-shastra:*

> Thus it is by giving that all wealth will be produced.
> Perfect ethics lead to high rebirth, while meditation rids
>   you of defilement.
> But the veils, emotional and cognitive, are both removed
>   by wisdom.
> Therefore wisdom is supreme. Its cause is study of this
>   teaching.

In the *Bodhisattva-pitaka* it is said:

> Through learning, you will understand all things.
> Through learning, you will put an end to sin.
> Through learning, senseless things will be abjured.
> Through learning, perfect freedom will be gained.

And in the *Jatakamala* it is said:

> Learning is a gloom-dispelling lamp,
> The best of riches that no thief can steal away,
> The best of arms that slays the foe, bewilderment,
> The best of friends revealing means and ways and pith
>   instructions,
> The best of friends, unchanging even in the face of poverty,
> The best of medicines whereby no ills can harm,
> The best of armies that can crush the foe, great negativity.
> It is the best of treasures, glory, and renown.
> If noble persons have it, they will be supreme.
> It rejoices learned ones in the assembly
> And is like sunlight scattering the dark.

Likewise in the abridged *Prajnaparamita-sutra,* it is said:

> The man of little learning is as if born blind.
> He knows not how to meditate. On what can he reflect?
> Diligently study, for from this will come
> The vast and perfect wisdom of reflection and of meditation.

And in the *Ganti-sutra* it is said:

> The hour of teaching of the holy Dharma
> Is marked by sounding of the drum or gong.
> If merely hearing this, one may attain enlightenment,
> No need to speak of meeting to receive the teachings.

In the *Maitreyamahasimhanada-sutra* it is said:

> Suppose one were to give in charity
> The universe three thousandfold all filled with gold,
> The benefit accrued would not compare
> With giving of a single four-lined verse.

> Whoever wants to do a beneficial thing,
> Who gives a single stanza of four lines
> Of Buddha's teaching to a single man,
> Will do more good than if he gave to him

> The happiness of all the beings in the triple world.
> By such a deed is supreme good achieved,
> For such an action will give freedom
> From all pain and suffering.

> One may with joyful mind make offerings to the Conqueror
> Of buddhafields, replete with seven treasures,
> Many as the grains of Ganga's sand;
> And one may give a verse of Doctrine to a single being.

> Such precious offerings, extremely vast,
> Do not approach in value even in the slightest part

The worth of giving with compassion but a single verse.
No need to think of giving two or three!

By such a comparison we may have some idea of the value of the Dharma teachings.

In the *Tattvanirdesha-sutra,* we find the text, "To concentrate, O Shariputra, on suchness for the time it takes to snap one's fingers brings an increase in merit greater than if one were to study the teaching for an entire kalpa! Therefore, O Shariputra, be assiduous in explaining to others the concentration on suchness!" By these and other texts we may perceive the benefits of correct meditation.

In short, the Buddha said that whoever takes a single step, or inhales or exhales a single breath, for the purposes of hearing or explaining the Dharma is an upholder of the teaching. As we find in the *Tathagata-acintyaguhya-sutra:*

If all the Buddhas were to tell,
With all their effort for a million kalpas,
The merits of upholding sacred Dharma,
They would not reach the end of such a discourse.

Such are the benefits of upholding and preserving the holy teachings.
In respect of all that has been said above, we find in the *Saddharma-smrityupasthana-sutra:*

'Tis possible that fire turn cold,
Or else the wind be taken in a noose,
That sun and moon fall down upon the plain—
But actions and their fruits will never fail.

And in the *Samadhiraja-sutra:*

The moon and all the stars may fall,
The earth with all its many hills can vanish into space.
And space can into earth be once more changed,
But you will never say an untrue word.

In accordance with such teachings, by being convinced that the karmic law is inescapable, we should strive to make meaningful our existence and our meeting with the supreme Teacher and his teachings.

1. CONCLUSION

2. HOMAGE PAID BY REMEMBERING THE KINDNESS OF MANJUGHOSHA

[verse 58] Shantideva declares that it was thanks to the kindness and blessings of Manjughosha that he was able to abandon every attachment to the futile behavior of the world and that he was able to make concentrated effort in the virtuous practices of learning, reflection, and meditation. Such an extraordinary attitude of mind has arisen, he says, through the Bhagavan Manjughosha. Therefore he pays respectful homage to him in his thoughts, words, and deeds. In the same vein he prostrates respectfully to the holy beings thanks to whose kindness he was able to take monastic ordination and receive the bhikshu vows—the same beings who spread and propagate the Dharma of transmission and realization, namely, the ordaining abbot Jinadeva and the other teachers of the glorious monastery of Nalanda and elsewhere. To all his spiritual teachers, therefore, Shantideva bows down.

In the same way, we too should consider as our teachers all those through whose kindness our minds have absorbed some of the qualities of the Dharma of transmission and realization. And remembering their kindness, we too should respectfully reverence them in thought, word, and deed.

Here ends the tenth chapter of the *Bodhicharyavatara*, on the dedication of merit, which brings to an end the *Bodhicharyavatara* composed by the great master Shantideva.

2. THE TRANSLATOR'S COLOPHON [239]

[Regarding the propagation of the teachings in Tibet] a division is made between the earlier and the new translations. The early translation period of the Nyingma tradition occurred under the aegis of the three religious kings, Songtsen Gampo, Trisongdetsen, and the sovereign Tri Ralpachen, who were themselves the manifestations of the noble lords of the three lineages. It was then that the sutras and tantras together with their commentaries were rendered into Tibetan by a series of translators from Thönmi Sambhota until the omniscient Rongdzom Dharmabhadra, under the guidance of the panditas Lha Rigpa'i Senge down to the great master Smritijnana. Subsequently, certain tantras and their commentaries, and some of the shorter sutras, were translated by Rinchen Zangpo and others, and these belong to the Sarma or new translation period. All these translated teachings are the precious Doctrine of our compassionate Teacher, the Buddha Shakyamuni. Moreover, all the holy upholders of the Buddhadharma possess the view marked by the four seals, on account of which it is impossible to discriminate between them with regard to their activities of the three secrets, which are as indistinguishable as space within the expanse of the dharmakaya. Therefore it behooves us to approach them all in a manner free from faction and sectarian bias.

The *Bodhicharyavatara* was composed in the well-ordered language of Sanskrit. While yet extant in the noble land of India, it was rendered into Tibetan during the early translation period by the great Indian scholar Sarvajnadeva and Kawa Peltsek, the Tibetan monk who was its translator and editor in chief. They used a manuscript from Kashmir. With reference to Kawa Peltsek, the great translator Ngok Loden Sherab declared:

> Vairotsana equals the unbounded sky;
> Kawa, Chokro, Zhang are like the sun and moon together,
> Rinchen Zangpo sparkles like the brilliant morning star.
> Compared with them we are but fireflies.

Kawa Peltsek and Sarvajnadeva also edited and finalized the translation through the exposition and study of the treatise, thereby bringing great benefit to fortunate beings.

Later, the Indian scholar Dharmashribhadra and the Tibetan monks, translators, and editors Rinchen Zangpo and Shakya Lodrö revised and finalized the text according to a manuscript and commentary brought from the central region of India (Magadha). At a still later date, the Indian scholar Sumatikirti and Loden Sherab, the monk and translator from Ngok, revised the text and finalized it in its [present] state of perfection. In his great commentary, Sazang[240] says that the text was corrected, edited, and finalized by the Nepali scholar Sumatikirti and three later translators. And he adds that by comparing the translation with the Sanskrit, he had himself corrected the slight imperfections that had crept into the text during the intervening period.

2. Khenpo Kunzang Pelden's colophon

This introduction to enlightened deeds, the perfect path of
    Bodhisattvas,
Composed by Shantideva whom the sweet-voiced
    Manjughosha took as his disciple,
Has been expounded in a marvelous treasure of a thousand
    teachings
In the words of Chökyi Wangpo, from the lords of the three
    lineages never parted.

Lest it be lost, my holy teachers have requested it,
That it become a healing cure for beings and the Doctrine.
And so I have compiled what I have noted and received,
Of such profound instruction.

Although I am untroubled by the poisoned wish for wealth
    and fame,
The demon of stupidity, of clinging to the self, is lodged
    within my heart.
My faults of understanding wrongly or of understanding not
    at all
I now declare before my teacher and the yidam deity.

All the virtue gathered in the triple time, the effort made to
    make this text—
Enjoined by holy beings, that the line of teachings be not
    spoiled,
That beings be assisted, and the holy Dharma be upheld—
I dedicate it in the manner of the Buddhas and their
    Bodhisattva heirs.

May the free, impartial teaching of the Conqueror increase
    and spread;

May faction be dispelled, may biased zeal and enmity be
   cleansed;
May all sectarian troubles be completely stilled;
And may the banner of the Dharma's victory be raised on
   every side.

May the holders of the teaching everywhere and always have
   long lives;
May the sangha's ranks increase; may benefactors prosper;
May the precious Doctrine of the Buddha, source of benefit
   and joy,
Everywhere and always be upheld and spread.

From this day forth, in this and future lives,
May I and others be accepted by our teachers and our yidams;
May we everywhere uphold the essence of the Doctrine
Through the perfect Way of Bodhisattvas, for the good of
   wandering beings.

May all who have connection with this text live long and
   healthy lives!
May they strive in goodness in their actions, thoughts, and
   words!
May the yidam and the teacher grant to us their blessing,
That we be sovereigns of the Dharma, with the twofold
   purpose naturally achieved.

May the teacher, may the Triple Jewel, may the Three Roots,
   ocean vast
(Through speaking of their words of truth) bring forth results
According to the prayers that I have made—
And at the same time send a rain of flowers: virtue and
   auspiciousness.

The time and place of composition of this commentary, as well as the
personal qualities of myself, the commentator, are all deficient. My intelligence (both native and acquired) is meager, and my efforts are feeble and

inadequate. Nevertheless, the great master of Kathok in the East, Situ Chökyi Gyatso, the sovereign of the entire Doctrine and doctor in the five sciences, commanded me, telling me repeatedly to compose a commentary on the *Bodhicharyavatara* according to the teachings of Patrul Rinpoche. And an earnest request to the same effect came from Gyurme Thegchog Shedrup Gyaltsen Pel Zangpo, the tulku of the monastery of Yilhung Trashul, who has in this present age pledged himself to the excellent work of expounding and accomplishing the precious Doctrine of the Buddha (source of every benefit) in its aspects of transmission and realization. As a token of his sincerity, this same master—whose ways conform to the life and manners of the holy beings, upholders of the teaching—made the gift of a silk scarf; of a thangka painted in gold of the twenty-one Taras, the Courageous Ones, the mothers of the Buddhas and embodiments of their activities; and of a vajra and bell, together with paper for the composition and a promise to have the printing blocks made.

But I took it into my head to leisure away my days in the solitude of the mountains, passing my time in relaxation and sleep, and I left the matter as it was. Finally, the sun of the teachings of the Old Translations, Shechen Gyaltsap Rinpoche, Gyurme Pema Namgyal, who was aware of this situation, presented me with a very long and precious silken scarf and with great insistence pressed me to complete the task, saying that he would be very pleased if I did it soon. The lama, mentioned earlier, who had requested the same commentary reiterated his promise to provide for the carving of the woodblocks for publication, toward which task certain lamas from Sharkha also contributed necessary provisions. In addition, two monks devoted to the three trainings, Sangye (otherwise known as Lodrö Chogden) and Thubten Gendün Pelgye, imbued with the utterly pure attitude [of bodhichitta], promised to act as scribes.

Therefore, in response to this wealth of excellent and favorable circumstances, and because of the great interest shown, and on account of these repeated requests, I wrote this commentary, basing myself on the teaching of the third incarnation of Palge Lama, the lord of the entire Doctrine of Shakyamuni and the very embodiment of Manjushri, Orgyen Jigme Chökyi Wangpo (Patrul Rinpoche), the white banner of whose renown is raised aloft above the three worlds of existence. When I had the marvelous opportunity to receive from the omniscient lord, Patrul Rinpoche himself, a detailed exposition of the *Bodhicharyavatara*, which he gave in the course of a six-month teaching at his seat at Chökhor Gegong, the Dharma encampment called Rigdzin Chime Drupa Shedrup Gatsel, I gladly undertook the task of writing notes in the periods before the teaching sessions. In addition, I also made notes during an explanation of the *Bodhicharyavatara* given in a detailed forty-day course by Patrul Rinpoche's heart-son, Önpo Rinpoche, Orgyen Tendzin Norbu, a teaching that I had the good fortune to receive twice. It is on the basis of these notes of mine, and thanks also to notes made by other close disciples of Patrul Rinpoche, and to their spoken explanations, that I, the ignorant and foolish Kunzang Chödrak, also known as Kunzang Pelden, the mere pretense of a monk of Shakyamuni, wrote this commentary, with a perfectly pure attitude and with a view to ease of comprehension. May virtue and well-being result. MANGALAM!

Notes

1. This date for the ordination of the *semi midun* (*sad mi mi bdun*) is in the writings of the Fifth Dalai Lama, as mentioned in the *Tshig mdzod chen mo*, p. 3204. According to the Vinaya, candidates for full ordination must have reached their twentieth year. Assuming the accuracy of the cited date, Kawa Peltsek could not have been born later than 747.
2. The Denkarma (*ldan dkar ma*) was a catalogue compiled by Kawa Peltsek and Namkha'i Nyingpo listing all the texts that until that time had been translated into Tibetan. Assuming the accuracy of the date given, Kawa Peltsek would have been in his eighties. See Kretschmar, *Shantideva's "Bodhisattvacharyavatara"* (hereafter Kretschmar), chap. 1, p. 13.
3. The five others were the *Mahayana-sutralankara* of Maitreya and Asanga, the *Bodhisattvabhumi* of Asanga, the *Shikshasamucchaya* of Shantideva, the *Jatakamala* of Aryashura, and the *Udanavarga*.
4. We are indebted to Gene Smith for information about Tsang Nakpa's commentary and a copy of his text, as also that of Sonam Tsemo's. Both these commentaries are of interest for the Madhyamaka tradition. They appeared at the time when Chandrakirti's works were being introduced to Tibet through the translations of Patsap Nyima Drak (1055–1145). The quotation from the *Madhyamakalankara* at the beginning of Sonam Tsemo's commentary on the *Bodhicharyavatara's* ninth chapter suggests that he propounded the view of the Yogachara-Madhyamaka school of Shantarakshita, which Chapa strenuously defended. By contrast, the *Blue Annals* reports that Tsang Nakpa followed the view of Chandrakirti "preferring it to that of his teacher Chapa" even though he apparently did not expect it to survive Chapa's onslaught! See *Blue Annals*, p. 334. See also Smith, *Among Tibetan Texts*, p. 326, n. 763.
5. See Kretschmar, chap. 1, p. 21.
6. Gene Smith lists a number of other commentaries composed in the earlier period especially by the masters of the Kadampa tradition. See *Among*

Tibetan Texts, p. 228.

7. See Smith, *Among Tibetan Texts,* pp. 227–72; and Dreyfus, *Recognizing Reality,* pp. 33–41.

8. See Kretschmar, chap. 1, p. 37.

9. Many of the details of this biographical note derive from the account of Patrul Rinpoche's life given in Tulku Thondup's *Masters of Meditation and Miracles* (hereafter *Masters*), pp. 201–10.

10. See Ricard, *Life of Shabkar,* p. xv.

11. Patrul Rinpoche was a disciple of Jigme Gyalwa'i Nyugu, himself a direct disciple of Jigme Lingpa, the revealer of the famous cycle of meditative and yogic practices known as the *Longchen Nyingtik.* Patrul Rinpoche composed a famous commentary on the preliminary practices to this cycle, a text entitled *Kun bzang bla ma'i zhal lung* and translated into English as *The Words of My Perfect Teacher,* in which he set down the oral instructions received from Jigme Gyalwa'i Nyugu.

12. See *Masters,* p. 203.

13. See *Masters,* p. 208.

14. See "Orgyan 'jigs med chos kyi dbang po'i rnam thar," in *Complete Works of Patrul Rinpoche,* vol. 8, pp. 221–222.

15. These details of Khenpo Kunpel's life are taken from the short biography given in *Masters,* pp. 258–59, which is itself a summary of a biographical poem composed by Jamyang Khyentse Chökyi Lodrö. Tulku Thondup follows this authority in giving Khenpo Kunpel's birth year as 1872. Patrul Rinpoche's teaching on the *Bodhicharyavatara* during which Khenpo Kunpel took the notes on which his commentary is based must have occurred in or, more probably, before 1884 when Patrul Rinpoche gave his last public teaching. If Khenpo Kunpel was born in 1872, this would mean that he was less than twelve years old when this event took place. However, Tulku Thondup also cites the biography of Patrul Rinpoche by Minyak Kunzang Sonam, according to which, Khenpo Kunpel was born in 1862. This seems a more plausible date.

16. A detailed biographical essay on Mipham Rinpoche composed by Khenpo Kunpel has been translated into English. See Pettit, *Mipham's Beacon of Certainty,* pp. 23–39.

17. Patrul Rinpoche himself remarked on the fidelity with which Mipham Rinpoche had reproduced his teaching style. See Kretschmar, chap. 1, p. 40.

18. The resulting book, *Wisdom: Two Buddhist Commentaries,* was produced in France by Editions Padmakara.

19. I.e., Maitreya.

20. The seven first fathers were the seven patriarchs who in succession led the Sangha after the Buddha's parinirvana.

21. The six adornments of the world are Nagarjuna and Aryadeva, Asanga and Vasubandhu, Dignaga and Dharmakirti. The two supreme ones are Gunaprabha and Shakyaprabha.

22. I.e., Sakya Pandita, Je Tsongkhapa, and Gyalwa Longchenpa. See Patrul Rinpoche's remarks as recorded in Tulku Thondup, *Masters*, p. 209.

23. Dza Patrul Orgyen Jigme Chökyi Wangpo (1808–87), the root guru of Khenpo Kunpel, from whom the latter received the teachings of the *Bodhicharyavatara*. For his life and work, see Tulku Thondup, *Masters*, and Patrul Rinpoche, *The Words of My Perfect Teacher*.

24. For the sixty aspects of melodious speech, see Khenpo Chöga (hereafter KCG) in Kretschmar, chap. 1, p. 265.

25. For a discussion of the qualities of buddhahood, see Longchen Yeshe Dorje, *Treasury of Precious Qualities* (hereafter *Treasury*), p. 297/387.*

26. See *Treasury*, p. 349/439, n. 6, and p. 350/440, n. 10.*

27. *nges pa gnyis*, i.e., confirmation that a given teaching is authentic Dharma and confirmation that the teaching is the Buddha's word. See KCG, Kretschmar, chap. 1, p. 276.

28. I.e., the tradition of Nalanda.

29. The principal sources in Tibetan literature for the biography of Shantideva are the histories of Butön and Jetsün Taranatha, which diverge on a number of particulars. Khenpo Kunpel follows Butön's account.

30. Shastra (*bstan bcos*), a commentary specifically illustrating the meaning of the Buddha's words. The three qualifications for composing shastras are a perfect realization of ultimate reality, a vision of the yidam deity, and a complete knowledge of the five sciences.

31. *na len dra'i bkod pa phun tshogs* (the perfect conduct at Nalanda). This refers to Shantideva's activities at Nalanda, the most obvious of which was the teaching of the *Bodhicharyavatara*, but also includes his secret studies, meditations, and visions.

32. In modern Gujarat.

33. Tib. *'Jam dpal rnon po'i sgrub thabs*, a sadhana, or meditative practice, based on the Bodhisattva Manjushri, performed with a view to the development of intelligence and sharp faculties. The fact that Shantideva had a vision of Manjushri means that he became fully accomplished in the sadhana.

34. Spiritual qualities that shine forth in proportion as the emotional and cognitive veils are removed from the mind. See *Treasury*, pp. 125–34/215–24.*

35. I.e., study, meditation, and activities such as printing books, making medicines, etc.

36. See chapter 5, verses 105–6.

37. This reference to the threats from Machala is unclear. We have been unable to verify the Sanskrit names given in the Tibetan text and have taken the

liberty of correcting them according to Butön, whose account Khenpo Kunpel has, in all other respects, followed closely.

38. I.e., beings with the ability to generate bodhichitta and follow the Mahayana path. For an explanation of the three scopes of spiritual practice see *Treasury,* pp. 41ff./131ff.*

39. For a discussion of the meaning of these important categories, see *Treasury,* pp. 246–52/336–42.*

40. The *Dartik,* of which there were four, were composed by Gyaltsap Darma Rinchen, one of the heart-sons of Je Tsongkhapa. They are so called because they are Darma Rinchen's *tika* (commentaries). The *Dartik* to the *Bodhicharyavatara* is one of the commentaries most widely used in the Gelugpa school.

41. Chogyur Lingpa was a great master and tertön (revealer of Dharma treasures), an important figure in the Rimé movement, and a close friend and collaborator of Jamyang Khyentse Wangpo and Jamgön Kongtrul Lodrö Thayé.

42. *skad rigs chen po mi 'dra ba bzhi.* According to tradition, there were three hundred and forty languages in Ancient India. Four of these were canonical (in the sense that sutras and shastras were composed in them): Sanskrit (*legs sbyar*), Prakrit (*rang bzhin*), Apabhramsha (*zur chag*), and Pishachi (*sha za*). Of these, Sanskrit was considered the most important. See KCG, Kretschmar, chap. 1, p. 329.

43. I.e., the language of the central provinces of Ü and Tsang.

44. The standard Sanskrit term for a being who is progressing toward buddhahood is *bodhisattva,* lit. "enlightenment being." See A. A. Macdonell, *Sanskrit Dictionary* (1929), p. 198. It should be noticed, however, that the Tibetan term (*byang chub sems dpa'*) is apparently a translation not of *bodhisattva,* but *bodhisatva,* where *sattva* (being) is replaced by *satva(n)* (warrior). See Macdonell, p. 331, and Kretschmar, chap. 1, p. 12, n. 69.

45. When the future Buddha Maitreya appears.

46. As stated in the colophon, the *Bodhicharyavatara* was first translated by Kawa Peltsek and Sarvajnadeva (early ninth century). The translation was revised twice, first by Rinchen Zangpo, Shakya Lodrö, and Dharmashribhadra (tenth century), and finally by Loden Sherab and Sumatikirti (eleventh century).

47. I.e., the kings Songtsen Gampo, Trisongdetsen, and Tri Ralpachen.

48. For a description of the five aggregates, eighteen dhatus, and twelve ayatanas, see *Treasury,* pp. 287/377, 409/499, and 404/494, respectively.*

49. For the Buddha's qualities of elimination and realization, see *Treasury,* pp. 125–33/215–23.*

50. *dpal gyi beu,* a poetic expression for the mind of the Buddha and one of the eight auspicious symbols referring to eight aspects of the Buddha's body, speech, and mind (the unending knot, the lotus, the canopy, the conch, the wheel, the banner, the vase, and the golden fishes).

51. This is taken from the prologue to Vibhutichandra's commentary on the *Bodhicharyavatara.*

52. For a discussion of fourfold faith, see *Treasury,* p. 124/214.*

53. See *Treasury,* p. 350/440, n. 7.*

54. Proportionately, if the stars visible at night correspond to beings in hell, the stars visible during the day correspond to the pretas. Again, if the stars at night correspond to the pretas, the stars visible during the day correspond to animals. And so on.

55. For a description of the ten innermost riches, see KCG, Kretschmar, chap. 1, pp. 392ff.

56. The expressions "powerful sage" or "sage" are intended to translate both the Sanskrit term *muni* (wise man, sage) and its Tibetan rendering *thub pa* or *thub dbang,* lit. the "powerful" or "capable one."

57. I.e., the enlightenment of oneself and the benefit of others.

58. The preparation, the commitment itself, and the conclusion (*sbyor dngos rjes gsum*) are respectively the mind-training, the taking of the Bodhisattva vow, and the act of rejoicing, as described in chapter 3.

59. For a discussion of these three kinds of virtue, see *Treasury,* pp. 61ff./151ff.*

60. See *Treasury,* p. 57/147.*

61. *mtshams med lnga.* These are to kill one's father, to kill one's mother, to kill an Arhat, to shed the blood of a Buddha with evil intent, and to cause a schism in the sangha. The sins of immediate effect owe their name to the fact that their effect is so great that they outweigh all other karmas and at death result in an immediate rebirth in the Hell of Unrelenting Pain.

62. Skt. *avici,* sometimes translated as Hell of Torment Unsurpassed. It is the lowest of the hot hells, where suffering is the most intense and protracted.

63. For a discussion of the main mind and mental factors, see *Treasury,* p. 294/384.*

64. See *Treasury,* p. 160/250.*

65. For a discussion of the eighty unceasing factors, see KCG, Kretschmar, chap. 1, p. 436.

66. A chakravartin, lit. "one who turns the wheel (of power)," is a universal king with power over several of the cosmic continents. See *Treasury,* p. 407/497.*

67. Reasoned proofs are constructed on the basis of evidence, in other words, valid knowledge, of which the Buddhist tradition of logic and epistemology recognizes three sources. The first two, which are universally valid both within the Buddhist fold and when Buddhists are debating with non-

Buddhists, are the commonly available evidence of sense perception and, based on this, the undeniable conclusions of correctly constructed inferences. The third source of valid knowledge, accepted by Buddhists, is the Buddha's word. Once one has accepted the truth of the Buddha's teaching (and it would be inconsistent to accept the Buddha as the Speaker of the Truth and then doubt him), it too can be used as the basis of reasoned arguments about objects that ordinarily lie outside the range of the evidence supplied by normal sense faculties. It is only thus that we have access to knowledge of extremely hidden phenomena, specifically, the workings of the karmic law. See also KCG, Kretschmar, chap. 1, p. 451.

68. Khenpo Kunpel is summarizing. The full story may be found in *The Words of My Perfect Teacher,* p. 224.

69. *tshangs pa'i gnas bzhi,* i.e., the four *brahmaviharas* or divine abidings. See KCG, Kretschmar, chap. 1, p. 454.

70. The seven attributes of royalty are the seven possessions of a chakravartin: the precious golden wheel, the precious wish-fulfilling jewel, the precious queen, the precious minister, the precious elephant, the precious horse, and the precious general. These symbolize the seven sublime riches: faith, discipline, generosity, learning, a sense of moral conscience with respect to oneself and others, and wisdom.

71. See *Enlightened Courage,* p. 62.

72. The taking of the Bodhisattva vows is a necessary preliminary to the reception of an empowerment.

73. This remark is not as self-congratulatory as it appears. Khenpo Kunpel was from Kham, the eastern region of greater Tibet that borders on China. Khampas very often do not consider themselves Tibetans since, for them, Tibet consists of the central provinces of Ü and Tsang that encircle Lhasa. This exhortation to respect the Tibetans takes on particular force when one considers the political and sectarian tensions, sometimes very acute, that had existed in previous centuries between Central Tibet and the eastern provinces of Kham, Amdo, etc.

74. *'jur 'gegs.* See KCG, Kretschmar, chap. 2, p. 162.

75. The six excellent substances are nutmeg, bamboo manna, saffron, cloves, cardamom, and castor oil. See KCG, Kretschmar, chap. 2, p. 168.

76. Lake Neverwarm (*ma dros pa; anavatapta*) usually refers to Manasarovar, the stretch of water lying at the feet of Mount Kailash on the southern border of Tibet. The rivers mentioned together with the Ganges are the Indus (Sindhu), Oxus (Vakshu), and Tarim (Sita). The seven seas are the seven oceans separating the seven concentric rings of mountain ranges around Mount Meru and the four continents. Their waters are said to be sweet and are the pleasure ground of nagas. See *Myriad Worlds,* pp. 110–12.

77. Manasarovar (*mtsho ma pham*), Tengri Nor (*gnam mtsho*), Yardrok (*yar 'brog mtsho*), and Koko Nor (*mtsho sngon po*).
78. In the northern cosmic continent of Uttarakuru, people are naturally endowed with ethical discipline. They are without craving since all that they could possibly wish for manifests spontaneously.
79. *mdzad spyod bsrung ba med pa.* The Buddhas' every thought, word, and deed is naturally virtuous. Consequently, Buddhas have no need to hide anything. See *Treasury,* p. 344/434.*
80. For an explanation of the four demons, see *Treasury,* p. 408/498.*
81. I.e., Manjushri, Avalokiteshvara, and Vajrapani.
82. For the thirteen articles of ordained livelihood, see KCG, Kretschmar, chap. 2, p. 180.
83. The seven elements leading to enlightenment are mindfulness, perfect discernment, diligence, joy, flexibility, concentration, and evenness. See *Treasury,* p. 303/393.*
84. Mahakashyapa was one of the foremost disciples of Buddha Shakyamuni. Renowned for his gravity, he was the leader of the monastic sangha after the Buddha's parinirvana.
85. The first level of the first samadhi of the form realm. See *Treasury,* p. 414/504.*
86. *bstan pa bu gcig.* See KCG, Kretschmar, chap. 2, p. 194.
87. These twelve places are specific locations, mentioned in the scriptures. See KCG, Kretschmar, chap. 2, p. 193.
88. Bhikshus (*dge slong*) are men who have taken the full monastic ordination of two hundred and fifty-three precepts. Shramaneras (*dge tshul*), are men who have the lesser monastic ordination of thirty-three precepts. Women who hold these ordinations are called bhikshunis (*dge slong ma*) with three hundred and sixty-four precepts, and shramaneris (*dge tshul ma*) with thirty-three precepts. For a detailed discussion of the pratimoksha vows, see *Treasury,* pp. 197–201/287–91.*
89. *dbang po lnga.* This refers to the five powers that affect the development of enlightened qualities in the path of joining: confidence, diligence, mindfulness, concentration, and wisdom. See *Treasury,* p. 302/392.*
90. See *Treasury,* p. 297/387.*
91. I.e., the great golden foundation that underlies the universe. See *Myriad Worlds,* pp. 109ff.
92. *bsnyen gnas.* The twenty-four-hour discipline. See *Treasury,* p. 198/288.*
93. Because the Vatsiputriyas take refuge in the Three Jewels, they are regarded as Buddhists by refuge. However, since their theory does not accord with the four seals, the possession of which are the hallmark of a Buddhist Doctrine, they are not considered Buddhist by precept. See *Adornment,* p. 402, n. 225.

94. The *Uttaratantra-shastra* is structured in a series of seven vajra points. The first three comprise an exposition of the Three Jewels, the remaining four correspond to the four chapters mentioned here: Buddha-nature, enlightenment, enlightened qualities, and enlightened activities.

95. That is, the commitment focused on oneself and the commitment focused on others.

96. The Buddha's eight qualities comprise three qualities related to his own benefit and three qualities related to the benefit of others. The combination of each group of three is regarded as a distinct quality, thus resulting in a sum total of eight qualities.

97. The "Great Mother" is a name for Prajnaparamita or transcendent wisdom. The ganti is a kind of wooden gong used to summon the monastic community to the temple.

98. I.e., something not to be touched.

99. It is said that when he was on the path of learning, Akashagarbha aspired to be a protector for beginners in the Bodhisattva discipline. Moreover, he is said to appear at dawn, which is why the confession is recited in the morning.

100. The first four branches are the acts of veneration, refuge, offerings, and confession of negative actions.

101. Knowledge of what is correct and incorrect is one of the ten strengths. See p. 108, and *Treasury*, p. 298/388.*

102. See *Essence of Refined Gold*, p. 137.

103. See *The Words of My Perfect Teacher*, pp. 230ff. The meaning of the text here (*gzhan srog chags des pa*) is obscure.

104. One of the Buddha's earlier incarnations.

105. The "intermediate kalpas of famine" are periods of extreme want occurring from time to time in the cycle of cosmic ages. These periods, when the span of human life is reduced to thirty years, are marked by three stages in which the want of food is increasingly severe. In the period of the secret eaters, food will be so scarce that even tiny quantities of it will be regarded as treasure, to be hidden and jealously guarded. During the time of the spoon eaters, food will be rationed and meted out only in tiny spoonfuls. Finally, in the time of the eaters of bleached bones, the only food left will be the remains of the dead: bare skeletons that will be crushed and turned into soup. See KCG, Kretschmar, chap. 3, p. 94.

106. Chö (*gcod*), lit. "cutting," is a meditative and ritual practice, based on the Prajnaparamita, involving a visualization in which the physical body is offered as food to evil or dangerous spirits, the purpose being to destroy or "cut" the four demons of one's own ego-clinging. Chö was introduced to Tibet by the Indian master Padampa Sangye and his Tibetan disciple, the yogini Machig Labdrön. See *Words of My Perfect Teacher*, chap. 5.

107. For the particular meaning of these terms, see *Treasury,* p. 385/475, n. 205.*
108. As long as one is attached to one's body, possessions, and merit, all practice done within the framework of ego-clinging will remain on the mundane level and will not directly lead to buddhahood. See KCG, Kretschmar, chap. 3, p. 107.
109. See *Treasury,* p. 356/446, n. 42.*
110. Nirvana according to the Mahayana is a result that emerges thanks to the separation from (or absence or elimination of) what is adventitious: the two kinds of veil that obscure the mind, together with the associated habitual tendencies (*sgrib gnyis bag chags dang bcas pa spang ba'am bral ba'i 'bras bu*).
111. I.e., in the case of those who in reality aspire only to the attainment of a good rebirth in their next lives.
112. By this, one considers that the Buddhas are invoked and stirred from the ultimate expanse.
113. That is, all together in the course of an empowerment.
114. See *Treasury,* pp. 183–84/273–74.*
115. They can materialize any kind and any number of objects. It is as if space were filled with whatever may be needed. This is what is called the "sky-treasure," *nam mkha' mdzod.*
116. I.e., as antidotes to desire, aversion, and ignorance respectively.
117. *kun shes,* or omniscience, the knowledge of all things (i.e., the truth of suffering, the truth of origin, the five skandhas, etc.), refers here to the wisdom that realizes the absence of self in everything.
118. I.e., respectively the mind-training, the taking of the Bodhisattva vow, and the act of rejoicing, as described in chapter 3.
119. As will be explained presently, the twenty root downfalls are the eighteen referred to plus the two downfalls of giving up bodhichitta in intention and action.
120. Through compassion, bodhichitta focuses on the welfare of others; through wisdom it focuses on perfect enlightenment. See chapter 1, p. 53.
121. These first five downfalls are the so-called downfalls of a king. The first four downfalls listed here, together with the sixth, constitute the downfalls of a minister. The following eight are the downfalls of ordinary people. Because four downfalls are common to kings and ministers, they are only mentioned once. All together, however, it is usual to speak of the eighteen Bodhisattva downfalls. See also *Treasury,* pp. 374–75/464–65.*
122. "The rest" is detailed in other texts as "a village, a small town, a large town, and an entire region." See *Treasury,* pp. 374–75/464–65.*
123. See KCG, Kretschmar, chap. 4, p. 111.
124. See *Treasury,* pp. 184/274.*
125. See KCG, Kretschmar, chap. 4, p. 118.

126. I.e., the *Bodhisattvacharyavatara-panjika* and *Bodhisattvacharyavatara-vritti-panjika*, both by Vairochanarakshita. See Kretschmar, chap. 4, p. 41.

127. I.e., the *Bodhicharyavatara-panjika* by Prajnakaramati. See ibid.

128. A root defeat (*phas pham pa*) is a grave transgression that destroys the monastic ordination. See *Treasury*, p. 200/290.*

129. Nirvana without remainder (*lhag med myang 'das*) occurs at the death of an Arhat, when all the previous karma is exhausted and the five aggregates dissolve.

130. In the present instance, the author of the commentary appears to overlook the "most grave acts" mentioned in the quotation from the *Abhidharmakosha*. He does not do so, however, when considering the matter again at the beginning of chapter 6. See page 198.

131. *bya byed kyi rigs pa, ltos pa'i rigs pa, chos nyid kyi rigs pa,* and *'thad sgrub kyi rigs pa.* See *World of Tibetan Buddhism*, p. 48, and *Adornment of the Middle Way*, p. 287.

132. For a discussion of this kind of Bodhisattva commitment, see KCG, Kretschmar, chap. 4, p. 162.

133. I.e., they avoid the ten negative, and strive in the ten positive, actions.

134. I.e., the realm of pretas.

135. See *Treasury*, p. 200/290.*

136. See KCG, Kretschmar, chap. 5, p. 158.

137. For a discussion of tutelary deities (*'go ba'i lha*), see KCG, Kretschmar, chap. 5, p. 159.

138. See *Treasury*, p. 293/383.*

139. I.e., when one is "proud among the proud," thinking that one is the best of an accomplished group.

140. Bodhisattvas are described as "perilous" (*gnyan po*) because evil actions done in their regard are particularly grievous, while good things done to them are very meritorious. It is therefore the responsibility of those who have become Bodhisattvas to act in such a way that others will respond positively toward them and not take offence.

141. For the full account of the story, see chapter 4, p. 145 .

142. See *Treasury*, p. 195/285.*

143. It was in fact the lama-king Yeshe Ö (Changchub Ö's uncle) who made this sacrifice in order to invite Atisha to Tibet. See Tsepön W. D. Shakabpa, *Tibet: A Political History*, pp. 56–57.

144. See *Treasury*, pp. 246ff./336ff.*

145. *pha rol gyi mi dad pa bsrung ba.* "To give scandal" here is used in the strict sense of "causing others to fall" and, in this case, to lose faith.

146. See *Treasury*, pp. 184–85/274–75.*

147. See KCG, Kretschmar, chap. 5, p. 266.

148. See *Treasury*, p. 227/317 and n. 205.*
149. See *Way of the Bodhisattva*, p. 203, n. 74.
150. See *Treasury*, pp. 269ff./359ff.*
151. I.e., the prophecy of their enlightenment from the Buddhas.
152. See *Treasury*, p. 363/453, n. 76.*
153. Gyalse Rinpoche or Precious Bodhisattva is a popular way of referring to Ngulchu Thogme Zangpo.
154. It will be remembered that Shantideva has already made the point that the essence of all the paramitas is a matter of the mind (see chap. 5, verse 9 following). In the present, rather difficult, passage, the commentary states that the effect of anger is to destroy the merit gained from physical and verbal, but not mental, acts. For this reason, generosity and discipline are vulnerable to anger in a way that the remaining (more elevated) paramitas are not. For unlike patience, diligence, concentration, and wisdom, which are entirely a matter of mental orientation, generosity and discipline are externalized in actions of word and deed. And although the author does define discipline as "perfect observance in thought, word, and deed," it seems that, in the present context, greater emphasis is placed on the merit generated by the physical and verbal aspects of these two paramitas.
155. *dam pa gsum*. The three supreme methods for any practice or action are first, to prepare the ground by cultivating bodhichitta; second, to perform the practice in a concentrated manner unimpaired by grasping at the object, subject, and action as really existing entities; and third, to conclude the practice by dedicating the resulting merit to enlightenment for the sake of others.
156. See M. Hiriyanna, *The Essentials of Indian Philosophy*, pp. 90–91.
157. See *Treasury*, page 100/190.*
158. I.e., the patience of accepting suffering, the patience regarding the ultimate reality of things, and the patience of making light of adversity.
159. I.e., with direct verbal aggression, together with the destruction of one's good name through malicious rumors.
160. See *Treasury*, p. 272/362.*
161. See note 140.
162. See *Treasury*, p. 297/387.*
163. "Wind" (*rlung; prana*) is the principle of motion, both in the external world (i.e., the displacement of air—wind in the usual sense) and in the body, where it is the principle of physical movement and the other anatomical processes. Generally speaking, wind is regarded as a kind of bridge between mind and body and is the means whereby the mind is "mounted" within its bodily support. The movement of wind thus accounts not only for a person's physical condition but also his or her mental state.

164. This is a rather free rendering of the meaning of the Tibetan expression *mgo gcig tu lung ston pa.*
165. See *Treasury,* p. 50/140.*
166. See *The Words of My Perfect Teacher,* p. 73.
167. *nga rgyal,* lit. pride. Here, and in the ensuing commentary, a distinction is drawn between two kinds of pride. On the one hand, there is the positive quality of self-confidence, which is the source of courage and perseverance, and, on the other, the negative quality of arrogance and conceit. Using the same term in both senses, Shantideva plays on the word "pride" in a way that might at first be confusing. For the sake of clarity, the two kinds of pride have been more pointedly distinguished in the translation.
168. This is a reference to Prajnakaramati, the author of a Sanskrit commentary on the *Bodhicharyavatara,* whose name, translated into Tibetan, is Sherab Jungne Lodrö.
169. *nyer bsdogs mi lcogs med.* See *Treasury,* p. 241/331.*
170. Aryas are those who have attained the paths of seeing and beyond (according to either the Hinayana or Mahayana). The expression "wise and learned" here refers specifically to the Bodhisattvas.
171. See *The Words of My Perfect Teacher,* p. 69.
172. Deer are traditionally said to be attracted by the sound of a lute. The hunters play such instruments in order to lure them within the range of their weapons.
173. The term *vidyadhara* (knowledge holder) refers here to sages endowed with the power of great longevity. The kinnaras are one of the eight classes of spirits; they are said to be vaguely human in appearance. The uragas are "ground-owning" spirits.
174. I.e., the state in which the duality of self and other is totally transcended. Here, the interests of oneself and others are indistinguishable and therefore an object of equal concern.
175. The force of this argument is rooted in the fundamental Buddhist axiom that, however closely associated, the material body and the immaterial mind are entities of a completely different nature. Pain is a mental event; physical discomfort arises in the presence of a mind. For that reason, corpses do not suffer. The intensity of pain depends on the degree (in most people very great) to which the mind appropriates and identifies with what, for the time being, is acting as its bodily support. Being of a different nature, however, the mind is not irrevocably yoked to such experiences. Through skillful practice, it can detach itself from the body's condition and remain serene even in the midst of grave illness. Many stories to this effect can be found in the biographies of great meditators. The capacity of the mind either to cling to or dissociate itself from the body has a bearing on

the way practictioners of the Bodhisattva path are able to relate to the sufferings of others. If, as Shantideva believes, clinging to the body as "mine" (and therefore adopting its ailments as "my suffering") is a matter of psychological orientation and habit, it follows that it can be redirected through mental training. When the object of identification and clinging changes, the experience of suffering will also change. The mind may be taught not only to overlook the discomforts of its own bodily support, but also to embrace the physical sufferings of others. When this is done, the urge to remove the pains of others will be as natural and imperative as the urge the mind now feels to remove the discomforts of the body with which it is associated.

176. It is recorded that once, when Maitriyogin was teaching, someone threw a stone at a barking dog so that the animal was badly injured. Maitriyogin gave a scream of pain and fell from the throne on which he was sitting. To the astonishment and embarrassment of the disciples, who had been inclined to dismiss the master's behavior as an exaggerated theatrical performance, Maitriyogin pulled up his shirt so that they could see a great wound on his side, in exactly the same place where the dog had been struck.

177. It is recorded in the *Mahabhinishkramana* that Devadatta, the cousin of Prince Siddhartha, took a bow and arrow and shot down a swan. The creature was grounded but not killed. The future Buddha took the bird upon his knees and comforted it. Devadatta sent to claim his prize, no doubt intending to kill it, but the Buddha refused to hand over the swan, saying that the bird was his. An exquisite description of the incident is to be found in *The Light of Asia* by Sir Edwin Arnold, p. 11:

> . . . Then our Lord
> Laid the swan's neck beside his own smooth cheek
> And gravely spake, "Say no! the bird is mine,
> The first of myriad things that shall be mine
> By right of mercy and love's lordliness."

178. This is a reference to Machig Labdrön, the great Tibetan yogini and disciple of the Indian master Padampa Sangye. She is particularly celebrated as the propagator of chö (*gcod*), a meditative practice in which an offering is made of one's own body as sustenance for malevolent spirits.

179. Khenpo Kunpel considers that Shantideva has constructed verse 94 in the form of a probative argument (*'byor ba; prayoga,* sometimes, though less satisfactorily translated as "syllogism"). According to the rules of Indian logic, a probative argument consists of a thesis or statement composed of a

subject and predicate, supported by a valid sign or reason, and illustrated by an example. The standard model of a probative argument runs as follows: "This hill has fire on it (thesis) because there is smoke there (sign or reason), just as we find in a kitchen (example)." Following the same format, Shantideva's argument runs, "I will eliminate the sufferings of others (thesis) because suffering does not benefit them (reason), just as I remove my own discomforts (example)." Given that probative arguments are normally understood to effect a demonstration or proof that "such and such is the case," to describe the justificatory statement in verse 94 in such terms may seem rather forced. But it is important to realize that for Shantideva, the decision to benefit others is a matter of logical necessity rather than a sense of duty experienced in response to moral exhortation.

180. *rigs 'dra rgyun mi chad pa*. This means that when a moment of consciousness ceases, a new one arises identical to it in nature—i.e., mere clarity and cognizance—but varying in "color" according to karmic circumstances. There is simply a continuum of interlinked moments; there is no subpositum, no underlying entity, that endures as the "experiencer" of a stream of extrinsic events.

181. In the root text, throughout this description of the exchange of self and other, Shantideva uses the contrasting pronouns "I" and "he." According to custom, these same pronouns are retained in the commentary without the meaning being obscured. In the translation, however, we have found it clearer to render the Tibetan word *bdag* ("I") as "you," since the "speaker" is Khenpo Kunpel addressing the reader. Needless to say, his reflections are directed at all readers regardless of sex, so that the third person pronoun (used to refer to one's "other self") could just as well be "she" as "he." Since the constant repetition of both pronouns would be very tedious, we have, in deference to Shantideva's own personal situation (that of a man living in a community of monks), kept the masculine pronoun.

182. *thub pa dgongs gsal*.

183. In other words, at this point in the root text, Shantideva discontinues the I/he division used in the previous meditation, where he created an imaginative division in himself, playing one side off against the other. He now returns to the more normal practice of soliloquy as he continues his introspective reflections.

184. I.e., in expectation (if you were cutting meat, it would).

185. This is a reference to Mipham Rinpoche, whose *Norbu Ketaka* is closely followed (almost verbatim) in this chapter.

186. Generally speaking in the present context, we translate the Tibetan word *shes rab* (Skt. *prajna*) as "wisdom," and *ye shes* (Skt. *jnana*) as "primordial wisdom."

187. The knowledge of the ultimate status of things and the knowledge of the whole multiplicity of things.

188. If, on the ultimate level, the two truths are taken to be distinct, it follows that (1) when the Aryas actually realize the ultimate truth they would still have to realize the relative truth; (2) ultimate truth would not be the ultimate nature of phenomena on the relative level; (3) when the empty nature of relative truth (e.g., the aggregates) is realized, it would not suffice as an understanding of ultimate truth; (4) the realization of the ultimate and relative truth would be mutually exclusive in a single mind. By contrast, if, on the relative level, the two truths are taken to be the same, it follows that (1) when ordinary people perceive sense objects, they would also perceive the ultimate truth; (2) since relative phenomena are not beyond conceptual elaborations, the ultimate truth would not be either; (3) since ordinary perception lies within the sphere of defiled emotion, the ultimate truth would not be free of defilements; (4) it would be impossible to show that ultimate truth is different from the relative truth that ordinary beings perceive.

189. See *Introduction to the Middle Way*, chap. 11, v. 13.

190. To affirm that the ultimate truth is an object of knowledge from the standpoint of detection amounts to asserting that emptiness is a truly existent thing (*dngos po*). A discussion of the terms "exclusion" and "detection" (*rnam bcad, yongs gcod*) can be found in Mipham Rinpoche's commentary on the *Madhyamakalankara*. See *Adornment of the Middle Way*, p. 275.

191. In the case of Buddhist practitioners, the expression "worldly being" refers to those who have not yet attained the Mahayana path of seeing.

192. According to the Vaibhashikas, it is the visual organ that directly apprehends its object (a material thing apprehends another material thing); the visual consciousness merely accompanies this process of perception. Conceptual consciousness then identifies the perceived form. The three factors (object, sense organ, and consciousness) being simultaneous, there is no relation of causality between them.

193. No doubt in a bid to keep things simple, Khenpo Kunpel makes no mention here of the fact that the Sautrantika school is commonly divided into two subgroups: Sautrantikas following scripture (*lung gi rjes 'brang gi mdo sde pa*) and Sautrantikas following reasoning (*rigs kyi rjes 'brang gi mdo sde pa*). The Sautrantikas following scripture are perhaps so called because, adhering strictly to the sutras, they reduced the number of scriptures regarded as authentic by relegating the seven sections of Abhidharma (accepted by the Vaibhashikas as the word of Buddha) to the level of shastras composed by Arhats (Shariputra, etc.) Their philosophical position, however, does not seem to have differed greatly from that of the Vaibhashikas in that they considered the indivisible instant of mind and

particle of matter to be ultimate truths, and extended objects as only relatively existent.

"Sautrantika following reasoning" denotes the doctrine of Dignaga and Dharmakirti. The naming of these masters as Sautrantikas reflects the fact that they appear to accept the existence of an extramental material world (which is in turn reducible to the agglomeration of partless particles). This identification, which is largely a matter of doxographical tidiness, is however called into question by the fact that on occasions, Dignaga and Dharmakirti seem to adopt a Yogachara position. The representationalist theory of knowledge implied in the doctrine of hidden objects and the distinction, on the level of relative truth, between functional (i.e., causally effective), specifically characterized phenomena (which are real), as contrasted with nonfunctional, generally characterized phenomena (which are unreal) are features typical of the epistemology and ontology of the Sautrantikas following reasoning, a system that has played a major role in the development of Buddhist thought down the centuries. A detailed presentation of the views of Dignaga and Dharmakirti, and their reception in Tibet, is to be found in Dreyfus, *Recognizing Reality.*

194. According to the Sautrantikas following reasoning, external objects, although existent, are known by means of the mental aspects that they cast upon the mind (like reflections in a mirror). It is only the aspect, which is itself mental by nature, that the mind cognizes directly. Although a causal relationship exists between them, the external, nonmental phenomenon is said to be "concealed" by the mental aspect, which, of necessity, comes between it and the cognizing mind.

195. *ldan min 'du byed;* a subsection of the skandha of conditioning factors; factors associated with neither mind nor form (e.g., impermanence, continuity, acquisition).

196. In the present context, we follow the convention of using *madhyamaka* to refer to the system of tenets and *madhyamika* to refer to its advocates.

197. I.e., they cannot be prevented from appearing and do affect us.

198. See *Treasury,* pp. 246–52/336–42.*

199. This is a reference to the "argument of neither one nor many," one of several classic arguments used in Madhyamaka to establish the ultimate status of phenomena. See *Adornment of the Middle Way,* p. 39.

200. This is a reference to the Buddhist teaching of impermanence, according to which an apparently stable object is in fact a series of point-instants, flashing into, and out of, existence at every moment. Each instant is a separate entity similar to, but not identical with, the entities that precede and follow it. In contrast with the Samkhya notion of a flexible and ever-evolving substrate, change according to the Abhidharma means *replacement.* An appar-

ently single phenomenon is in fact a sequence of separate, but like, events. Its apparent solidity and continuity is as illusory as the circle of light created by a firebrand whirled in the air.

201. See *Adornment of the Middle Way*, p. 240.

202. This crucial point should be born in mind throughout the ensuing discussion. Khenpo Kunpel, following Mipham Rinpoche, is asserting that *rang rig*, the self-knowing mind, has no existence on the ultimate level. It is Mipham's view, however, following Shantarakshita (see *Adornment of the Middle Way*, p. 202) that the self-knowing mind exists on the level of relative truth. In this he differs from Je Tsongkhapa, one of whose *Eight Difficult Points* is the assertion that the self-knowing mind is nonexistent even on the conventional level (see Dreyfus, *The Svatantrika-Prasangika Distinction*, p. 324).

203. I.e., *gzhan don rig gi shes pa*, a consciousness that cognizes objects other than itself (as distinct from self-aware consciousness, *rang rig gi shes pa*). In other words, the process of illumination is understood in terms of a subject-object polarity.

204. One has a wound and one remembers that it was inflicted by a water rat. But the present condition of the wound (it is now festering) reveals something about the bite that one does not remember (for one was not aware of it at the time), namely, the fact that it was poisoned. According to the terms of the comparison, the simple memory of the color blue corresponds to the simple memory of the bite; the thought "I saw blue" corresponds to the thought "I was poisoned." Just as the present understanding that one was poisoned does not require the awareness (at the time of the bite) that one was being poisoned, by the same token, the thought "I remember blue" does not require the self-awareness "I am seeing blue" at the time when the color was experienced. According to the Madhyamaka argument, because subject and object are necessary interdependent aspects of all experience, the memory of blue automatically implies the thought "I remember blue." In itself, memory is no proof of the self-cognizing mind.

205. The False Aspectarians consider that the mental aspect is completely unreal and nonexistent. See *Adornment of the Middle Way*, p. 247.

206. These eight examples are mentioned in the *Uttaratantra-shastra*. The glory of Indra's reflection seen in the crystal floor before him is such that, without intending to do so, it effortlessly inspires respect in others and the desire to emulate him. See *The Changeless Nature*, by Arya Maitreya and Acarya Asanga, translated by Ken and Katia Holmes, p. 123.

207. A mythical bird that preys on nagas, serpent-like beings which are said to cause certain types of disease.

208. The sendhavas were a group of Shravakas opposed to the Mahayana. See Taranatha, *History of Buddhism in India,* p. 279.

209. See *Treasury,* p. 283/373.*

210. I.e., of the Shravakas, Pratyekabuddhas, and Bodhisattvas. The goal of the first two is arhatship; the goal of the third is buddhahood.

211. Perception, inference, and scriptural authority.

212. The belief that, in any given action, the subject, object, and act are real entities.

213. Maudgalyayana was ignorant of where his mother had been reborn, and Shariputra did not know when the seed of liberation had arisen in a certain person's mind stream. See p. 16.

214. Tom, the father of Dick, is the son of Harry. It is only in terms of his connections with Dick and Harry that Tom can be simultaneously described as both father and son. The mistake of the Samkhyas is to absolutize relations, which are by definition relative. If the definition of Tom is completely exhausted in the fact of his sonship (which must be the case if he is indivisibly "one" and *by nature* a *truly existent* son), he is locked for all eternity in his relation with Harry. There is no room for his relation with Dick. The same is true, mutatis mutandis, regarding his fatherhood.

215. As with the discussion of sense consciousnesses of form and sound.

216. In other words, the opponents complain that the Madhyamaka denial of an existent self renders karma unintelligible. The Madhyamikas reply that their opponents' doctrine of a changeless self does the same.

217. See *Introduction to the Middle Way,* chap. 6, v. 61.

218. It is helpful to remember that the pairing *"imputed self* versus *innate or co-emergent self"* (*brtags pa'i bdag* and *lhan skyes kyi bdag*) is not the same as the pairing *"the self as mere designation* versus *the inherently existent self"* (*btags pa'i bdag* and *rang bzhin kyis grub pa'i bdag*). In the first case, a contrast is made between the intellectual belief in the self, which is inculcated by incorrect religious and philosophical tenets, is acquired anew in any given existence, and may be demolished by reasoning, and, on the other hand, the innate sense of self, which is deeply ingrained in the mind, remains active from one life to the next, and can be dislodged only by prolonged meditative practice. In the second pairing, which is the one referred to in the present context, the conviction that the self is truly real is contrasted with the mere, unreflective, designation of self, which is no more than a convenient label and is useful in interpersonal discourse (when we talk to other people) and subjective reflection (when we talk to ourselves). Refutation of this mere designation is unnecessary, since it is not the deep-seated clinging that forms the basis of karma and defilement. It is also impossible, for no amount of reasoning will convince people to stop using the

pronoun "I." In comparing these two contrasted pairings of notions of the self, it will be found that the imputed self and the coemergent self are subdivisions of the supposedly inherently existent self.

219. See commentary to verse 2 of the present chapter, p. 315.

220. If the phenomena of the relative truth are not specifically characterized (extramental) phenomena, they must be mental projections. If the relative is a mental projection, it follows that it (that is, samsara) must last as long as the mind lasts.

221. Objects, senses, and consciousness.

222. See *Introduction to the Middle Way*, chap. 6, v. 53.

223. To return to the comparison just employed, it would be like someone continuing to dream even after waking up.

224. See *Introduction to the Middle Way*, chap. 11, v. 17.

225. It is perhaps worth remembering that the Buddhist critique here is directed at the pantheistic notions of Indian philosophy, not the beliefs of the three monotheistic religions of Semitic origin, Judaism, Christianity, and Islam, to which only some of Shantideva's arguments are relevant.

226. See commentary on chapter 9, verses 68 and 69.

227. The pairing "thing-nonthing" (*dngos po-dngos med*) is familiar from the classification of phenomena in the Sautrantika system of Dignaga and Dharmakirti. Here it refers to the distinction between concrete, extramental, functioning things (*dngos po*), which are the objects of perception, and general ideas, mental aspects, and so on (*dngos med*), which are the objects of conception. In the Madhyamaka context, however, the contrast between thing and nonthing refers to the difference between "things that are existent" and "things that are nonexistent"—the existent pot (*bum pa*) and the nonexistent pot (*bum med*). Without going into the (considerable) philosophical complexities implied by such expressions, the point being made here is that, in the bid to understand and establish emptiness, we might use reasoning to prove that a concrete object, such as a pot, has no true existence. We thus arrive at the idea of the nonexistent pot as compared with the existent pot that we had previously thought of. To prove that a phenomenon is not truly existent in the way that it appears is a major step toward understanding its emptiness (for that reason it is referred to as an "approximate or lesser emptiness"). This, however, is not the Madhyamaka view, which is a refutation of all four ontological extremes. The true status of phenomena is beyond conceptual and verbal expression. Phenomena are empty not only of existence, but also of nonexistence and of both and of neither.

228. Since the referent (the existent phenomenon) is unreal, that which is based on it (the nonexistent phenomenon) is also unreal.

229. These are a dream, an illusion, a trompe l'oeil, a mirage, the moon's reflection in water, an echo, a city in the clouds, and an apparition.
230. These prayers are taken from the *Prayer of Good Action* found in the *Avatamsaka-sutra.*
231. A unit of measurement in ancient India, corresponding to one quart.
232. See *Treasury,* p. 35/125.*
233. A kind of ancestral spirit.
234. *snying gi thur ma,* a text composed by Butön Rinchen Drup.
235. The basic code of Tibetan law, founded on Buddhist principles and established by King Songtsen Gampo (616–49).
236. In this context, "four medicines" is a technical term used in monastic parlance. These are *dus rung* (the food taken at the proper time, namely, before noon, in order to "cure" hunger), *thun tshod* (liquid food that may be taken in the afternoon), *zhag bdun pa* (a preparation taken for a period of seven days to reduce disturbances of phlegm), *'tsho bcang* (a preparation in order to dispel phlegm, which may be taken throughout the course of one's life).
237. See *Treasury,* p. 380/470, n. 174.*
238. See *Treasury,* p. 57/147.*
239. This is a commentarial gloss on the colophon appearing at the end of the *Bodhicharyavatara* itself.
240. Sazang Mati Panchen, Jamyang Lodrö Gyaltsen, was one of the main disciples of Dolpopa Sherab Gyaltsen of the Jonangpa school.

*Page number references to *Treasury of Precious Qualities* are given for both the original hardcover and revised paperback editions. The page number in the hardcover edition appears first, followed by a slash and then the page number in the paperback edition.

Works Cited

Arnold, Edwin. *The Light of Asia.* London: Routledge & Kegan Paul, 1971.

Chandrakirti and Mipham. *Introduction to the Middle Way.* Boston: Shambhala Publications, 2002.

Dalai Lama. *Essence of Refined Gold.* Translated by G. Mullin. Ithaca, N.Y.: Snow Lion Publications, 1982.

Dalai Lama. *The World of Tibetan Buddhism.* Boston: Wisdom Publications, 1995.

Dilgo Khyentse. *Enlightened Courage.* Translated by the Padmakara Translation Group. Ithaca, N.Y.: Snow Lion Publications, 1994, 2006.

Dreyfus, Georges. *Recognizing Reality.* Albany, N.Y.: SUNY Press, 1997.

Dreyfus, Georges and McClintock, Sara. *The Svatantrika-Prasangika Distinction.* Boston: Wisdom Publications, 2003.

The Great Tibetan-Chinese Dictionary (bod rgya tshig mdzod chen mo). Chengdu: Minorities Publishing House, 1984.

Hiriyanna, M. *The Essentials of Indian Philosophy.* Delhi: Motilal Banarsidass, 1995.

Jamgon Kongtrul. *Myriad Worlds.* Translated by Kalu Rinpoche Translation Group. Ithaca, N.Y.: Snow Lion Publications, 2003.

Khenchen Kunzang Pelden and Minyak Kunzang Sonam. *Wisdom: Two Buddhist Commentaries.* Translated by Padmakara Translation Group. St. Leon sur Vezere: Editions Padmakara, 1993, 1999.

Kretschmar, Andreas. *Shantideva's "Bodhisattvacharyavatara," "Entering the Conduct of the Bodhisattvas,"* accompanied by a translation of *"Drops of Nectar,"* an important Tibetan commentary on the *"Bodhisattvacharyavatara"* by Khenpo Kunpal (1862–1943), a direct student of Patrul Rinpoche (1808–1887). www.kunpal.com (accessed July 2004).

Longchen Yeshe Dorje, Kangyur Rinpoche. *Treasury of Precious Qualities.* Translated by the Padmakara Translation Group. Boston: Shambhala Publications, 2001.

Macdonell, A. A. *Sanskrit Dictionary.* Oxford: Oxford University Press, 1929.

Maitreya and Asanga. *The Changeless Nature.* Translated by Ken and Katia Holmes. Kagyu Samye Ling Tibetan Centre, Eskdalemuir, Dumfriesshire, Scotland, 1985.

Mipham. *Shes rab le'u tshig don nor bu ke ta ka.* Chengdu: Sichuan People's Publishing House, 1993.

Patrul Rinpoche. *The Words of My Perfect Teacher.* Translated by the Padmakara Translation Group. Boston: Shambhala Publications, 1998.

Patrul Rinpoche Orgyen Jigme Chokyi Wangpo. *The Collected Works (dpal sprul o rgyan 'jigs med chos kyi dbang po'i gsung 'bum).* Chengdu: Minorities Publishing House, 2003.

Pettit, John. *Beacon of Certainty.* Boston: Wisdom Publications, 1999.

Roerich, Georges. Trans. *The Blue Annals.* Delhi: Motilal Banarsidass, 1988.

Shabkar. *The Life of Shabkar.* Translated by M. Ricard. New York: Snow Lion Publications, 2001.

Shantarakshita and Mipham. *Adornment of the Middle Way.* Boston: Shambhala Publications, 2005.

Smith, Gene. *Among Tibetan Texts.* Boston: Wisdom Publications, 2001.

Taranatha. *History of Buddhism in India.* Translated by Lama Chinpa and Chattopadhyaya. Simla, India: Debi Prasad Chattopadhyaya, 1970.

Tsepön W. D. Shakabpa. *Tibet: A Political History.* New York: Potala Publications, 1984.

Tulku Thondup. *Masters of Meditation and Miracles.* Boston: Shambhala Publications, 1996.

Index

tenet system, 319–21, 332
True Aspectarians, 326
two truths according to, 320
chö, practice of, 126, 285, 450n106,
    455n178
Chogyur Lingpa, 28, 446n41
close mindfulnesses, four, 357–67
compassion,
    and realization of emptiness, 315,
        383–84, 388, 398
    as property of Brahma, 57
    compatible with no-self, 354–55
    definition of, 401, 404
    insufficiency of compassion alone,
        84
    nonreferential, 88, 126
    not pure in beginners, 190
    one of two features of bodhichitta,
        53
    pain of, 290
    root of bodhichitta, 397–98
    root of Mahayana, 420
completely existent.
    See three natures
concentration
    as antidote to desire and attachment,
        270
    conditions necessary for, 259–60;
        solitude, 260, 263–64, 266, 280–81
    faults of being without, 169–70
    obstacles to, 200, 259, 311
    of the "treasury of space," 422
    one of five powers on path of join-
        ing, 449n89
    one of seven elements leading to en-
        lightenment, 449n83
    weariness with samsara and, 222
    wisdom is cause and effect of, 260
    See also samadhi; shamatha; three
        higher trainings
confession
    antidote to negativity, 112–13
    faults not purified by, 96
    four strengths of, 95
    made in the morning, 450n99

necessity of, 113–14
thirty-five Buddhas of, 193
three supreme methods of, 112
consciousness(es)
    attracted to their objects, 277
    sense consciousness according to
        Vaibhashikas, 457n192
    continuum of discrete moments,
        287–88, 456n180
    consciousness and object both un-
        real, 370–71
    do not meet their objects, 363–66
    indivisible moment of, 318; rejected
        by Chittamatrins, 319–20
    permanent consciousness according
        to Samkhyas, 348–51
    self-cognizing, 319–21, 328–30
    six types of, not the self, 347
continuum
    illusory nature of, 289, 353
    mental continuum not the self,
        353–54
    of consciousness, 456n180
corpses
    and *tsun-lha* spirits, 412
    contemplation of, 268, 275
    essentially the same as our own bod-
        ies, 268
    swamp of, 403, 405
craving
    afflictive and nonafflictive, 342
    arising from feeling, 342, 362, 364
    cause of existence, 341
    cause of the lower realms, 280, 405
    conceptual elaboration, the root of,
        332
    illusory nature, 364
    not found in Uttarakuru, 449n78

Dartik, xvii, 28, 446n40
dead, the
    cannot return, 412
    impersonated by spirits, 412–13
    offerings on behalf of, 412, 421
deafness, karmic causes of, 416

The Padmakara Translation Group

Translations into English

The Adornment of the Middle Way. Shantarakshita and Jamgön Mipham. Boston: Shambhala Publications, 2005, 2010.

Counsels from My Heart. Dudjom Rinpoche. Boston: Shambhala Publications, 2001, 2003.

Enlightened Courage. Dilgo Khyentse Rinpoche. Dordogne: Editions Padmakara, 1992; Ithaca, NY: Snow Lion Publications, 1994, 2006.

The Excellent Path of Enlightenment. Dilgo Khyentse. Dordogne: Editions Padmakara, 1987; Ithaca, NY: Snow Lion Publications, 1996.

A Flash of Lightning in the Dark of Night. The Dalai Lama. Boston: Shambhala Publications, 1993. Republished as *For the Benefit of All Beings.* Boston: Shambhala Publications, 2009.

Food of Bodhisattvas. Shabkar Tsogdruk Rangdrol. Boston: Shambhala Publications, 2004.

A Guide to The Words of My Perfect Teacher. Khenpo Ngawang Pelzang. Translated with Dipamkara. Boston: Shambhala Publications, 2004.

The Heart of Compassion. Dilgo Khyentse. Boston: Shambhala Publications, 2007.

The Heart Treasure of the Enlightened Ones. Dilgo Khyentse and Patrul Rinpoche. Boston: Shambhala Publications, 1992.

The Hundred Verses of Advice. Dilgo Khyentse and Padampa Sangye. Boston: Shambhala Publications, 2005.

Introduction to the Middle Way. Chandrakirti and Jamgön Mipham. Boston: Shambhala Publications, 2002, 2004.

Journey to Enlightenment. Matthieu Ricard. New York: Aperture Foundation, 1996.

Lady of the Lotus-Born. Gyalwa Changchub and Namkhai Nyingpo. Boston: Shambhala Publications, 1999, 2002.

The Life of Shabkar. Albany, NY: SUNY Press, 1994; Ithaca, NY: Snow Lion Publications, 2001.

Nagarjuna's Letter to a Friend. Longchen Yeshe Dorje, Kangyur Rinpoche. Ithaca, NY: Snow Lion Publications, 2005.

The Nectar of Manjushri's Speech. Kunzang Pelden. Boston: Shambhala Publications, 2007, 2010.

The Root Stanzas of the Middle Way. Nagarjuna. Dordogne: Editions Padmakara, 2008.

A Torch Lighting the Way to Freedom. Dudjom Rinpoche, Jigdrel Yeshe Dorje. Boston: Shambhala Publications, 2011.

Treasury of Precious Qualities: Book One. Longchen Yeshe Dorje, Kangyur Rinpoche. Boston: Shambhala Publications, 2001. Revised edition with root text by Jigme Lingpa, 2010.

Treasury of Precious Qualities: Book Two. Longchen Yeshe Dorje, Kangyur Rinpoche. Boston: Shambhala Publications, 2013.

The Way of the Bodhisattva (Bodhicharyavatara). Shantideva. Boston: Shambhala Publications, 1997, 2006, 2008.

White Lotus. Jamgön Mipham. Boston: Shambhala Publications, 2007.

Wisdom: Two Buddhist Commentaries. Khenchen Kunzang Pelden and Minyak Kunzang Sonam. Dordogne: Editions Padmakara, 1993, 1999.

The Wish-Fulfilling Jewel. Dilgo Khyentse. Boston: Shambhala Publications, 1988.

The Words of My Perfect Teacher. Patrul Rinpoche. New York: HarperCollins, 1994; Boston: Shambhala Publications, 1998.

Zurchungpa's Testament. Zurchungpa and Dilgo Khyentse. Ithaca, NY: Snow Lion Publications, 2006.